Subordination *or* Empowerment?

Subordination *or* Empowerment?

*African-American Leadership and
the Struggle for Urban Political Power*

RICHARD A. KEISER

New York   Oxford • Oxford University Press   1997

Oxford University Press

Oxford   New York
Athens   Auckland   Bangkok   Bogota   Bombay   Buenos Aires
Calcutta   Cape Town   Dar es Salaam   Delhi   Florence   Hong Kong
Istanbul   Karachi   Kuala Lumpur   Madras   Madrid   Melbourne
Mexico City   Nairobi   Paris   Singapore   Taipei   Tokyo   Toronto   Warsaw

and associated companies in
Berlin   Ibadan

Copyright © 1997 by Oxford University Press, Inc.

Published by Oxford University Press, Inc.
198 Madison Avenue, New York, New York 10016

Oxford is a registered trademark of Oxford University Press

Library of Congress Cataloging-in-Publication Data
Keiser, Richard A.
Subordination or empowerment? : African-American leadership and
the struggle for urban political power / Richard A. Keiser.
p.   cm.
ISBN 0-19-507569-2
1. Political participation—United States—Case studies.   2. Afro-
American leadership.   3. Community power—United States—Case
studies.   I. Title.
JK1764.K45   1997
303.3'089'96073—dc20   96-41161

1 3 5 7 9 8 6 4 2

Printed in the United States of America
on acid-free paper

Preface

In 1983 mayoral elections were held in both Chicago and Philadelphia. Both cities elected Black mayors for the first time, and in both cities less than 20 percent of the White voters cast ballots for the Black candidate. But the respective elections of Harold Washington and Wilson Goode were very different in their tenor. In Chicago the racial polarization was thick enough to cut with a knife. On Palm Sunday in Chicago, graffiti spray-painted on the side of a church read, "Harold sucks. Nigger die." Campaign buttons for Washington's opponent, Bernard Epton, read, "Educated People To Oust Niggers—EPTON." Pamphlets passed through White neighborhoods called Washington and other Blacks "Mr. Baboon." The locker-room racism and the lack of any repudiation of those responsible for this sickening display drew the attention of the national media and citizens across the country. In Philadelphia no examples of vitriolic rhetoric or any other form of racism were evident. Many Philadelphians were disappointed with the election result, but the city's social fabric was not shredded by this event. This stark contrast drew my attention, and my attempt to explain these events led me to write this book.

In the process of researching this book I read much on Black leadership, but the original plan of the book did not include developing the typology of Black leadership that is presented here. Two factors suggested that considerable attention to this topic was warranted. The first was a conversation I had with Cornel West about the negative evaluation of Black political leadership over the past thirty years that he presented in *Race Matters*. West came to Carleton College to speak at a convocation, and because of the foresight of the dean of the college I had the pleasure of sitting next to him for an entire dinner and monopolizing his conversation. The second factor, the transformation of Louis Farrakhan from a leader marginalized in the Black community to a leader who commands considerable respect and legitimacy, convinced me that a fuller treatment of the dialectic that exists between types of Black leadership was necessary.

In *Race Matters* West condemned the state of Black leadership in America, asserting that Black mayors like Wilson Goode of Philadelphia and Tom Bradley of Los Angeles "stunt progressive development and silence the prophetic voices in the black community by casting the practical mainstream as the only game in town." Who are the prophetic voices that West looked to for leadership? He mentioned Harold Washington, Jesse Jackson, and Adam Clayton Powell Jr., and argued that the shortage of such leaders is "at the center of the crisis of black leadership" (see *Race Matters* [Boston: Beacon, 1993] pp. 39–40). In his book West offered no elaboration of the faults or flaws of the first group, nor did he explain what attributes the second group possessed that distinguish them from it. He offered no empirical evidence, not even a telling anecdote, to support these claims. He did enumerate positive leadership characteristics such as morality, maturity, humility, and boldness, but he offered no basis for identifying these characteristics in individuals, nor did he offer any reason to believe that Washington, Jackson, Powell, or others shared these traits while others did not. Moreover, there is no indication in *Race Matters* of what kinds of circumstances produce positive leadership (In a seminal article, James Q. Wilson explained how Powell and his leadership style were the products of the political environment of the New York City politics from which he emerged. See "Two Negro Politicians: An Interpretation," *Midwest Journal of Political Science* 4:4 [November 1960], pp. 346–369).

Over dinner, West conceded that his book offered no empirical substantiation of his claims about Black mayors, but he argued that because he was not writing as a social scientist he should not be held to the standards of social science evidence. The more telling aspect of our discussion was that when it came to national-level Black politics, West was able to persuasively document the absence of Black leaders who could make a difference for Black people and successfully address issues that would be on the agenda of that diverse group. In other words, the differences between urban Black leadership and national Black leadership came to the fore.

West and other progressive Black scholars have been critical of the claims to leadership and moral authority of Louis Farrakhan. Yet it is clear that although Farrakhan has refused to recant any of the views or statements that have offended the sensibilities of Blacks, Whites, and others, he is now viewed as one of the leading spokespersons for Black America. The view I share with these scholars is that it is not Farrakhan who has changed but the terrain of Black leadership and the articulated alternatives to him. More precisely, the progressive alternatives to him are much less evident and less frequently heard than they have ever been.

My disagreement with Cornel West was about whether Black leaders who champion political and economic empowerment and deliver this empowerment do exist at the urban level. Not only do they exist, but they pose a powerful and popular alternative to those at the urban level who preach the separatism of Louis Farrakhan. An explanation of the urban dynamic that produces these leaders—who orchestrate Black empowerment and shun separatism—would tell us much about urban Black politics and help us to understand the Farrakhan phenomenon at the national level. *Subordination or Empowerment?* offers such an explanation.

In the process of writing this book I have accrued many debts, and I am pleased to thank those who have helped me so much. Ray Wolfinger has been a model adviser, colleague, and friend, and whatever merit is in this work owes much to his patience, teaching, and scholarship. Drafts of parts of this book were improved by sound advice from Amy Bridges, Rufus Browning, Steve Erie, Paul Green, Bill Grimshaw, Judy Gruber, Charles Henry, Bryan Jones, Norton Long, Dale Rogers Marshall, Jim McGuire, John Mollenkopf, Nelson Polsby, Raphael Sonenshein, Clarence Stone, David Tabb, and James Q. Wilson. I also received advice, guidance, and support from my colleagues in the political science department at Carleton College. My former colleagues at the University of Denver deserve thanks as well; I would not be where I am were it not for them. I would also like to thank the two anonymous reviewers at Oxford University Press, as well as my editor, Thomas LeBien. Any remaining errors are mine.

Many people in the four cities that are the focus of this book helped me immensely in gathering data and interpreting events. In Philadelphia, Margaret Tartaglione and the staff of the Office of the Election Commissioners deserve thanks, as do journalists Acel Moore, Chris Hepp, and S. A. Paolantonio. Ed Schwartz, Karen Warrington, and Benjamin Ramos gave unselfishly of their time. A number of business executives and elected officials who requested anonymity also deserve thanks. John Guinther, formerly of *Philadelphia Magazine*, gave me detailed comments on a draft of the Philadelphia chapter, and I remain grateful. The staff at the Temple University Urban Archives also deserve thanks. In Chicago, Samuel Ackerman opened many doors for me and taught me a great deal about biracial liberal politics in the Daley era and after, and I offer him my sincerest appreciation. Al Raby, Warren Bacon, Ron Stevens, Alderman Leon Despres, Jackie Grimshaw, Congressman Charles Hayes, Monroe Anderson, Basil Talbott, Alderman Roman Pucinski, Alderman Richard Mell, David Cantor, Rev. Claude Wyatt, Addie Wyatt, Carl Scheer, and a number of other people who requested anonymity deserve thanks as well. The staff of the Municipal Reference Library of Chicago was very helpful and deserves the recognition it receives from every scholar who has done research on Chicago politics. In Atlanta, I was fortunate to have the opportunity to meet with Mayor Maynard Jackson and to receive assistance from Delores L. Washington and Emmanuel W. Jones, both of whom served in the administration of Andrew Young. Susan J. Ross, acting director of the Office of Contract Compliance in Mayor Jackson's third administration, was most helpful. In Gary I received considerable help from the librarians at the Gary Public Library, for which I am grateful.

The Institute of Governmental Studies at the University of California, Berkeley, gave me considerable financial support in this project, as well as space to write and revise. Each of the librarians there was very helpful, and I am grateful for this and for their friendship. I look forward to continuing my relationship with this fine resource for scholars. The National Endowment for the Humanities provided a summer research grant for travel to Atlanta, and I am thankful for its support. Carleton

College provided me with a faculty development grant that enabled me to leave teaching for one term and complete the writing of this book. I am very grateful for this financial support.

Finally, I want to thank my parents for developing my interest in politics and for the encouragement they gave me throughout the writing of this book. My profoundest thanks go to my wife, Teena, who let me borrow her strength during every difficult moment that this book produced. Her support carried this project to fruition. I dedicate this book to her.

Contents

Subordination *or* Empowerment?

One

Electoral Competition and the Emergence of Political Leadership

During the 1980s and 1990s the world witnessed victories in the global struggle for democratization. In South Africa, an apartheid police state relinquished power, and that nation is taking major steps in the democratizing process. In Eastern Europe, the former Soviet Union, and South America dictatorial regimes have collapsed and democratically elected regimes with representative governments have emerged. In the United States, the struggle for democratization within the formal democratic structure has been ongoing in cities. *Subordination or Empowerment?* documents and analyzes this struggle.

Democratization means much more than holding elections and allowing political parties to form. Democratization also means the reduction, and movement along a continuum toward the ultimate elimination, of *political inequality.*[1] The struggle for democratization is a struggle to end the second-class political status of some groups that prevents them from influencing agenda-setting, decisionmaking, and other aspects of politics that directly affect their interests. Outside the United States, the first step in the struggle is ending the de jure exclusion of many citizens from political participation. Both outside the United States and in our cities, the next step in the battle is to level the playing field, so that institutions like elections and political parties are not props in a charade of domination and resistance but tools for the exercise of meaningful political participation that yields political influence to all groups. The process of democratization is not a one-time battle but an ongoing clash, in which some groups strive to overcome subordination while other groups may face threats to the political access they have achieved.

The text of the struggle for political power in the United States by subordinated groups is found in the histories of many groups, most notably the Irish, Italians, Poles, Jews, African-Americans, Latinos, and women. The democratization struggle has been waged in all levels and branches of government; this book concentrates on the urban trenches—specifically, the struggle for political power of one group, African-Americans, in four cities: Chicago, Gary, Philadelphia, and Atlanta. The time frame is the twentieth century, particularly its second half, the period of the great migrations from rural to urban areas within the South and from the rural South to the urban centers of the North. It was during this period, when Blacks settled in big cities, that their political struggle finally began to resemble the experiences of White ethnic groups.[2] Here I will briefly describe the struggle for Black political power in these four cities; each is presented in detail in chapters 2 through 5.

In the early part of the twentieth century, noteworthy steps toward democratization for Blacks were evident in Chicago more than in any other city. There Black politicians were able to broker Black votes in exchange for breakthroughs in political empowerment that benefited both individual politicians and their constituencies. Martin Kilson has argued that between 1915 and 1940, Blacks in Chicago were junior members of the governing coalition of the city, an achievement that was "extremely rare in those years" and made Chicago a "notable exception."[3] In the 1950s a puzzle that has captured scholars' attention began to emerge: some cities with large Black populations matched Chicago's earlier achievements, but Blacks in other quite similar cities were not moving toward greater political empowerment. In Philadelphia and Atlanta, the situation was evolving: coopted, clientelistic relationships with White leaders had typified Black politicians in the early twentieth century; now they were able to demand new levels of political power and influence over the policy agenda. Yet in other cities with significant Black populations, like Gary, political development remained stagnated, and Black politicians remained subordinated. In Chicago, meanwhile, Black political leaders no longer had the power to defend public policy gains, and during the 1950s and 1960s Black political power was dramatically rolled back.[4]

In the 1970s the number of Black leaders in Philadelphia and Atlanta capable of commanding respect and support in both the Black and White communities continued to grow. Even when political turbulence prevented these leaders from playing a decisive role in electoral outcomes and forced them out of governing coalitions, their former allies worked with them to protect political gains that previously had been made. In Gary, the nearly total exclusion of Blacks from political power by a White ethnic machine came to a sudden, unanticipated end due to crippling scandals. Richard Hatcher was elected mayor of Gary in 1967, one of the first Blacks elected as mayor of a major city. In numerous subsequent elections the Black community rallied around Hatcher; he had become a folk hero because of his status as a pioneer. Black opponents were denigrated as race traitors, and White opponents were stereotyped as "great White hopes." In Chicago, White ethnic political domination (in alliance with a downtown growth coalition) and Black subordination lasted much longer. But in 1983 Harold Washington became the first Black mayor of Chicago, an election outcome that was just as sudden and unexpected as Hatcher's. However, when Washington died shortly after his reelection, the fragility and underdevelopment of Black political power in Chicago again became evident.

Understanding Chicago's pattern of Black political development and accounting for the decay there of what Ralph Bunche labeled the "seventh heaven" of Black political power will help explain the process of the *rollback* of Black political power, a process that is currently transpiring in New York City, took place in Cleveland during the 1970s and 1980s, and may await Los Angeles.[5] Comparing the incremental development of Black political power in northeastern, partisan, ethnic Philadelphia and southern, nonpartisan Atlanta makes it possible to take significant steps toward specifying the structural and environmental factors that enhance opportunities for the empowerment of subordinated groups; these two cases are the referent for the empowerment alluded to in the book's title. Similarly, comparing Chicago and Gary makes it possible to present specific evidence about the structural conditions that impede incremental Black political empowerment and are more likely to produce sudden, unstable polity transformations; these two cases elaborate the causes of the maintenance of subordination. Finally, this study will reveal which of the variables that seem to foster or impede minority empowerment in the urban political arena actually have an impact across the four cases.

Before embarking on a discussion of minority empowerment, it is necessary to define this concept and discuss how it can be measured.

Defining Minority Empowerment

Empowerment is the process by which a minority group, or representatives of that group, gains a greater ability to influence political outcomes in its favor. A clear distinction must be made between nonempowering participation and political participation that yields empowerment. Minority group members may increase their political participation, and even win benefits or offices from the power-holding groups, without achieving any gains in empowerment. When benefits are symbolic and imply no reallocation of political power, that is, no authority to influence political decisionmaking outcomes for the benefit of the power-seeking minority group, I label this subordination. In contrast, empowerment implies both a reallocation of power to the minority group and an independent base of support in the minority electorate for their leaders, that is, these leaders are not anointed and coopted by the established power-holders.[6] (The differences in the relationships between followers and leaders are fully addressed later in this chapter.)

The *reallocation of political power* is the defining feature of empowerment. Reallocation of power can be identified and assessed along two dimensions.[7]

First, a group gains empowerment as it wins a more favorable distribution of public offices. Most significant for empowerment are the capturing of high-status, visible, appointed, and elected offices from which political power can be exercised. For example, if an African-American captures a seat on the city council and works to advance the interests and agenda of African-Americans (this caveat forces us beyond mere head-counting to an examination of behavior), this signifies an increment of political empowerment. The capture of offices that entail no political decisionmaking does not represent empowerment and may indicate the maintenance of subordination. When enough offices like that of the mayor and city council have been captured by African-Americans and their allies, they will be in a position to dominate the city's governing coalition. Becoming part of the governing coalition and playing an increasingly important role in it signify further reallocations of political power and increments of empowerment for African-Americans. From a position within the governing coalition, African-American political leaders are in an advantageous position to enact aspects of the Black political agenda.

A group also incrementally gains empowerment when it wins a more advantageous distribution of public-sector jobs. All public-sector job increases are significant to subordinated groups because the alternative may be unemployment or underemployment in the private sector due to discrimination. But particularly when African-Americans capture a greater share of those municipal government jobs that are higher paying and possess greater decisionmaking authority and status—for example, when they are employed as "officials and administrators," "professionals," and "technicians," as classified by the Equal Employment Opportunity Commission (EEOC)—they are capturing positions held and sought by other groups in the zero-sum struggle for urban political power. Even in the case where the African-Americans who occupy such positions do not make decisions that positively advance group interests, these positions still represent increments of political empowerment because they are the kinds of political plums for which even better-off groups still compete vigorously.

Second, political empowerment can be identified and assessed in terms of group influence over public policy agenda-setting and decisionmaking. Such influence is typically exercised in two ways. African-Americans can use political pressure or work through decisionmakers to block the emergence of policies inimical to Black interests, or they can influence decisionmaking and shape the agenda in ways that positively affect group interests. Examples of public policies that were or are high on the agenda of African-Americans include the creation of civilian police review boards that can punish police brutality, the creation of better housing and schooling opportunities for minorities, the implementation of affirmative action programs that enable African-Americans to penetrate all levels of the bureaucracy, the creation of provisions that set aside city contracts for African-American business enterprises, and combating the underemployment and poverty that disproportionately plague minority communities.[8]

In evaluating African-American empowerment, the crucial issue is whether there is evidence of a reallocation of political power, that is, whether Blacks are able to win offices and make policies that represent new accomplishments in the face of resistance from other competing power contenders. In the zero-sum arena of urban political power, the achievements of one group represent defeats for other groups, and such victories constitute evidence of genuine political power. This approach to political empowerment is based on the historical experience of groups in the United States who have struggled to increase their political power and been judged to have made admirable progress by group members as well as outsider laypeople and scholars. The Irish- and Italian-Americans, for example, are universally considered to have made great strides in political empowerment. Members of these groups have held most of the important political offices in settings where the groups constitute sizable proportions of the electorate and group members have been able to help formulate public policies that removed barriers to group advancement (i.e., curbing discriminatory practices) and that advanced the interests of the group (i.e., redistributive policies).

It is important to recognize at the outset that sharp economic inequalities continue to exist within each of these groups, in part because all group members have not received the same benefits from the process of political empowerment. Political empowerment, as it has always been defined and as it is defined here, does not include the eradication of poverty among all group members; if it did, it would be a concept with no empirical referents. Economic divisions as well as differences in political efficacy exist within all ethnic and racial groups and will probably continue to exist as long as people devote differing amounts of time to politics and have different levels of education, ambition, and acquisitiveness; however, these differences have not kept members from mobilizing together to seek increased group empowerment. Nor have these differences kept the rewards of empowerment from benefiting all members of the group, albeit unequally. Unlike cooptation, the benefits of political empowerment are not particularistic benefits that go to only a handful of individuals; empowerment has a diffuse impact, yet the benefits do not have to be distributed equally or disproportionately to the neediest. To struggle for an egalitarian or progressive pattern of distribution of benefits in one's personal politics is laudatory; but from the perspective of social science, to equate political empowerment with the equitable distribution of benefits within the group, and to measure empowerment against this standard, would be to deny that the Irish-Americans or other groups have gained political empowerment and to transform the idea of political empowerment into an empty set with almost no comparative utility. Each ethnic group that has struggled up from the bottom of the ladder of political empowerment has developed a higher-status political leadership cadre that overlaps considerably with a growing middle class. The reasons for this are rooted in the unequal distribution of benefits that are synonymous with a capitalist economic system, the kinds of traits that Western society in general sees as desirable for leaders, and the ways in which ethnic, racial, or nationalist struggles differ from, and undermine the bases for, class struggle.[9]

Political Competition and the Process of Empowerment

This book argues that electoral competitiveness creates opportunities for African-American leadership to step forward and gain political empowerment. Competition and contestation are not the same.[10] Most elections in the United States are contested; many are noncompetitive. If the same coalition consistently wins elections for important offices by overwhelming margins, that political system should be considered noncompetitive.

What is an overwhelming margin? What margins of victory define competitive elections? Highly competitive elections are defined here as those in which the victor captures 50–54 percent of the vote, competitive elections are those in which the winner receives 55–58 percent of the vote, and noncompetitive elections are those won with 59 percent or more of the vote. Following William H. Standing and James A. Robinson, I consider the number and continuity of wins relevant in distinguishing between competitive and noncompetitive elections.[11] One mayoral victory achieved with less than 59 percent of the vote should not signify an urban political system that is competitive when this election falls in the midst of a series of noncompetitive elections. Therefore, the criteria for competitive mayoral elections are twofold: One faction must win (1) by a margin of less than 18 percent (e.g., less than 59–41 percent) (2) two out of the four consecutive primary and general elections that constitute two mayoral election cycles. If the margin of victory is greater than 18 percent in any three of these four elections, electoral politics are noncompetitive.[12]

Assaying political competitiveness is not a purely quantitative exercise, in scholarship or politics. Robert T. Golembiewski said as much when he suggested that the problems inherent in devising a universal measure of party competition may be "insoluble," and that "awareness of the problems and a realization of the limitations of any measure of party strength are the student's only real bench marks at this time."[13] Two qualitative political factors should also be considered. First, do excluded groups and other potential challengers perceive that the dominant group or coalition is invincible? If so, serious electoral competition, regardless of the actual margins of victory, is unlikely. Second, given competitive electoral conditions, do the competing groups actually seek the Black vote? Competing for the Black vote in an electorally competitive polity is rational, unless a faction or party perceives that to do so will cause unacceptable defections. In such an instance, it is the task of Black leaders and the leaders of losing factions to finesse this problem—to devise a way an alternative coalition can pursue Black votes without experiencing an unacceptable hemorrhage. Because of the complexity of defining competitiveness, the case studies present a variety of relevant data in an unambiguous manner, so that readers may evaluate for themselves whether these elections and city political systems are competitive or not.

As the case studies demonstrate, the significance of politically competitive polities is that they create strong incentives for coalitions between White factions and subordinated Blacks. In competitive conditions, winning the electoral support of a Black voting bloc often means the difference between victory and defeat. In these situations, Black leaders have come to the forefront and been able to successfully bargain with the competing groups and win a reallocation of political power. Empowerment has been an incremental and iterative process. When the votes of subordinated Blacks produced an electoral victory, Blacks received the visible and tangible benefits of empowerment discussed earlier. These small successes increased the legitimacy of Black leaders who forged these bargains, in comparison with other potential Black leaders who advocated different strategies. Augmented legitimacy often meant an improved ability to deliver Black votes, and a greater ability to capture White electoral support as well, which enhanced these leaders capacity to bargain for further empowerment in the next electoral iteration.

In competitive polities, leaders of the power-holding White factions may seek to bargain with Black leaders and satisfy them with cooptative personal rewards; they may attempt to divide Black leadership and find the least expensive bargain; or they may try to anoint new Black leaders who will seek less "expensive" benefits.[14] But if these factions hope to win elections, their leaders ultimately must deal with Black leaders who are legitimate, in that they can deliver votes. The case studies show that the Black leaders who have bargained for benefits that yielded group empowerment and membership in the "governing coalition" have increasingly gained legitimacy from Black voters. On the other hand, those who at best delivered only particularistic, cooptative rewards and token membership in the "electoral coalition" gradually lost legitimacy.

Conversely, I argue that noncompetitive polities hinder political empowerment and help to maintain the subordination of unincorporated groups. In noncompetitive polities the monopolistic coalition has no incentive to reallocate power to African-Americans or other excluded groups, because that coalition is already large enough (i.e., could mobilize enough votes) to win. The monopolistic coalition sometimes receives sizable numbers of votes from the excluded group—for intangible reasons such as partisan loyalty (in partisan systems), disdain for the feeble opposition, or a desire to get on the bandwagon. And members of the excluded group might vote for the monopolistic coalition, or organize a clientelistic network that delivered votes to it, out of a desire to win low-level, particularistic benefits for themselves or their families, such as patronage jobs. But none of these behaviors add up to the incremental growth of group political power defined here as political empowerment. As long as the threat of defection of Black voters to an opposing faction is not perceived as likely to create a coalition that could defeat the monopolistic coalition, a reallocation of power to African-Americans is not forthcoming. Such a reallocation of power would redistribute status and authority from some groups in the dominant coalition and could easily destabilize the coalition.

A Typology of African-American Leadership

To say that successful African-American political empowerment is to a large degree dependent on the quality of African-American political leadership is to proffer a truism. It does little to explain why a cadre of Black leaders with biracial support emerged in Philadelphia and Atlanta prior to the elections of their first Black mayors and such a cadre failed to emerge in Chicago and Gary. Long after the elections of Harold Washington and Richard Hatcher, the absence of other Black leaders capable of mobilizing broad support persisted in their cities. The explanation for this nonrandom distribution of leadership talent is not found in the voluminous literature on Black leadership; yet it is crucial for understanding the contrasting evolution of these two pairs of cities and the patterns of incremental empowerment or subordination. The nonrandom distribution of leadership types is not due to differences in the quality of the air or the purity of the water; rather, the emergence and flourishing of types of leaders is a function of the polities within which latent leaders are located. This argument is developed more thoroughly in a later section of this chapter and is empirically demonstrated in the case studies.

The following tripartite typology of Black leadership includes the leadership type that delivered African-American political empowerment in Philadelphia and Atlanta (and other cities not analyzed here, such as New Orleans, New York, and Milwaukee), as well as the two other leadership types that historically have been found in all cities. The purpose of this typology is to help in our understanding of urban leadership and political empowerment in cities. But because this typology is being presented prior to the case studies and their relevant actors, the discussion must be more theoretical, and I refer to more widely known national-level Black leaders to exemplify the types. In the concluding chapter, I will provide a richer discussion in which these ideal-type descriptions are illustrated by empirical referents drawn from the cases.

The defining feature of leadership in the typology presented here is the strategy of leaders and followers toward changing their status as a politically subordinated numerical minority. What is the approach of leaders and followers toward coalitions with other contenders for political power such as Whites, Latinos, Asians, gays, and lesbians? (Our analytical concern is with cities where Blacks are a numerical minority, the typical situation of subordinated groups.[15]) Is political empowerment a goal? How do these minority leaders pursue it? Can Black empowerment be pursued through the political system? Can African-Americans achieve the reallocation of political power in their favor while being part of a coalition with other groups?

The vast literature on Black political leadership provides a detailed illustration of two types of leadership: those who enter into patron-client relations with established White politicians that do not alter the subordinate status of the group, hereafter called clientelistic-subordinates, and those who reject even short-term political coalitions with non-African-Americans, hereafter called separatist-messianics.

Clientelistic-Subordinates

Within the literature, what I call clientelistic-subordinate leadership resembles what others have labeled accommodationist, conservative, moderate, Uncle Tom and Race Diplomat, Black boss, and traditional-brokerage types.[16] Such leaders do not pursue genuine group empowerment; they recognize that accommodation to the status quo is likely to yield privileges and their own individual advancement, even though it will maintain the *subordinate* status of the Black community. Typically such Black leaders have existed in a *clientelistic* relationship with a White patron. The patron provides enhanced prestige and, concomitantly, material rewards to the Black leader, individually and for him to distribute to others; these favors enable him to carry out his duty in this relationship: the generation of political support and compliance for the White patron. Black subordinates are often anointed or coopted into the ranks of the larger political organizations or networks in which their patrons serve. In anointment, an individual with little connection to politics and no prior standing as a community spokesperson is enlisted by the patron and the organization to be their liaison to a segment of the Black community and, by virtue of this designation, is endowed with heightened status and power. In cooptation, a person with some prior standing (political or otherwise) and potential for leadership is persuaded to join the patron's organization, which is committed to the maintenance of African-American subordination, and to lend his or her prestige and standing to the patron's efforts. For instance, some Black ministers, enticed by the potential for heightened status and material gain for themselves and their congregation, have been coopted as subordinates.

Are clientelistic-subordinates "Uncle Toms" and traitors to their race? Certainly they are often labeled with these terms of derision. These leaders access, by virtue of race, to segments of the Black citizenry and their promotion of the patron's agenda maintains the subordination of Blacks. In the words of Martin Kilson, the task of the subordinate is "to guarantee the Negro vote for [the patron's political party] . . . and when necessary discourage Negro voting altogether rather than allow Negro voting power to grow and diversify."[17] Carter G. Woodson captured the nature of subordinate leadership when he wrote:

> The oppressor must have some dealing with the despised group, and rather than having contact with individuals he approaches the masses through his own spokesman. . . . Leadership is usually superimposed for the purpose of "directing the course of the ostracized group along sane lines." . . . These supervisors of the conduct of Negroes would prevent them from learning the truth which might make them "unruly" or ambitious to become free. . . . This "racial racketeer" might be a politician, minister, teacher, director of a community center, or head of a "social uplift agency." As long as he did certain things and expressed the popular opinion on questions he lacked nothing, and those who followed him found their way apparently better paid as the years went by. His leadership, then, was recognized and the ultimate undoing of the Negroes in the community was assured.[18]

Many of the empirical descriptions of clientelistic-subordinates suggest that these leaders confuse the granting of cooptive concessions by patrons and the achievement of small changes by clients with empowerment and the actual reallocation of power. For example, Oliver C. Cox differed with Kilson and Woodson and argued that the subordinate is not an enemy of his people: "he merely decides that in the given situation it is expedient to avoid the common cause and make peace with the enemy."[19] My view is that by shunning nearly all direct challenges to the political arrangements that institutionalize White domination, by serving as spokespersons for the dominant exclusionary coalition, and by advancing the retail strategy of material cooptation of individuals as opposed to the wholesale reduction of group inequalities in political power, these leaders have contributed to the maintenance of Black political subordination.

The foregoing probably conjures up an image that would seem to exclude Black mayors. Yet if a Black mayor won election as the leader of a biracial coalition with a sizable Black segment, had the means to govern and affect change (i.e., was not blocked in every effort by a hostile city council or elected to a position that had little formal or actual power), yet did not advance the agenda of the Black constituency and otherwise foster Black empowerment against a status quo of subordination, then to consider that person an example of a clientelistic-subordinate would be justified.

A number of scholars have indeed suggested that Black mayors have done little to empower their Black constituents.[20] However, I believe these claims are far too sweeping. Evaluation of whether Black mayors have had success in empowering their Black followers should proceed on a case-by-case basis prior to the formulation of any generalizations about such a diverse group. One of the goals of this book is to explain, through the analysis of cases, why some Black politicians (not just mayors) have been able to empower their Black constituents while others have maintained Black subordination.

Separatist-Messianics

Those leaders and their followers who demand Black empowerment but refuse to work in coalition with other groups contending for political power and often abstain from working within the political system, which they define as "corrupt" or "racist," have been profiled in detail in the literature. They have been called nationalist or radical leaders, militants, cultural nationalists or secular revolutionaries, rhetorical leaders, religious nationalists or faddist-rhetorical leaders, and Pan-Africanist leaders.[21] Underlying this variety of designations are differences regarding the importance of cultural, religious, or economic variables in explaining and abolishing African-American oppression.[22] Although the Black Panthers, SNCC, the Republic of New Africa, the Nation of Islam, Malcolm X, Eldridge Cleaver, Stokely Carmichael, Amiri Baraka, and the less well-known separatist crusaders who emerge in the case studies have often perceived their differences in an invidious, sectarian manner, this does not contravene Alphonso Pinkney's conclusion that "the ideology of Black nationalism has always contained a core of widely shared beliefs."[23] Certainly this fact helps to explain the ease with which prominent theorist/leaders like Carmichael, Baraka, and Malcolm X have shifted from one camp to another.[24] Those shared beliefs include an emphasis on Black political unity that is a product of the exclusion of Whites (and rarely honors the rhetoric of rainbow coalitions); rejection of the strategy of working within the political system in general, and electoral politics specifically, to advance African-American goals; and demands, made on a demonized and undifferentiated power structure, for nonincremental reallocations of wealth and political power (in the United States and globally) that are sometimes justified as reparations.[25] By shunning political coalitions and often rejecting political participation, separatism is produced and maintained. This desire for a separate identity and an independent (not interdependent) fate in politics is why such leaders are so often called either *separatists* or nationalists. In that they demand dramatically redistributive reallocations of power and dismiss incrementalism as an unadulterated tool of White hegemony, and in that they make such demands from a separatist position that undercuts their electoral and political effectiveness, the *messianic* designation is earned. When separatist-messianics do enter electoral politics, the candidacies they support exclude all other groups and are often stillborn.[26]

Separatist-messianics would probably agree with Francis Fox Piven and Richard Cloward's contention that "whatever influence lower-class groups occasionally exert in American politics does not result from organization, but from mass protest and the disruptive consequences of protest."[27] Their rejection of both the strategy of working within the political system and the process of incremental redistribution of power suggests that separatist-messianics refuse to recognize the accomplishments of the expanding Black middle class and working class in gaining political and economic power. Discussing the achievements of the last two decades, Manning Marable has argued that "Black nationalists as a group were unaware of the major changes within the American economy that were taking place during the 1970s. . . . Through a combination of affirmative action programs, the desegregation of corporate middle-management positions, and federal grants to black corporations, the elites as a whole did not suffer nearly as much as the great black majority."[28] During the 1980s, according to Marable, "African-American managers and professionals had larger income increases than whites with identical educational backgrounds and vocations."[29] Although I would disagree with Marable's inference that only a small Black elite benefited from affirmative action and other such empowering concessions—unless the numerous Black police and fire officers and lower-level denizens of city halls and state agencies who have obtained their positions from such programs are, unbeknownst to themselves, part of the Black elite—I embrace Marable's larger point that Blacks gained power at that time through the political system and that separatist-messianics have long been stuck in denial about this hard fact.[30]

Another important feature these leaders share is a messianic perception of African-Americans as a chosen people who will be delivered from subordination and redeemed.[31] Wilson Jeremiah Moses has argued that "People develop a messianic view of themselves because of the historical experience of being oppressed as a group. Messianic traditions persist because the heritage of oppression persists. Ancient African roots are much less important to Black messianism than is the experience of white domination in the modern world."[32] The expectation of messianic redemption is crucial for understanding how these leaders and their followers can shun involvement in the political process and, at the same time, hold such an ambitious agenda for the reallocation of political power.[33] It is not simply their goals that are messianic or millenarian; one generation's extreme demands become the next generation's moderate goals.[34] And tactics such as protest do not clearly distinguish messianics from subordinates.[35] Rather, the separatist-messianics' belief that political power will be reallocated in the absence of a political struggle (a struggle that involves more than rhetoric), their failure to recognize the veracity of Harold Washington's favorite adage, that "politics ain't beanbag"—in essence, their failure to recognize that separatism and rejection of political coalitions are nonstarters in the efforts of numerical minorities to become empowered—is what defines such leaders and their followers as messianic and what makes them so vulnerable to marginalization by outsiders.[36]

Max Weber's ideal-type of charismatic leadership also captures some crucial aspects of the relationship between separatist-messianic leaders and their followers. Followers perceive leaders as charismatic when they accomplish heroic tasks that previously seemed undoable. Ann Ruth Wilner, in her study of charismatic leadership, explained that such accomplishments do not have to be tangible. "The gain of benefit resulting from the heroic act need not be material or intangible but can be psychic. Thus, a deed of restoration involving the recovery for people of land that once was theirs and was then taken from them is a tangible benefit; restoring their pride and dignity after they have been subject to humiliation is conferring a psychic benefit."[37]

In other words, separatist-messianics' open rejection of submissiveness and deference, their vitriolic articulation of Black pride and Black rage, and their condemnation of White racism and evil are heroic and confer psychic benefits on followers, because they are public declarations of what James C. Scott has called the "hidden transcript" that so many Blacks have shared and articulated among themselves but usually found too dangerous to articulate directly to Whites.[38]

The charisma and inspirational rhetoric that such leaders exude and the well-attended demonstrations that they lead give the impression that they command the allegiance of huge numbers of supporters; yet when separatist-messianics do deign to enter electoral politics, they have a poor record of mobilizing their supporters behind candidates.[39] Such leaders face difficulties in their attempts to garner the support of a Black middle class that considers separatism impractical, views a non-incremental approach to empowerment as extremist, and is attracted to radical rhetoric only as long as it does not conflict with their hopes for bourgeois success.[40] For the support of working-class and poor Blacks, separatist-messianics face competition from clientelistic-subordinates. The experience of less well-off Blacks may corroborate the separatists' claim that coalitions and compromise are merely code words for domination. But in many cities, lower-income Blacks risk losing the meager yet vital material benefits—such as patronage jobs, preferred access to public housing, or help in negotiations with street-level bureaucrats—that Black subordinate leaders historically have provided to them if they support the candidates of the dominant White faction.

The Undemocratic Nature of Subordinate and Messianic Leadership

Separatist-messianics and clientelistic-subordinates both fail to abide by liberal democratic ideas of representative leadership, accountability to followers, and political legitimacy resulting from popular consent. Messianic leaders have very narrow constituent bases; sometimes they head organizations with small memberships, and at other times they are simply self-declared leaders. They declare their authenticity and then seek to capture media attention and provoke negative responses from White elites in order to provide evidence of their de facto leadership status. That they are representatives of people and possess a constituency has not been established prior to their claims of leadership status. The heroic articulation of the hidden rage and the venting of the pent-up anger that so many African-Americans share provide their followers with a sense of empowerment, albeit only a *vicarious form of empowerment*, as in wearing a Malcolm X cap or an African dashiki.[41] Another source of separatist-messianics' legitimacy in the eyes of their followers is the promise of retributional justice they offer. Finally, they cite the fact that White elites aim so much criticism at them and seem so often to try to silence them (excepting media elites, who understand that rhetorical conflict yields an increased audience) as evidence of their own legitimacy and heroism.

Subordinates also are not representatives of the broad constituency for which they claim to speak. Although subordinates are often freely and fairly elected to their positions, turnout in these elections is often low because of the successful Black electoral demobilization that the dominant, anti-inclusionary coalition typically enjoys. Thus subordinates, like messianics, have narrow bases. They are typically recruited and anointed by White elites rather than selected by any majority segment of their constituency. Their claims to legitimacy, and whatever benefits they capture for themselves or other Blacks, are *vicariously derived*, that is, they have been given by the White patron and they can be withdrawn.[42]

The Negative Dialectic of Subordinates and Separatists

Between the subordinate who is deprecated and delegitimized as an Uncle Tom and the separatist who is dismissed as politically naive and irrelevant to efforts at reallocation of political power, usually there is a no man's (or woman's) land. Few leaders have arisen outside of the two types presented, because the dialectical relationship between separatists and subordinates typically creates and maintains a leadership vacuum. The two types portray each other and all fledgling alternatives as illegitimate, preventing any leaders from having broad-based legitimacy, either biracially or even among the Black voting age population. I call this leadership vacuum the *negative dialectic* between subordinates and separatists.

When individuals emerge who call for genuine reallocation of power through participation in electoral politics, they face high hurdles. Subordinates undermine such protoleaders by rhetorically blurring important distinctions between them and separatist-messianics. By being "reasonable" Black leaders—in other words, by being willing to settle for minor adjustments and other cooptive benefits that do not amount to any real reallocation of power, advising their constituents to do the same, and publicly condemning the demands of these protoleaders—subordinates serve the interests of dominant White elites. Dominant White political leaders can (a) marginalize fledgling Black leaders as individuals with an unreasonable, overly ambitious agenda; (b) sustain their own claim of being reasonable and flexible by making cooptive, nonempowering concessions to subordinate Black leaders, and (c) brandish the threat that if radical, unreasonable demands continue to be forwarded by Black spokespersons, Black citizens may jeopardize the goodwill of the White leadership, unleash a backlash, and lose their paternalistic, clientelist ally.

The separatist-messianics also undermine these protoleaders' efforts. Separatist-messianics, refusing to recognize the significant distinctions, delegitimize these fledgling leaders among Black citizens by labeling them Uncle Toms, the same epithet widely used to describe the subordinate leaders. Once the negative label of Uncle Tom is brandished against these protoleaders it is a steep uphill battle to gain legitimacy and credibility in the eyes of potential Black constituents. Moses has stressed the unusual power of this epithet.

> It is significant that courageous militants, who demonstrated exemplary heroism in confronting violent racism with techniques of passive resistance, simply could not withstand the pressure of being named "Uncle Toms." The emotional violence of Black-power rhetoric had far more power to undermine the non-violent civil rights protests than did the actual physical violence of Southern mobs.[43]

Participation in the institutions of a political system that was created by Whites and helps Whites to maintain political domination, and participation in coalitions that force compromise with groups that have benefited from the subordination of African-Americans, are unheroic, noncharismatic actions that threaten to adulterate the messianic stance that binds separatist leaders to their followers; therefore, such actions must be rejected.[44] In fact, separatist-messianic's refusal to recognize the gains made through working within the political system, evokes the image of a person or group in denial, speaking psychologically. Such gains *cannot* be recognized, because they would provide both concrete evidence of the incremental empowerment that can be derived from participatory, coalitional strategies and a competing heroic paradigm. Certainly all observers can cite numerous instances in which participation in the electoral system and entry into coalitions have yielded few if any benefits to African-Americans. Yet surely this has not always been the case, and it behooves leaders and scholars to try to systematically discover under what circumstances such strategies have advanced African-American political empowerment.

Typically, clientelistic-subordinates consider all other leadership types to be advocating goals that are unreasonable, unattainable, messianic, and dangerous because of the potential for inciting backlash. Conversely, separatist-messianics dismiss all other leaders as advocates of goals that are too accommodating, spineless, and likely to lead to cooptation and the frustration of efforts toward genuine empowerment. When no alternatives to these two kinds of leadership emerge, where do Black constituents turn? One answer is that they opt out, that is, they withdraw from participation in politics, and turnout declines become evident. Another consequence of the negative dialectic is that those willing to work through the political system for change become frustrated and turn toward the separatists' messianism out of desperation. Scholars such as Cornel West and Adolph Reed Jr., have suggested that the current national Black leadership void is producing such results. Reed has suggested that the recent popularity of the messianic message of Louis Farrakhan is linked to the absence of an alternative Black leadership with a progressive, empowering vision: "In the midst of the Reagan counterrevolution and Black elites' typically uninspired and ineffectual responses, that sort of demagogic appeal found a popular audience. With no more promising agenda available, racial cheerleading at least offered a soothing catharsis."[45]

Finally, to offset the possibility that Blacks are turning to the separatists out of frustration with a lack of alternatives, the White patrons may increase the flow of (nonempowering) benefits to the subordinates to nourish these leaders' credibility. As Daniel C. Thompson argued, "Most of the favors the Uncle Toms receive are due to the fact that in order to be serviceable to the White community, they must maintain prestige among Negroes. They must, therefore, evince some influence with White authorities . . . without which a leadership vacuum would be created that might be filled by a really radical Negro leader, who is not under the control of White authorities."[46]

Given the destructive negative dialectic that preserves a leadership void, under only certain polity circumstances will those leaders who try to stake out a position between separatists and subordinates, forging coalitions within the electoral system and pursuing genuine empowerment, be able to gain the foothold of credibility and legitimacy necessary to build a constituency within the Black community and to fend off subordinates' and separatists' claims, that such strategies are fruitless diversions.

I label this type of leadership coalitional-incrementalist. What criteria define such leaders, who are usually not recognized in typologies of Black leadership, and what kinds of circumstances foster their emergence?

Coalitional-Incrementalists

Coalitional-incrementalists seek political empowerment. They believe that the most effective way to use liberal democratic institutions for this purpose is to form coalitions with other groups; hence they are *coalitionist* rather than separatist. They participate in electoral coalitions as a means to elect responsive officials and exert influence over political appointments, all toward the ultimate goal of influencing policy agendas and outcomes and exercising political power to advance the interests of their electoral constituency. Like separatist-messianics, coalitional-incrementalists are, to borrow Ronald Walters's terminology, "system-challenging" leaders;[47] both believe that the benefits bestowed on subordinates do not constitute a real reallocation of political power. But unlike the separatists, coalitional-incrementalists are willing to achieve these gains *incrementally* and frame their goals in a piecemeal manner; indeed, they believe that this is the only realistic strategy for redistributing power.

If subordinates have political authority because they have been anointed as the local agents of a politically dominant White faction, and separatists have authority by virtue of their charismatic relationship with followers, what is the coalitional-incrementalists' source of the authority? The answer to this question takes us an important step toward answering the question that launched this discussion of leadership—what are the particular circumstances that lead to the nonrandom emergence and distribution of coalitional-incrementalists across polities?

For coalitional-incrementalists to be successful in their goal of reallocating political power in a way that is more beneficial to African-Americans, one of two things must happen: either (1) they must persuade leaders of other power-contending groups (e.g., Irish-Americans, downtown business groups, WASPs) that it is in their best interests to willingly relinquish some power to Blacks, so that these other power-contenders can gain Black electoral support and preserve their remaining political power, or (2) coalitional-incrementalists must work to have Blacks and their allies oust other power-contending groups from the governing coalition and capture some of the political power previously held by them.[48] In either case a process of elite negotiation takes place, in which Black coalitional-incrementalists seek greater empowerment and negotiate with other leaders who also are seeking either to enhance or maintain their power.

The leverage that coalitional-incrementalists possess in such a bargaining situation is derived from the impact that the votes that they claim to be able to mobilize will have on the ultimate outcome of an election. If coalitional-incrementalists can mobilize enough votes to shift the outcome of elections, and therefore affect the standing of other power contenders, then these Black leaders are poised to have considerable leverage and are in an excellent position to win greater Black empowerment. Delivering decisive votes in exchange for incremental gains in political empowerment leads to coalitional-incrementalists' political legitimacy from the Black electorate, who benefit from these gains. When elections are competitive, even a

Black voting population that represents only 10 percent of the electorate, but is mobilized as a bloc vote (a contingent factor and a test of the leader's capabilities), can swing the outcome of an election. Even in less competitive polities, *if* the Black electorate is sizable, coalitional-incrementalist leaders are in a position of strong leverage in negotiations about the distribution of political power if the candidate they support wins by a margin that is smaller than the mobilized Black bloc vote. Thus *polity environments* play a very important role in the creation of opportunities for potential leaders to thrive and gain legitimacy. In noncompetitive polities coalitional-incrementalists are unlikely to flourish, because they will find themselves without negotiation leverage. Even if they can mobilize a sizable Black bloc vote, in non-competitive elections this bloc does not affect the outcome. To power-contending groups in the opposition, Black electoral support can often be welcome, but if it does not change the outcome of the election, then bargaining and promises of Black empowerment are moot. The losers of elections are not in a position to alter the allocation of political power. To those in the governing coalition, Black incrementalist electoral support would be merely icing on the cake. Agreeing to demands made in exchange for votes that are unnecessary would, in most instances, be irrational and could produce instability in a dominant coalition, because such a reallocation of power *to* African-Americans implies a reallocation of power *from* some other power-contending group already in the coalition. If a coalitional-incrementalist leader is unable to negotiate a genuine reallocation of power, and is instead forced to settle for cooptive benefits (or receives nothing), he or she will then be very vulnerable to the separatist-messianics' delegitimating charges that coalitional-incrementalists are no different from clientelistic-subordinates. Thus, noncompetitive polity environments foster the negative dialectic between separatists and subordinates that results in the decimation of alternatives to these two types of leadership.

In the environment of competitive politics, on the other hand, coalitional-incrementalists can gain legitimacy iteratively. Each election, and each of the many battles over policy, provides such leaders with an opportunity to exchange *decisive* Black votes for increased shares of political power; and each time electoral success does yield incremental Black empowerment (i.e., the bargain is kept), the coalitional-incrementalist leadership can point to concrete achievements that distinguishes it from both subordinates and separatists and augments its legitimacy in the eyes of current and potential Black constituents.[49] The success of coalitional-incrementalists alters the dialectics of leadership legitimacy. The warnings of clientelistic-subordinates—that if Black leaders demand genuine reallocation of power they will be rebuffed and may precipitate a backlash that jeopardizes clientelistic relations—are not borne out and are exposed as hollow and unnecessarily cautious. The criticism offered by separatist-messianics, that the incrementalists deliver the same plantation-style subservience as the subordinates, is also demonstrated to be invalid. Politically attentive followers of both subordinates and separatists may recognize the virtues of the coalitional-incrementalists' leadership strategy and shift their allegiance to them. In competitive electoral polities, therefore, the opportunity exists for a reversal of the negative dialectic and a flow of power centripetally rather than centrifugally.

Examples of coalitional-incrementalist Black leadership at the national level are sparse. The Congressional Black Caucus, as a group and individually, has been able to exercise political power to advance items on the agenda of African-Americans such as the economic embargo against the South African apartheid regime. Their primary leverage has been the threat of withholding votes on legislation important to the Democratic party's congressional leadership. In the post-1964 national political scene, the Republican party has ceased to compete for Black electoral support; in fact, the party has successfully played the race card to drive a wedge into the old New Deal coalition and recruit White voters who believe that the Democratic party has advocated a program that gives too much preference to goals shared by most African-Americans.[50] Facing no competition for African-American votes, the Democratic party has been able to take Black voters for granted. Blacks vote for Democrats, even when they are unwilling to accede to the demands of African-American leaders for greater empowerment, because Republican candidates rarely even acknowledge the needs of Black citizens. Under these noncompetitive electoral conditions, the best that African-Americans are able to achieve as members of the Democratic party coalition is a maintenance of the status quo and a defense of the gains previously made against those who would roll them back. The contemporary inability of national-level Black leadership to make progress toward further Black empowerment illustrates the contention that noncompetitive polity environments represent conditions under which Black leaders have little leverage and power. If Black leaders hope to advance group empowerment, they must devise a strategy for making Black voters the object of the parties' competition.[51]

The current situation has not always been the case at the national level. From 1932 until 1964, the two parties competed for Black votes in presidential elections. For example, in Franklin D. Roosevelt's 1944 presidential defeat of Thomas Dewey, the Black vote played a decisive role. A shift of slightly more than 303,000 votes in 15 states outside of the South would have given Dewey a victory. In 8 of these 15 states the margin of Black votes won by Roosevelt exceeded his overall margin, meaning that without his Black electoral support, he would have lost those states.[52] Recognition of the importance of the Black vote for FDR probably contributed to the decision by the recently ascended President Harry Truman to request that Congress, in 1948 (just prior to his first presidential election bid), pass the legislation that would establish the permanent Commission of Civil Rights and Civil Rights Division in the Department of Justice, provide federal protection against lynching, protect the right to vote, and establish the Fair Employment Practices Commission to prevent unfair discrimination in employment.[53] An analysis of Truman's surprising victory over Dewey concluded, "[T]he incumbent President received 69 per cent of the Black vote. It was this large Black vote that was responsible for his narrow margins in three key states—Illinois, 33,612; California, 17,865; Ohio, 7,107."[54] Similarly, a number of scholars contend that the significant increase in Black support for Dwight Eisenhower in 1956, in response to both Democratic congressional intransigence on civil rights and the strong civil rights record his administration accomplished through executive orders, played a crucial role in Ike's performance in Louisiana, Tennessee, and Alabama.[55]

The dynamic of electoral competition producing leverage for Black leaders and opportunities for Black advancement has also been observed at the state level. According to Weiss, the entry of Blacks into elected and appointed positions in state and local Democratic politics also brought greater political opportunities for Black Republicans. The GOP finally awakened to the reality that Blacks would in fact desert the party of Lincoln and, in a number of northern states, began to slate Black candidates for office in the hope of wooing Black voters back into the Republican fold. The invigoration of Black politics showed up in the election results. Between 1925 and 1929, twenty-seven Blacks served in state legislatures; between 1932 and 1936, the number increased to thirty-eight. In the election of 1932, ten Black Republicans and three Democrats won seats in the legislatures of eight states. In 1936, twelve Black Democrats and five Republicans were elected to nine state legislatures. Four years later, twenty-three Blacks—fourteen of them Democrats—won election to ten legislatures.[56]

The contemporary absence of such competition for the Black vote and of coalitional-incrementalist leadership at the national level points to what may be the most significant constraint on Black empowerment today, the lack of leverage that extant and fledgling Black leaders have in the councils of either party. The case studies in this book demonstrate that at the local level, partisan or factional competition for the Black vote creates the conditions within which coalitional-incrementalist leadership can flourish.

The Positive Dialectic between Incrementalists and Messianics

Hanes Walton Jr. has asserted that few scholars have "bothered to analyze the role that Black nationalism plays in Black politics or how it translates itself into political action in the Black community. In fact, most scholars have argued that Black nationalism is *apolitical*. They fail to see the different manifestations of Black nationalism as both a force for separation and a politically motivating vehicle."[57] I have already discussed how Black nationalism becomes a force for separation in the environment of noncompetitive polities. The negative dialectic in particular has contributed to the underdevelopment of Black leadership and the retarding of Black empowerment, as messianic leaders play a huge role in denying legitimacy to other leaders by condemning them as Uncle Toms. Yet separatist-messianics also play a role in augmenting the legitimacy of coalitional-incrementalist leaders.

As Walton suggested, separatist-messianics can play a positive role in the struggle for empowerment—given the environment of a competitive polity. In that environment, separatists' charges of Uncle Tomism threaten the legitimacy of the coalitional-incrementalists and lead them to make their goals ambitious enough to convince the majority of Blacks that they are still working toward African-American empowerment. At the same time, the separatist-messianics' continuing active advocacy of a considerably more radical agenda leads the leadership of the power-contending groups to view the coalitional-incrementalists' demands as more realistic and appropriate. In contrast to the negative dialectic that produces a leadership vacuum, the interaction between separatist-messianics and coalitional-incrementalists in competitive polities can enhance the legitimacy of the latter leadership cadre and advance the struggle for empowerment.[58] This interaction can be labeled the *positive dialectic* of Black leadership.

Separatist-messianics do not have this kind of positive impact in polities where no coalitional-incrementalist cadre has been established—in noncompetitive polities. In such circumstances, neither subordinates nor incrementalists have the leverage to make demands on power-holders or other power-contenders for the kind of reallocation of political power that constitutes empowerment. These leaders have meager defenses against charges leveled by separatist-messianics that they contribute to the subordination of African-Americans. But the separatists themselves have equally little defense against the efforts by defenders of the status quo, both Black and White, to marginalize them and individually portray them "as a lunatic fringe [that] actually impede the progress that the movement might be making were it not for the backlash which they evoke."[59]

A Note on Jesse Jackson's Leadership

Jesse Jackson's leadership has deservedly drawn much attention from scholars and journalists.[60] Because Jackson's activities were centered in Chicago in the 1960s and 1970s, I discuss his local activities in chapter 2. Here I want to briefly address a question that may be on the minds of readers—where does Jesse Jackson fit in this typology?

Although Jackson is not a clientelistic-subordinate, he does not fit neatly into either of the other leadership types. It is not simply that Jackson is enigmatic or fickle; rather, he combines important traits of the messianic type with defining features of coalitional-incrementalist leadership. In keeping with the antidemocratic nature of messianic leadership, Jackson anointed himself as the heir of Martin Luther King Jr.; subsequently, he declared himself the single political vehicle for the political hopes of Black America. Jackson regularly invokes messianic images of himself and is treated as a messianic figure by others. Adolph L. Reed Jr., more than any other scholar, has highlighted Jesse Jackson's messianic self-presentation. Reed reminds us that Jackson was

> told of a terminally ill Virginia supporter who insisted on leaving his hospital bed to attend a campaign rally at which his condition improved so dramatically that his doctor ordered new tests, only to find no evidence of his earlier cancer. Always given to drape himself in the cultural authority of King's image, Jackson thus assessed his success in the New York primary: "What was a crucifixion in April of 1968 [became] a resurrection in April of 1984." The message is clear: the campaign's mission was divinely inspired. Only apostates could refuse to accept it on its own terms.[61]

Following Jackson's mission to Syria to negotiate the release of a Black navy flier, Lieutenant Robert Goodman, Louis Farrakhan said: "As Jesse handled the press with such skill, I didn't see Jesse. I saw God. . . . When he pleaded a case before the president of Syria, Hafez Assad, we didn't see Jesse, we saw God. . . . You should hurry and see God working in one of the children of the slaves."[62] Jackson has also called Black reporters who criticize him traitors to the Black race, publicly attacking many of them.[63]

Although clearly a messianic, Jackson is not a separatist. He has worked, since his days in Chicago, to secure a reallocation of political power to Blacks within the

Democratic party. His two presidential campaigns demonstrated a willingness to work within the electoral system and to reform political institutions so that they can be vehicles for advancing Black empowerment. In both these campaigns he sought votes outside the Black community, while giving greater attention to shoring up his base. His platform did not solely address the plight of Blacks but offered a broad-based economic and moral appeal. Particularly in 1988, his agenda became more concrete, more incremental, and less messianic. Finally, through his willingness to compete in elections and let voters be the arbiters of his political legitimacy, Jackson took a big step away from the tenets of separatist messianism.

Jackson's evolving leadership style was evident in the struggle for Black political empowerment in Chicago, to be discussed in chapter 2. Chapter 2 presents two case studies: of intraparty and interparty competition in the Thompson and Kelly eras that yielded Black empowerment; and of electoral monopoly in the Richard J. Daley regime, in which Black political power was rolled back and Blacks became politically subordinated. The chapter also discusses the breakthrough of Harold Washington and the negative Black leadership dialectic that has paralyzed his erstwhile successors and enabled Richard M. Daley to halt Washington's dramatic efforts at Black empowerment. Chapter 3 presents a case study of Black political subordination in Gary's noncompetitive polity and the special conditions that enabled Richard Hatcher to displace the conservative Democratic machine polity. It traces the underdeveloped Black leadership structure in Gary from the early part of the century through the Hatcher era. Chapters 4 and 5 turn from subordination to empowerment. Chapter 4 examines the struggle for political empowerment in Philadelphia, which began as part of the effort to overthrow a long-dominant Republican machine. Intraparty and interparty electoral competition made Black votes significant and created numerous opportunities for a cadre of Black leaders to emerge and win incremental empowerment. Even in defeat, Blacks and White liberals remained allies and built the trust that enabled them to elect Wilson Goode as the city's first Black mayor in 1983. The chapter also addresses the significance of Edward Rendell's election in 1991, which returned the mayor's office to a White liberal. Chapter 5 presents a case study of the nonpartisan electoral competition between growth activists and segregationists that raised Black votes to a position of decisiveness in Atlanta elections and resulted in six consecutive terms in which the city has been led by a biracial coalition headed by Blacks.

Gary and Atlanta were specifically chosen as companion complementary cases. Because they are cases that have been well documented by other scholars, they offer the properly skeptical reader an independent check on the theoretical implications drawn from all four cases in the final chapter. I believe there is no methodological flaw in the strategy of nonrandom selection of cases to test and refine these theoretical arguments. The goal of this book is not to offer the only theory that explains all cases of these dependent outcomes; rather, my purpose is to build a midrange theory that explains a fair number of cases and is, therefore, a useful analytic tool. In chapter 6 I discuss the theoretical significance of the relationship between electoral competition and Black political empowerment. In chapter 6 I also use the four case study arguments to illustrate the typology of Black leadership presented in this book. Finally, I explore explanations for the transformation from noncompetitive to competitive political regimes.

Two

Black Political Subordination
in Chicago

I n no U.S. city had Blacks achieved more substantial political empowerment by the first half of the twentieth century than in Chicago. Ralph Bunche declared that Chicago was "the seventh heaven" of political activity for Blacks.[1] Harold Gosnell argued that "Negroes in Chicago have achieved relatively more in politics than have the Negroes in other cities of the United States."[2] Allan Spear concluded that during this period Blacks "had more political power in Chicago than anywhere else in the country."[3] Yet from the 1950s to 1983 (when Harold Washington was unexpectedly elected as the city's first African-American mayor), the political gains of Blacks were rolled back so thoroughly that a new generation of analysts viewed the Windy City as an extreme example of Black political subordination and powerlessness.[4] Out of the midst of this subordination, labeled plantation politics by local participants and scholars, emerged a movement that swept Harold Washington into the mayor's office and dramatically increased the political power of African-Americans in Chicago. But in the aftermath of his sudden death, African-Americans have again become divided and have squandered most of the political power they so quickly accrued in his brief tenure.

Why were Blacks so successful in their struggle for political power in early-twentieth-century Chicago? How can the dramatic rollback in the political progress of Blacks in Chicago from the late 1950s to 1983 be explained? This chapter contrasts these two successive periods in Chicago's history (in effect, holding many factors constant) and shows that one factor that varied significantly between the two periods, and that can contribute to an explanation of the progress and rollback of Black political power in Chicago, is the degree of *electoral competitiveness*.

First, an analysis of politics in Chicago from 1900 to 1947 provides evidence that electoral competitiveness created the conditions for the empowerment of formerly subordinated groups, with the result that Black empowerment in Chicago surpassed that of any other major city in the United States during this period.[5]

Second, this chapter documents the dramatic shift of Chicago's political environment from competitive to noncompetitive, which began with the election of 1959 and resulted in the monopolization of political offices by the Democratic party organization. Third, I argue that a crucial consequence of this shift was that Black political empowerment was halted and rolled back. The impact of the Democratic party's electoral monopoly on the structure of political leadership in the Black community is examined. Finally, I show how an unprecedented split between White factions of the Chicago machine created the opportunity that enabled Harold Washington to unify African-American voters and dramatically increase registration and turnout enough for a victory. I argue that the structure of Black leadership created by the electorally noncompetitive environment had detrimental implications for Washington's governing coalition and largely accounted for the inability of African-American citizens to unify in the aftermath of his death.

Electoral Competitiveness and the Empowerment of Blacks in Chicago, 1900–1947

The Thompson Era and Black Electoral Power

When Republican William Hale Thompson entered Chicago politics in 1900 to run for the office of alderman of the Second Ward, he was a political novice and a relative stranger to the city.[6] He turned for help to Rev. Archibald Carey; Carey tutored him in the ways of the Second Ward and introduced him to other Blacks capable of organizing and mobilizing voters. To the surprise of all observers, Thompson defeated the incumbent alderman, Democrat Charles Gunther. Thompson publicly credited Carey for the victory and rewarded him and the voters of the Second Ward by shepherding an ordinance through the city council that placed the city's first public playground in the heart of the Second Ward across the street from Carey's church. Thompson and Carey repeatedly reminded constituents that Black children had a playground to play in before White children did in Chicago.[7]

Alderman Thompson introduced Carey to many other White politicians as the "ambassador of the Black Belt." The most important of these politicians was Senator William Lorimer (1909–12), who was the leader of one of the two Republican party factions—the one to which Thompson belonged. The other was headed by Charles S. Deneen (governor, 1905–13; senator, 1925–31).[8] Lorimer and Thompson put Carey in touch with the Swift and Armour families and other packinghouse owners, who became important suppliers of jobs for his parishioners. Carey's ability to provide jobs to Blacks—who often faced discriminatory employment barriers—enhanced his ability to build a network of election-day workers and to deliver large numbers of Black votes.[9]

In the 1915 Republican mayoral primary, candidates of the two factions—Thompson and Harry Olson—faced each other. Thompson won a narrow victory with less than 51 percent of the vote. The 2,508-vote margin of victory (Thompson, 87,333–Olson, 84,825) was a result of Thompson's strong support in the 70 percent–Black Second Ward. With the help of Oscar DePriest, Carey delivered the ward with an almost 7,000-vote margin (Thompson, 8,633–Olson, 1,870).[10] After the close primary, Thompson defeated Democratic mayoral candidate Robert Sweitzer with 52 percent of the vote.[11]

"Big Bill" Thompson (1915–1919, 1919–1923, 1927–1931) would not have won the Republican nomination in 1915, and probably would have lost the subsequent mayoral elections of 1919 and 1927, without the support he received from Black voters. In 1919 Thompson captured 52 percent of the approximately 690,000 votes cast, winning the election by about 21,000 votes. Thompson's margin in the predominantly Black Second (80 percent) and Third (70 percent) wards was over 15,000. That is, approximately 71 percent of Thompson's victory margin in the 1919 mayoral election came from the two wards in which Blacks were most concentrated. To quiet charges of corruption in his administration, Thompson skipped the 1923 election. Running again in 1927, he received 54 percent of the votes and narrowly defeated incumbent mayor William Dever. Blacks gave Thompson 92 percent of their vote, and the two predominantly Black wards generated 56 percent of Thompson's victory margin. Harold Gosnell concluded that even though Black voters were less than 10 percent of the voting population, they spelled the difference between victory and defeat for Thompson and his coalition of native stock Americans and Italian immigrants:

> In the four primary elections at which [Thompson] was a candidate for mayor he received over 80 per cent of the total Republican primary vote cast in the Second Ward, the ward which contained the largest proportion of Negro voters. . . . In every other mayoralty primary at which he was a candidate except the one in 1927, the plurality which he piled up in the wards inhabited largely by Negroes was decisive in winning the nomination. . . . [In mayoral elections] upon a number of occasions the pluralities received in the districts inhabited largely by Negroes have been decisive. Without these pluralities Thompson could not have defeated his Democratic opponents in the mayoralty elections of 1919 and 1927.[12]

The Growth of Black Political Power

"Big Bill" Thompson's victories—the 1915 mayoral primary and the 1919 and 1927 general elections—all were highly competitive elections, according to the definition presented in chapter 1. Did the decisive role that Black votes played in these elections matter? Were Black leaders able to empower themselves and their community? Mayor Thompson rewarded DePriest's hard work in organizing Black voters by supporting his bid to become the first Black alderman in 1905 and later by slating him to be the GOP committeeman for the ward.[13] For DePriest and his constituents, this was a steppingstone toward election as the first Black congressman from the North. Carey was appointed civil service commissioner, a post from which he was able to aid many Blacks seeking city employment; Gosnell called this "one of the most outstanding appointive positions held by a colored man in Chicago."[14] Thompson later supported two other aspiring Black leaders, Louis Anderson and Robert Jackson, in their successful aldermanic campaigns.[15] More than two-thirds of the Black employees in the school system (about eight hundred) owed their positions to the political influence of Carey, DePriest, Anderson, and Jackson.[16] In 1920 Edward H. Wright, earlier appointed by Thompson as a city attorney, received Thompson's support for the position of Second Ward Republican committeeman. As committeeman, Wright controlled patronage distribution in the ward and influenced the slating of candidates.[17] St. Clair Drake and Horace Cayton explained that this was an "indication that they [Blacks] had been really admitted into the inner councils of the Republican party."[18] In his last administration the mayor again appointed six Blacks as assistant corporation counsels, five as assistant city prosecutors, one as assistant city attorney, and an unspecified number as legal investigators. About 14 percent of the city's Legal Department was Black in Thompson's last term.[19] The large numbers of Black appointees led the mayor's enemies at the city's newspapers to label City Hall Uncle Tom's Cabin.[20]

By 1932, Blacks were about 7 percent of the city population and held 6.4 percent of the jobs in the city workforce. Blacks did not capture important positions in every city bureaucracy. But in the Health Department, the Bureau of Parks and Recreation, the Water Department, and the city's library system, Blacks held proportions of the top jobs that approached parity with the Black proportion of the population.[21]

Short-Term Alliances with Democrats

Carey, DePriest, and other Black leaders did not support Thompson and the GOP exclusively. They also mobilized Black majorities to cross party lines if Democratic candidates offered significant rewards.[22] For instance, in 1911 Carey stumped for incumbent mayor Carter Harrison II against Republican Charles E. Merriam. In exchange, Harrison appointed Carey to the Motion Picture Censure Board, from which he led the protest against racially insulting films such as *Birth of A Nation*.[23] Similarly, in 1912, in exchange for supporting Democratic gubernatorial candidate Edward Dunne, Carey and another Black organizer, Robert Jackson, were selected to head the state commission (with an appropriation of $25,000) commemorating the fiftieth anniversary of Lincoln's Emancipation Proclamation. Carey's church was chosen as the headquarters of this commission.[24]

When Thompson decided not to run for mayor in 1923, Arthur Lueder, a candidate from the opposition Deneen faction, emerged as the GOP candidate. Black alderman Louis Anderson and former alderman DePriest openly backed Democrat William Dever. Dever captured 62 percent of the vote in the predominantly Black Second and Third wards and won the election.[25] Dever appointed a Black to the city's library board and steered patronage positions to Alderman Anderson.[26] Unlike the concessions won from the Republicans, the rewards from the Democrats did not further empower Blacks. Still, these rewards did mean more jobs, offices, and "pieces of the pie" for Blacks, and they served notice to the local GOP that Black votes could not be taken for granted.

The consistent ability of Black voters to play a decisive role in elections drew the attention of others besides Gosnell. The *Hyde Park Property Owners Journal* in 1927 issued the following warning:

> Their solid vote is the Negroes' great weapon. They have a total vote in Chicago of about 40,000. This total vote is cast solid for the candidate who makes the best bargain with them. . . . This vote situation is the foundation of the Chicago Negro's effrontery and his evil designs against the white man's property. He feels that he holds the balance of power and that he can dictate the policy of any administration that happens to be elected by his controlling black vote. He therefore becomes arrogant, insulting, threatening. He abuses his rights and liberties and feels that he is perfectly safe in doing so for the reason that as he controls this bloc of votes he believes that he can practically dictate to the police department, the city administration and the courts.[27]

Their own arrogance was reprehensible, but the authors of this statement offered an explanation of the increasing political power of Chicago's Blacks that corresponds to the argument made in this book. For the first third of the twentieth century, politics in Chicago was characterized by intraparty factional competition as well as interparty competition. This environment increased the importance of Black votes. When the Black voters of the Second and Third wards were mobilized as a bloc, they often determined the outcome of important city elections. Because political leaders like Carey and DePriest were not bound to one faction or party, they had significant leverage with which to negotiate the delivery of large numbers of Black votes in exchange for benefits, including political empowerment. Each time any of the Black organizers won concessions from White power brokers, the status of these leaders within their own communities grew and their ability to speak on behalf of their constituents undoubtedly increased.[28]

In 1931 Thompson was finally defeated in a mayoral election by Democrat Anton J. Cermak, who captured 58 percent of the vote. Cermak's rise to power, which has been analyzed in detail elsewhere, was the product of a number of factors.[29] Cermak built a coalition of his own native Czechs, as well as Jews, Germans, and Poles, that elected him to the presidency of the Cook County Board of Commissioners in 1922. This patronage-rich position enabled him to centralize a Democratic party that included warring Irish factions and Eastern European ethnic groups whose empowerment was hindered by the Irish dominance of the party. Thompson also made the foolish mistake of belittling Cermak's foreign origins during the campaign, further solidifying Eastern European animosity toward himself.[30] In addition, violent gang wars, recurring tax scandals, and an insolvent school system discredited the Thompson administration and led Republican civic and business leaders to defect from the GOP and support Cermak, whom they hoped would bring good government and political order. Finally, Cermak was the beneficiary of national factors that improved the political fortunes of local Democrats, including the presidential candidacy of Al Smith and the Great Depression. Blacks, however, remained loyal to Thompson and gave him 82 percent of their votes, but this was not enough to defeat Cermak.

If Cermak was interested in including Blacks in a New Deal coalition, his approach would have to be characterized as one of forced submission.

> The better part of [Mayor Cermak's] first day in office was black Thursday for Ne-
> groes. He discharged almost 3,000 workers, most of them colored people. . . . Cermak
> was determined to make blacks pay a handsome price for boycotting the Democratic
> party. . . . [Cermak] instructed Captain Martin Mullen to form a special vice and gam-
> bling detail to work under his direct orders. Cermak's first command to Captain Mullen
> and John Stege was to give the black policy [numbers gambling] barons and their ilk
> holy hell. Stege's Forty-eight Street gestapo-like troops arrested an average of two
> hundred black men and women a day.[31]

But Cermak was mayor only until February 1933, when he traveled to Miami to
meet with President-elect Roosevelt. He was shot by a gunman, who—most believe—
was aiming at Roosevelt, and died 19 days later.

The Kelly Era

On Cermak's assassination, power shifted to Democratic party chairman Pat Nash,
who picked Edward Kelly (1933–47) as mayor. With power back in the hands of
Irishmen Nash and Kelly, Cermak's multiethnic coalition was weakened. As the electoral data in table 2–1 indicate, from 1935 to 1955, politics in Chicago remained
competitive. The electoral edge had shifted from the Republicans to the Democrats.
Yet in no mayoral election, except that of 1935, did the Democrats capture 60 percent of the vote; the Republicans remained a competitive force in the city's politics,
largely because of continued Black electoral support.[32]

If the Democrats were to become the majority party of the city, as they rapidly
were becoming at the national level, they would have to win more of the Black vote.
To do this, Black leaders told Mayor Kelly, they would have to slate more Blacks for
offices.[33] To his credit, Kelly raised his share of the Black vote to more than 50 percent, about three times the percentage that Cermak had received.

Yet, as table 2–2 shows, except in 1935, Kelly, Dawson, and the local Democratic
organization still were unable to command the huge proportions (i.e., 80–95%) of
the Black vote that Thompson had regularly captured.[34] In 1939 and 1943, Blacks

Table 2–1 Democratic Party Victories in Competitive Mayoral Elections, 1931–1955

Year	Democratic Percentage of mayoral vote	Republican Percentage of mayoral vote	Democratic winner
1931	58	42	Cermak
1935[a]	83	17	Kelly
1939	56	44	Kelly
1943	55	45	Kelly
1947	59	41	Kennelly
1951	56	44	Kennelly
1955	55	45	Daley

Source: Board of Election Commissioners, City of Chicago, "Official Election Returns, General Elections" (City of
Chicago, 1931–1955). All calculations by me.

[a]As discussed in note 34, all observers agree that Kelly's strength in this election was an anomaly that resulted from a
political bargain between the Democratic organization and Republican party leaders, who agreed to slate a lackluster
candidate.

Table 2–2 Voting in Chicago's Black Wards: Mayoral and Presidential Elections, 1927–1976

Year	Percentage Black vote for Democrat, mayor	Percentage Black vote for Democrat, president	Black[a] wards
1927–28	8	29	2, 3
1931–32	18	22	2, 3
1935–36[b]	79	49	2, 3
1939–40	56	52	2, 3
1943–44	52	65	2, 3
1947–48	52	72	2, 3
1951–52	52	75	2, 3
1955–56	77	64	2, 3, 20
1959–60	84	78	2, 3, 20
1963–64	85	97	2, 3, 4, 6, 20, 24
1967–68	87	94	2, 3, 4, 6, 20, 24
1971–72	75	91	2, 3, 4, 6, 17, 20, 24, 29
1975–76	88	92	2, 3, 4, 6, 17, 20, 24, 29

Source: For mayoral data: see Board of Election Commissioners, City of Chicago, "Official Election Returns, General Elections" (City of Chicago, 1927–75). For presidential data, see the relevant years in Richard Scammon, *America Votes* (Washington, D.C.: Congressional Quarterly).

[a]All Black wards were more than 90 percent Black, except during 1927–32, when they were more than 70 percent Black.

[b]As noted in note 34, all observers agree that Kelly's strength in this election was an anomaly.

cast, respectively, 56 and 52 percent of their ballots for Kelly. Continued Republican vigor was most evident in the predominantly Black Third Ward, where Oscar DePriest was elected as alderman in 1939. In 1943 DePriest was succeeded by Archibald Carey Jr. (son of Thompson's longtime ally) who defeated Democrat Roy Washington (father of future mayor Harold Washington) and continued the Republican party's control over the Third Ward aldermanic office until 1955. At the end of Kelly's tenure in 1947, electoral politics remained competitive (as defined earlier)—the Republican party still had not been licked in Chicago.[35]

Kelly's elections were competitive; in his four victories his percentage of the vote was 58, 83, 56, and 55 (table 2–2). Because his margins of victory were not overwhelming, he knew that he had to expand his party's electoral coalition. At the national level, FDR was broadening the party's tent by appealing to Blacks, and Kelly followed the same strategy. In these efforts, he yielded significant political benefits to Blacks. He reversed Cermak's policy of cracking down on gambling operations in the Black wards. He also dispensed more patronage jobs to Blacks than any previous mayor, including Thompson. He not only increased the quantity of jobs that went to Blacks, but he also upgraded the quality of these positions. Mayor Kelly was the political sponsor of Arthur Mitchell, the first Black elected to Congress as a Democrat. He returned Black lawyers, forced out by Mayor Cermak, to the offices of the corporation counsel.[36] He also appointed Blacks to the positions of chairman of the Chicago Housing Authority, civil service commissioner, assistant city prosecutor, assistant attorney general, assistant state's attorney, member of the school board, and judge of the municipal court, and he named the first Black police captain.[37] Although naming a Black to head the Chicago Housing Authority was an unequivocal real-location of political power that angered many White ethnics, some of these other appointments obviously do not represent empowerment as I have defined it; they might even be dismissed as tokenism. One member of the school board, or a single police captain, do not have the authority to influence decisionmaking in a bureau-cracy weighted against the interests of Blacks. Yet, because they represented firsts or breakthroughs in areas that were very sensitive to the Democratic party's White constituents, and because there was a long history of resistance to allowing Blacks to hold such positions, these appointments by Kelly must be viewed as meaningful and significant. In part, they explain why Kelly came to be viewed by Blacks as a Democratic Thompson, just as Thompson had come to be known as "the second Lincoln."[38]

Mayor Kelly went beyond personnel appointments in his rewards to the Black community for its electoral support. Blacks demonstrated unprecedented influence over the mayor in the important policy areas of schools and housing. In 1934 the Board of Education attempted to diminish overcrowding at Morgan Park High School by creating high-school classrooms in existing elementary schools. All first-year Black students were transferred to Shoop School. Blacks repudiated this policy as segrega-tion, because many White students from outside the Morgan Park district boundaries had been allowed to remain enrolled. A Black state representative, along with a dele-gation from the NAACP, the Urban League, and the parents of the students person-ally lobbied Mayor Kelly. Kelly overruled the Board of Education and ordered the Black students reinstated at Morgan High. This prompted two hundred White pro-testers to storm the mayor's office and demand that he "respect the authority of the Board of Education." Kelly refused to buckle under to these demands by White par-ents; a boycott of Morgan Park by White students failed to budge him.[39] Kelly's rec-ognition of Black electoral allegiance, as well as his commitment to desegregated education, led him in 1939 to appoint an African-American to the Board of Educa-tion. According to Michael W. Homel, this position was "the highest municipal po-sition that Negroes coveted."[40]

Mayor Kelly also demonstrated his responsiveness to the Black policy agenda in housing policy. He endorsed the Chicago Housing Authority's (CHA) efforts to in-tegrate public housing in overwhelmingly White neighborhoods, and he protected the CHA from the city council, which sought to derail this policy.[41] When approxi-mately one thousand protesters gathered at the Airport Homes project to protest the arrival of Black tenants, he mobilized four hundred police officers to disperse the crowd and protect the new residents. Martin Meyerson and Edward Banfield explained that Kelly's commitment to his Black constituents remained firm even in the face of this strong resistance:

> Kelly had encouraged the Authority not to be concerned about opposition; he was the Boss, and he would see that the CHA program and projects were protected. . . . [Mayor Kelly] issued a strong statement prepared by the Commission on Human Relations which endorsed CHA's policy of selecting tenants "according to need" and he had declared that "all law-abiding citizens may be assured of their right to live peaceably anywhere in Chicago."[42]

Further evidence of his commitment to the Black community was his establishment of the nation's first permanent and independent city department devoted to race relations.[43]

Mayor Kelly also intervened on behalf of African-Americans in the sacrosanct area of ward politics and patronage control. For years the objections of the predominantly Black residents of the Second Ward to White committeeman Joseph Tittinger's practice of distributing most patronage to the ward's small White population had been ignored. More than 50 Black precinct captains petitioned Mayor Kelly to remove Tittinger in 1939, and Tittinger relieved them of precinct work and fired them from their patronage jobs. Kelly stepped in on behalf of the Black precinct captains against Tittinger and replaced him with William Dawson, a Black politician whom Kelly had lured away from the GOP.[44]

Of course, Mayor Kelly's actions can not be claimed to be exclusively responsible for the Democrats' substantial increase in the proportion of the Black vote. Part of the credit obviously must go to the popularity of Franklin D. Roosevelt and his New Deal policies.[45] Simply put, because a national Democratic administration was organizing relief efforts and a local Democratic organization was distributing relief, WPA jobs, and federal patronage, it was important for Black leaders—whose communities often were harder hit than White communities by the economic depression— to make new alliances with the Democrats. With this carrot, Kelly persuaded one of the GOP's most promising Black ward leaders, William L. Dawson, to switch to the Democratic party. Dawson was given the patronage-rich position of committeeman in the Second Ward. From this base, Dawson distributed patronage and built an organization that regularly delivered the largely Black votes of Wards 2, 3, 4, 6, and 20. In 1942, Dawson was elected representative from Chicago's First Congressional District, an office that he held until his death in 1970.

Mayor Kelly took these steps that fostered Black empowerment because he was fighting for his political life. The continuing strength of the local GOP and the splintering of the Democrats after the death of Cermak created a competitive electoral polity. Because of the competitive electoral environment he faced (three of his mayoral elections were competitive), a mobilized bloc of Black voters represented a potentially decisive element; he made the rational choice to pursue the huge bloc of Black votes, even if this cost him pockets of White support. Yet the fact that this was the rational strategy should not obscure the possibility that Mayor Kelly was to some extent a liberal on civil rights. Some historians of the Kelly era endorsed this judgment. Reed labeled the mayor "Kelly the egalitarian," and described him as "a leader who was not afraid of incurring the wrath of his fellow whites when speaking out for justice" and who encouraged Blacks "to pursue their law-given rights."[46]

Unfortunately for Black voters, party chairman Jacob Arvey led a machine effort to dump Kelly and forced him not to enter the 1947 mayoral race. Although he had suffered much negative media coverage because of crises in the city's schools and transportation services, the prime reason for the removal of Kelly seems to have been the negative reaction of many of Chicago's White ethnic voters to his integrated housing policies.[47] He refused to capitulate to the violent reaction of White voters opposed to his anti-discrimination stance;[48] but the party's committeemen and aldermen who ran the city's fifty wards had a different calculus. Rather than trying to build a citywide coalition, they were interested in maintaining the support of the White ethnic voters, who were the majority in most wards (due to segregation and ward homogeneity). After the Republican victories in the 1946 election, which "marked the biggest setback for county Democrats since 1930," the ward leaders ousted Kelly and selected someone they could control.[49]

Political Competitiveness and Black Empowerment

Chapter 1 hypothesized that competitive elections create circumstances in which Black voters can play a decisive role in electoral outcomes. This position affords Black leaders who can mobilize voters great leverage and bargaining power vis-à-vis leaders of White electoral factions or parties. Used wisely and with skill, this bargaining power can result in individual and group political empowerment of Blacks.

The foregoing discussion of politics in Chicago provides evidence in support of this hypothesis. In the first half of the twentieth century it was rare for one faction to win a mayoral primary and general election with 60 percent or more of the vote. Elections were at least competitive and often highly competitive. In many of these elections, Black votes played a pivotal role in determining the winner. Black leaders like Archibald Carey, Oscar DePriest, and William Dawson were able to barter the votes of the Second and Third wards for significant political opportunities and rewards. What kinds of gains did Blacks make? They included the slating and election of aldermen and, even more important, party organization committeemen (who distributed jobs and favors); the election of Blacks to the U.S. Congress; the appointment of a Black as civil service commissioner and the related capturing of about 6.5 percent of the civil service jobs by Blacks, who were about 7 percent of the city population; the appointment of a Black to the sensitive position of chairman of the Chicago Housing Authority; the creation of the nation's first city department devoted to race relations; and victories, with mayoral support, in battles (not the war) for school desegregation and open housing policies. These gains amount to much more than symbolic, cooptive rewards. And all of these achievements that indicated a genuine reallocation of political power were made prior to 1950. For these reasons I conclude that Chicago's Blacks took real steps forward in the struggle for political empowerment.

From Competition to Monopoly: The Transformation of Politics in Chicago

Although the Democratic party had been growing more powerful in Chicago politics since the election of Anton J. Cermak as mayor in 1931 (see table 2–2), it was not until Richard J. Daley became mayor (1955–76) that the Democratic machine established the political monopoly for which it became famous. Once Mayor Daley consolidated power in the aftermath of his 1955 mayoral election, electoral politics in Chicago shifted from the pattern of interparty competition to noncompetitive elections in which the Democratic party monopolized the mayor's office, the city council, and other important local offices. Because the Democratic organization monopolized electoral politics in the city, the Black vote played a decisive role in only two mayoral elections between 1955 and 1976. Paradoxically, as the Black proportion of the city's population was rapidly growing (as table 2–3 illustrates) Black voters were becoming superfluous to the Democratic machine's electoral coalition. The consequence of this transformation of Chicago from a competitive to a monopolistic polity was the political subordination of Blacks.

As the following discussion of Mayor Richard J. Daley's administration shows, electoral politics became noncompetitive and winning the Black vote became unnecessary during most of his tenure.

Black Political Realignment Behind Daley

Martin Kennelly, a reform-oriented businessman, was slated by party chairman Arvey and the other Democratic organization leaders to run for mayor in 1947 in place of the deposed Mayor Kelly. Kennelly was mayor for two terms (1947–51, 1951–55) before Richard J. Daley defeated him in the 1955 Democratic primary.

In his eight years in office, Mayor Kennelly alienated many of the regular party leaders. He earned considerable scorn when he removed more than 12,000 city jobs from discretionary patronage coffers and placed them into the hands of the reinvigorated Civil Service Commission.[50] Among his enemies in the party organization was the city's leading Black politician, Representative William Dawson. As a result of the nationwide crime investigation by Senator Estes Kefauver in 1952, Mayor Kennelly cracked down on the "policy wheel" operation (Chicago's term for numbers gambling) that flourished in Dawson's Second Ward and of which Dawson was a major beneficiary.[51]

Kennelly's reelection strategy in 1955 was to run a typical reformer campaign and charge that his principal opponent, Richard Daley, was merely a naive front man who would be controlled like a puppet by Dawson and other corrupt elements within the organization.[52] The Chicago media gave prominent attention to the mayor's charges and characterized Daley as the "candidate of the hoodlum element."[53]

Kennelly's innuendoes about Dawson produced a backlash in the Black community. In part because crime had long been endemic to Al Capone's town, Blacks felt that

Table 2–3 Growth in the Black Proportion of Chicago's Population, 1940–1980

Year	Total population	Percentage Black
1940	3,394,049	8
1950	3,620,962	14
1960	3,550,404	23
1970	3,362,825	33
1980	3,005,072	40

Source: Bureau of the Census, Census of the Population, General Social and Economic Characteristics, Illinois, Vol. 1: Characteristics of the Population.

Kennelly's anticrime stand was merely a front for a racist appeal to the White community.[54] The *Chicago Defender*, the newspaper of the Black community, editorialized:

> Kennelly's strategy is clearly designed to arouse the indignation of whites against a powerful Negro leader and influence them to vote their prejudices rather than their well-founded convictions. . . .
>
>   The basic issue is not policy [numbers gambling]—it is politics. . . . Hitler rose to power in Germany by accusing high-placed Jews of treason and whipping up anti-Semitism. . . . By building up a powerful Negro congressman as a symbol of hatred, the Kennelly forces can exploit racial prejudice for all it is worth, while at the same time pretending to be crusading against corruption. This is a greater crime than any attributed to Dawson. It is the responsibility of all decent citizens of both races to make certain that race-baiting will produce no victories in Chicago.[55]

Blacks rallied around Dawson and the candidate who was not critical of him, Richard Daley. Running in his first Democratic mayoral primary, Daley, the Democratic organization's candidate, captured 49 percent of the vote; Kennelly won 35 percent, largely from the liberal, reform faction of the party; and Benjamin Adamowski, a Polish-American candidate, won 15 percent.[56] *Daley lost the White vote*, but he won the election by garnering 72 percent of the vote in predominantly Black wards.

In the general election, Daley faced Alderman Robert E. Merriam, a Democrat running on the Republican ticket. As a city councilman, Merriam had established a favorable record on issues of concern to Blacks. Although he promised to appoint Blacks to high offices within his administration, Merriam, like Kennelly, was an opponent of patronage, something Black leaders avidly sought. Merriam also refused to curtail his attacks on the city's corruption, in which Dawson was embroiled. He made continued insinuations about Dawson, insuring that he would receive little Black support.[57]

Merriam appealed to the same reform constituency as had Kennelly, as well as to the largely Republican business community, and won virtually the same wards. But Daley won the election with 55 percent of the vote, rolling up huge margins in organization-controlled wards, especially in Black wards, where he captured 77 percent of the vote. Because Kennelly and Merriam attacked Dawson, while Daley remained silent, Dawson's precinct workers were able to portray Daley as a leader with a favorable attitude toward Blacks. This enabled Daley to finish the job begun by Mayor Edward Kelly (and President Franklin D. Roosevelt) and bring Chicago's Black voters fully into the Democratic party. Riding on Daley's coattails, Black Democratic aldermanic candidates in three South Side Black wards (Wards 3, 4, and 6) unseated incumbent Republicans. The 1955 mayoral election of Richard J. Daley signified the end of Black allegiance to the Chicago GOP.[58] As table 2–2 indicates, Daley's share of the Black vote represented a 50 percent increase over the share captured by Kennelly, and by Kelly in his last election.

The 1955 mayoral election was one of two elections in which Daley owed his victory to the support he received from Black voters. Yet this support came very inexpensively. In exchange for voting for Daley, what did Blacks receive? Before becoming mayor, Daley had been instrumental in the appointment of Ralph Metcalfe, a former sports star, as committeeman (hence dispenser of patronage) of the Third

Ward. But Metcalfe was merely a replacement for another Black committeeman. With Daley's aid, Metcalfe was elected Third Ward alderman in 1955 (finally defeating Archibald Carey Jr.), and two other Black aldermanic candidates broke new ground by defeating White Republicans in the Fourth and Sixth wards.[59] Judging from their records of almost no accomplishments that reallocated authority to Blacks, the anointment of these new aldermen did not represent empowerment.[60] However, it is plausible that Daley viewed the slating of Blacks for aldermanic positions not as tokenism but as real rewards for crucial electoral support. But the significance of the machine slating Blacks against White Republicans in these wards can easily be overstated. These wards had rapidly turned predominantly Black. The machine had long ago conceded that the predominantly Black areas of the South Side could be represented by Black aldermen and Congress members. These were not offices that put a Black in a position of authority over Whites. Moreover, because of the ironclad control that Daley exercised over the city council, these anointed Black leaders possessed almost no independent political power or decisionmaking authority. Realistically, Black voters won little other than the intangible benefit of a mayor who was perceived to be a friend of Blacks solely because he refrained from attacking Dawson. Where Daley stood on issues of open housing or school desegregation was unstated.

Beyond this, the rewards that Blacks received in exchange for their votes, *in this and future Daley elections*, amounted to a halt of the city investigations of the lucrative policy wheels (enabling the illegal operation that greatly benefited Dawson to continue unfettered), aid in applying for and obtaining federal welfare, and low-paying, nondecisionmaking patronage jobs in the park district, sanitation department, and other city bureaucracies. Neither Dawson nor other Black leaders were able to win a reallocation of political power. Blacks surely did not receive from Mayor Daley the same treatment they had received from Mayor Kelly. Under Daley there would be no more support for integrated schools or scattered-site housing. Nor would Blacks make further gains in obtaining positions of citywide political power in Chicago.

Regime Change: From Political Machine to Growth Machine

Black political empowerment was halted under Richard J. Daley because in his initial mayoral term he took steps that significantly diminished the potential for electoral opposition to the Democratic organization. *The most important segment of the machine's traditional opposition, and the major backers of Kennelly and Merriam, were the business and civic leaders; Daley successfully captured their support.* He realized that the principal leaders of the opposition to his election in 1955—the city's business, banking, and civic leaders, and the major newspapers that usually echoed their growth- and good-government-oriented agendas—did not trust him, because he was the candidate of a graft-riddled organization, and because he sought to depose the reform-oriented Kennelly. To his credit, he recognized that unless he could assuage their distrust, these groups would continue to finance and support mayoral challengers. He immediately began to reshape his image among these groups. Soon after he took office, he wrote to some of the city's most prominent businessmen asking them what the mayor could do to advance the interests of business.[61] The result was an urban growth program of immense proportions in the downtown Loop. A *Chicago Daily News* reporter explained:

> He put big bond issue referendums on the ballot to raise funds for the start of public works projects. The banks were delighted at the prospect of bidding on the profitable bonds. He announced that high-rise apartments were the administration's official answer to the suburban exodus, and that the lake front and the central city would someday bristle with the residential skyscrapers. The banks and real estate interests were enthralled. Planned expressways, all of them leading to the downtown business section, would be put on a crash, priority, hurry-up, round-the-clock schedule, and more parking garages would be built to accommodate the motorized shoppers, and the downtown stores were ecstatic. O'Hare Airport, then used only by the air force, would be rushed along to meet the jet age, bringing more and more convention business to the city. And a convention hall would be built on Chicago's lake front, despite the protests of conservationists.[62]

In addition, when the Democratic national convention was held in Chicago in 1956, Daley took the credit for bringing the party to his city and for bringing the revenues the convention produced to Chicago businesses. The upshot of his actions was the transformation of his image from political machine boss to growth-machine CEO.

In exchange for providing many of these "wish list" items to Chicago's business and civic leaders, Daley set ground rules for the involvement of these leaders in the political affairs of the city. On any matters that directly impinged on their interests, the city's business and civic leaders would have easy and personal access to the mayor. But on all other matters, they were to defer to him and the leaders of the groups whose interests were affected.[63] The corollary of this was that Chicago's White business leadership played a minimal role in economic development and job training efforts in the Black community (especially in comparison to the role played by the business communities of Philadelphia and Atlanta), because these issues were the domain of Black elected officials and City Hall.[64] Moreover, nearly all political liaisons between business and Black leaders in Chicago were mediated—and obstructed—by the Daley organization. Seeking to prevent direct contact between Blacks and business leaders, contacts that might have sown the seeds of future political alliances, Daley insisted on interpreting the business community to Blacks, and vice versa.[65] As one longtime business executive explained,

> Whenever we had a problem we could just pick up the phone and call the mayor, have a friendly chat, and action would be taken. . . . But when we would call . . . about something that we viewed as a problem with the city overall—not an economic problem but a political problem about the city's image—he would become perplexed and react defensively. Like when Martin Luther King marched in Chicago. Daley had no patience for advice from me or any other of the concerned businessmen who I know tried to talk to him. He made it clear, in the kind of language that you knew you had better not press him, that King was none of our business.[66]

Within four years of the election of Richard J. Daley as mayor, the good-government versus machine basis of competition in Chicago politics had become irrelevant. The business and civic leaders who had supported Kennelly and Merriam (e.g., the president of United Airlines, the president of Carson, Pirie, Scott, and the president of the Association of Western Railways) now staunchly backed Daley in 1959 and continued to support him throughout his career.[67] The upshot of Daley's efforts to win the favor of the city's business community was the separation of this group of leaders from the liberal/reform elements of the Kennelly and Merriam coalitions. The political demands of leaders of liberal reform organizations, like the Independent Voters of Illinois (IVI) and the Independent Precinct Organization (IPO), went beyond increasing governmental efficiency, an absence of scandals, and enhancement of the city's infrastructure, all of which the business community sought and Daley delivered. The IVI wanted increased participation in the affairs of the Democratic party, a greater degree of openness in the selection of candidates, and intervention by city government to remove the barriers to employment, housing, and political participation faced by the city's minorities—demands that Daley refused to consider. By dividing the business community from their former allies in the liberal organizations, Daley eliminated the likelihood that he would be challenged by the same coalition that almost defeated him in the 1955 primary and general elections.

Daley partially deflected the opposition of the IVI and the IPO by supporting such liberal candidates as Paul Douglas, Adlai Stevenson III, and Sidney Yates. But these candidates were always slated for state and national offices rather than the local offices, which were considered much more important by the Democratic organization.[68] The liberal organizations represented small, relatively powerless enclaves with little money and tiny geographical bases; to the Daley organization, they were a nonthreatening opposition.[69]

The consequence of Richard J. Daley's capture of the support of Chicago's business and civic leaders, the newspapers that echoed their views, and the voters (largely Republican) who took cues from them was nothing less than a transformation of a competitive into a noncompetitive polity. Although elections would be contested in the Daley era, electoral politics would not be competitive. Milton Rakove did not exaggerate when he stated that "the Democratic party in Chicago is so strong vis-a-vis its Republican and independent oppositions that it can operate essentially in the same way that a party can in a one-party totalitarian system."[70]

As table 2–4 shows, from 1959 to 1975 Mayor Daley faced only one competitive challenge from the Republican party for the mayor's office. Within the Democratic

Table 2–4 Noncompetitiveness of Chicago Mayoral Elections, 1959–1975

Year	Daley's vote	Opponent's vote	Daley's percentage
1959	776,806	312,230 (Sheehan)	71
1963	677,497	540,705 (Adamowski)	56
1967	792,238	272,542 (Waner)	74
1971	740,137	315,969 (Friedman)	70
1975	542,817	139,335 (Hoellen)	80

Source: Board of Election Commissioners, City of Chicago, "Official Election Returns, General Elections" (City of Chicago, 1959–1975). All calculations made by me.

party he faced no primary challengers in the four mayoral elections between 1959 and 1974. Under his leadership the Chicago Democrats enjoyed an electoral monopoly reminiscent of southern Democratic politics. The upshot was that the votes of Blacks were no longer relevant in most mayoral elections. Black political leaders no longer had bargaining leverage; therefore, Black political empowerment was arrested in the Daley era.

Electoral Monopoly and One-Party Politics

Mayor Daley faced no challenger in the 1959 Democratic primary. In the mayoral election the Democratic machine rolled over the Republican candidate, Timothy Sheehan, with Daley winning 71 percent of the vote. Sheehan won only one ward (recall that four years earlier Merriam won 21 of 50 wards), while Daley won by more than five thousand votes in 46 of the city's 50 wards.

Daley again was unopposed in the 1963 Democratic primary. However, the general election, which he won against former Democrat Benjamin Adamowski, was competitive. As in 1955, Adamowski attempted to mobilize the Polish vote to displace the Irish. He criticized the mayor for raising the real estate tax—and consequently squeezing the city's homeowners—to pay for his massive building programs and the city's expanding payroll (bloated by patronage). But the support Adamowski received from White ethnic homeowners was not solely the product of a "tax revolt"; it was also a response to White ethnic fears of Black encroachment into their neighborhoods, which he had incited.[71] He charged that the national Democratic party and, by implication, the Democratic organization locally were succumbing to the demands of the civil rights movement and were no longer sympathetic to the interests of White constituents, especially with respect to protecting their neighborhoods from Black encroachment by opposing open occupancy housing policies.[72] As was the case in 1946, when White Democrats defected to the GOP in response to Mayor Kelly's support for integrated housing, in 1963 White ethnics again demonstrated their willingness to defect to the GOP on the basis of this issue. But Adamowski did not win enough White votes to overcome the support for Daley among Blacks, support that was no doubt buttressed by the nature of Adamowski's appeal. Daley won a still-impressive 56 percent of the vote. Of the 10 wards in which Daley achieved his largest pluralities, 6 were predominantly Black. They accounted for 63 percent of his total margin of victory over Adamowski.

What did Blacks receive from Mayor Daley in exchange for their decisive support? Again it appears that Black political leaders were able to negotiate few concessions from Daley that amounted to political empowerment or the reallocation of political power. Daley slated Blacks as ward committeemen (with the power to distribute patronage in the ward) in middle-class Wards 17 and 21. William Grimshaw has argued convincingly that Daley anointed these Black leaders not as rewards for electoral support (Daley won by less than a thousand votes in Ward 21) but in a belated effort to regain control of wards where independent (nonmachine) Blacks were having success against the machine's candidates.[73] Instead of slating Whites, Daley was now slating Blacks; but he was still doing the slating and giving the marching orders.

Daley's response to the strong challenge mounted by Adamowski in 1963 was not to reward Blacks for their crucial support. Rather, he and the Democratic organization chose to appease the White voters who defected to Adamowski; the Daley administration became even more steadfast in its unwillingness to promote residential desegregation or the integration of schools. From 1955 to 1969, only one of the 33 public housing projects built in Chicago was located in an area less than 84-percent Black. As for public housing apartments, 99 percent of those built after 1955 were located in all-Black neighborhoods.[74] A federal court found the Chicago Housing Authority guilty of discrimination in 1969 and ordered future public housing to be constructed in White areas. Rather than complying, the Daley administration ended the construction of public housing in the city. Similarly, in 1967, when federal officials from the Office of Education withheld elementary and secondary education funds allotted to the Chicago public schools until they moved forward on desegregation efforts, Mayor Daley persuaded President Lyndon Johnson to overrule this decision. Chicago's school system received its funding without complying with federal rules on desegregation.[75]

Why didn't Daley choose to build a coalition around Black voters who were so loyal to him and his party, rather than trying to win back the votes of White ethnics who had defected to Adamowski? There are a number of possible answers to this question. From a rational and pragmatic perspective, Daley may have believed that Blacks would not defect to the GOP even if he retarded progress on open housing and school desegregation. He knew that Blacks had developed a strong loyalty to the party of FDR and the New Deal. And given Daley's background, he probably believed that ethnic group voting was motivated largely by opportunities for patronage employment, and that in their pursuit of such opportunities Blacks would remain loyal to the Democratic party, which controlled federal, state, and local patronage.

Coalition decisions are not made solely on the basis of rational pragmatism; as J. David Greenstone and Paul E. Peterson have argued, ideology plays an important role as well.[76] Daley may have been uncomfortable, for racial reasons, with the idea of empowering Blacks, and on this basis he may have chosen not to build a coalition around the Black voters who were so loyal to him and his party.[77] Perhaps his behavior was not racial but was a more generalized group xenophobia that typifies the blood sport of urban ethnic politics. Characteristically, ethnic leaders seek to win as much political power as possible for their own group and view all other ethnic groups as challengers bent on displacing them. Perhaps Blacks to Daley were just one more ethnic group (like the Poles behind Adamowski) threatening the superordinate status of the Irish in Chicago politics. He would take Black votes to fend off the Polish challenge, but before ceding real power to Blacks he would exhaust all efforts at appeasement and cooptation.

Four years after Adamowski's challenge, Daley looked stronger than ever. In 1967 he defeated Republican John Waner with 74 percent of the vote. Waner failed to win even one of the 50 wards and, as was the case in 1959, Daley won 46 of them by more than five thousand votes.

In 1971 Daley faced Richard Friedman, a highly touted reform Democrat running on the GOP ticket. Friedman had been the president of the Better Government Association, a municipal watchdog organization that received substantial funding from the city's major corporations. He solicited these corporate acquaintances for financial support, but they were nearly unanimously committed to Daley. Friedman also had the endorsement of Rev. Jesse Jackson, the Chicago-based civil rights leader, but this proved to be of little value. Daley captured 70 percent of the vote, including 75 percent of the Black vote. Friedman won just two of the 50 wards.

In 1975 Daley faced his first Democratic primary challenger since his initial bid for the mayor's office twenty years earlier. His opponents were liberal, Lakefront alderman William Singer, Black state senator Richard Newhouse, and former Cook County state's attorney Edward Hanrahan. Hanrahan, a former Daley protégé, was a law-and-order politician who had gained notoriety for ordering a raid on the Chicago Black Panthers' headquarters in which two Panther leaders had been murdered. In the primary, Daley won 58 percent of the vote. The inability of White liberals and Blacks to unite behind one candidate (discussed at length later) split the anti-Daley vote between Singer, who won 29 percent of the vote, and Newhouse, who received 8 percent. Hanrahan won the remaining 5 percent. This election can only be viewed as an affirmation of Daley's domination of the city's politics. The mayor demonstrated continued citywide support by winning 47 of the city's 50 wards. Even if the votes for Singer and Newhouse were combined, Daley still would have outpolled this hybrid by more than 20 percent of the vote and won 38 of the city's 50 wards.[78]

In the 1975 mayoral election Daley faced Republican John Hoellen, who for many years was the lone GOP city councilman in that Daley-controlled body. Daley won 80 percent of the vote against Hoellen, who failed to capture a single ward—and also lost his bid for reelection to the city council. Daley won by more than five thousand votes in 47 of the 50 wards.

Richard J. Daley failed to win with more than 60 percent of the vote in only two of the 10 elections (primary and general) that he entered from 1959 through 1975. According to the definition of competitiveness set forth in chapter 1, electoral politics clearly were monopolistic, not competitive.

The extent of the Democratic organization's monopoly on local politics is equally evident when one compares the electoral performance of the Republican mayoral candidates with that of Republican gubernatorial candidates in the city. As table 2–5 illustrates, the latter fared significantly better. In the five gubernatorial elections from

Table 2–5 Comparison of Chicago Wards Won by Republican Mayoral and Gubernatorial Candidates during the Daley Era

Year	Mayoral elections	Gubernatorial elections
1959–60	1	1
1963–64	18	10
1967–68	0	11
1971–72	2	9
1975–76	0	20

Source: Board of Election Commissioners, City of Chicago, "Official Election Returns, General Elections," and "Official Election Returns, Gubernatorial Elections" (City of Chicago, 1959–1976).

1960 to 1976, the average number of wards in the city won by Republican candidates was 10. In contrast, in the five mayoral elections held during the same period, only once did the GOP win more than two wards. This suggests that there were voters in Chicago who did support the Republican party—but not in local elections when the Republican candidates had no reasonable hope for victory.

That the Republican party offered no competition and had in fact been coopted by the Democratic organization is suggested by more than electoral data. Both Timothy Sheehan, Daley's opponent in 1959 and a former chairman of the Republican organization, and John Waner, the GOP candidate for mayor in 1967, publicly admitted that the Republican organization had thrown in the towel:

> There is no other power structure left, so the net result is that even the news media doesn't want to beat the incumbent mayor over the head. . . . Many Republican workers and even Republican ward committeemen were and still are obligated to the Democrats. They get jobs from the city, or have jobs in their organization. Many of them feel that it is a hopeless task and why kill themselves trying to get somebody elected when they know they can't elect him.[79]

Given that the local Republican party was little more than a hollow shell, disaffected Black voters largely lost the option of defecting to the GOP. But if Blacks had defected in large numbers, would the Democratic organization's hegemony have been challenged?

The Inconsequentiality of Black Votes

How much of an electoral monopoly did Mayor Daley have? To what extent could he afford to ignore the demands of Blacks for school desegregation, integrated housing, or a role in the internal affairs of the party? Could he have won elections if all of the Black voters who cast ballots for him had stayed at home on election day? An even more convincing indicator of the superfluousness of the Black vote to his electoral coalition would be if he still could have won his reelection bids if all of the Blacks who voted for him had defected to his Republican opponents. Table 2–6 estimates that he indeed could have won four of his five reelection bids (he would have lost the 1963 election simply without the Black vote) if his opponents had received all the Black votes he received.

Because votes are not recorded by race, there is no way to determine precisely how many Blacks voted for Mayor Daley in a given election. Table 2–6 displays my estimates of Daley's citywide Black vote on the basis of his vote in predominantly Black (90 percent or more) wards. Census data are then used to discover what percentage of all Blacks in Chicago live in these predominantly Black wards. Once one knows how many voters in these Black wards voted for Daley in a given election and what percentage of the city's Black population live in those wards, one can estimate Daley's total Black vote citywide. For example, if one hundred thousand votes were cast for Daley in predominantly Black wards, and the population of those wards comprised 50 percent of the total Black population in the city, one would estimate that the other 50 percent of the Black population would also have delivered one hundred thousand votes to Daley, for a citywide total of two hundred thousand votes.

Table 2–6 Estimated Election Outcomes if Black Votes Cast for Mayor Daley were Cast for Republican Opponent in Four Mayoral Elections

Year	A Total Daley vote and percentage	B Total opponent vote and percentage	C Vote for Daley in predom. Black wards	D Percentage of total Blacks living in predom. Black wards	E (C÷D) Estimated total Black votes cast for Daley	F (A-E) Recalculated Daley vote and percentage	G (B+E) Recalculated opponent vote and percentage
1959	778,612 71%	311,940 29%	100,716	51.3	196,327	582,285 53%	508,267 47%
1967	792,238 74%	272,542 26%	88,058	38.0	231,731	560,507 53%	504,273 47%
1971	740,137 70%	315,969 30%	98,693	50.3	196,208	543,929 52%	512,177 48%
1975	542,817 80%	139,335 20%	58,507	40.0	146,267	396,550 58%	285,602 42%

Source: Board of Election Commissioners, City of Chicago, "Official Election Returns, General Elections (City of Chicago, 1959–1975). All calculations made by me.

One can then determine approximately how many votes Daley would have received if he had received no Black votes by subtracting from his official number of votes the estimated total of Black votes he received. By adding the estimated total number of Black votes cast for Daley to the GOP candidate's original total, one can estimate how many votes Daley's Republican opponent would have received. Table 2–6 shows the results of these calculations for four of Mayor Daley's five reelections. (The 1963 reelection, which Daley would have lost without the Black vote, is omitted.) *In each of the elections illustrated in table 2–6, Daley still would have been victorious even if all of his Black supporters had defected to the GOP.* Daley, a master vote counter, surely was aware of this.[80]

Granted, the conditions imposed in these calculations are extreme. On the one hand, the partisan loyalty of Blacks to the Democratic party almost surely would prevent a 100 percent defection rate of Black votes to a Republican candidate. Conversely, the kinds of real-world events that could possibly precipitate a mass defection of Black voters to the GOP might also spur a higher level of Black turnout. Still, the data presented in table 2–6 provide strong additional support for the contention that Black voters were superfluous to Mayor Daley's electoral coalition. There were no electoral incentives for him to redistribute political power from his White ethnic electoral base to Blacks. Black votes were unimportant to him, and in large part this explains why he treated Black voters accordingly.

Black Subordination in the Post-Daley Era

Mayor Daley's death in December 1976 led to a special mayoral election in 1977. Three major candidates emerged in the Democratic primary: Michael Bilandic, the organization's candidate and a long time ally of Daley; Alderman Roman Pucinski, a powerful Daley ally who believed the opportunity was ripe for a Polish ethnic to lead the party; and Black state senator Harold Washington.[81] Bilandic won with 51 percent of the vote, Pucinski received 33 percent, and Washington captured 11 percent. Bilandic then won 78 percent of the mayoral vote against Republican candidate Dennis Block, demonstrating that the GOP was as weak after Daley's death as it had been before.

Like Pucinski, Washington had run as a machine candidate, hoping to improve the position of his ethnic group within the organization. He did obtain the endorsement of the IVI, but he refused to condemn the patronage system.[82] He received the endorsement of only one of the city's Black aldermen, and he did not win the crucial endorsement of Ralph Metcalfe.[83] Washington's almost 11 percent of the vote was a small improvement over Newhouse's 1975 total, but he was unable to capture a majority of the city's Black vote.[84] He also received little support from the Lakeshore "liberal" wards, which split between Bilandic and Pucinski.

Under Mayor Bilandic, Black subordination continued. After the death of Congressman Metcalfe in 1978, the party organization planned to install Alderman Bennett Stewart, a Black machine politician, as the new congressman.[85] But Blacks and liberal Whites, who had been inspired by Metcalfe's break with Daley (precipitated by the mayor's refusal to curb mounting police brutality) wanted to have a special election to allow the voters to determine Metcalfe's replacement. Samuel Ackerman, First District state central committeeman of the Democratic party and an influential member of the IVI, chaired the meeting at which the replacement of Metcalfe was discussed. Ackerman tried to steer the meeting to a vote for a special election, but the other committeemen forced Stewart's name into nomination and won a hasty vote.[86] These efforts of Ackerman, and other liberal Whites, represented a first step toward overcoming disillusionment with the idea of a biracial reform coalition. In 1980 the Democratic organization was unable to hold the First Congressional District seat; Harold Washington defeated Stewart.

Bilandic continued Daley's policy of refusing to support the busing of Black students to White schools by blocking a plan proposed by his superintendent of schools. Siding with a vociferous group of White mothers of students at Bogan High School, he announced a three-year moratorium on busing.[87]

All observers expected an easy victory for the incumbent in the 1979 mayoralty race. In the Democratic primary, Bilandic faced Jane Byrne, who had been appointed commissioner of consumer sales by Mayor Daley in 1968. Daley befriended Byrne, and in 1975 he appointed her as cochair (with himself) of the Democratic Central Committee of Cook County. After Daley's death, Byrne was relieved of her position by party regulars who resented her meteoric rise through the party ranks.[88] When she announced her mayoral candidacy 10 months before the primary, few observers considered her a serious challenge to Bilandic. She campaigned not as a reformer but against a "cabal of evil men" who were leading the party (and Bilandic) away from the style of governance and quality of service delivery created by Daley. Milton Rakove assessed Byrne's candidacy as follows:

> It was not a candidacy to be taken seriously. Byrne had no money, no precinct workers, no programs of any note, and no support from any of the elements of the power structure of the still extant machine—the ward committeemen, the bureaucrats and public officials and the business/banking/labor elites. She was unknown in the Black

community, unwanted by the white-ethnic constituencies, and unpopular with the lakefront liberals who had known her to be a part of the machine during the Daley era. And she was a woman in a city and political system where no woman had ever achieved major public office.[89]

Mayor Bilandic would have been reelected in 1979 but for the incompetent and impolitic ways that he reacted to a massive snowstorm that paralyzed the city. Byrne's charges of deteriorating city services suddenly resonated after five massive snow-storms during December 1978 and January 1979 brought snow removal, public trans-portation, and air traffic in "the city that works" to a halt. Part of Bilandic's response was a plan to speed up public transportation during rush hours by having trains from the outlying suburbs speed through to the Loop without making the normal stops. Most of the skipped stops were in African-American neighborhoods. After less than a week of protests charging that the mayor's policy was racist, Bilandic rescinded this decision. But the African-American community was already enraged.

People from all over the city, but especially Blacks, wanted to vote *against Bilandic*, and Byrne was the only alternative. White ethnics had nothing to fear from her because, as Paul Kleppner wrote, "she identified herself with Daley's image and evoked memories of what the city had been like when he was in charge, she reas-sured White ethnics that she posed no threat to their continued control of their neigh-borhoods and schools."[90] Byrne won by a narrow margin of 16,000 votes out of more than eight hundred thousand. Her surprise victory did not precipitate defections to the Republican mayoral candidate; she won 84 percent of the vote and became Chicago's first female mayor. Four years later, she herself would become the object of Blacks' rage, and her defeat by Harold Washington and a biracial coalition would interrupt twenty-eight years of Black political subordination in Chicago.

Noncompetitive Electoral Politics and the Political Subordination of Blacks

The political subordination of Blacks in Chicago was most clearly evident in the decline of their ability to influence public policy outcomes on issues that were of the utmost importance to them. Two policy areas in which Black powerlessness was most evident were integrated housing and school desegregation.

Public Housing Policy

The full story of the nexus between public housing and race in Chicago has been extensively analyzed elsewhere.[91] By the late 1940s there were nearly 1.2 million families in the city and less than one million housing units. In addition, a sizable portion of the housing in the area south of the downtown Loop, an area that over the next twenty years would be inhabited solely by Blacks, was substandard.[92] Through the Housing Act of 1949, the federal government offered subsidies for the redevel-opment of blighted areas and the construction of low-rent housing. In Chicago the problem was that Blacks were the largest group of slum-dwellers and the fastest-growing population group, but the areas of the city with the most vacant land were lower-middle-class neighborhoods in the South and Northwest sides of the city.

The riots that were incited by the efforts of the Chicago Housing Authority (CHA) to integrate Airport Homes and the Fernwood Project in 1946 and 1947 made it clear to Mayors Kennelly and Daley that their White constituents opposed integration.[93] Daley rolled back the political influence that Blacks had won in the struggle for open housing in Chicago. He installed a new CHA director, under whom the CHA ceased playing the role of advocate of open occupancy housing policies.[94]

The Democratic organization's solution to the compound problems of increasing Black population and overcrowded Black ghettos was the construction of massive high-rise public housing projects in areas that were already Black or in the process of racial transition. High-rise public housing alleviated much of the need for vacant land; each of the 28 buildings in the Robert Taylor Homes project housed about a thousand people. In 1966 Dorothy Gautreaux and a group of other Black CHA tenants, with the help of the American Civil Liberties Union, filed suit in U.S. District Court charging that the CHA's tenant and site selection procedures were discriminatory. They also sued the federal government for its financial support of these segregated accommodations. In 1969 Judge Richard Austin, ruling in favor of the plaintiffs, issued guidelines for future CHA construction in White neighborhoods and tenant selection processes that included residents beyond the immediate neighborhood.[95] Little came of this decision. From 1969 to 1983, Mayors Daley, Bilandic, and Byrne delayed. They appealed some court orders, agreed to others and then proceeded to ignore them, signed letters of intent, raised hopes, and then stalled until the process went back to the courts. All the while Black overcrowding was worsening, leading the Chicago Urban League and Operation PUSH to request in 1978 that exceptions be made to Austin's ruling so that new public housing could be built in all-Black neighborhoods.[96] Daley had decided that ending the construction of public housing in Chicago was a safer option politically than allowing integration to proceed, and his successors did not challenge his political acuity.

The School System

To deal with a rapidly expanding Black population, already overcrowded Black schools, and underutilized White schools, Mayor Kelly had taken a position favoring school desegregation. In contrast the politicized School Board, which was comprised of representatives from White ethnic neighborhoods, had favored confining the Black students to the overcrowded Black schools. Black parents opposed the School Board because schools in White neighborhoods contiguous to the Black neighborhoods had empty desks. On three separate occasions, at the Morgan Park, Englewood, and Calumet schools, White students and parents boycotted school, protested, and went directly to Mayor Kelly. Kelly rebuked the White protestors and declared, "I am definitely opposed to any movement that will deny the free right of any citizen of Chicago the privilege of attendance at any public institution of learning regardless of race, color or creed."[97] He stood firm against the protesters, threatened to jail anyone who persisted in disrupting school sessions, and watched the resistance dissipate.[98]

In Mayor Martin Kennelly's administration, the parochial, White-ethnic-dominated city council ended Kelly's policy of desegregating the schools; Kennelly's administration stood by as overcrowding in the Black schools increased. Under Mayor Daley and his new schools superintendent, Benjamin Willis, the situation dramatically worsened. By 1961 the overcrowding of Black schools had become so acute that two lawsuits were filed against the city's Board of Education alleging deliberate segregation and overcrowding. In the latter, the national NAACP provided evidence that 15,000 Black students were attending school on double sessions (meaning fewer class hours than White students who attended a full school day), while in nearby White schools there were enough empty desks to accommodate all of them. In 1963 the School Board passed a pilot plan for the transfer of selected groups of talented Black students to White schools. With Mayor Daley's support, Superintendent Willis refused to implement the plan. In the face of a court order to implement the transfer plan, Willis offered his resignation. This dramatic gesture provoked large demonstrations by White parents who demanded that the School Board reverse itself and keep Willis as superintendent. The riotous White parents again won out.[99]

By 1965 the battle between Black civil rights organizations and Mayor Daley's superintendent had reached crisis proportions. The federal Office of Education ordered $32 million in education funding withheld from Chicago's schools. To many of the civil rights activists, it looked like the federal government's financial inducements would force the city to desegregate its schools.[100] But after a private conversation between Mayor Daley and President Lyndon Johnson, federal funds were restored, and federal authorities retreated from Chicago. The powerlessness of Blacks in Chicago was plainly evident.

One would be hard-pressed to find a major city with a sizable Black population that has had success in desegregating housing and schools. This fact might suggest that successful desegregation of housing and schools are unrealistic criteria for evaluating the empowerment of Blacks in Chicago. Yet what should be stressed is that nonnegligible steps were being taken in a positive direction under Mayor Kelly, who was providing the mayoral leadership necessary to sustain such unpopular policies. Under Kelly's successors this forward progress was stopped and rolled back. These successors, particularly Daley, enjoyed an absence of competitive elections that Kelly did not. The argument here is that these successors ignored Black demands because they were unaccountable to Black voters, and that this shift from competitive to noncompetitive elections is a crucial part of the explanation for the rollback of Black political empowerment.

Employment in the Urban Bureaucracy

To compare the levels of Black political empowerment prior to Mayor Daley with the Daley era, a parity scale, on which a score of 100 percent signifies that the proportion of jobs held by Blacks is equivalent to the Black proportion of the population, can be created. If aggregate Black employment figures for 1932 (the end of the Thompson era) and 1976 (the end of the Daley era) are compared, a sharp decline on a parity scale is evident. In 1932, Blacks were 6 percent of the city workforce and 7 percent of the population, for a parity score of 86 percent.[101] In 1976, 24 percent of the city workforce and 37 percent of the population were Black, for a 65 percent parity score.[102] To the extent that a decreasing proportion of city jobs indicates the reduction of political power for a particular group, these data indicate that Blacks were not winning empowerment through the urban bureaucracy and had suffered a setback from earlier achievements. As for their influence in decisionmaking, in 1932 Blacks held about 2 percent of the highest-status positions in the city workforce and were 7 percent of the city's population, for a 29 percent parity score.[103] In 1965, after Blacks helped Daley overcome the serious electoral challenge of Benjamin Adamowski, they held only 5 percent of the policymaking positions in city government but were about 20 percent of the city's population, for a parity score of 25 percent.[104] This represents a small decrease in the proportion of high-status jobs Blacks held in the city bureaucracy. These data strongly suggest that Black empowerment did not increase in the era of the Daley machine.

Political Offices

During Mayor Daley's 21 years in office, only one Black was elected with the support of the Democratic organization to a powerful citywide office (city treasurer). No nonmachine Blacks were elected to such offices until 1983 when Harold Washington captured the mayor's office.

In the city council the picture *appeared* to be more positive. Three Blacks successively held the position of president pro tem of the city council; the political significance of this office was that its holder was assumed to be first in the line of mayoral succession. However, when Mayor Daley died in December 1976, and Black city council president pro tem Wilson Frost sought to become acting mayor, White city officials and city council members denied him access to the mayor's office.[105] The definition of empowerment presented in chapter 1 stressed that the crucial distinction between cooptation and empowerment was that empowerment involved a reallocation of political power. The denial of the right of the city council president pro tem to succeed the mayor suggests that the capturing of this office by a Black did not indicate a reallocation of political power to Blacks.

As table 2–7 indicates, the proportion of Blacks on the city council did increase throughout the Daley-Bilandic-Byrne era. Blacks held about 80 percent of the number of seats on the city council they would have held if that number was at parity with the Black proportion of the population. Even though not 100 percent, this score still appears to be impressive testimony to a significant degree of Black political empowerment.

However, skepticism is in order.[106] These elections did not represent—a reallocation of political power to the Black community, but were examples of Black political cooptation. For the most part, Black city council members did not articulate the interests of their constituencies on open occupancy housing and school desegregation, nor did they raise issues of civil rights, police brutality, or almost any other cause of concern to Blacks. They did not substantively represent their constituents but were agents of the machine domination of the Black wards. The Daley organization anointed, or coexisted with, Black leaders who agreed to accept personal material rewards, increased status, discretion over limited numbers of low-level patronage jobs,

Table 2-7 Growth in the Number of Black City Council Members

Year	Number of Blacks on city council	Percentage of Blacks[a] on city council	Percentage of parity[b]
1967	10	20	83
1971	14	28	85
1975	14	28	76
1979	16	32	80

[a]The city council comprises the 50 aldermen elected from the 50 wards. The percentage of Blacks on the city council is the result of dividing the number of Blacks on the city council by 50.

[b]The percentage of parity is the result of the percentage of Blacks on the city council divided by the percentage of the total city population that is Black for each year. In 1967, 24 percent of the Chicago population was Black, in 1971, 33 percent, in 1975, 37 percent, and in 1979, 40 percent.

and the power to help ward residents in obtaining federal welfare money or segregated public housing. Although these perquisites in no way approached what has been defined as the benefits of political empowerment, they were conspicuously more than noncoopted Black leaders could provide. In exchange for the increased personal status that flowed from being the distributor of these benefits, these clientelistic-subordinate politicians helped the machine to maintain its support in Black wards by allowing it to operate through Black rather than White representatives, by serving as advocates for the candidates and policies approved by the machine, and generally by stifling any efforts to overcome Black political subordination.

In the era of Richard J. Daley, Blacks did not control any more decisionmaking positions in the urban bureaucracy than they had more than forty years earlier. The Chicago political machine clearly was not providing a ladder of status and power for Blacks to climb toward political empowerment. Rather than a ladder leading upward, a more accurate metaphor to describe the machine's impact would be a lid or low ceiling blocking advancement.

The Black Leadership Structure

In the first part of this chapter it was argued that competitive elections provided leverage to Black leaders by creating bargaining opportunities. Competing White factions were persuaded by Black leaders to give up some increment of real political power in exchange for the delivery of votes that were decisive in the outcome of crucial elections. Black leaders who were successful bargainers enhanced their legitimacy among Blacks by delivering politically empowering benefits, and they enhanced their credibility with White leaders by delivering those decisive votes. The analysis of the Daley period portrayed the sharply contrasting impact that noncompetitive elections have on the structure of Black political leadership. Because Black leaders had little leverage with which to bargain with the Daley organization, the Black leadership structure atrophied. The stunted Black leadership structure as it existed through the Daley years may be described as follows.

Clientelistic-Subordinates: Machine Cooptation of Black Leadership

By the early 1960s, six wards (Wards 2, 3, 4, 6, 20, and 24) in Chicago had predominantly Black populations. Although William Dawson had begun organizing in five of these wards, Mayor Daley did not allow the power of the aging congressman to grow unchecked. When Daley stated, "There can be no organization within The Organization," he sounded the death knell for the Dawson "submachine."[107] Daley anointed Black ward and precinct leaders who would be loyal to himself, not Dawson, so that Dawson could not shift the votes of these five Black wards into some mayoral opponent's camp.[108]

Daley weakened Dawson's claim to be the political boss of Black Chicago by anointing Blacks of his own selection, including former sports star Ralph Metcalfe.[109] The aldermen and committeemen picked by both Daley and Dawson to organize these wards were chosen in part because they had no political or economic power base of their own. Often they had no other source of income aside from their job as committeeman or alderman.[110] In the same way that the Democratic organization designated these men as leaders (i.e., they were not promoted by constituents), it could dispose of them and create others to replace them.[111]

The price these designated chieftains of the Black wards paid to the Democratic organization for their elevated status was unquestioning loyalty. The six Black aldermen rarely introduced legislation in city council, always voted as instructed by Daley or his council floor leader, Alderman Thomas Keane, and never criticized the mayor or his administration.[112] The inactivity of the Black aldermen earned them the epithet Silent Six. None of them sponsored any civil rights legislation or questioned the Daley administration's policies enforcing the segregation of schools and preventing scattered-site housing.[113] I label these leaders *clientelistic-subordinates* for two reasons. First, they acted as if the only means to redress the grievances of the Black community was through a patron-client, dominant-subordinate relationship with the leaders of the regular Democratic organization. They did not believe that electoral participation outside of the control of these patrons, that is, as independents, could achieve much. They also did not believe that the goals of the Black community could be achieved outside of electoral politics, that is, in protests or demonstrations. Second, because they accepted the task of mobilizing votes for the organization in exchange for an allotment to Blacks of municipal jobs that gave them the lowest-paying and least powerful jobs, and no power to pursue the agenda of the Black community, these leaders facilitated the maintenance of the subordination of the Black community.

Clientelistic-Subordinates in the Black Church

In Chicago, as in most other cities, politicians who have sought Black electoral support have long recognized the important intermediary role played by Black ministers. The most significant source of Black electoral support for Mayor Thompson was Archibald Carey, who repeatedly opened his pulpit to Thompson and campaigned for him.

Under Mayor Daley a symbiotic relationship between Black clergymen and the Democratic organization developed. If a minister needed to find jobs for congregants, summer employment for students, money for a congregational day care center, or a social center to entertain youths and senior citizens, he turned to Daley. Money from banks for such projects was not forthcoming, except at exorbitant interest rates. But Daley could arrange for funds to be forthcoming from the city or the federal government or could by arranging special terms with a bank.[114]

In exchange, the minister had to be totally loyal to Daley, his organization, and his candidates.[115] For instance, after insurgent Charles Chew defeated the organization in the 1963 aldermanic elections in the Seventeenth Ward, he stated, "the majority of the Negro clergymen worked against me. One pastor would not even let me stand on the sidewalk in front of his church and hand out literature."[116]

A striking example of the control the Daley organization exerted over the city's Black clergymen came when Martin Luther King Jr. decided to shift his activities from the South and chose Chicago as his northern beachhead. King's Southern Christian Leadership Conference (SCLC) sent Dorothy Tillman (who became the alderman of the Third Ward in 1984) to Chicago to do advance work. She discussed the negative reception that King and the SCLC received in Chicago from Black preachers.

> Chicago was the first city that we ever went to as members of the SCLC staff where the black ministers and black politicians told us to go back where we came from. . . .
>
> Although there were Uncle Toms in every city that we went to across the country, nobody ever had nerve enough in any other town to stand up and tell Dr. King and his staff members to leave. Blacks in Chicago actually allowed other blacks to go on television and say that we were not wanted in Chicago. . . . As a matter of fact, we could not find a church pastored by a black minister on the west side that would give the SCLC office space. Therefore, we ended up with a white minister.[117]

Congressman William Dawson, demonstrating his subservience to the Democratic organization, denounced King as an "outside agitator."[118]

Because of the efforts of clientelistic-subordinates in the machine and the churches, Daley received steady electoral support from the Black community. As table 2–8 indicates, he consistently captured 70 to 80 percent of the Black vote, except in the 1975 Democratic primary when he faced both an antimachine Black and a White liberal. Table 2–8 also indicates the declining rate of Black turnout, especially in general elections.[119] Black politicians earned their rewards from the mayor by making sure that, of those Blacks going to the polls, the majority were supporting him. Mobilization of the Black vote (i.e., increasing turnout) was not necessary because Black votes were a superfluous part of Daley's electoral coalition.

Separatist-Messianics: A Disorganized Movement versus the Machine

The Black subordinate leadership and the Daley organization paid scant attention to demonstrations during the early 1960s that called for reform of the segregated school system. Black children were taught in trailers because of overcrowding while desks

Table 2–8 Mayor Daley's Vote in Predominantly Black Wards: Stable Support amid Declining Turnout

	Percentage Daley	Percentage turnout
Primary elections		
1955	82	45
1959[a]	80	32
1963[a]	85	34
1967[a]	84	33
1971[a]	90	27
1975[b]	48	33
General Elections		
1955	72	55
1959	84	44
1963	77	50
1967	81	41
1971	72	43
1975	83	24

Source: Board of Election Commissioners, City of Chicago, "Official Election Returns, Primary and General Elections" (City of Chicago, 1955–1975). All calculations made by me, from wards that were 90 percent Black or greater.

[a]Uncontested primary.

[b]Black candidate Richard Newhouse ran in the primary.

remained unoccupied in White schools. Investigative committees were formed, reports critical of city policies were issued, and promises were made, but few changes were forthcoming.[120] As the community leaders and the people they mobilized grew increasingly frustrated, their approach shifted from trying to elect and influence public officials to a separatist disdain for biracial coalitions; their tactics moved from negotiation to protest; and their goals shifted from specific policy reforms to more diffuse demands for community control.[121] These leaders are appropriately labeled *separatist-messianics* because they generally disdained participation in an electoral system that they saw as serving only the interests of domination, and when they did participate they preferred to remain separate from Whites, not join them in coalitions. Through charismatic presentations and messianic promises to transform subordination into domination and empowerment, these leaders hoped to rally a force to redress the grievances of the Black community. In Chicago the separatist-messianics included Dick Gregory, Lawrence Landry, Robert Lucas, Jesse Jackson, and Lu Palmer.[122] The well-attended demonstrations and protests they led indicated that they commanded the attention of huge numbers of supporters; yet such leaders had great difficulty in translating this support into electoral mobilization and the accomplishment of their goals. Their attempts to become autonomous spokesmen for their communities were frustrated by the Daley organization and the subordinate Black political leaders.[123] The role in Chicago politics of Jesse Jackson, the most outspoken and least radical of the extraelectoral leaders, exemplifies the constraints under which such leaders operate and the limitations of this type of leadership.

Because of Jackson's prominence as the director of Operation PUSH (People United to Save Humanity), before whose Saturday-morning meetings he regularly spoke, many politicians expected that he could mobilize large numbers of voters. One such politician was Sammy Rayner, the antimachine Black alderman, who lost two bids for the Second Congressional District seat—to William Dawson in 1968 and to Ralph Metcalfe in 1970. Metcalfe evaluated Jackson's role as follows:

> [Jesse Jackson] doesn't have the people who are willing to go from door-to-door and do the precinct work. They may pack his Saturday meetings, but the people don't go out and ring doorbells. . . . I know that he does not have the forces to move votes. He has not been able to cultivate teams of people who are dedicated enough to do this. When I ran against Sammy Rayner for Congress, I found that his [Jackson's] volunteers are basically interested in a lot of rhetoric, attending meetings, and social affairs, but they have to operate as a team. They have to be able to go into a precinct like a hardened precinct captain and sit down and talk with people. But they do the most talking in a friendly climate to receptive audiences that are already espousing their viewpoints.[124]

Why didn't Jackson's disciples register Black voters and construct precinct organizations to mobilize votes? For that matter, why wasn't the Coordinating Council of Community Organizations (CCCO), led by Lawrence Landry, Albert Raby, and officials from TWO, able to mobilize sustained support from the Black community in its efforts to desegregate the Chicago public schools?[125] These separatist-messianic efforts were thwarted for two reasons: First, these leaders were unable to wrest away from the machine the support of lower-income Blacks. Poor Blacks did crowd into Jackson's weekly Operation PUSH meetings. They listened to the diatribes against political alliances with Whites voiced by Lu Palmer on his radio show, *On Target*. But lower-income Blacks had the most to lose from working in the campaign of an anti-Daley candidate like Rayner. The benefits of low-level patronage jobs, opportunities for public housing, and the avoidance of bureaucratic red tape in obtaining federal welfare were more significant to poor Blacks than any other group. And the Democratic machine was known for exacting retribution from those who failed to vote the party line.

Second, middle-class Blacks, who were a potential antimachine constituency, turned away from the separatist-messianic crusaders.[126] According to Alan B. Anderson and George W. Pickering, the militant leaders of the CCCO considered negotiations with Whites a "sellout" and preferred to adopt a tough, no-compromise posture.[127] Lu Palmer often suggested that Black interests could not be represented by White politicians. In contrast, middle-class Blacks were typically repelled by the separatist-messianics' divisive rhetoric, and their tactics of demonstration and the threat of violence.

The Failure to Legitimate
Coalitional-Incrementalist Leadership

For middle-class Blacks in Chicago who refused to vote for Mayor Daley or his Black subordinates and refused to follow the separatists, the choices became increasingly meager. Many of them were disgruntled with the lack of leadership provided by Black aldermen and committeemen in South Side wards, as well as by the maintenance of machine control through White politicians in the increasingly Black West Side wards.[128] The machine's rewards of menial patronage jobs, welfare, and public services were not attractive incentives to middle-class Blacks, who wanted the power to choose their own representatives within the organization and on the city council.[129] The machine was unwilling to yield on this matter, leading increasing numbers of Blacks to support independent aldermanic candidates, often with the organizational and financial support of the IVI. However, these fledgling biracial alliances did not produce coalitional-incrementalist leaders or Black political empowerment; once elected, independent Black candidates quickly realized that because they were heavily outnumbered by Daley loyalists in the 50-seat city council, they were unable to legislate any changes or in any way improve the conditions of their Black constituents.[130] Rather than facing what was always a bare-knuckles effort by the machine to reclaim a lost office, these Black independents often accepted the Daley machine's offers of cooptation. The careers of Charles Chew and Fred Hubbard demonstrate this pattern.

In 1963 the city council's lone White liberal, Leon Despres, was joined by Charles Chew, a Black independent who was elected in the rapidly changing Seventeenth Ward. Because of a migration into it of middle-class Blacks from the Second and Third wards, the Seventeenth changed from 50 percent Black in 1959 to 90 percent Black in 1963. Chew won 55 percent of the vote and defeated the Democratic organization's incumbent White alderman. In the council, Chew criticized Daley as well as the subordinate Black aldermen, but he accomplished little except gaining notoriety. The city council at the time comprised 47 Daley aldermen, Despres, Chew, and Republican John Hoellen. After one term Chew left the council, ran for the state senate, and defeated a former aide to both Daley and Dawson.[131] On election night Chew declared that his victory represented a "direct rebuff of the Daley organization and its attempt to dictate policy for my people."[132] Hours later he emerged from a secret meeting with a Daley representative in which he had cut a deal with the organization. In exchange for certain perquisites and the promise of no serious future challenges from organization candidates, Chew agreed to take voting cues from the organization and "make no waves."[133] An IVI leader spoke of the hopes that were raised in Chew's campaign.

> Charlie Chew's [State] Senate campaign was a really special experience, even more so than his aldermanic victory. It represented a coming together of independent leaning Blacks and the liberal reformers like IVI, who had long supported Despres and had been impressed with Charlie's impassioned rhetoric in the council. That race was a real test of strength against the Daley machine because there was no incumbent. And there was a feeling that this election could be a validation of the things that Dr. [Martin Luther] King stood for when he came to Chicago. That is why Chew's abandonment of the cause represented such a devastating blow.[134]

Prior to Chew's election, Despres, together with a handful of White and Black liberals, had founded the Committee for an Effective City Council. Dedicated to the election of an integrated slate of reform-minded candidates, the committee offered platform positions, political and strategic advice on campaigning, and some money to prospective candidates. Three Black council candidates in which the committee took a special interest in 1967 were A. A. "Sammy" Rayner (Sixth Ward), William Cousins (Eighth Ward), and Fred Hubbard (Second Ward). Rayner and Cousins both defeated the organization's candidates and won seats on the city council. Rayner tried to use his office as a steppingstone to the U.S. Congress but was twice defeated by machine candidates. In 1971, after his defeat in the aldermanic contest by Daley loyalist Eugene Sawyer, the ward committeeman, he withdrew from politics. Cousins continued to serve on the city council and remained independent. But like Despres he was relatively powerless.[135] In the Second Ward, Hubbard was defeated by William Harvey, Dawson's aide, in 1967.

Hubbard was viewed as a shining star in the dim sky of independent politics. He was a graduate of the University of Chicago, where he had been the president of the NAACP chapter, and he had acquired exposure and a "can-do" reputation as the director of the Clarence Darrow Community Center. In 1966 he had given Congressman Dawson a real scare, running against him and losing by only 1,500 votes in the congressional primary. In 1969 Hubbard ran against Lawrence Woods, designated by Dawson to succeed Harvey in the Second Ward. Hubbard entered the race against Woods with the endorsements of the IVI and the Committee for an Effective City Council.[136] White liberals and independent Blacks put much time, effort, and money into his campaign.[137] When Hubbard defeated Woods, there was celebration among Black and White independents. Alderman Despres said, "This is the biggest possible defeat the Democratic machine could have suffered. The 2d Ward always has been the most secure position of the machine."[138]

Again the celebration did not last long. Hubbard seemed to have understood from the start that the city council was an inhospitable place for independents. After Daley arranged his appointment to a $25,000-a-year administrative position in a federal job-training program for minorities, Hubbard threw aside his independence and consistently voted with the organization. He eventually was sentenced to two years in prison for embezzling $100,000 from the program and gambling it away in Las Vegas.[139]

I have discussed just a few examples of the pattern of the Daley organization's cooptation of electorally successful independent Black politicians.[140] For their supporters, the occasional victory over the Daley organization was a heady experience. But the victories were hollow and ultimately demoralizing. The independents who were elected learned that, as one of five independent votes in a 50-member city council, there was little they could do to increase their constituents' political power.

It is arguable that it was not irrational for Black politicians to pursue cooptation. They secured a safe, often well-paying position with some degree of status. They also were in a position to help limited numbers of their constituents (most often family and friends) find jobs, get ahead on waiting lists for public housing, and cut through the red tape often involved in receiving public services. However, each instance of the cooptation of a formerly independent Black who was elected with support from the IVI drove a wedge of further distrust between IVI and other independent Black leaders. This distrust made the formation of biracial, antimachine coalitions more difficult and severely undermined the hopes of forming a coalitional-incrementalist Black leadership. The devastating impact of this problem was illustrated in the 1975 mayoral election.

Black Political Subordination in Chicago

The Leadership Vacuum

The mayoral campaign of 1975 represented a genuine opportunity for anti-Daley forces in Chicago. By the time of the election Daley would be 72 years old. He had suffered a stroke in 1974 and was visibly older and more tired. Some of his closest political allies had been convicted of various forms of corruption, including Governor Otto Kerner, Daley's city council floor leader Alderman Thomas Keane, and his longtime friend and press aide Earl Bush.

Alderman William Singer (Ward 43) recognized Daley's potential weakness, and in October 1973 he announced his intention to run in the Democratic mayoral primary. Elected in 1969 on an anti-Daley, anti–Vietnam War platform, Singer was one of the small handful of independent liberals in the city council.[141] This primary would be the first in which Daley faced a challenger since his original mayoral bid in 1955. Singer sought to forge a coalition of White liberals, independent Blacks, and any other groups disaffected with the machine.[142]

Within the Black community others recognized that the 1975 mayoral elections presented a greater opportunity than any in recent history—not only because of Daley's health and the corruption around him, but also because the most widely recognized Black politician in Chicago, Congressman Ralph Metcalfe, had recently broken with Daley and the Democratic organization. Metcalfe had worked his way up from precinct captain to alderman to the organization's designated successor to Dawson in Congress. He had always played politics strictly by the rules of the organization. But when two friends of his, both middle-class Black dentists, were separately brutalized by the police (one died soon afterward) and Metcalfe found that he was unable to initiate any action against the policemen, he decided to break with the party organization and lead a fight against police brutality and for a civilian police review board. A Committee to Elect a Black Mayor was quickly formed as a vehicle to raise money and generate support; but Metcalfe's candidacy was still born. A veteran political reporter who was a close observer of the city's Black politicians described what transpired:

> Ralph Metcalfe was really afraid to buck the machine. He was no different than any other Black politician in that way. But he knew what it took to win. Metcalfe looked around and saw people were upset about police brutality, but the Black businessmen were not ready to support him in a challenge to Daley. They were afraid of retribution. He went to the churches and they agreed with him on the police issues, but would not help him in an election. He went to the Black ward committeemen who controlled patronage workers that would be needed for precinct operations in an election and they refused to help. Metcalfe had been stripped of patronage by Daley and they weren't looking for the same fate. He went to the unionists and they said they could provide manpower but no endorsements or money. There wasn't enough there and Ralph was neither a martyr nor a fool.[143]

After Metcalfe's withdrawal a number of lesser-known Black aspirants began seeking the endorsement of the Committee to Elect a Black Mayor. State Senator Richard Newhouse emerged at the head of this field, but the committee refused to endorse him. He was not well known outside his state senatorial district, and he had few contacts within the White community. Within the Black community his support was also very weak.[144] Jesse Jackson, who most observers believed was planning to run once Daley was no longer a candidate, warned that a poor showing by a Black candidate such as Newhouse might hinder the future of Black independent politics.[145] Congressman Metcalfe, Alderman Anna Langford, Jackson, and longtime political activists Richard Barnett and Jackie Grimshaw endorsed Singer and urged Newhouse to withdraw from the race because the issue was defeating Daley and only Singer could do that.[146] After contemplating a change in its name that would allow it to back Singer, the Committee to Elect a Black Mayor endorsed no candidate and lamented, "there is no moving together of Newhouse and Singer."[147]

The reaction from the separatist-messianic camp to the display of Black support for Singer was scathing. The *Chicago Metro News* called Langford's request that Newhouse withdraw and support Singer "asinine" and issued this volley: "The recent defection of a few more Uncle TOM Negroes to support a Jewish candidate for Mayor of Chicago, who has never shown any interest in Blacks in his tenure in City Council, proves again the stupidity of some white brainwashed Negroes."[148] Newhouse denounced the committee as a "self serving, shuffling, backside-scratching cadre of worse than Uncle Toms . . . compared to whom Judas is a paragon of virtue."[149]

Langford, Barnett, Grimshaw, and NAACP director Andrew Barrett all spoke out against pressure they received from Black activists not to support Singer. Those who urged support for Singer had trouble avoiding the Uncle Tom epithet because, as Barnett said, many Black Chicagoans had never learned that "it is possible for one to work for black political power while supporting a Singer over a black candidate."[150] Jesse Jackson came under intense criticism and was labeled "a major sellout" by Black nationalist leader Lu Palmer.[151] He eventually retreated from his support for Singer.

Singer and Newhouse failed to take any steps toward joining forces against Daley. Daley emerged victorious while Blacks and White reformers continued to exacerbate the distrust and tension that had long characterized their relationship in Chicago. Daley won 58 percent of the vote and 47 of the city's 50 wards, Singer captured 29 percent and won 3 wards, while Newhouse received 8 percent.[152] Singer captured more votes than Newhouse in every ward. Added together, the antimachine votes of Singer and Newhouse still would not have defeated Daley, but together they would have won 12 wards.[153] Yet White liberals, Blacks, and Republicans remained too estranged to initiate the dialogue necessary for uniting either behind Republican mayoral candidate John Hoellen or in support of a slate of aldermanic candidates. In the general election the mayor received 78 percent of the vote, winning every ward overwhelmingly.

The 1975 Democratic mayoral primary exemplified the distorted pattern of Black political leadership in Chicago. Aside from Anna Langford (who was defeated in the following aldermanic election by a Black female organization candidate), all the Black aldermen and committeemen backed Mayor Daley. The city's Black ministers and churches also overwhelmingly opened their pulpits and gave their support to Daley.[154] When Newhouse charged that an alliance with the White liberals who were led by Singer was the equivalent of exchanging one plantation master for another, the credibility of these charges was not challenged by any historical record that showed the benefits of such alliances. Such intimidation tactics were successful because moderate Blacks had historically failed to demonstrate that benefits could be gained through a biracial reform coalition. The middle-class leaders of the Committee to Elect a Black Mayor retreated from their open support of Singer and relinquished their role in fielding an alternative to Daley to separatist-messianics who equated supporting a White liberal with selling out.

With the elevation in 1977 of Michael Bilandic after Daley's death, little changed for Blacks. As late as 1978 there was only one independent Black alderman of the 14 Blacks on the 50-member city council. David Rhodes (Ward 24) was the only Black alderman to endorse Harold Washington's first mayoral bid in the special 1977 mayoral election necessitated by Daley's death. Rhodes was defeated in his reelection bid by the ward committeeman. Others, such as Aldermen Clifford Kelly (Ward 20) and Timothy Evans (Ward 4), liked to call themselves "independent" and sometimes introduced legislation that was not approved by the organization. But neither supported Ralph Metcalfe's congressional candidacy after he broke with the machine, nor did they support Harold Washington's 1977 mayoral candidacy. In the 1979 mayoral campaign, in which Black voters helped Jane Byrne become mayor, every Black alderman supported Mayor Bilandic. This indicated not only that the Black aldermen were not independent of the Democratic organization, but also that they were out of touch with the sentiments of their constituents. Even after Byrne defeated Bilandic and proved that the Democratic organization was not invincible, most of the Black aldermen remained subordinated to the Democratic machine. For example, in 1981 the Democratic organization drew up a new ward map that shifted the boundaries of the Fifteenth Ward, giving it a White instead of Black majority population. Only 4 of the 16 Black aldermen voted against this racially motivated gerrymander.

The Division of the White Vote and the Election of Harold Washington

Once in office, Mayor Byrne quickly discarded her reform rhetoric and tried instead to make the machine work to her benefit. Her overriding goal was to win reelection in a nonfluke election in 1983 and fill the shoes of her hero, Mayor Richard J. Daley. She believed that only one thing stood in her way—Richard M. (Richie) Daley, the eldest son and heir apparent of the late mayor. During her four-year term she tried ceaselessly to discredit Richie Daley and insure her continued domination over the Democratic organization.

Her strategy for building a firm base of support in the city's White ethnic communities was to earn a reputation as the leader who would best hold the line against the political demands of Blacks.[155] She repeatedly antagonized Blacks and steadfastly worked to roll back the minimal political gains they had made. Examples of her contempt for the Black community included: (a) selecting as police superintendent the only White on the list of recommendations from the Police Board, skipping over the Black acting superintendent; (b) replacing two Black members of the School Board with two White women who had been leaders of the antibusing movement; (c) skipping over the Black deputy superintendent of schools to pick his subordinate, a White woman, for the post of school superintendent; and (d) replacing two Black members of the Chicago Housing Authority with two White members.[156]

Byrne's actions had a second rationale, aside from attracting White voters fearful of Black encroachment. She sought also to provoke the African-American community to produce a challenger against her for the Democratic primary, in order to prevent Richie Daley from capturing much of the Black antiadministration vote.[157] Jane Byrne arguably did more to organize and mobilize the Black community to overthrow machine domination in Chicago than any other person, serving to unify that community by becoming the enemy against whom it could rally. Her demonstrations of contempt for it reinvigorated the historically weak efforts of those Black leaders and organizations that called for radical changes in Chicago politics. She stimulated the emergence of a number of antimachine organizations, including Chicago Black United Communities (CBUC), led by the Black nationalist Lu Palmer.[158]

Harold Washington's decision to make a second bid for the mayoralty in 1983 marked the fruition of Byrne's strategy. She did not consider a victory by Washington possible (nor did most pundits) for two reasons: Blacks had never before united as a voting bloc behind a nonmachine Black candidate; and Blacks and White liberals had never been able to overcome their differences and unite against the Democratic organization. Not until the very last weeks of the 1983 primary campaign did Mayor Byrne realize that the real threat to her reelection was Harold Washington, not Richie Daley. This late realization by herself and her allies produced the divisive and ugly racism that marred the 1983 elections.[159]

In the 1983 Democratic primary, Mayor Byrne captured 34 percent of the vote and Richie Daley received 30 percent. Because they split the White vote, Washington was able to emerge as the winner with 36 percent of the vote. In the predominantly White wards (excluding the liberal, Lakefront wards) Washington won about 2 percent of the vote, Daley received 51 percent, and Byrne captured 47 percent. In the six Lakefront wards, Byrne received about 44 percent, Daley 34 percent, and Washington 22 percent. Washington won about 79 percent of the vote in the predominantly African-American wards, with Byrne winning 15 percent there and Daley 6 percent.

In the mayoral election, Washington faced Republican candidate Bernard Epton. Prior to Washington's victory, Epton had been viewed as the chosen sacrificial lamb whom Byrne would easily defeat. However, because Washington had vowed to abolish machine politics and reform the city's government, and because Washington was an African-American, White Democratic party leaders joined forces with Epton. Epton won 48 percent of the total vote, including 88 percent of the White vote. Washington's 52 percent of the vote was the product of the votes of Blacks (99.7 percent), Hispanics (75 percent), and Lakefront liberal voters (42 percent).[160]

Harold Washington's victory was not the culmination of a process of incremental, evolutionary African-American empowerment, as when Atlanta elected Maynard Jackson or Philadelphia elected Wilson Goode. Rather, the election of Harold Washington was the product of a sudden volcanic eruption of a long-subordinated African-American community. Byrne's efforts to deny Blacks high-level appointments would not have been enough to alienate Black voters who were linked clientelistically to the organization. It was the fissure in the hegemony of the White Democratic organization caused by the leadership struggle between Byrne and Richie Daley that gave Harold Washington a serious chance at winning and created an opportunity that even the most jaded in the African-American community recognized was unique.

White Ethnics Remain Loyal to the Ancien Regime

Washington immediately faced a challenge to his ability to govern from a city council that was dominated by his regular organization foes. Black machine politicians were forced to side with him because to do otherwise would have been to guarantee defeat in the next election at the hands of an aroused Washington constituency. Quite similarly, White ethnic voters would have punished any alderman who defected from the opposition and voted with Washington. The city council divided into the "Vrdolyak 29," led by Cook County Democratic party chairman Edward Vrdolyak, and the "Washington 21." "Council Wars" began, Chicago became nationally known as Beirut on the Lake, and the Washington agenda became the victim of gridlock. The mayor could sustain a veto of any legislation advanced by Vrdolyak and his allies, while they in turn could scuttle any legislative initiatives he forwarded. The city council was not the only battlefield for the struggle between the Washington administration and the regular Democratic organization. As was the case in Gary in Mayor Richard Hatcher's first term, Washington appointees faced hostility and sabotage from the entrenched bureaucracy.[161]

The stalemate was finally broken in December 1985 by the settlement of a lawsuit over the post-1980 census reapportionment of the city council. Latino and Black activists (but not sitting city council members) had contended that the new ward map approved by the council was gerrymandered in a manner that discriminated against their groups. Special elections were held in seven wards in 1986, and the net effect was a shift of four wards to the Washington coalition. With the warring forces tied 25 to 25, the mayor was able to cast the decisive vote on city council legislation. After two years of unproductive wrangling with the council, his administration finally passed landmark ethics legislation that increased legal scrutiny of the city's 50 council members and the lobbyists who make their living trying to influence them. Lobbyists were forced to report their lobbying activities, their clients' identities, and their expenses. City council members no longer could accept gifts valued at more than $50 or campaign contributions that exceeded $1,500. Aldermen who were attorneys no longer would be able to represent clients who are suing the city, a practice that had resulted in special treatment for clients.[162] Washington also took significant steps to open up government to the scrutiny of outsiders. Earlier he had issued a freedom-of-information executive order that gave citizens access to nearly all city documents. He also opened the city's budget process by holding budget hearings in the summer and introducing the budget by mid-October; previously the proposed budget had remained secret until it was presented for passage.

Washington appeared to be on the verge of consolidating power after his successful 1987 election. Speculation was rife that he would serve as long as Daley had and that he would seek no higher offices. He defeated Jane Byrne in the 1987 Democratic primary with 53 percent of the vote, and he captured 54 percent of the vote against three White candidates, including the rapidly fading Edward Vrdolyak, who ran as an independent. The 1987 election exhibited an air of inevitable victory for Washington. The tenor of the rhetoric was nondivisive, and turnout among both Blacks and Whites fell from 80 percent of registered voters in the 1983 elections to the low 70 percent range.

Once he was no longer under siege from Vrdolyak and his allies, Washington's separatist supporters became more critical of him. Affirmative action and minority business enterprise set-asides were not improving the lives of CHA residents, who were living in high-rises that candidate Washington had many times said should never have been built. Failing public schools and a lack of affordable housing were two other issues that activist outsiders in the Black community had long complained about to previous mayors. Now that they had Washington inside city hall and many Blacks wearing pin stripes and occupying inner offices of the bureaucracy, these messianic activists expected miraculous change and were disappointed. When the mayor explained that federal funds to Chicago had been dramatically cut by the Reagan administration, these allies wondered whether he and his appointees had lost touch with them now that they were in power.[163] The fact that Washington tripled funding for the homeless and enabled community organizations to take over abandoned buildings was significant, yet it was evident that the problem was getting worse.

Mayor Harold Washington died of a heart attack less than eight months after his reelection, on November 25, 1987. The city council had the responsibility of picking the interim mayor. Aldermen Danny Davis and Timothy Evans were the most legitimate successors to Washington. Davis was the most progressive of the Black aldermen; Evans, a convert from the ranks of the clientelistic-subordinates, had become Washington's legislative floor manager in the city council. Neither could muster a majority of the city council votes, however, because many other Black aldermen were not interested in continuing on the reform path. After debates and negotiations that lasted all night and into the morning. Alderman Eugene Sawyer was selected. He was well schooled in patronage politics, having served on the city council longer than any other Black. The more clever of the White city council members realized that backing him was an excellent strategy for promoting the festering dissension in the Washington coalition. It was a foregone conclusion that Sawyer was not the kind of candidate the progressive Whites and Latinos would want; conversely, Blacks who were nonplused by Washington's calls for reform and simply wanted the spoils that had long been the perquisites of the Irish would avidly support Sawyer.

After his election, Mayor Sawyer could count on little meaningful support from the White organization members of the city council. They did not obstruct his governance; they merely took no steps during his 15-month term to make him look good. In 1988 Richie Daley entered the Democratic primary against Sawyer early enough so that any other White entrant would risk being labeled a spoiler. He dispatched incumbent Sawyer in the primary (outspending him 3–2, capturing 56 percent of the vote, and winning by more than one hundred thousand votes), and in the general election he defeated Timothy Evans and Ed Vrdolyak, who further embarrassed himself by running as the Republican candidate for mayor.

Vrdolyak ran a puzzling campaign, rarely seeming to have the spirit of mortal combat that had always characterized the way he played politics. The Daley campaign had a monopoly on money, and the leaders of the state Republican organization, particularly Governor Jim Thompson, did nothing to dispel the widespread rumor that they preferred Daley. Hence, although two White candidates were in the race with Evans, they did not divide the White vote and create the kind of situation that could foster Black unity behind Evans.[164] Sawyer was unwilling to endorse Evans's candidacy (just as Evans had refused to back Sawyer); the feuding between the two camps yielded divisive rhetoric that divided the Black community and made Daley's victories a foregone conclusion.[165]

Richie Daley's administrations have not returned Blacks to the plantation politics that existed under his father; nor has he pursued racially antagonistic policies as did Jane Byrne. But under Daley Black empowerment by every measure has been rolled back. Although his administration took steps to create a local ordinance for affirmative action for minority and female contractors that would pass muster in the aftermath of the Supreme Court's *Croson* decision, Black political empowerment through top policymaking positions has been rolled back; conversely, Latinos have gained in the new Daley regime.[166] Of the contracts awarded to minority-owned firms in 1994, Hispanics received 34 percent, Asians received 29 percent, and African-Americans, who outnumber both groups, received only 27 percent.[167] Daley endorsed for the U.S. Congress a Latino who was formerly an ally of Washington. The mayor also replaced the retiring Black police superintendent with a Latino appointee. The composition of Daley's new hires in 1989 was 62 percent White, 17 percent African-American, and 14 percent Latino. In the midst of city hall cutbacks that also hurt Blacks the most, this distribution transformed the breakdown of top administration jobs from 44 percent Black, 43 percent White, and 7 percent Latino during the Sawyer administration to 50 percent White, 34 percent Black, and 12 percent Latino. In terms of all public-sector jobs, Whites held 55 percent, Blacks held 35 percent, and Latinos held about 8 percent.[168] Since Daley has been mayor, there have been numerous reports of unwarranted stops and verbal mistreatment of Blacks by the police department and an episode in which police abandoned two Black youths in all-White Bridgeport to be chased and beaten by a White gang.[169] Although one can cite numerous differences between Richard J. Daley and his son, the present mayor, Chicago scholar Paul Green suggested that with respect to Black votes the current mayor's regime is quite similar to that of his father: "Governmentally and morally, Daley needs to go after black support but politically, he really doesn't need it. His support among white ethnics, white liberals and Hispanics just continues to go up and up."[170] Daley's electoral support has increased among Blacks as well, but Black turnout has fallen dramatically since his first election.

The Black political leadership vacuum remains, and no Black candidate in the 1991 or 1995 mayoral elections was able to unify the divided Black political community, let alone rebuild Washington's multiracial coalition. The future for Black mayoral aspirants in Chicago is not promising either. Demographically, flight from the city to the suburbs is both a White and Black phenomenon in Chicago, and the prime political beneficiaries of this are likely to be Latinos. Moreover, Black unity is unlikely to emerge unless one of three circumstances materializes. If Daley were to dramatically change his policy and personnel approach and become the kind of enemy to Blacks that Byrne was, unity could be forged. If Daley left the Chicago political scene and a succession crisis led multiple White candidates to enter the mayoral race, a single Black candidate might be able to eke out a victory in a party primary. Finally, if the Daley administration is crippled by serious scandals, a strong Black candidate (untainted by the corruption scandal) might have a chance at election in a crowded field. And the history of the Council Wars are a reminder that the difficulties any Black faces in getting elected may be surpassed by the dilemmas of governing.

The Black Leadership Structure in the Era of Harold Washington

During his first mayoral campaign, and while Harold Washington was mayor, his organization was plagued by divisions and distrust that mirrored the fault lines of Chicago's Black leadership structure already discussed. Separatist-messianics were willing to participate in voter registration drives and political education efforts to a degree that had never been approached before. For once the job of precinct-level organizing was not beyond those who typically preferred bombast to doorbell-ringing. But when they entered the campaign they brought with them their litmus tests, which yielded tension and divisiveness. They regularly accused other Blacks in the campaign apparatus of being too devoted to the agendas of White liberals and Latinos. These separatists formed the Task Force for Political Empowerment, but they were better known by their unofficial name, "the 47th Street Crowd." The leaders of the task force, Conrad Worrill and Robert Starks, rejected electoral politics in the United States, believing that the government was little more than a colonial force of occupation.[171] Like other separatists, including Lu Palmer and Rev. Al Sampson, Starks and Worrill saw the downtown campaign officials as a force trying to subvert and moderate Harold Washington. Washington's replacement of Renault Robinson, his first campaign manager, with Al Raby, a veteran of the civil rights movement, was seen as a major setback in the separatist struggle to influence Washington. Journalist Gary Rivlin, one of the few observers who recognized the significance of this internecine struggle, wrote:

> Worrill, Starks, and Palmer felt the campaign they helped launch was being snatched away from them. ACTIVISTS FEEL BETRAYED, read the headline over a column by Nate Clay in the *Metro News*. In an attempt at downtown respectability, Clay wrote, "bourgeois professionals with strong ties to the white establishment" were given control of the campaign. . . . Downtown they felt superior in their knowledge that electoral politics was more than rousing speeches and bullhorns. They laughed among themselves that these activists who for years dismissed politics as some honkie scam were suddenly experts on winning elections. Even those seeing the Third Force [the Task Force] as a godsend—how else could they reach the disenfranchised?—were put off by their stridency.[172]

Once Washington was elected the same divisions surfaced, as he tried to simultaneously build bridges to the White community, solidify his Black base and empower Black citizens, and reform a city administration long mired in machine politics. Lu

Palmer railed against Washington's pride that his administration's service delivery record demonstrated his fairness to White ethnic neighborhoods; fairness was not a privilege that Whites had earned when it came to services or personnel policy, according to Palmer and most of the separatist-messianics.[173] Palmer charged that Washington seemed more interested in proving to the IVI and Jewish liberals that he was a reformer than in rewarding Blacks who deserved compensation after years of subordination. According to Rivlin, the separatists openly talked about how there were too many Jews in the administration, that Latinos were demanding too much, and that Washington was too friendly with gays and lesbians.[174] "Some, too, were angry with the presence of so many whites. What did Washington owe the white community? The white liberals had rejected him in the primary and then hardly made amends in the general election. . . . And the Latinos, who accounted for a seven percent share of Washington's vote in 1983; what had they done to earn Washington's attention?"[175]

Black Chicago's distorted leadership structure led directly to the loss of the mayor's office after the death of Harold Washington. Eugene Sawyer's selection and his 15-month lame-duck term exemplified the dilemma of the clientelistic-subordinate style of leadership, the lack of broad legitimacy in the Black community. On the night he was selected as mayor, Sawyer was dubbed "Uncle Tom Sawyer," and Black citizens jeered him with slogans like "Sawyer's in a Cadillac, driving for Vrdolyak." Timothy Evans from the start cast himself as the heir to Washington awaiting coronation, and many in the Black community (as well as progressive Latinos and the few progressive Whites) saw Sawyer as anathema to the Washington legacy. When Sawyer removed Evans and White progressive Larry Bloom from the chairmanships of two powerful city council committees, appointments that Washington had made immediately after he gained control of the council, he confirmed for all that he was not trying to follow the path of his predecessor. The most devastating episode of Sawyer's tenure was the Steve Cokely affair. Cokely was a Black nationalist with fiery oratorical skills who served Sawyer as a liaison to the separatist-messianic community. In plain terms, he was a foil to Evans's supporters, who claimed that Sawyer didn't have the proper messianic movement credentials. When Cokely articulated the anti-Semitic statements that are a common refrain from the separatist-messianic camp (i.e., that a conspiracy of Jewish doctors was infecting Black children with the AIDS virus), Sawyer responded indecisively. He failed to decide quickly whether to support Cokely (e.g., refuse to allow the White media to tell him who to fire while distancing himself from specific statements) and strengthen his support among separatists or fire him and buttress his support among Whites, particularly liberals. His indecision reduced his standing among all groups.

Evans, like Sawyer, came from the clientelistic-subordinate leadership, originally having learned his politics at the feet of Claude Holman, one of the most infamous of the Silent Six. When the Black political world was turned upside down by the election of Harold Washington, Evans chose to recast himself.[176] Blacks who didn't want merely a bigger slice of the pie but wanted to bake the pie and do the slicing would back Evans. When one of Evans's closest allies (a separatist who had caused similar problems for Mayor Washington) called Sawyer "a shuffling Uncle Tom," the legacy of Chicago's vacuum of coalitional-incrementalist leadership became evident, as it had in 1975.[177] Some in the Black community agreed with this characterization, but others felt that the city's sitting Black mayor deserved much more respect. Because both Black candidates could mobilize only part of the Black electorate, Daley was elected easily. Given the absence of coalitional-incrementalist Black leadership, it is unlikely that Chicago will elect a Black mayor until a major regime-disturbing event produces the conditions for a dramatic coalitional realignment.

Political Monopoly and the Maintenance of Black Subordination in Gary

This chapter examines the evolution of Black political power in Gary, Indiana, as a complement to the analysis of Chicago. Important similarities in the patterns of Black political development in Chicago and Gary suggest that the Chicago case was not unique. Economically the two cities are similar. Both were the locales of heavy industry and large unionized blue-collar work forces. Due to shifts in the international political economy that precipitated changes in the structure of the U.S. economy, both suffered economic setbacks. (Because of the lack of diversity of Gary's economy, the city's overall economic decline has been more severe.) Demographically the cities are also similar: both have large Eastern European and Black populations that are residentially segregated. In ways that are salient for this analysis, Gary and Chicago are also similar politically. In both cities one can trace the historical development of dominant, electorally monopolistic political party organizations and the institutionalized political relationship between superordinate Whites and subordinate Blacks that is produced by these monopolies.

Excellent literature is extant on the political surbordination of Blacks and the struggle to overcome this powerlessness in Gary. My study builds on such fine work as James B. Lane's *City of the Century* and William E. Nelson Jr.'s fine dissertation, "Black Political Mobilization," but I offer a unique interpretation that emphasizes the absence of electoral competition for Black votes. I argue that after the New Deal realignment, White ethnics built the Gary Democratic party into a dominant organization, and the local GOP offered no meaningful competition in the governance of the city. I will show that by the time Black voters were solidly in the ranks of the Democratic party in Gary, two factors mitigated against their ability to demand a reallocation of political power: (1) Black votes were superfluous to Democratic mayoral victories and domination of the city council, and (2) Black leaders could not seriously threaten the Democrats with defection because the moribund nature of the local GOP deprived them of the institutional vehicle necessary to do so. Even though the proportion of Blacks in Gary more than doubled from 1940 to 1960, as table 3–1 indicates, the Democratic machine's empowerment of Blacks stalled at the lowest levels. Finally, I will show how the absence of electoral competition distorted Gary's Black leadership structure. When Richard Hatcher became the city's first Black mayor, as the result of a sudden split in the dominant party organization, he became chief executive of a city that had never experienced Black leadership in any powerful political offices. Moreover, he was elected by a Black community with decades worth of pent-up frustration and demands. The frustrations of Black citizens and the worst fears of the unknown that White voters harbored led to a polarized, explosive political environment.

Building a Democratic Political Monopoly

A Republican Company Town

Gary was founded in 1906 as a company town by U.S. Steel and was named after Judge Elbert H. Gary, chairman of the board of U.S. Steel until his death in 1927. A logical site to bring together by water or rail the iron ore of Minnesota, Michigan limestone, and Appalachian mountain coal, Gary was created in the midst of the Indiana dunes to satisfy the growing demand for steel in the Midwest. U.S. Steel officials and local Republican party leadership exerted unchallenged influence over the policies of the city, the content of the newspapers, and the curricula of the schools, as well as the activities of the churches and settlement houses.[1] Immigrants from all parts of southeastern Europe lived in Gary, and by 1920 the proportion of foreign stock (foreign-born or native-born with at least one immigrant parent) had reached

Table 3–1 Growth in the Black Proportion of the Population of Gary, Indiana

Year	Total population	Percentage Black
1920	55,378	10
1930	100,426	18
1940	111,719	18
1950	133,911	29
1960	178,320	39
1970	175,249	53
1980	151,953	71

Sources: Bureau of the Census, *Negroes in the United States, 1920–32* (Washington, D.C.: 1935), chap. 5, p. 49; Bureau of the Census, *Sixteenth Census of the U.S., 1940, Population, vol. 3, pt. 1* (Washington, D.C.: 1943), pp. 20–23.

60 percent of the city's population.[2] To address labor shortages caused by immigration restrictions during World War I, the mills advertised job opportunities in southern newspapers and drew large numbers of Blacks to the city. By 1920 Gary was 10 percent Black, and the workforce at U.S. Steel was almost 14 percent Black.[3]

After 1930 the steel company and its Republican allies could no longer dominate Gary's politics. The death of Judge Gary in 1927, the retirement of most of those who had participated in the founding of the company and the city, the impact of the depression, and the growth of countervailing union power brought a new generation of leadership to U.S. Steel.

Early Black Politics in Gary

Gary's Black voters were loyal supporters of the Republican party, the party of Lincoln and of the city's most prominent employer. In fact, White ethnic racial hostility toward Blacks was exacerbated by widespread rumors that U.S. Steel had recruited them simply because they could be counted on to vote for the GOP.[4] Black leaders such as Charles Gregory, W. C. Hueston, and A. B. Whitlock organized and delivered Black votes to the Republican organization by urging voters to "vote for your friends—those who employ you."[5] In exchange, these leaders were personally rewarded.[6]

The individual successes of these Black officials did little for the Black population of Gary. Wilbur J. Hardaway, a Black Republican who served on the city council from 1925–1934, thought that the "Negroes of Gary have been humiliated and discriminated against more than in any other city north of the Mason-Dixon line."[7] Blacks were not welcome in public parks or beaches, nor were they allowed in some city theaters; they had separate, lower-quality hospitals and separate cemeteries.[8] City officials caved in to the demands of White high-school youths who boycotted Emerson school in 1927 after 18 Black students were transferred there to relieve overcrowding in an all-Black school. The mayor and the city council removed all the Black students from Emerson and promised to build a temporary school building; no building was built.[9]

In 1929 former mayor R. O. Johnson (1914–18, 1922–25, 1930–34) was released from jail and pardoned by President Calvin Coolidge of conspiracy to violate prohibition laws.[10] In the 1929 Republican mayoral primary, Johnson defeated the incumbent mayor, Floyd Williams, capturing 58 percent of the vote. In the general election, Johnson received 56 percent of the vote and defeated Democrat Emmet N. White (who had the support of many Republicans who feared that another Johnson administration would increase the level of municipal corruption).[11] In the three wards where Blacks lived, in which they comprised 25, 46, and 72 percent of the population, Johnson won by about 3,800 votes. On this basis, Black leaders such as Chauncey Townsend, editor of the *Gary American*, the city's Black newspaper, and former city council member A. B. Whitlock argued that Blacks were deserving of significant largesse from the mayor. They presented a petition signed by three hundred Black voters that demanded particular appointments and policies. Mayor Johnson penned a reply that stated he had "immediately deposited [the petition] in the wastebasket" without reading it.[12] This incident persuaded some in the Black community that the

Republican party would not reward Black supporters; but loyalty to the party of Lincoln and U.S. Steel precluded many from defecting.[13] Republicans had good reason to believe that the Black vote could be taken for granted.

In the county elections of 1930, the level of support among Blacks for Republican party candidates did fall from about 80 percent to 60 percent.[14] The increase in Black voting for Democratic candidates, coupled with heavy Democratic voting from White ethnics who had rallied around the 1928 presidential candidacy of Al Smith, produced across-the-board Democratic victories in 1930.[15] These successes surprised the Democrats and infused new leadership into the party.[16] Still, Gary's Blacks were not yet converts to the Democratic party. In the 1932 presidential election, Gary was one of only 12 cities in the nation with a population over one hundred thousand in which Herbert Hoover defeated Franklin D. Roosevelt. Hoover's success was due in large measure to his ability to win 85 percent of the vote in the predominantly (at least 80 percent) Black precincts of Gary.[17]

One tactic by which the new Democratic administration could gain control was to eliminate Republican strength on the city council. One area of Republican strength was the Black wards of the Central District (Wards 3, 4, and 5), where the population had nearly doubled sine 1920 (see table 3–1). In 1932, the Democratic administration redistricted Gary's city council ward boundaries, and Black voters were gerrymandered into a single ward. The structure of the city council was changed from 10 ward council members and 5 at-large members, to nine members elected at-large, six of whom would represent the city's six wards. The *Gary American* predicted that "the ultimate end" of the redistricting would be the "disfranchisement of the Negro in Gary."[18] Undoubtedly, the potential for the city council to serve as an avenue for the assertion of Black political power was sharply restricted. Blacks would not occupy more than one seat on the city council until 1947, whereas under the old arrangements the prospects for Black city council representation from Wards 3, 4, and 5 had looked excellent.

Black Voters Lag behind the Democratic Realignment

Riding Franklin D. Roosevelt's coattails, Democrats were able to sweep all the major offices in Gary in 1934.[19] Barney Clayton, the first Democrat since 1909 to be elected mayor, captured 50.4 percent of the vote and defeated Republican John Holloway by a razor-thin margin of 268 votes. Clayton owed his victory to the largely Irish and Polish voters of Tolleston and Glen Park, who gave him from 60 to 75 percent of their votes. These voters were mobilized by an organization built on the more than three hundred numbers runners controlled by syndicate racketeer Walter Kelly, which had defected intact from R. O. Johnson after a split between Kelly and Johnson.[20]

Clayton did better among Black voters than Roosevelt had done two years earlier, capturing about 28 percent of that vote compared to the president's 15 percent. Yet with 70 percent of their vote going to the GOP, Blacks remained in no position to secure from Mayor Clayton their goals of increased patronage and a greater share of the payoffs derived from official tolerance of vice operations in the Black districts.[21]

As the 1938 mayoral election approached, some Black leaders continued to support the GOP, others, like the editors of the *Gary American*, leaned to the party of

FDR (who had received more than 60 percent of the vote in Gary's predominantly Black precincts in 1936).[22] Republican candidate Dr. Ernst Schaible charged that Clayton had allowed corruption to run rampant. With vocal backing from the *Gary Post-Tribune*, Schaible ran on a reform platform against the gambling, vice, and corruption that earned Gary the name Sin City.[23] Schaible was elected by a narrow margin of 1,200 votes. He captured about 56 percent of the vote in predominantly Black precincts, a sizable decline from the 72 percent that had gone to the GOP four years earlier.[24] The tepid support Black voters gave to Gary's GOP could only diminish the position of Blacks in the queue for mayoral largesse. Blacks received no major political appointments; on the contrary, "Negro policemen were shifted to the dog catching detail and . . . Negro city employees were all working with picks and shovels."[25]

Schaible's victory did not represent a reassertion of Republican dominance; the Democrats won almost every other electoral contest and captured all but two seats on the city council.[26] White ethnics (Irish, Poles, Serbs, Slovaks, Hungarians, Greeks, and Italians) built a Democratic organization that thoroughly dominated the city's politics by 1940. Part of the credit for Schaible's victory rested with Democratic party factionalism; Clayton's rivals, led by Joseph E. Finerty and city clerk Tom Knotts, had depressed turnout for Clayton to prevent him from consolidating control over the party. Schaible's campaign was also a referendum against the corruption of the Clayton administration. It delivered a severe blow to Clayton's faction of the Democratic party: Schaible's antivice commitment forced underworld boss Walter Kelly out of town, never to return.[27]

The 1942 election signalled the ascendance within the Democratic party of Finerty's faction.[28] Finerty defeated Clayton, his former ally, in the 1942 Democratic primary with a coalition of southeastern European voters organized and mobilized by Fourth Ward leader George Chacharis. In the general election the Republican party's inability to compete was again evident. Finerty captured 58 percent of the vote and easily defeated the incumbent, Schaible, while Democratic victories reduced the GOP presence on the city council from two to one.[29] In the nearly all-Black Fifth Ward, Finerty won 54 percent of the vote, marking the first mayoral election in which the Democrats won the majority of Black votes. Yet Finerty's 302-vote margin in the Fifth Ward was only a fraction of the 5,277-vote margin by which he defeated Schaible. Black political leadership, still divided between the two parties, remained unable to mobilize a bloc of Black voters that was relevant to electoral outcomes. Black leaders failed in their efforts to win equal treatment in Gary and to create a nondiscriminatory environment. Seeking legal respite from police brutality, they were forced to settle for a dubious program in which the director of the Gary Urban League addressed each new cohort of police recruits (the majority of whom were White ethnics) about how to work most effectively in the Black community.[30]

School Politics

The influx of Blacks and the related exodus of White ethnics from the Central District (Ward 4) to Glen Park (Ward 6) precipitated racial tensions in the rapidly changing Fourth Ward. By 1945 Blacks constituted more than 40 percent of the ward's population, and the percentage of Black students at Froebel school had gone from about 30 to 50 percent in two years.[31] In September 1945 a few hundred White students boycotted classes at Froebel, demanding that Black students be transferred to other schools and that Principal Richard A. Nuzum be relieved of his duties. Students, later joined by parents, accused Nuzum of treating them like "guinea pigs" in "racial experiments." Since 1942 when Nuzum became principal, he had taken a number of steps to reduce the marginalization of Black students; he had founded a biracial PTA, halted the routine classification and segregation of most Black students as "incorrigibles" and brought them into academic courses, integrated the student council and the boys' swimming pool, and opened up the orchestra to Blacks.[32] Student leader and integration opponent Leonard Levenda cleverly staked out the position that all the city's other White schools, including the higher-income North Side schools, should be integrated, not just Froebel. Such a policy probably would have triggered a citywide school boycott. After two weeks of boycott at Froebel, the School Board agreed to an investigation of Nuzum's activities and temporarily relieved him of his duties. At a School Board meeting the city's most prominent Black minister, Rev. Lester Kendall (L. K.) Jackson, appealed to the audience to keep Froebel integrated. Mayor Finerty publicly supported the goals and actions of Principal Nuzum. Students returned to the classroom, but their victory was short-lived; three weeks later Nuzum was exonerated and reinstated. The boycott was resumed, but by the second week of November parents and students, worried that the high school basketball games would be canceled, called for an end to the boycott. The episode closed with a School Board resolution to end discriminatory practices in the other schools (beginning with the primary grades only) in September 1947.[33]

This ambitious-sounding plan became a major issue in the 1947 elections. Mayor Finerty withdrew from the mayoral race after segregationists began attacking him. He claimed that his decision was motivated by his desire to administer the desegregation of the schools without being constrained by reelection prospects. He may also have wanted to retire to an estate worth more than three million dollars. In the Democratic primary of May 1947, Finerty backed Eugene Swartz, former Lake County auditor, whose honest administration of that office and two-year stint as a bank vice-president had earned him the nickname Clean Gene. Swartz supported the antidiscrimination resolution; his opponent, city clerk Anthony Dobis Jr., opposed it. But the campaign had little to do with school issues and much to do with intraparty factional competition to divide the spoils generated by the alliance of rampant organized crime (gambling and prostitution) with a city administration that was accustomed to looking the other way. Dobis was the founder of the Sportsman Club, an ethnic club and drinking association for Poles and other White ethnics who lived in the Tolleston area of Gary, and he was part of the Clayton faction of the party. Faced with an intraparty choice between a candidate favoring school desegregation and another favoring the status quo, Black voters voted decisively. Swartz defeated Dobis by only 287 votes on the strength of a huge Black vote. Swartz won nearly 75 percent of the vote in the Black Fifth Ward and the predominantly Black precincts of the Fourth Ward.

When school started in September, 116 Black children enrolled in five formerly all-White schools. School boycotts were immediately initiated. But according to Lane, the integrationist forces were ready. "The CIO informed its members that union bylaws prevented them from supporting racist actions, and the Gary Bar Association threatened to censure any attorney who aided the 'mass truancy.' Msgr. John A. Sullivan called the boycott un-Christian and undemocratic."[34] This civic censure, combined with the hard line taken by the School Board, the juvenile courts, and the police, squelched the boycott and forced the students back to school.

In the November general elections, neither party gave much attention to the School Board issue. The Democrats were trying to patch up their divisions so that they did not lose control over the spoils of governance. Swartz received the endorsement of Dobis, which indicated to many that Swartz had agreed not to pursue more than token school integration. The GOP candidate, Clarence H. Smith, opposed the School Board's policy, yet the *Gary Post-Tribune*, which had strongly backed the School Board, endorsed him.[35] The explanation for this confusion is that the schools were only a minor issue in the election; corruption was what divided the two parties. Circumstantial evidence had begun to accumulate that linked Mayor Finerty to illegal gambling and vice.[36] Smith ran an anticorruption, good-government campaign against the Democratic organization and the Finerty administration.[37] The *Post-Tribune*, discounting Swartz's ability to set a course that differed from the corrupt ways of his mentor and the Democratic organization, supported Smith. Much to the chagrin of Black Republicans, the GOP showed no interest in competing for Black votes. The party's anticorruption platform clashed with the view, widely held in the Black community, that the only problem with corruption and vice was that Blacks were not getting a large enough share of the spoils. Moreover, Smith was a known enemy of the race and opposed school integration.

Rather than emphasizing their support for school desegregation, which had cost Swartz considerable support from his own partisans, the Democrats opted for the machine-politics strategy of anointing Blacks for political offices while ignoring Black policy demands. Incumbent Benjamin Wilson was reslated for the Fifth Ward seat and Terry Gray, a patronage officeholder in the school system, was slated for council-at-large. Both were elected.[38]

Swartz captured 52 percent of the vote and defeated Smith. Smith won the middle-income Irish First and Third wards, while Swartz had put together a biracial, working-class coalition. Swartz's entire margin of victory (1,629 votes) and more was provided by the predominantly White ethnic Fourth Ward (2,192 vote margin), which was skillfully organized by George Chacharis. Swartz padded his lead by capturing 56 percent of the vote in the all-Black Fifth Ward.[39]

Even though they had contributed to Swartz's victory, Black votes had helped elect a candidate who was beholden to the poorest of the White ethnics, the southeastern Europeans. These voters were in direct competition with Blacks for machine patronage, real estate and housing opportunities to alleviate overcrowding, use of public facilities like schools and beaches, and unionized jobs in the steel industry. The consolidation of power by this southeastern European community meant the continued marginalization and cooptation of Blacks. Once elected, Mayor Swartz refused to side with Black citizens in a longstanding battle with Whites over the Marquette Park beach. Police protection was denied for protest marches and a Beachhead for Democracy rally, leaving public authority in the hands of White mobs.[40]

Blacks were still expected to avoid beaches in Gary that were designated all-White. During the entire decade no change was brought about in this discriminatory arrangement. As well, the agreements to initiate school desegregation translated into little more than token integration. The two Black members of the city council repeatedly ignored the pleas of their constituents to take action on these issues.[41]

The Consolidation of Party Domination: George Chacharis and Club SAR

In 1946 the Democrats further solidified their political power by capturing the patronage-rich Calumet Township offices of trustee, assessor, and constable. The three respective winners, Peter Mandich, Steve Gersack, and Nick Schiralli, were all members of Club SAR (Social, Athletic, Recreational). This election provided the first glimpse of the important role this organization would have in the internal politics of the Democratic party for the next two decades.[42] Club SAR accomplished the major feat of uniting the formerly exclusive communal blocs of immigrants from southeastern Europe. Formed in 1932 in response to the depression, Club SAR became known for dispensing food baskets, promoting political candidates, sponsoring prizefighters, and holding fund-raising dances. Club SAR was the local face of the New Deal, and more. The organization was led by George "Chacha" Chacharis, who had come to the United States as a child from Thebes, Greece, with his parents. While rising through the ranks of the steel mills to become a chief project engineer, he became involved in politics and founded Club SAR. Chacharis's ethnic organization, which was aligned with the Finerty-Swartz faction of the party, was responsible for mobilizing the voters of the Fourth Ward, which gave the two mayors their largest margins of victory. By the 1950s, this organization was a "tightly organized political instrument" that dominated the Democratic party and Gary politics.[43]

In 1951 long-simmering party tensions within the Irish-Polish faction that had been led by Mayors Clayton, Finerty, and Swartz came to a head. Dobis ran again, but this time Verne Bauldridge received the support of former mayors Finerty and Swartz.[44] Chacharis and Club SAR took this opportunity to break with the Finerty-Swartz faction, and Peter Mandich, a Serb, entered the primary. Mandich, who as township trustee had doled out relief payments during a 1949 steel strike, was quite popular and well known. A fourth candidate, Hylda Burton, ran on an anticrime platform that grew out of the violent robbery and murder of a beloved schoolteacher, Mary Cheever.[45] Mandich won the primary with 37 percent, Dobis received 28 percent, and the other two candidates split the remainder.[46]

The general election was a replay of 1947, the two major issues being lawlessness in Gary, for which the openly partisan *Gary Post-Tribune* blamed the Democrats, and racial integration. Republicans seemed to have a good chance at recapturing the mayor's office. The Democrats' base was in the White ethnic communities, and Mandich quickly patched up his differences with Dobis and Bauldridge. They sought to expand their support among Black voters by slating a third Black candidate for the city council. The all-Black Fifth Ward was already represented by Benjamin Wilson, and Black incumbent Terry Gray held an at-large seat. The Democrats nominated political novice David Mitchell (a patronage employee of the Park

Board) to represent the racially changing Fourth Ward. The GOP did not match these efforts to win Black voters, leading a last wave of Black voters to leave the local GOP.[47] Republican candidate Clarence Smith made no credible efforts to capture the Black vote, and Black citizens finally seemed to realize the painful truth that the GOP was no longer the party of Lincoln. Longtime Republican L. K. Jackson warned that the Democrats were a party of White ethnics who would not pursue integration with any seriousness. But his efforts were undermined by candidate Smith's behavior. When Smith was asked whether he would maintain the racial exclusivity of the beach at Marquette Park, he replied, "Should a man ask me could he take a bath on Saturday night?" This answer not only avoided the question, but was taken by many Blacks to suggest that he believed they took baths only on Saturday nights.[48] When a concerned property owner telephoned Smith to press him on his answer, Smith said that Blacks would not be able to use the beach if he was elected. This "voter" turned out to be an ally of Mandich who tape-recorded the conversation and played it throughout the Black precincts.[49]

Mandich captured 52 percent of the vote and defeated Smith by 1,364 votes. Mandich lost three of the city's six wards, but his margins in the all-Black Fifth Ward, the White ethnic Sixth Ward, and the mixed Fourth Ward were large enough to deliver victory. In the predominantly Black precincts of the Fourth and Fifth Wards, Mandich received 70 percent of the vote and won with a margin of about 3,600 votes. In the predominantly White ethnic precincts of the Fifth and Sixth Wards, Mandich received about 56 percent of the vote and had a margin of about one thousand votes.[50] *Without the strong support that Peter Mandich received from Black voters, he would have lost the 1951 mayoral election.* The *Gary American* brought this fact to the attention of Mayor Mandich and other readers in two postelection editorials. One editorial stated, "We sincerely pray that the heads of the Democratic party recognize the Negro vote for its worth and do something about keeping it intact for the party. For, just as they turned on the Republican party, so can they turn on the Democratic party."[51]

But this threat of defection, which is necessary if Black leaders are to be able to gain leverage in an electorally competitive polity, was hollow. Gary's Blacks really had no place to go. The Republican party had been beaten and would not be resurrected until after 1951. The local GOP was content to live off the patronage that flowed from the governor's office and the state legislature, both of which were controlled by Republicans.[52] Moreover, the local party was still dominated by politicians like Smith who personally were unable to make a credible appeal to Black voters. Conversely, Black loyalty had been transferred almost completely at the national level to the Democratic party, so local Democrats did not have to make much of an effort for Black voters. Demands made by the editors of the *Gary American*—for "better appointments than those of alley inspectors and assistant city attorney," such as "full-fledged street commissioners, building commissioners . . . some top flight office in his cabinet, along with increasing the openings in employment," and public policy goals such as integrating the 19th Avenue fire station and desegregating public recreational facilities—went unmet.[53] By 1955 the intraparty competition among the Irish, the Poles, and the southeastern Europeans (which had led to defections to the GOP in the Irish First and Third Wards in 1947 and 1951) was settled. The party had become a big tent under the direction of Chacharis. Black voters had made their decisive break to the Democrats just as the party had forced the local GOP to cease its electoral efforts.

In the 1955 Democratic primary, incumbent mayor Peter Mandich won 67 percent of the vote and defeated Rocco Schiralli. In the 1955 general election, Mandich became the first Gary mayor to win a second consecutive term when he captured 59 percent of the vote to defeat Republican candidate Emery Badanish. The Democratic organization again captured all but one of the seats on the city council.

In 1958 Mandich resigned to run for sheriff of Lake County. Controller George Chacharis, who had emerged as the undisputed boss of the Democratic party and who was always the power behind Mandich, was next in the line of mayoral succession and became acting mayor; he would be elected outright in 1959.[54] Chacharis was a very popular figure. He had a reputation for unusual generosity, he was a highly visible community figure, and even after he became mayor he answered his own phone at home to discuss the mundane problems of citizens.[55] He also imbued his organization with a locally resonant populism that charged that U.S. Steel was paying much less in taxes than it should because of fraudulently low property assessments. Chacharis spent much of his career battling with U.S. Steel and the corporation's staunch defender—H. B. Snyder, publisher of the Gary *Post-Tribune*—over the issue of property tax assessment.[56]

Chacharis and the candidates he backed typically received heavy support from Black voters. In the 1940s Chacharis gained the admiration of many Blacks because he refused to allow his Community Chest donation to go to the local YMCA, which was all-White. The dispute remained unresolved for close to a decade, but Chacharis finally prodded the YMCA into accepting token integration.[57] Above all else, however, Chacharis captured the support of Gary's Blacks with the classic machine cooptation recipe: a heavy serving of low-level patronage and a sprinkling of visible offices dished out to loyal Blacks. Even these minor rewards might not have been possible if the prosperity of the 1950s had not benefited the Democratic organization's constituency of southern and eastern European ethnics so directly. Union wages steadily rose at the steel mills, and homeownership and a middle-class lifestyle became increasingly common for these children of immigrants.[58] As they became much less dependent on the political patronage positions at the disposal of the Democratic machine, the Chacharis organization became able to dispense more patronage to Black precinct leaders and bring Black voters more fully into the machine's electoral coalition. Chacharis had more than a thousand patronage appointments at his direct discretion through the mayor's office, as well as another two thousand jobs on the staffs of mayoral appointees (e.g., city controller, city attorney).[59] According to Peter H. Rossi and Phillips Cutright, as well as Warner Bloomberg Jr., Mayor Chacharis anointed reliable and subservient middle-class Blacks to "represent" the Black electorate, distribute patronage jobs and other benefits, and instruct Black voters on whom to vote for in elections.[60] But aside from his appointment of Harry O. Schell as city attorney (the first Black cabinet member) and his approval of the selection of David Mitchell as titular president of the city council, Blacks were in no positions of decisionmaking authority in the city.[61]

In the 1959 elections, Chacharis faced no competition in the primary. In the general election, he won 73 percent of the vote and defeated Republican Elmer K. Bailey. Democratic party strength was evident throughout the ticket. Incumbent city judge A. Martin Katz defeated his Republican opponent with 75 percent of the vote. And the lone Republican city council member was also defeated in the 1959 elections.[62]

Black Political Subordination

Black voters did receive extensive patronage during the three mayoral terms of Mandich and Chacharis.[63] But few gains were made in the struggle for political empowerment. Of the nine seats now on the city council, three were held by Blacks (two of the six district seats and one of the three at-large seats) after 1955. This 33 percent of the council membership is close to parity, the Black proportion of the city's population grew from 29 percent in 1950 to 39 percent in 1960. Observers of politics in Gary have discounted the significance of these Black city council members, arguing that "blacks refused to accept them as legitimate spokesmen for the black community" because they "were selected by the dominant party leadership based upon their ability to adhere to the subservient form of politics."[64] I will discuss the nature of the subordination of these leaders later. The argument here is that the Black political leadership did not involve itself in efforts to accomplish any aspect of the Black community's agenda, other than accruing low-level patronage positions. By 1960 Blacks held about 25 percent of the jobs in the city bureaucracy, but "the bulk of this number [were] laborers for the street department."[65] Thomas F. Thompson could cite no Blacks who held positions of any authority in the bureaucracy. Gary's Black (and White) elected officials paid no more than lip service to the demands by Blacks that economic discrimination be outlawed. Mayor Eugene Swartz and the city council created the Fair Employment Practice Commission (FEPC) in 1950. By early 1956 the one Black member of the FEPC had resigned in disgust, and a prominent pastor had led a group of Black citizens in public criticism of its failures and the token hiring of Blacks. (The goals of the FEPC were *only* equal opportunity on the basis of merit, it should be noted, not some early version of affirmative action.[66]) But the FEPC was ineffective by design; it lacked both adequate funding to provide a full-time administrator and enforcement power. Denied any real tools to force compliance (e.g., the ability to levy fines or evaluate the qualifications of applicants), the FEPC accomplished almost nothing in a decade of operation. Perhaps its greatest impact was that its resounding failure spurred Gary's Black citizenry to favor a more confrontational approach.

Mayor Mandich also rejected the entreaties of L. K. Jackson and refused to force Gary Railways, the municipal transportation franchise holder, to end discriminatory practices in the hiring of drivers.[67] The city council finally passed legislation in 1954 banning discrimination in the use of park and beach facilities, yet nothing changed. Even as late as 1961, when Blacks tried to use the beaches, mobs formed, and as police looked the other way, they beat the Black citizens so severely that they were hospitalized. Internal police investigations never found "conclusive" evidence.[68]

The limited successes of the most noteworthy Black leader of the 1940s and 1950s, L. K. Jackson, confirm the lack of political power that Blacks held in Gary. These few instances of progress in breaking down discriminatory barriers came through private negotiations with individual businesses, not through political channels or mayoral clout. Jackson dismissed the anointed clientelistic-subordinate Black leadership as "Uncle Toms and Aunt Sallys."[69] He used the same kind of economic boycott tactics to win hiring concessions from Gary businesses that later produced successes for Rev. Leon Sullivan in Philadelphia and Jesse Jackson (with Operation Breadbasket) in Chicago. Threats by Jackson and other ministers to lead a boycott of the Gary Transit Company ended the discriminatory policies of that company and produced modest hiring. A similar approach by Jackson forced the Gary National Bank to increase its loans to Black depositors seeking loans. Goldblatt's Department Store began hiring Black clerks after Jackson threatened to lead a boycott of Black shoppers during the Christmas season of 1946.[70]

The Role of Noncompetitive Elections

Thus the following paradox emerged: Even though the Black proportion of the population had grown from about 18 percent in 1930 to about 40 percent in 1960, the political status of Gary's Black population had improved only a small degree. Why were Black leaders and Black voters unable to gain real decisionmaking authority within the party or any influence over the governing coalition's agenda? Why did Black leaders continue to function as the subordinated intermediaries of a White ethnic power structure?

The explanation for this paradox rests largely on the noncompetitive nature of politics in Gary and the inability of Black leaders to organize and mobilize a unified Black bloc vote to take advantage of those instances in which highly competitive elections presented opportunities for group empowerment. Writing in 1965, Edward Banfield and James Q. Wilson noted that along with the Daley machine in Chicago, the Gary Democratic organization represented one of the few remaining examples of vibrant political machines.[71] Discussing the awesome power of Gary's Democratic party, William E. Nelson and Philip J. Meranto noted, "Republicans have generally avoided competing in local political contests. Rather than using their limited resources to drum up support for party candidates running as sacrificial lambs, Gary Republicans have appeared to prefer to concentrate their political activities on securing patronage and other benefits from key state—and national—party officials."[72] The rapid shift from Republican domination to a Democratic electoral monopoly in Gary's politics has previously been established; its causal relationship to Black political subordination has not been previously documented, however.

By 1934 Gary's Democrats had ridden Roosevelt's coattails to the mayor's office and redesigned the city council to reduce the power of the Republicans' largest non-upper-income constituency, Blacks. By 1938 the Democrats had captured seven of the nine seats on the council. After the 1942 election, the Republicans did not again win the mayor's office or capture more than one-third of the city council seats (see table 3–2). From 1940 on, the Republican organization was moribund, and Republican officeholders were an endangered species in Lake County and the city of Gary, even though the governor's office and the state legislature were dominated by the

Table 3–2 From Competition to Noncompetition: Mayoral Elections in Gary, 1929–1959

Year	Winner	Political party	Percentage of vote
1929	R. O. Johnson	Republican	56
1934	Barney Clayton	Democrat	51
1938	Ernst Schaible	Republican	54
1942	Joseph Finerty	Democrat	58
1947	Eugene Swartz	Democrat	52
1951	Peter Mandich	Democrat	52
1955	Peter Mandich	Democrat	59
1959	George Chacharis	Democrat	73

Source: "Complete Report of Election Returns," *Gary Post-Tribune.*

Republican party.[73] Although particular mayoral elections were competitive, these did not represent opportunities from which Gary's Black citizenry were likely to gain. Gary's Blacks did not give more than 50 percent of their votes in local elections to the Democrats until 1942; this figure did not reach 70 percent until 1951. The divided loyalty of Black voters was a recipe for neither party to consider them an important part of its electoral coalition. In the mayoral elections of 1947 and 1951, two in which a Black bloc vote could have altered the outcome in favor of the Republicans, the GOP candidate was an open advocate of Jim Crow segregation. Moreover, in both elections it was the southeastern European faction, not Blacks, that was able to unify and take advantage of intraparty splits between the Irish and the Poles. The local Republican party had largely ceased to be a serious competitor except at the mayoral level, where the unremitting charges of corruption against Democratic candidates by the highly partisan *Gary Post-Tribune* occasionally reduced the Democratic margins of victory. Republicans in Gary functioned to deliver votes for statewide races like the governor's office, which the GOP dominated. They were not about to join with Blacks in advocating open occupancy housing laws and the desegregation of schools. Conversely, Blacks heard little of interest in the GOP's harangues against Democratic corruption and the machine spoils system. What many Blacks wanted was a greater share of these spoils, not an end to the system, which had enriched White ethnics. (Richard Hatcher's classic reform opposition to spoils politics would run smack into this sentiment.)

By the time Blacks were more than 30 percent of the city's population and were voting as a bloc for the Democrats (about 1955), the local electoral system was noncompetitive. Republicans had stopped seeking to expand their local electoral coalition, and the Democrats were winning with such large majorities that the Black vote became inconsequential. The mayoral elections of 1955 and 1959 were won by Democrats who captured 59 and 73 percent of the vote, respectively. Moreover, the Democratic organization's monopolization of politics was so thorough and machinelike that very few other groups showed any interest in urban problems and public affairs in Gary.[74] Given these conditions, Black leaders were in no position to make demands for a greater share of political power, nor did they have any leverage with which to negotiate for their public policy goals.

The Breakdown of the Democratic Organization's Monopoly

In 1962 the Gary Democratic organization was crippled by scandal. After an investigation that implicated a number of other city officials, Mayor Chacharis was indicted and convicted of tax fraud (failing to pay taxes on hundreds of thousands of dollars of corrupt kickbacks and payoffs that he had received).[75] Many of the city's White voters withdrew their support from the Democratic organization While some sought to coalesce into a genuine reform movement, others simply wanted a change. Whatever their motivation, more than two-thirds of them defected from the machine's previously popular mayoral candidate, A. Martin Katz, in the 1963 Democratic primary.[76] The machine leadership responded by focusing their efforts on increasing mobilization in the Black community.[77]

To solidify its support in the Black community, the organization slated machine critic Richard Hatcher for the office of councilman-at-large. Traditionally, Blacks held one of the three at-large seats on the city council. Because the Black incumbent was implicated in the Chacharis scandals, he had to be replaced, and Hatcher was selected. This choice of Hatcher for the at-large council seat was, to an important extent, an effort by the Democratic organization to defeat another at-large candidate, Hilbert Bradley, who was perceived to be a militant Black power advocate.[78] The organization viewed its support of Hatcher "as just another token concession that the machine had to give to the black community to keep blacks voting strongly in support of regular organization slates."[79] Both William E. Nelson Jr. and Charles H. Levine said that the leadership of the Democratic organization expected that once Hatcher was elected he would cease his reform activity (discussed later) and toe the machine's line just as his Black predecessors had done.[80]

Shortly after settling in Gary in 1959, Hatcher had became involved with the Lake County Democratic organization (as a deputy prosecutor) and joined the NAACP. He served as one of the NAACP attorneys in a federal lawsuit to halt de facto school segregation in Gary. Together with a handful of other middle-class Blacks disgusted by the prevalence of vice and graft in the city, he founded a reform-oriented political organization called Muigwithania, meaning "we are together" (in Kikuyu, a language spoken in Kenya) in a determination to reform Gary.[81] This small organization served as the cornerstone for his future political career.

A field of five candidates entered the 1963 Democratic primary. The regular organization's candidate, Martin Katz, won the election with 38 percent of the vote. With Hatcher on the ticket, and most of the subordinate Black leadership untarnished by the scandals, the regular Black precinct organization was able to maintain its grip on the votes of Blacks. Katz received 51 percent of the Black vote and 22 percent of the White vote. Of the total votes he received, 67 percent were cast by Blacks.[82] The strong showing of Emery Konrady (32 percent of the vote), who ran on the issue of reforming the corrupt city administration, led him to enter the general election as an independent against Katz and Republican candidate Ted Nering Jr. Katz easily won the general election with 53 percent of the vote, while Konrady received 26 percent and Nering 20 percent. Again, Katz's victory was a result of the support he received from about 80 percent of the voters in predominantly Black precincts. As was the case in the primary, Katz lost in the city's White wards.[83]

Mayor Martin Katz recognized the heightened electoral power that Blacks had as a consequence of the division of the White electorate between the Konrady-led reform faction and the Democratic machine faction. Katz could not help but realize that if he was to be able to govern Gary he would need the support of the Black city council members and the mobilized segments of the Black community. Moreover, if he was contemplating running for a second mayoral term in 1967, building a base within the Black community would be essential.

Indeed, Katz did initiate an unprecedented effort to reward Blacks politically. However, these efforts generally were perceived by Blacks to be too little, too late. With Katz's support, a Black was elected coroner. Along with the city attorney, a Black who had been appointed in 1959 by Mayor Chacharis, this meant that Blacks headed 2 of the 26 departments in the city's bureaucracy as late as 1967. Although much of the White community was disillusioned with Mayor Katz because of his efforts to woo Blacks,[84] among Blacks (excepting subordinate leaders) these efforts were evaluated as falling far short of what was deserved for having delivered victory to him. The numbers of Blacks holding city jobs of all types increased under Katz, yet in 1965 Blacks still held only 28 percent of the city's jobs at a time when they formed more than 50 percent of the city's population. Blacks held only 3 percent of the positions of decisionmaking authority in the bureaucracy. Only 12 percent of the police force was Black, and no Black held the rank of captain.[85] Blacks were still excluded from decisionmaking positions in the city government and slatemaking positions in the city and county Democratic organizations.[86]

Yet Mayor Katz's efforts represented larger concessions than many others within the Democratic organization were willing to make. On two major issues—the racial integration of schools and open occupancy housing—the efforts of Blacks, led by councilman Hatcher and vociferously aided by Mayor Katz, were blocked by a school board and city council dominated by officeholders beholden to the machine (including Black subordinates).[87] The ambiguity of Katz's position vis-à-vis Black political power became moot; the White leadership of the Democratic organization was unwilling to relinquish its domination of the political system and allow Blacks to move beyond token roles to policymaking. If the Black community was to achieve a significant degree of political empowerment, a united Black community would have to break with Mayor Katz and the Democratic organization. The subordinate Black leadership, including the Black precinct organization that had historically delivered the Black vote, assured Mayor Katz and the White leadership of the Democratic organization that a sizable Black defection was unlikely.[88]

The Election of Mayor Richard Hatcher

The candidates in the 1967 Democratic mayoral primary were incumbent Martin Katz, councilman Richard Hatcher, and Bernard Konrady, brother of the deceased reform candidate Emery Konrady. Katz, following a strategy mapped out by George Chacharis, sought to put together a coalition of White and Black Democratic party organization loyalists, as well as Blacks who believed Katz had done a commendable job of increasing Black political power in his first term.[89] Katz had the support of most of the established Black leadership, including coroner Alexander Williams. Hatcher expected to mobilize an unprecedented Black bloc vote (about 50 percent of the registered Democrats were Black) and a small number of liberal Whites.[90] Konrady expected Hatcher and Katz to split the Black vote while he would win most of the White votes, combining Whites seeking governmental reform (which the Katz administration had not advanced) with segregationists who felt that Katz had been far too liberal in his appeasement of Blacks.[91] Konrady's chances looked good in light of the results of the 1964 Democratic presidential primary race, in which segregationist George Wallace had overwhelmingly won the White vote in Gary. To help him mobilize a Black electorate that was cynical and alienated from politics, Hatcher built an organization of two thousand volunteers. According to Lane, "Hatcher defined the issue in *messianic* terms as a battle between good and evil. 'Each and every one of us will sing in unison in one huge chorus in one polling booth after another,' he told blacks. 'No longer will we be stampeded to the polls like a bunch of cattle by a cynical, corrupt political machine. Plantation politics is dead.'"[92]

The Democratic primary election results gave Hatcher a narrow victory with 38 percent of the vote. Katz won 34 percent, and Konrady received about 25 percent. Hatcher received 69 percent of the vote in predominantly Black districts, with Katz getting most of the rest. Katz and Konrady split the White vote, with each getting about 47 percent and Hatcher receiving about 5 percent.

In the general election Hatcher faced Republican candidate Joseph Radigan, who had never run for political office. He was selected by the GOP leadership because he was an honest merchant whose family was well known in the city. The scene was set for an easy victory based on Hatcher's vote-getting ability in the Black community (48 percent of the electorate and 55 percent of the city's population was Black), the strength of the Democratic organization, and the longstanding weakness of the Republican organization. But the leadership of the Democratic organization turned against Hatcher and used all of its resources—legal and illegal—to try to defeat him.[93]

Lake County Democratic organization chairman John Krupa had indicated, after the primary defeat of its candidate, Martin Katz, that Hatcher would receive the regular organization's support in the general election.

> When Hatcher first won the primary, party leaders gave strong indications they intended to support Hatcher in the same way they had mayoral nominees in the past. For example, on 4 May County Chairman John Krupa scotched rumors that the regular organization would field an independent ticket in the fall election. Rather he said that he intended to get together with Hatcher to work out arrangements for the support and assistance of the party central committee in his fall campaign. The political picture did not begin to change until several months later.[94]

What caused Krupa to change his mind and withdraw his support of Hatcher? Why did Krupa explain this action by saying that his job as county chairman was "to elect 'red-white-and-blue Democrats' not men who would 'risk our way of life for some other ism' and who thought that being an American was 'nasty, old fashioned, and corny?'"[95]

Krupa had approached Hatcher after his surprising victory in the Democratic primary with what Krupa must have considered a fair-minded request; he wanted Hatcher to grant him control over the selection of a range of major cabinet appointees (i.e., the heads of bureaucratic departments that had large numbers of patronage positions). Hatcher refused, remaining committed to make reforms in city government that would prevent the corrupt distribution of patronage and payoffs to any party.[96] Because Hatcher was unwilling to allow the Democratic organization to maintain control of the distribution of city patronage, Krupa turned the party's support away from Hatcher. To Krupa and the Democratic organization it was most important that control of the patronage-rich mayor's office remain in the hands of a machine loyalist.[97]

Their strategy for defeating Hatcher was to portray him as a militant advocate of Black power who was under the influence of left-wing extremists, and to incite a stampede of White voters to his opponent. Krupa publicly demanded that Hatcher denounce Stokely Carmichael, H. Rap Brown, and the antiwar position of Martin Luther King Jr. Although about 55 percent of the population was Black, Whites held a two-thousand-vote edge in registration. Hatcher won the mayoral election by less than two thousand votes (out of a total of almost 78,000). He captured about 96 percent of the Black vote and 12 percent of the White vote, largely from liberal Jewish enclaves of the city. A biracial coalition of Blacks and White liberals came together to elect Richard Hatcher. But this coalition had not materialized previously in any elections, nor had White liberals played a major role in organizations like the Fair Share Organization (FSO) that spearheaded the civil rights activism in Gary.

Hatcher's election, like the election of Harold Washington in Chicago, was not the product of an incremental process of Black empowerment. The political subordination of Blacks had been maintained by the strong Democratic party organization from the 1930s to 1967, when Hatcher was elected. Blacks dramatically displaced an entrenched conservative (with respect to empowerment of the powerless) regime; there was no gradual transition from Black subordination to Black empowerment, nor was there any biracial power-sharing in Gary after 1967. This dramatic regime change was the result of a two-step process. First, the Chacharis corruption scandal destabilized the electoral coalition that had guaranteed electoral victories to the monopolistic Democratic machine regime. White voters turned away from the machine's candidate, Martin Katz, and defected to the Konrady brothers in the 1963 and 1967 elections. The *Gary Post-Tribune* and other interests seeking municipal reform had not found such a receptive audience since 1938, when Ernst Schaible won election on a reform platform. The corruption scandals created a political opportunity for Blacks in Gary by dividing the White vote and destroying the image of electoral invincibility that the Democratic machine had cultivated. Second, Black organizations and Black voters severed their ties to the machine or roused themselves from nonvoting, united around the candidacy of Richard Hatcher, and turned out to vote in large enough numbers to elect him as mayor. This second step was not predetermined or the inevitable product of the corruption scandals; Blacks could have remained divided. But this second step of Black unity would not have occured at this time (even with the contemporaneous expansion of the civil rights movement) were it not for the corruption scandals that divided the White vote.

Overview of the Hatcher Administrations

Hatcher won the mayoral election, but he came to power lacking many of the resources necessary to govern. He did not put together a slate of candidates to run with him for city council, and once he was elected he had great difficulty pursuing his agenda because of the composition of the council. Four of the nine city council members were Black, but two were holdovers from the Chacharis-Katz organization and were sympathetic to Lake County Democratic party chairman John Krupa. A third Black city council member, Dozier Allen, was a Muigwithania member, but his own mayoral ambitions put him at odds with Hatcher on many issues. Of the five White city council members, three consistently opposed the initiatives of the Hatcher administration. Charles H. Levine blamed Hatcher's poor relationship with the city council (which had functioned as a rubber stamp during the Mandich-Chacharis era) on the clash between the mayor's dedication to good-government reform principles and the desire of city council members to partake in traditional patronage perquisites. Some city council members, both Black and White, sought control over contracts and patronage jobs as well as a revival of the lucrative illegal businesses of prostitution and gambling.[98] Mayor Hatcher was successful in eliminating the infamous Adams Street red-light district, and he reduced gambling almost to nothing in the city. In sharp contrast to his predecessors, his administrations were scandal-free. But these accomplishments cost him support from the city council and from a police department whose senior ranks had been infiltrated by organized crime. Moreover, Gary's rapidly rising crime rate drew more attention than any of his administration's accomplishments.

Hatcher was able to gain control of the city Democratic organization (although Krupa maintained control of the county organization). Minority employment in decisionmaking posts of the city bureaucracy and appointments of minorities (Blacks and Latinos) to city boards and commissions rose dramatically. Levine reported:

> By 1969, blacks or Latin-Americans headed fourteen of Gary's twenty-seven departments including the police, fire, general service, and planning departments, as well as manning the offices of the city controller, city attorney, and corporation council. Many of the operating units of the city government became almost all black or Latin-American, and their number and influence increased in the police and fire departments. The control of sensitive boards and commissions like the school board also changed from white to black.[99]

Black businesses and construction firms also received a much greater share of city contracts than they had previously (only anecdotal data is available to document this).[100]

In 1971 an attempt by the remnants of the White Democratic organization and the city's business leadership to sponsor a Black mayoral candidate against Hatcher failed.[101] Hatcher was able to elect a city council dominated by his supporters; subsequently, all levels of the city's bureaucracy, from housing to the police force, were dominated by Blacks (although White machine loyalists protected by civil service continued to disrupt the implementation of Hatcher administration initiatives).[102] Unusually generous funding from the federal government (e.g. Model Cities, Office of Economic Opportunity, and the Law Enforcement Assistance Agency) subsidized promising change in Gary. But this ran out in the mid-1970s and revealed a city in dire economic straits because of a mass desertion by businesses and banks to a first-ring suburb. Symbolic of this desertion of Gary by many of the city's growth elites (except U.S. Steel) was the Gary National Bank's name change to Gainer Bank and the construction of a new main branch in suburban Merrillville. Similarly, the *Gary Post-Tribune* dropped the city from its name.[103] Nearly all White (except for a growing contingent of middle-class Blacks seeking safety and amenities), the suburb of Merrillville quickly became the economic center of the area and drained away the commercial lifeblood of Gary.[104]

The Structure of Black Political Leadership

Because of Gary's noncompetitive political environment, in which the Chacharis Democratic organization seemed invincible until it was crippled by scandal, Black votes were not crucial for victory. Black leaders had no leverage with which to bargain for political empowerment. Realizing this, many Black politicians accepted anointed positions of clientelistic-subordinate leadership and, offering low-level patronage jobs and personal favors, they organized Black voters to jump on the Democratic bandwagon. The weak Republican party made little effort to contest elections or seek Black votes. This meant that a cadre of coalitional-incrementalist leaders did not emerge in Gary because they were unable to find partners with whom they could form biracial reform coalitions capable of winning elections. Only two types of Black political leaders existed in Gary: clientelistic-subordinates and separatist-messianics.

The Clientelistic-Subordinate Leadership

During the 1940s there were two Black city council members in Gary, and in the 1950s Black representation increased to three of the nine members. The entire precinct organization structure in the Black wards of what was known as the Central District (a local synonym for the Black Belt) was staffed by Black party loyalists. These individuals participated in a clientelistic relationship in which they received patronage jobs in some part of the public bureaucracy in exchange for their political work to organize and mobilize Black voters on behalf of Democratic party candidates. These Black party functionaries, from the council members to the precinct organizers, consistently placed their own self-interest and the interests of the party ahead of their constituents, and by so doing they contributed to the maintenance of the political subordination of Blacks in Gary. Nelson has written:

> [B]ecause of their ties with the downtown organization, black councilmen have been unable or unwilling to forcefully articulate the desires of their constituents for thorough going reforms of the social and economic life of the city. Rather, as ambassadors from the machine, they have assumed the role of "responsible Negro leaders" counseling patience, respect for authority and acceptance of the status quo to the black masses.[105]

Gary's Black clientelistic-subordinates were selected and anointed by the White party leadership, and they owed their allegiance to it, not to the voters who actually elected them. The anointees were typically men of no independent means, and the political reward of a decent job that they gained for their service insured a significant degree of loyalty. Millender observed, "The so-called Negro leader was so close to his own days of poverty, that he thought only of himself and his prosperity and would sell his people to any white politician who offered him something."[106] Nelson reports that his interviewees "[t]ime and again . . . referred to them as 'Uncle Toms' and political 'prostitutes', and accused them of selling their people down the river in return for token rewards from the dominant white political machine."[107] Because these so-called Black leaders could be replaced at will by the party leadership, they assiduously followed the agenda set by the party. Since they were not replaced by Black voters they gave little heed to Black voters' agendas. According to Nelson,

> It is clear that this role of black councilmen has sprung fundamentally from the fact that while they have been elected by the black masses, they have not been selected by them. Because black people have not selected them they have not had the ability to control their behavior once they assumed their councilmanic positions. For the most part, black councilmen in Gary have owed their allegiance not to the black community but to the leaders of the white machine who are their real masters. As a result, they have played the role of keeping the black community firmly within the clutches of the machine rather than working to promote independent black political power.[108]

Until Richard Hatcher's election to the council in 1963, Black council members always voted in accordance with the Democratic organization's dictates. Levine noted that prior to Hatcher, "every other black politician who had ever been elected to the city council had been cooperative."[109] Aside from making no waves, these Black anointees were charged with the duty of criticizing those—Black or White—who sought to raise issues of racial inequity that might embarrass the Chacharis machine. Finally, the Black politicians delivered the Black vote to machine candidates. Even when Hatcher ran for mayor, Black subordinates worked to defeat him. According to Oden, Black precinct workers "intimidated welfare mothers with threats of having child support payments cut off if they registered to vote for Hatcher."[110] In exchange, these anointed leaders received such rewards as liquor licenses for taverns, low property assessments, or immunity from raids by the city vice squad on their gambling and prostitution operations. But the most sought-after rewards were city (and to a lesser extent county) patronage jobs and plentiful pocket money during election times. Thompson wrote:

> Negroes have learned, or have been educated, to depend on these party officials [precinct leaders, ward committeemen] for intercession with governmental functionaries in many activities impinging on the daily life of members of the group. Seasonal jobs with the city, food orders from the Township Trustee's relief funds, help in interpreting and sometimes a softening of the impact of court rulings, and unadorned handouts of money are all dispensed through the precinct committeemen.
>
> In return . . . [the party organization] expects and gets . . . dutiful behavior at the polls.[111]

As in Chicago, Black politicians were not the only leaders whose acquiescence to and cooptation by the machine contributed to the subordination of Blacks in Gary. The Democratic machine was equally successful in coopting many of the most prominent Black ministers, often through large financial contributions to their church building programs. In exchange the ministers opened their pulpits for Sunday morning speeches from machine politicians and instructed their membership to "go out and take care of this man because he is taking care of us."[112] According to one observer, from the 1920s through the 1960s Black preachers received cash "donations" from White politicians. In exchange the preacher "was expected to sway his followers in the direction of the thinking of that donor."[113] Officials from the NAACP and the Urban League also were coopted and seemed to have no political legitimacy or leadership status among Blacks.[114] Black politicians and Black ministers were unreceptive when Hatcher approached them about supporting his mayoral bid, and they even organized a committee to undermine his efforts among Blacks.[115]

Also as in Chicago, Gary's political system provided no real alternative to the Democrats. The Republicans had largely withdrawn in defeat from the politics of Gary and surrounding Lake County. Nelson wrote:

> [M]any black voters continued to vote for machine candidates without very much conviction or sense of purpose. . . . Many blacks expressed disgust from time to time with the monopolistic control of the Democrats over the black vote. . . . It was a product too of the fact that blacks had no choice in elections except a choice among two or three equally unacceptable candidates. The machine stubbornly refused to sponsor black candidates for major elective office other than the one at-large seat reserved for a black on the city council, and one county position, the coroner's office. White candidates sponsored by the machine never addressed themselves to black problems in Gary in any meaningful way in their political campaigns.
>
> Having no alternative in elections, those blacks who voted accepted the recommendation of their precinct captains or ministers and voted without much enthusiasm or sense of mission the slate put forth by the machine.[116]

Because the candidates slated by the Democratic machine were going to win regardless of the Black vote, if a Black citizen was going to vote, it made some sense to jump on the Democratic bandwagon, especially if the five- or ten-dollar bill that many voters got from precinct captains on election day was much of an incentive.[117] This was never more true than in the period of the most dynamic growth of the Black population, between 1950 and 1960, when the proportion of Blacks grew beyond 40 percent of the city's total and the Chacharis organization was winning elections with 70 percent or more of the vote.

The Separatist-Messianic Leadership

Not all Blacks were stymied by the absence of articulated alternatives to the Chacharis organization. Middle-class Blacks, for whom the patronage and favors of the Democratic organization meant less, attempted to organize politically outside the party. They sponsored a series of protest marches and political demonstrations to voice more forcefully the discontent and political demands of the Black community.[118] Their direct action efforts were at best only modestly successful in producing positive changes in either the quality of life of Blacks or the relationship between Blacks and Whites in Gary.[119] L. K. Jackson continued his struggle through the 1960s, when his efforts were supplemented by the Gary Fair Share Organization (FSO). The FSO, established in 1958 by militant activist Hilbert Bradley as a response to the antiactivist philosophy of the NAACP, forced a number of local merchants to increase their hiring of Blacks by organizing picketing and boycotts.[120] The FSO relied more on mobilizing large numbers of Black demonstrators than on the personal bargaining and negotiation of a single leader like L. K. Jackson. But the FSO was crippled when it lost a legal battle (that went from the local courts to the U.S. Supreme Court) that resulted in a damage claim award of $15,000 to two local businesses.[121]

Another group that challenged the Democratic organization's control of the political agenda was the Combined Citizens Committee On Open Occupancy (CCCOOO). In 1962–63, CCCOOO brought together Blacks from the FSO and liberal Whites. The focus of these new efforts became segregated housing and the fight for open occupancy laws. Again Gary's elected officials steadfastly opposed integration; the city council (by a six-to-three vote) rejected a CCCOOO-sponsored open-housing ordinance.[122] But after the Chacharis scandals and the election of Mayor Katz, the new mayor recognized his debt to the Black electorate by creating a powerful Human Relations Commission (to supersede the FEPC) that could enforce antidiscrimination laws in housing.

Extraelectoral activities (protest, boycott) were not enough (to paraphrase Browning, Marshall, and Tabb), but such activities yielded gains that were unattainable through negotiation with public officials. Although the various protest actions played an important role in awakening a quiescent population, the Democrats faced no threat from Black defection to the GOP. Party insiders recognized that there was much greater danger in appearing to be too accommodationist with Gary's Black population. Gary's White voters demonstrated through their overwhelming support for George Wallace in the 1964 Democratic presidential primary that they were willing to bolt from mainstream Democrats who were liberal on civil rights.

Much as in Chicago, the separatist, Black-power tendencies of a significant segment of the Black leadership became more discernable after the election of Richard Hatcher. They had united with Hatcher in the goal of electing him as mayor, but once this was accomplished, the divergence between his biracial reform goals and the separatist-messianic goals of those around him became increasingly evident. Hatcher had sought to win a proportionate share of political power for Blacks, without excluding Whites or Gary's growing Hispanic population; others, however, sought to monopolize political power among Blacks. Hatcher had sought to reform an unfair political system; in contrast, separatists were more interested in turning the tables and becoming the beneficiaries of a style of monopolist spoils politics that had long exploited them. Nelson wrote:

> The number one source of discontent among Hatcher supporters . . . has been his failure to use his office to build a base of power in the Black community. Many Hatcher volunteers viewed his election as the opening wedge in a larger movement culminating in a Black takeover of every facet of city and county government. . . .

Many were unhappy because Hatcher's cabinet was, from their point of view, "too white." Some of them had advised Hatcher to make his cabinet mostly Black, but he refused, feeling he had to live up to his promise to bring to the city a truly multi-racial administration. Many were more than mildly piqued, too, by the character of Hatcher's Black appointees. They complained that Hatcher tapped for major positions black men who were mainly moderate in their political attitudes. . . . Such appointments, they argued, effectively muted the influence of militant Black elements on the administration's policies.[123]

Levine agreed that Hatcher lost the support of those who "believed that once Hatcher was elected mayor, graft, patronage, and power would be funnelled exclusively into the black community."[124]

The Absence of Coalitional-Incrementalists

The political monopoly of the Gary Democratic organization influenced the political paths chosen by potential Black leaders. Their choice was either to join with the Democratic organization and abet Black subordination or to use extrainstitutional tactics such as protest to seek thoroughgoing changes of the political system. Prior to Hatcher's success, those few insurgent, nonmachine Black leaders who had sought to mobilize their political followings in ways other than protest marches were largely unable to resist cooptation.

Co-optation of the black precinct organization by the leaders of the white machine has provided them with the leverage they needed to force other black politicians into active membership in the black machine. *Independent black politicians willing to fight with diligence and integrity in behalf of race goals, have from time to time emerged but their careers as leaders in the black community have been almost universally short-lived.* In many instances they have just plain and simply been bought off. That is, they have been given by the white machine large sums of money or lucrative jobs in city government in return for their cooperation. Others have been destroyed by massive machine opposition. Possessing a paucity of resources for wooing the black vote away from the machine, they have had either to become a part of the machine's structure in the black community or accept the inevitability of defeat.[125]

In a pattern very similar to that observed in Chicago, an independent group of Black leaders, seeking genuine reforms and building biracial alliances to win political empowerment—the kind of leadership that I have labeled as coalitional-incrementalist—failed to emerge in Gary.

Conclusion

In the midst of a rapidly decaying local economy, Blacks were achieving gains in Gary.[126] With the help of huge infusions of federal dollars, Hatcher was able to point to 4,500 new public housing units in the city by 1976.[127] The political empowerment of Blacks proceeded rapidly after his election. When Mayor Katz left office in 1967, Blacks were only 3 percent of the city's workforce. Of the city's 26 department heads, only two (8 percent) were Black. At the time, Blacks were about 50 percent of the population of Gary. By the close of Mayor Hatcher's second term, the Black proportion of Gary's population had grown to about 70 percent. At the same time, the proportion of Blacks in the city's workforce grew to about 62 percent. Of the city's 40 departments, 22 (55 percent) were headed by Blacks.[128] Richard Hatcher's ascension as mayor and the emigration of Whites from the city largely explain these dramatic examples of Black political empowerment in Gary.

What required explanation, however, was the absence of Black empowerment from the 1940s to 1967. Why were Blacks unable to gain political power and influence while the proportion of the Black population was rising? In the discussion of the causes of political empowerment in chapter 1, I hypothesized that political competitiveness among power-holding groups creates the conditions in which subordinated Blacks can win political empowerment, if leaders can mobilize a unified Black vote to play a decisive role in elections. Conversely, in the absence of political competitiveness, empowerment of Blacks is not likely to proceed. The analysis of Gary has shown that Black empowerment was stalled until the election of Hatcher in 1967. Electoral politics in Gary from the 1940s to the mid-1950s was competitive, but the Black vote was divided between two parties. By the time the Black vote was unified, in the mid-1950s, the Democratic party organization monopolized politics, and Black voters were superfluous members of the Democratic coalition of unionized White ethnics. Moreover, Black leaders could not credibly threaten defection to a Jim Crow Republican party. Black political and ministerial leaders were coopted with the inducements of patronage jobs, and their Black constituencies remained subordinated. Given the political conditions of noncompetitiveness, better opportunities for trading votes for political power were not likely to emerge. Some Black leaders like Hilbert Bradley tried to achieve their political goals through the tactics of protest and demonstration. But Gary's elected officials were not electorally accountable to Black demands. Only because of political scandals did a sizable reform faction emerge among Whites to challenge the political monopoly of the Chacharis machine. And Richard Hatcher was able to mobilize the Black community, which for the most part had been resigned to subordination, primarily because of the divided, hence vulnerable, condition of the White community.

The analysis in this chapter provides further evidence that contradicts the conventional explanation of the empowerment of formerly subordinated groups promulgated by James Q. Wilson and others. Wilson argued that Black opportunities for political empowerment were greatest in cities with strong political party machines. Yet this case study has shown that in Gary, a city dominated by one of the most powerful political machines of the postdepression era, Blacks were unable to achieve political empowerment. In contrast to the arguments of Wilson, the Lake County Democratic machine succeeded in coopting individual Black leaders and maintaining the subordination of the growing Black population. The empowerment of Blacks in Gary began only after scandals severely weakened the party organization. Blacks made significant progress in reallocating the lopsided distribution of political power only after Richard Hatcher was elected and began to dismantle the Democratic machine.

Immediately after his election, Hatcher confronted problems that were a product of the bifurcated Black structure of political leadership. He clearly was not a subordinate; his refusal to let Krupa control the naming of administrators to head the city departments that were rich in patronage demonstrated that he would not be a Black puppet of the Democratic organization. But he was unwilling to commence the whole-sale takeover of the city's departments that his separatist-messianic supporters demanded. It took him almost two terms to carve out the political space for a third segment within the Black leadership structure dedicated to reforming an unfair political system; by that time most of the Whites who could afford to leave Gary for the suburbs had done so.

Four

Not Quite Brotherly Love

Electoral Competition and the Institutionalization of Biracial Political Cooperation in Philadelphia

In 1983 Wilson Goode was elected as the first Black mayor of Philadelphia. He was one among a cadre of prominent Black politicians in Philadelphia who had gained legitimacy and could garner votes in both the Black and White communities. Unlike the situation in Chicago, or other cities in which Blacks enjoyed a sudden and unexpected breakthrough to political power after a long period of political subordination that left the Black community with few leaders capable of commanding diffuse support, in Philadelphia Black leaders had been participating in biracial coalitions that had been delivering incremental political empowerment for quite some time and that continue to do so in the post-Goode era. This chapter presents a history and analysis of the formation of the biracial, reform-oriented alliance in Philadelphia that was the forerunner of the coalition that elected Wilson Goode as mayor in 1983. I explain how and why biracial coalitions emerged from the conditions created by competitive electoral politics in the "City of Brotherly Love." The chapter also documents the intermittent success of the biracial reform coalition in gaining the political empowerment of Blacks, and the strategies that the coalition members used to maintain their trust during periods when they lost elections and were excluded from the dominant coalition. I also examine the opposition a biracial coalition dedicated to an incrementalist strategy faces from within the Black community and from Whites. Concluding with a discussion of the current biracial coalition, which is headed by a White Democrat with liberal credentials, this chapter suggests that such alliances are no longer limited to the reform variety.

The End of Republican Machine Domination

Charges of corruption, denials, evidence of malfeasance, additional charges, a widening web of corruption, suicides of public officials implicated in the scandal, and suicide notes further implicating other city officials—they all added up to a serious scandal and the disintegration of the Republican machine in Philadelphia between 1947 and 1951.[1] That Republican machine had survived the depression, FDR, and the New Deal. In the four elections prior to Roosevelt's presidential election (1919, 1923, 1927, 1931), GOP mayoral candidates stomped their Democratic opponents with an average of 82 percent of the vote. In all four subsequent elections, the Republican mayoral candidates still triumphed (1935, 1939, 1943, 1947), although their share of the vote averaged a competitive 55 percent. Yet the Republicans also captured at least 20 of the 22 seats on the city council in these four elections, suggesting that the mayoral data may understate GOP domination.[2] While Roosevelt's coattails were dragging big-city Democrats into office around the country, Philadelphia's Democratic organization remained a minor force that "acted in effect like a group 'kept' by the dominant Republican party, receiving the crumbs that the Republicans threw from their heavily laden patronage table."[3] But the GOP machine regime was felled by scandals, and by the end of the 1950s Philadelphia was the scene of intense partisan competition.

Joseph Clark, a reformer who promised "good government" in the wake of this corruption, led a coalition that ushered in a period of Democratic party domination of the city's politics when he was elected mayor in 1951. Since then, politics in Philadelphia has been characterized by competition between (a) an amalgam of White liberal activists and good-government reformers, including many of the city's business leaders, and (b) the regular organization ethnic politicians of the Democratic party (sometimes very loosely labeled a "machine"), many of whom defected with their neighborhood ties intact from the discredited Republican organization. The reformers and the organization politicians have battled largely within the confines of the Democratic party (e.g., in primary elections); however, when either the reformers or the ethnic pols have been defeated in such battles, they have not hesitated to shift their support to Republicans and use this otherwise moribund party as an alternative front for the ongoing battle. One of the major battle lines in this competition has been for the votes of the expanding Black electorate. These conditions of electoral competitiveness have made Black voters a potentially decisive force in electoral outcomes and given Black political leaders bargaining leverage. Although the Democratic organization preferred to dispense personal, cooptative rewards to Black leaders, both the reformers and regulars have been obliged to yield to Black leaders' influence over public policy and to accept their appointments to major citywide political posts that have represented milestones in Blacks' political empowerment. As a result of this iterative process, the election of Blacks to powerful offices and the satisfaction of Black public policy demands has become typical and accepted as legitimate. White fears of a Black takeover of political power have been reduced by the gradual (hence less threatening) capture of political power by Blacks.

The Origins of Philadelphia's Biracial Alliance

The earliest charges of corruption would not have received the newspaper coverage and exposure that led them to snowball into a massive scandal were it not for the efforts of two young idealists, Joseph Clark and Richardson Dilworth. Both scions of blue-blooded families and Republicans by birthright, Clark and Dilworth imposed themselves on the decrepit Democratic organization and used it as a vehicle to defeat the disgraced Republicans. James Finnegan, chairman of the Democratic organization, recognized that having blue-ribbon amateurs at the head of the ticket would sharpen the contrast with the corrupt GOP. Sharing with Finnegan the task of rebuilding the Democratic party—largely with remnants of the Republican machine—was Congressman William J. Green.[4] Green was highly skilled in ward-level organization and mobilization and had no sympathy for the antipatronage reformers. But the success of Clark and Dilworth in arousing anti-GOP fervor led Green to reluctantly support them. Dilworth lost in a mayoral bid in 1947 (receiving 44 percent of the vote), but two years later Clark won the strategic office of controller, enabling him to document the corrupt financial practices of the Republicans. In 1951 Clark received 58 percent of the vote and was elected mayor, ending 68 years of Republican control of city hall.

The reform coalition comprised big business and disaffected gentry (both were in the Republican camp before the scandals) who felt that the city's reputation had been stained by Republican corruption; the city's vibrant Americans for Democratic Action (ADA) chapter; and a cohort of postwar reformers from local universities and numerous civic and business organizations. The common thread that bound this coalition was anticorruption zeal. The reformers were not interested in improving the lot of the Democratic party per se, but in bringing "good government" to Philadelphia. The Democratic party was a useful vehicle for "throwing out the rascals" of the Republican party.

Responding to the revelations of Clark and Dilworth, the business and civic establishment severed ties with the local GOP and called for a new reform-oriented city charter that would alter the rules of politics to prevent future corruption. The organizational apparatus that Philadelphia's business establishment created (in 1949) for this task of civic improvement was the Greater Philadelphia Movement (GPM), an umbrella business organization committed to influencing the social, economic, and governmental development of the Philadelphia metropolitan area.[5] The GPM dominated the commission that produced the 1951 Home Rule Charter, a reform-minded document that set new parameters within which future governments of the city would have to operate.[6]

Many of the GPM's executives subsequently entered city government at the highest levels and helped to transform the city's politics.[7] The GPM's impact and influence on Philadelphia politics continued through the creation of the Community Leadership Seminar Program (CLSP), a course of studies including classroom and field research designed to train the city's promising young executives to assume important roles in Philadelphia's civic leadership structure. The formation of the GPM had extraordinary significance because, along with a few other organizations, it institutionalized the ethos of reform and good government in Philadelphia. In other words, reform was not a flash in the pan that lasted only as long as it took to "throw the rascals out."

A second influential reform organization was ADA. The Philadelphia chapter had long been a meeting-place for reform elements from both parties. Both Clark and Dilworth were past presidents of the Philadelphia ADA and relied on their contacts within the organization while they governed.[8]

Once the reformers rejuvenated the Democratic party, conflicts arose with the regular organization. Many in the Democratic organization had worked loyally during the years of GOP domination with the hope of eventually controlling patronage. Instead Mayor Clark alienated the organization by adhering to the new charter and filling city jobs through competitive civil service examinations. The organization also repeatedly tried to prevent Clark from hiring administrators from outside the city for good jobs that the regulars viewed as plums.[9] In 1953, when Finnegan stepped down and was replaced by Green, the struggle between the reformers and the regulars intensified.

The Contribution of Blacks to Democratic Victories

Although President Franklin D. Roosevelt was a popular figure among Philadelphia's Blacks, his coattails were trimmed by the ample patronage of the local GOP. Roosevelt received 67 percent of the vote in the city's predominantly Black wards in 1944, but in the mayoral elections of 1943 and 1947 the local Democrats won, respectively, 45 and 37 percent of the vote in these wards.[10] If the reform movement was to defeat the Republicans, winning a larger share of the Black vote, which comprised about 19 percent of the city's total registration, was imperative; Clark and Dilworth met this challenge.

In 1951, Clark won about 60 percent of the vote in predominantly White wards and 54 percent in predominantly Black wards. In Black middle-class wards, Clark won 59 percent of the vote, while in the poorest Black wards he won only 35 percent of the vote. Virtually the same educational and class differences among Black voters were evidenced in the referendum vote on the city's reform-oriented charter passed in 1951.[11] Poorer Blacks were remaining loyal to the patronage-rich Republican party, even as the employment policies of the New Deal were leading them to vote for Democrats at the national level. But among middle-class Blacks, support for the Democratic reformers who promised merit-based hiring was growing.

In 1955 Clark stepped aside, and Dilworth (elected district attorney in 1951) was elected mayor with 59 percent of the vote. Dilworth publicly credited Black voters for his victory.[12] He won 66 percent of the Black vote and about 56 percent of the White vote. The gap between middle-class (68 percent for Dilworth) and poor (62 percent for Dilworth) Blacks narrowed significantly.[13]

Table 4–1, which summarizes the data on Black mayoral voting presented in the preceding discussion, shows that in the 1951 and 1955 mayoral elections, Black voters made a decisive shift from the GOP to the Democrats, a defection that was crucial for the Democratic victories. The 54 percent of the vote in predominantly Black wards that Mayor Clark received was a significant increase from the 37 percent of 1947. Dilworth's even larger share (66 percent) signified a growing Black

Table 4–1 Reformers Capture the Black Vote for
the Democratic Party

Year	Percentage Black vote for Democratic mayoral candidate
1943	45
1947	37
1951	54
1955	66
1959	73

Source: Charles A. Ekstrom, "The Electoral Politics of Reform and
Machine: The Political Behavior of Philadelphia's 'Black' Wards,
1943–1969," pp. 92, 94, 97, and William J. McKenna, "The Negro
Vote in Philadelphia Elections," p. 78, both in *Black Politics in
Philadelphia*, ed. Miriam Ershkowitz and Joseph Zikmund II (New
York: Basic Books, 1973).

role in the Democratic mayoral victories. This shift earned Black voters a variety of
benefits, as follows.

Rewards of Alliance: Group Benefits and Incremental Empowerment

In chapter 1 I suggested that empowerment can be measured by examining the
progress made by Blacks in (a) increasing their proportion of the municipal workforce,
particularly in decisionmaking positions; (b) capturing visible and powerful political offices; and (c) influencing public policy outcomes. The new charter's rigid civil
service criteria for city jobs benefited Blacks immensely. Because of private-sector
discrimination, an especially well-educated pool of Blacks was available to take the
examinations and win city employment. One campaigner recalled that the reformers' message was that civil service examinations meant a halt to municipal employment discrimination.

> The Democrats really captured the Negro vote when Joe Clark and Dick Dilworth prom-
> ised to institute a civil service program, giving Negroes equal opportunities. I can re-
> member campaigning with a broom telling Negroes that Clark and Dilworth would take
> the mops and brooms out of their hands and give them a chance to work with their
> brains. It worked. . . . Dilworth immediately began hiring Negroes in the District
> Attorney's office.[14]

Because data on the distribution of Blacks in specific municipal employment classifications are not available for this period, it is impossible to quantify the progress
that Blacks made in this area. According to Lowe, "[a]t the time Clark became Mayor,
there were only four Negro secretaries in municipal jobs, and there had never been a
Negro sergeant on the police force."[15] Under the reform administrations of Clark
(1951–55) and Dilworth (1955–1962), the proportion of Black city employees rose
from less than 10 percent to about 30 percent.[16] At the same time, as table 4–2 indicates, the Black proportion of the population grew from 18 to 26 percent. The reformers also attempted to curtail discriminatory practices in private-sector hiring.

Table 4–2 Growth in the Black Proportion of the
Population of Philadelphia, 1950–1980

Year	Percentage Black
1950	18
1960	26
1970	34
1975	37
1980	38

Source: Bureau of the Census, Census of the Population,
General Social and Economic Characteristics, Pennsylvania, Vol. 1: *Characteristics of the Population.*

The Commission on Human Relations declared that companies would be penalized if they failed to "tak[e] affirmative steps to guarantee and promote equal employment opportunities."[17]

The significance of breaking the barriers to Black employment in city hall should not be diminished by our present-mindedness. Yet the pivotal role that Blacks played in the reform electoral coalition netted even more significant gains. Mayors Clark and Dilworth supported Black community leaders (especially clergymen) for elected and appointed offices that previously had not been held by Blacks. For example, Black allies of the reform movement were elected as city council members in 1951 and in 1955. Blacks were also elected recorder of deeds (1951) and commissioner of records (1953). Blacks were appointed to powerful and visible positions, including the chairmanship of the newly formed Commission on Human Relations (a watchdog agency for race relations), and as members of the boards of the Civil Service Commission, the Redevelopment Authority, and the Board of Education.

Blacks demonstrated significant influence on public policy as well. The best example was the creation by Mayor Dilworth of the first civilian police review board in the country, in response to Black demands for the curbing of police brutality. He also named a Black to this board.[18] Another major policy decision that directly benefited Blacks was in the housing field. A group of Black ministers persuaded the reform administration to use the city's housing resources to pursue integration rather than increased segregation. The reform administrations took what Lowe described as the "unusual and pioneering step" of rejecting high-rise public housing—which would have increased ghettoization and segregation—and opted instead for a combination of rehabilitation of existing housing and the construction of low-rise, single-project-per-site housing. Through the Commission on Human Relations, the reformers worked with the ministers to recruit Black families interested in purchasing houses and to educate them about the tricks of housing discrimination.[19] Most of these employment and housing opportunities went to better-off Blacks. Aside from creating a system of redress against police brutality, the value of which should not be gainsaid, poorer Blacks received little other than the vicarious satisfaction of seeing better-educated members of the race employed in city government.[20] These rewards would not prove sufficient to maintain the loyalty of poor Blacks to the reform wing of the Democratic party.

Rollback and Response: The Resilience of the Reform Alliance

Although Richardson Dilworth's election as mayor in 1955 continued the control of that office by the reformers, the regulars were gaining momentum in their struggle with the reformers for control of the party and city government.[21] Most significantly, in 1955 Democrat George Leader took office as governor of Pennsylvania. Leader's decision to dispense Philadelphia's share of state patronage through the Democratic organization rather than the mayor's office was perhaps the most important factor in the alteration of the power balance.[22] Prior to this, party chairman Green had controlled only a small number of patronage jobs in the School District, the Board of Revision of Taxes, the city judiciary, and other bureaucracies that fell outside the jurisdiction of the city's charter.[23] But in giving the organization approximately three thousand jobs, Governor Leader gave Green a position of strength from which to compete with the reformers for the allegiance of Philadelphia's voters.[24]

The regulars competed with the reformers for Black support by offering low-paying patronage jobs to Blacks as an incentive to organize votes for antireform candidates.[25] The Democratic organization also coopted the respected Black councilman Raymond Pace Alexander by promising him a judgeship. Alexander formerly had been allied with the reformers. In 1958 Green capitalized on Alexander's willingness to support the organization—and scored a coup in the battle for the Black vote—by having him actively campaign for Green's anointed Black nominee for Congress, Robert N. C. Nix. If the Democratic organization could claim credit for the election of the first Black Pennsylvanian to Congress, they would enhance their ability to attract Black votes. The reformers matched the ante of the regulars in the bidding war for Black electoral support. A coalition of Black church and civic leaders, ADA, Mayor Dilworth, and Clark (now U.S. Senator) endorsed a Black lawyer, Harvey Schmidt, for Congress. Nix overwhelmed his opponent, giving the regular organization a big victory. Hence the regular organization (not just White liberal reformers) deserved some credit for early advances of Black empowerment, and the impetus for this was the imperative of winning competitive elections.

Still, Green and his organization were not ready to mount a primary battle against Dilworth in 1959. Dilworth was elected by a landslide margin of 207,000 votes, winning 66 percent of the vote. Among Blacks, the class differential in support of the Democratic party candidate disappeared, as Dilworth won about 73 percent of the Black vote. However, in 1962 Dilworth resigned to enter (unsuccessfully) the 1963 gubernatorial race. With Dilworth's resignation, the president of the city council, James H. J. Tate, became the interim mayor. An Irish Catholic, Tate was a product of Democratic organization ward politics.[26]

The conventional wisdom holds that the ascendance of Tate was synonymous with the vanquishing of the reform movement. Edward Banfield argued that reform was "nice while it lasted" but the Democratic "machine" solidified its control over the city's politics and "put reform out of business."[27] The superficial evidence for this conclusion was that Tate won the mayoralty in 1963 and 1967. But a closer examination reveals that Philadelphia's politics remained competitive, both within the Democratic party (between the reformers and the organization) and between the Democrats and the Republicans, whose efforts were greatly aided by defections of Democratic reformers and middle-class Blacks, as well as White ethnics who sought greater "law and order" in the face of Black political mobilization.

One reason the Democratic organization was unable to sink the reform movement was that it lost its major source of patronage; the governor's office and gubernatorial patronage was captured by Republicans William Scranton in 1963 and Raymond Shafer in 1967. At the same time, the organization also lost its "boss"; party leader and congressman William Green died in 1963. With no heir apparent, his death engendered a succession crisis in the organization. Rather than obliterating the reform movement, ward leaders battled each other in a scramble to become the next boss; those who opposed Tate allied with the reform faction of the party and installed Francis Smith as the new chairman of the Democratic organization. Without control of the organization's electoral machinery for the 1963 mayoral race, Tate was forced to strike an expensive bargain with the city's unions, which, in his words, served as "a parallel organization to the regular party structure in areas where the ward leaders were against me."[28] For students of Philadelphia's fiscal crisis of the late 1980s, Tate's actions represent a starting point.

Although the White, working-class, largely Catholic support that the unions mobilized was crucial to Tate's electoral success, the Black vote was equally important. In 1963 Tate captured 54 percent of the vote and defeated Republican James McDermott by a comparatively narrow margin of 61,000 votes, as table 4–3 indicates. *Tate lost the White vote*, but his victory margin in Black wards (he won almost 75 percent of the vote in predominantly Black wards) was large enough to overcome his deficit among Whites. The *Philadelphia Bulletin* presciently commented, "The political fist of the Negro, particularly in a close election, is a weapon both parties are courting with increasing respect. Its potency is illustrated in the returns of the 1963 mayoral election."[29]

Because of heavy White defections to the GOP, Republican Arlen Specter won the district attorney's office in 1965 and was reelected in 1969.[30] The GOP candidate, Thomas Gola, also captured the office of controller in 1969. In the 1967 mayoral elections, White defections from the Democratic organization were unabated. Registered Democrats outnumbered Republicans 562,166 to 373,994; yet Tate defeated Specter by less than 11,000 votes (51 percent). Mayor Tate lost the White vote again in 1967, but he won the election on the strength of a margin of 58,000 votes in

Table 4–3 Margins of Victory for Democratic Mayoral Candidates, 1951–1971

Year	Candidate	Margin	Percentage
1951	Clark	124,700	58
1955	Dilworth	132,706	59
1959	Dilworth	208,460	66
1963	Tate	61,633	54
1967	Tate	10,928	51
1971	Rizzo	48,155	53

Source: *Philadelphia Bulletin Almanac and Year Book* (Philadelphia: Philadelphia Bulletin, 1971).

predominantly Black wards. Tate was suffering the consequences of the increased policy responsiveness (discussed earlier) that his Democratic predecessors Clark and Dilworth (as well as the Kennedy and Johnson administrations) had shown to Black demands. This was particularly true for White homeowners, who saw Blacks infiltrating their neighborhoods with the help of city agencies.[31] Only a year later Richard Nixon would capture the White House on the strength of these defecting traditional Democrats.

Locally, however, the support the GOP received was not solely from Whites fearful of Black encroachment. The reform movement defected from the Democratic party once it became clear that Tate was diverging from the path of Clark and Dilworth. Both the GPM and ADA supported liberal-Democrat-turned-Republican Arlen Specter in his 1965 election as district attorney and in his unsuccessful mayoral bid in 1967. Similarly, Specter won, respectively, 40 and 37 percent of the vote in predominantly Black middle-class wards (about 9–15 percent more than he won among non-middle-class Blacks), indicating that middle-class Blacks were willing to defect to the GOP to support a reform-oriented candidate.[32]

Philadelphia's reformers were not "mornin' glories [that] looked lovely in the mornin' and withered up in a short time."[33] The reform movement remained resilient because *the reform ethos had become institutionalized* in organizations like the GPM and ADA, as well as in the commissions created by the charter to implement the reform agenda.[34] The fact that the alliance of business leaders, reformers, and a sizable share of the Black middle class supported challengers to Tate in the Democratic mayoral primary and then crossed party lines to support the Republican candidates in two highly competitive mayoral elections (and in the district attorney and controller's races) was of crucial importance.[35] This fact signified that the good-government alliance would not shrink from political involvement once Clark and Dilworth were no longer at the helm. As a result, Philadelphia politics remained quite competitive; it was premature to write an epitaph for the reformers, and it is inaccurate to elevate the fragmented Democratic organization to the status of a political "machine," as some scholars have.[36]

Empowerment at a Standstill: Cooptive Benefits and Policy Nonresponsiveness

That politics in Philadelphia was highly competitive is significant because it meant that Tate and the regular Democratic organization were forced to court Black voters at the same time that they were trying to keep the blue-collar White ethnic vote from defecting to the GOP, as was the case nationally in the 1968 presidential election of Richard Nixon. As already discussed, Tate would have lost both elections were it not for the votes he received from Black wards, especially lower-income Black wards. What did Blacks receive in exchange for their electoral support? In contrast to the empowering benefits won predominantly by the middle class during the Clark-Dilworth era, Mayor Tate pursued a classic machine politics strategy of cooptation of Black support through the distribution of jobs that held no political power to individuals who could deliver the votes of family and friends. Tate earned his electoral support by delivering nearly 43 percent of the city's jobs to Blacks.[37] Although these were entry-level jobs or menial labor, for most of the recipients the alternative was to belong to what we today call the underclass.[38] The mayor pursued this strategy by capturing complete control of the federally funded antipoverty program and, in classic machine fashion, rewarding loyal Blacks with jobs through this program. Thus Blacks, who were not even 34 percent of the city's population, received more than their parity share of city jobs. That these jobs were not in decisionmaking positions shows the limits on Tate's willingness to reallocate power to Blacks. But given the significance of these jobs for the lives of those who held them, it is fair to say that the above parity allocation of municipal jobs to Blacks was a function of the competitive electoral polity.

Tate's first task was to shut down the efforts of the reform-business alliance to fight Black poverty. During Dilworth's administration, the business community had created the Philadelphia Council for Community Advancement (PCCA) to disburse federal, Ford Foundation, and locally generated dollars. These funds strengthened the political ties between the reform-business alliance and Blacks through, for example, assistance to Rev. Leon Sullivan's Opportunities Industrialization Centers.[39] Once Tate became mayor, he insisted that all federal antipoverty funds be channelled through city hall and he created the Philadelphia Anti-poverty Action Committee (PAAC). This action deprived the PCCA of its mission and main sources of funding.[40]

Tate and the PAAC promised "maximum feasible participation" to the Black community but delivered rules that insured that those who were elected could be manipulated by his Black intermediaries, Samuel Evans and Charles Bowser.[41] PAAC funds created patronage jobs for clientelistic-subordinates. In exchange for these patronage positions (there were 286 people on the PAAC payroll), the staff and elected representatives of the PAAC were pressured to do political work for the mayor.[42] The mayor also used the Philadelphia public school system, which fell outside of the control of the civil service regulations, as a patronage resource and hired many Blacks as teachers, albeit at the lowest salary levels.[43]

The regular Democrats also rolled back Black empowerment in other ways. They reapportioned electoral districts to spread out the Black electorate, so that fewer districts would be controllable by Black voting blocs; during the 1960s the number of state assembly districts in Philadelphia with a Black majority was reduced from 11 to 6.[44] Moreover, Blacks were not slated for visible public offices from which they could influence the formation of policy as they had been under the reformers. Although the number of Blacks on the 17-member city council rose from two to four during Tate's two terms, only one of these was slated by the Democrats.[45] Quite significantly, Blacks who aspired to positions of leadership within the organizational structure of the party were rebuffed and forced to accept either their subject status or expulsion from the party. For example, in 1965 the Democratic regular organization blocked the election of a Black, Edgar Campbell, to the vacant ward leadership of the Fifty-second Ward, which was about 65 percent Black. Campbell was the expected successor because he held the post that was next in command in the ward organization. Instead the organization leadership appointed the brother of the former leader. Because of his protestations, Campbell lost his job as assistant to the city council Democratic majority leader; moreover, the Black committeeman from the same ward who had led the efforts to promote Campbell was fired from his city job.[46]

Public policy also became less responsive to Black demands during the Tate years. For instance, Black leaders were for most of the 1960s unsuccessful in their efforts to lobby city hall to end discrimination in the school system. Similarly, the Tate administration refused to obey existing contract provisions prohibiting discrimination in city building projects. The Tate administration was also heavily criticized in the Black community for not enforcing existing housing codes—created during the Clark and Dilworth administrations—that would have forced an improvement in the quality of housing in the Black wards. Finally, Black leaders were unable to halt either the growing problem of police brutality or punish the offending officers. Mayor Tate even took the step of abolishing the civilian police review board created by his predecessor, decisively rolling back access to city hall on one of the most crucial issues for the Black community.[47]

Tate was betting that Black levels of electoral support for Democratic party candidates could be maintained through a generous distribution of low-level patronage even as the party adopted a less sympathetic view toward the policy concerns of Blacks.[48] The growing unresponsiveness to Black policy demands on the part of Tate and the Democratic organization was part of their attempt to halt the massive electoral defections of White voters. Many White voters identified the Democratic party with housing policies that fostered integration as well as a policy of appeasement of Black protest leaders, whose tactics, though not illegal, were obtrusive and disquieting.[49] The next step the party would take in this effort would be to promote a charismatic Italian-American policeman, Frank Rizzo, to the post of chief of police.

Cecil Moore's Politics of Racial Separatism

The party organization's decision to reject the demands of Blacks on policy and to preclude them from decisionmaking roles produced different reactions in the segments of the Black leadership structure that were not coopted by the Democratic organization. The Tate administration's inattention to Black advancement provided a political opening for a more radical agenda. Cecil Moore, a charismatic activist and flamboyant lawyer, seized this opportunity and quickly catapulted himself to the presidency of the Philadelphia chapter of the NAACP. He led demonstrations against the discriminatory practices of labor unions that were awarded contracts with the city. He also led the battle to force an all-White orphanage held in trust by the city to open its doors to Black children. Although he won only a few battles, and provoked a few brutal responses by the police, his accomplishments were significant. He shocked the more conventional leaders and led them to redouble their efforts. He made White leaders recognize that by ignoring the demands of Black leaders who seemed "reasonable" they risked contributing to the legitimization of others who seemed far less reasonable.[50]

Mayor Tate's PAAC was one of Moore's targets; Moore's aggressive messianic rhetoric and the mayor's material inducements both appealed to low-income Blacks.

Moore attempted to discredit Charles Bowser, Tate's nominee as executive director of PAAC, and to gain control of the PAAC by demanding that his assistant at the NAACP, Isaiah Crippens, be given the position. Moore's efforts failed, and he personally was dealt a setback when Tate coopted Crippens by offering him the high-paying post of PAAC legal counsel.[51]

Moore also sought to expand his power by promoting Black electoral separatism. He argued that only Blacks—preferably militant Blacks—could electorally represent Black constituencies. He rejected any differences between those Black politicians who subordinated themselves to the regular Democratic organization and the minister-politicians who were aligned with the White reform-business faction. Cooperation in political alliances with Whites was inherently bad, and he castigated those "so-called Negroes" who entered such alliances. For example, in the elections of 1964, Moore sponsored five Black candidates whose appeal was racial, that is, only Black candidates should represent Black people. *But four of their five opponents were Blacks.* He branded these four "tools of the White power structure."[52] All the candidates he backed lost.

Moore's rapid rise and fall in the struggle for political power in Black Philadelphia was reflected in the membership statistics of the Philadelphia chapter of the NAACP. In the first six months after Moore's election as NAACP president in 1963, membership rose from approximately 6,000 to 19,000 and peaked at 23,400. By the end of 1965, however, NAACP membership had fallen below four thousand.[53]

The rapid decrease in membership had two causes. First, some of those who had joined thinking they had found a messiah who would solve the ills of the Black community became disaffected with Moore. Second, the defection of the Black middle class from the NAACP was nearly total; they formed a rival organization after a Black middle-class minister failed to recapture the presidency.

The Resilience of the Cooperation between Reformers and Blacks

The rapid expansion of Moore's flock worried reform-oriented Blacks and their White allies. Black leaders and GPM officials realized that if Moore increasingly was perceived to be an effective spokesman for Blacks, the legitimacy of the Black reform leadership would be correspondingly diminished.[54] Moore's appeal to lower-income Blacks threatened the reformers' prospects for appealing to them.

After a group of four hundred Black ministers led a series of well-coordinated boycotts against selected Philadelphia businesses that had failed to respond to requests that they hire more Blacks, the business community initiated major efforts to create employment and training programs specifically for the Black community.[55] The most notable effort was the Black Coalition and its successor, the Urban Coalition. More than a million dollars were pledged to the Urban Coalition by the local business leadership. Together with federal funds, this created the Philadelphia Employment Development Corporation, which provided job training for the hard-core unemployed.[56] In announcing this initiative, the GPM candidly suggested that part of their motivation was to deter an escalation from peaceful boycotts to violent riots.

Their statement echoes the pragmatism of Atlanta's business leaders, who also formed a political coalition with Blacks that struggled successfully for Black empowerment: "Most of greater Philadelphia's business and industrial leaders realized that unless the plight of the Black Americans became the central concern for all Americans, there will be no racial peace in this nation for possibly generations to come."[57]

Two accomplishments of these biracial efforts deserve emphasis. First, Black leaders and businesspeople agreed that the coalitions helped convince Blacks that some business leaders sincerely wanted to ameliorate the economic problems of the Black community. Second, business and Black leaders got a chance to discuss these problems face to face and get to know each other.[58] The city's business leaders scored a victory in their battle against Mayor Tate for influence in the Black community by enticing Charles Bowser to cut his ties with the mayor and become the executive director of the Urban Coalition in 1968.[59]

Another noteworthy example of cooperation between the Black leadership and the business community was the Opportunities Industrialization Center (OIC), created in 1964 by Leon Sullivan and his Zion Baptist Church to provide job training and business skills for Blacks. The OIC trained thousands of Blacks in Philadelphia and across the United States in technical, industrial skills.[60] As Sullivan stated in testimony to the U.S. Congress, a large share of the credit for OIC belonged to Philadelphia's business community, which backed OIC when it was largely an untested idea. Local businesspeople helped to plan the curriculum, provide training equipment, screen instructors, and, most importantly, insure that jobs were available for those with skills.[61]

On a less tangible but no less important level, the cooperation of White business leaders with OIC disabused Black leaders, including Sullivan, of the misgivings they had about biracial economic and political alliances. Although self-interested electoral rationality in a competitive political system had originally brought White reformers and Blacks together, their alliance was now building bonds of trust that went beyond expediency. Moreover, the appeal of Moore's separatist approach and anti-coalition rhetoric was checked by the successes that moderate Blacks continued to achieve through biracial cooperation, even though White liberal reformers no longer occupied city hall.

Rizzo Unifies the Opposition

The Reform-Black Alliance of the 1970s

Because Mayor Tate was prevented by the city charter from running for a third consecutive term, the 1971 Democratic primary became a pivotal contest. Police Commissioner Frank Rizzo entered the campaign with the endorsements of Tate and the Democratic organization. Tate believed that his own electoral coalition could be expanded by Rizzo. He believed that the majority of Blacks would remain loyal to the Democratic organization while Rizzo's law-and-order appeal (as well as his ethnicity) would bring working-class Whites back to the party.[62]

Rizzo had become a household name in Philadelphia. He claimed credit for preventing the kind of racial rioting that was engulfing other major U.S. cities. However, many felt Rizzo's tactics were heavy-handed. Blacks and liberal Whites had repeatedly filed lawsuits against Commissioner Rizzo and the Police Department for alleged police brutality.[63]

Aside from Rizzo, the other candidates in the Democratic primary were Black state representative Hardy Williams, liberal city councilman David Cohen, and Congressman Bill Green Jr., son of the former party chief.[64] Cohen was the leader of the New Democratic Coalition (NDC), a prominent liberal reform organization closely aligned with ADA.[65] Green, Williams, and Cohen were all competing for the anti-Rizzo vote. Green persuaded Cohen to withdraw and endorse him, but he was unable to persuade Williams that dividing the anti-Rizzo vote insured a Rizzo victory. With only 48 percent of the vote, Rizzo emerged victorious. Green captured 35 percent, Williams won 12.5 percent, and Cohen, whose name remained on the ballot, received the remainder.

In the mayoral election Rizzo faced GOP candidate Thacher Longstreth, executive vice-president of the Philadelphia Chamber of Commerce. Rizzo confined his appearances to working-class White neighborhoods. He promised their residents safe streets, no unwanted public housing projects, opposition to racially motivated school busing, and no tax hikes. He won the endorsement of every union in the city. He ignored the Black third of the city's population that had been the party's staunchest supporters;[66] however, he predicted, "I will win every black ward with the exception of maybe one."[67]

Longstreth campaigned tirelessly throughout the city. He had the support of the rejuvenated Republican organization, many of Philadelphia's business and civic leaders, including the GPM, former mayors Clark and Dilworth, and the endorsement of the *Philadelphia Bulletin*. He also had the support of a number of Black leaders, including OIC director Leon Sullivan.[68] But with a record turnout of 77 percent of the city's registered voters, Rizzo defeated Longstreth by just under 50,000 votes, winning 53 percent of the vote in another highly competitive election.

The results bore out Tate's view that Rizzo could recapture the White vote for the Democratic party, as Rizzo won 34 of the city's 42 predominantly White wards. However, Tate was incorrect in thinking that Black voters would passively accept Rizzo and remain loyal to the party. Rizzo's unabashed stances against busing and public housing and his contempt for campaigning in the Black wards catalyzed a previously unseen degree of mobilization in the Black community, as revealed in the voting patterns in predominantly Black wards. In the Democratic primary, 51 percent of the Black voters supported the reform candidate Green, the only candidate who could defeat Rizzo, rather than Williams, who received about 37 percent of their vote.[69] In retrospect, Williams's candidacy has been viewed as a milestone in Philadelphia's independent Black politics, both because it represented a first Black mayoral candidacy and because a young housing activist named Wilson Goode was the campaign manager. Williams, however, was the wrong person for the job of mobilizing a united Black vote to take advantage of the split in the White vote and, quite significantly, the majority of Black voters recognized this.[70] Leon Sullivan and Charles Bowser had much greater name recognition and legitimacy in both the Black and White communities. But from this study's perspective, the most salient feature of the 1971 Democratic primary was that together the votes garnered by the liberal-reform candidates and the Black candidate would have beaten Rizzo.

Table 4–4 Black Voting Shift in Mayoral Elections, 1967–1971

Wards in which at least 90 percent of registered voters were black	Percentage of total vote Democratic 1967 Tate	Percentage of total vote Democratic 1971 Rizzo
3	67	20
4	64	16
6	74	22
11	57	21
16	75	22
28	72	23
29	73	26
32	74	21
44	69	27
47	76	32
60	70	20
AVERAGE	70	23

Source: Conrad Weiler, *Philadelphia: Neighborhood, Authority, and the Urban Crisis* (New York: Praeger, 1974), chap. 8.

In the general election, White liberals and Black voters were not blindly loyal to the Democratic party. Instead they unified behind Longstreth and came close to defeating Rizzo. This was most noteworthy because it represented the first massive defection of Blacks from the Democratic party to join in alliance with White liberals and reformers. As table 4–4 indicates, in the 11 wards in which more than 90 percent of the registered voters were Black, Rizzo won only 23 percent of the vote.[71] Of the voters in predominantly Black wards, 64 percent cast ballots, and Rizzo was rejected by an amazing 77 percent of them. That Mayor Tate only four years earlier had captured approximately 70 percent of the vote in these wards (then also at least 90 percent Black) indicates that the Black vote represented a sophisticated defection from Rizzo. If contrasted to Chicago, where Mayor Richard J. Daley consistently won more Black votes than any candidate he faced, including White liberal and Black challengers, this demonstration of Black independence from the Democratic party seems particularly significant.

Because Frank Rizzo's anticrime statements were widely perceived to be code words for an anti-Black message, and because of his disregard for campaigning in the Black wards, he provided the Black middle class and working class with an external enemy against whom they could unify. As table 4–5 recapitulates, in nearly every mayoral election examined so far, the Black middle class and working class/poor have had distinct voting patterns. In the years when reform mayors Clark and Dilworth were ascendant (1951–58), the Black middle class more solidly supported the reformers, while less well-off Blacks remained loyal to the formerly patronage-rich Republican party. In the 1963 and 1967 mayoral elections, less well-off Blacks gave a greater degree of support to the antireform Democratic organization candidate, James Tate. The Black middle class was more amenable to supporting reformers and less willing to support regular organization candidates than the Black working class. But the animosity that Frank Rizzo generated was equally strong among

Table 4–5 Class Differences and Black Voting Behavior for
Mayoral Candidates, 1951–1971

	Percentage Black middle-class vote	Percentage Black working-class vote
Reform Candidates		
Clark (1951)	59	35
Dilworth (1955)	68	62
Dilworth (1959)	72	74
Regular Candidates		
Tate (1963)	67	74
Tate (1967)	63	72
Rizzo Candidacy	23	24

Source: For 1951–1967: William J. McKenna, "The Changing Pattern of Philadelphia Politics, 1914–1955," *Economics and Business Bulletin of the School of Business and Public Administration, Temple University* 8:3 (March 1956), and Charles
A. Ekstrom, "The Electoral Politics of Reform and Machine: The Political Behavior
of Philadelphia's 'Black' Wards, 1943–1969," in *Black Politics in Philadelphia*, ed.
Miriam Ershkowitz and Joseph Zikmund II (New York: Basic Books, 1973), pp. 94,
97. For 1971: calculations made by me from data from the Office of Election Commissioners, City and County of Philadelphia, "Report to the People of Philadelphia."

well-off and less fortunate Blacks, as demonstrated by the fact that more than 75
percent of both groups defected to the candidate of the Republican party.

The mobilization of Black voters against Rizzo helped to elect two reform-minded
Blacks in the 1971 city council elections. In the race for the Fifth District city council seat, Republican candidate Dr. Ethel Allen defeated machine stalwart and Rizzo
supporter Thomas McIntosh, a 12-year veteran of the city council. Allen won by
making the campaign a referendum on McIntosh's support of Rizzo. In the Eighth
district, Joseph Coleman, a prominent Black member of ADA and other predominantly White liberal organizations, was elected; a decade later he would emerge as a
leading spokesman for the biracial reform coalition and become president of the city
council.

Frank Rizzo versus the Democratic Organization

When Tate and Democratic party organization chairman Peter Camiel first considered Rizzo for the mayor's office, they viewed him as someone whom they would
be able to control. However, he quickly emerged as a more shrewd politician than
anyone had imagined him to be. Rizzo recognized that the party needed his image
much more than he needed the party's organizational machinery. He methodically
began to dismantle the regular organization and reconstruct it as a personally controlled organization staffed by individuals loyal to him. Three factors—his phenomenal success at fund raising, his selection of advisers with no links to the Democratic
organization, and his ability to directly mobilize voters without organizational intermediation, were crucial to his ability to take control of the Democratic organization.[72]
In pursuit of this goal, he battled its powerful chairman, Peter Camiel.[73]

Mayor Rizzo persuaded Democratic governor Milton Shapp and the state legislature to transfer control of such bureaucracies as the Philadelphia Housing Authority and the Redevelopment Authority from the state to the city. Because these agencies had been state-controlled, they were not included in the civil service regulations of the city charter. At the same time, Rizzo was dismantling the leadership structure in these bureaucracies, forcing adversaries to resign and appointing new members who gave him control over a substantial number of jobs. By the time he ran for reelection in 1975, he personally dispensed about 5,500 jobs.[74]

In the regular organization's mayoral slating session, Camiel announced that the party would not endorse Rizzo's candidacy in 1975. Charles Bowser, the most well-known Black political figure in the city, also sought the party's endorsement. Since 1968 Bowser had headed the Urban Coalition, the business community's antipoverty effort in the Black community. Bowser's conversion to the good-government wing of the party (evidenced by his long tenure at the Urban Coalition) suggested that he would be no friendlier to the regular organization than Rizzo. Camiel rejected Bowser and instead slated state senator Louis Hill to face Rizzo in the primary.

By allegedly pressuring firms that hoped to do business with the city, Rizzo's campaign raised a record $1.5 million for the primary battle.[75] One week before the Democratic primary, Rizzo bolstered his popularity by approving a 12.5 percent pay hike for the municipal employees' union. With little Black support, Hill captured only 43 percent of the vote and was easily defeated by Rizzo.[76] But the real loser was not Hill; Rizzo slated him for a judgeship within a year. Rather, Camiel and the Democratic organization suffered a humiliating defeat, not only against Rizzo but also at the hands of "Rizzocrats" running against regular organization candidates for nomination to the city council.[77]

After Bowser failed to win the endorsement of Camiel and the Democratic organization, he decided to articulate the mounting grievances that the Black community and White liberals had with Mayor Rizzo by running as an independent in the general election. In addition to condoning a policy of police brutality against Blacks that ultimately led to a federal investigation of the police force, Mayor Rizzo systematically waged war on the city's Black leadership. He engineered the removal of one of the city's most prominent Black ministers from the School Board. He also removed Samuel Evans, Mayor Tate's most trusted Black advisor, from the vice-presidency of the Bicentennial Commission. Bowser's 1975 mayoral candidacy represented the first effort of the biracial reform alliance to channel Black disgust with Rizzo's performance behind a Black mayoral candidate. Bowser drew financial support from White liberals and received the endorsement of the Philadelphia ADA and Joseph Clark. But as an independent, Bowser had only an ad hoc campaign organization that proved unable to register or mobilize Black voters in large enough numbers to defeat Rizzo.

Additionally, some anti-Rizzo support was taken away from Bowser by the Republican mayoral candidate, city councilman Thomas Foglietta. With Bowser and Foglietta dividing the anti-Rizzo vote, the election was widely viewed as a contest for second place. When the votes were counted, Rizzo had won with 57 percent, Bowser had garnered 25 percent, and Foglietta had received 18 percent of the votes. Bowser's effort was encouraging because he received more votes than 1971 Democratic primary mayoral candidate Hardy Williams as well as Foglietta. But in comparison with Black support for GOP mayoral candidate Thacher Longstreth in 1971, Bowser's candidacy was a step back for Blacks and for the anti-Rizzo reform-Black alliance. Black turnout in the 1971 general mayoral election was 64 percent, yet in 1975, even with a Black candidate on the ballot, turnout declined to 54 percent.[78] Still, it was significant that voters in the city's White reform wards demonstrated their willingness to support a qualified Black candidate by giving Bowser 41 percent of their vote. Even in the face of certain defeat, Black and White leaders who favored a moderate, biracial coalition continued to work together to preserve the trust and norms of mutual support created under Clark and Dilworth and reaffirmed in the Longstreth campaign.

The 1975 elections were proof that Rizzo had taken personal control of the Democratic organization. More telling than the 57 percent of the mayoral vote he captured were the results of the city council elections. Only two of the five Democrats who held at-large seats were reelected. (The remaining two of the seven total at-large seats on the 17-member council are legally reserved for the minority—Republican—party.) Three Rizzocrats, Al Pearlman, Francis Rafferty, and Earl Vann, were elected on Rizzo's coattails. Vann's election is noteworthy because he was one of the few Black politicians in the city who supported Rizzo.

Electoral Mobilization and the Formation of a Dominant Biracial Coalition

Immediately after Rizzo's second term began, revisions of the city's budget revealing a deficit of at least $80 million were released. Rizzo's campaign claims that his economic stewardship had averted the fiscal crises that were crippling other major cities now sounded very hollow. His announcement of massive tax increases spurred a recall movement in April 1976 that united the anti-Rizzo biracial coalition of White reformers and Blacks, as well as middle-class taxpayers who had to bear the burden of the tax increases.[79] Enough signatures to put a recall referendum on the ballot were collected, but the Pennsylvania Supreme Court declared the recall process unconstitutional.[80]

Soon after his court victory, Mayor Rizzo began a campaign to strike from the charter the prohibition against more than two consecutive mayoral terms. Although the official rhetoric of the campaign pitted the need for institutionalized checks and balances against the unobstructed rights of the people to choose the city's leadership, the real issue was whether Frank Rizzo would continue as mayor.

The groups arrayed against Rizzo were largely the same as those that he had defeated in the 1971 and 1975 mayoral elections.[81] A coalition of prominent Black leaders, the ADA, and the Greater Philadelphia Partnership (formerly the GPM) organized, financed, and provided the leadership for the movement.[82]

Before a meeting of White supporters, Rizzo elaborated his approach to the campaign:

> I'm just starting to get my adrenalin going. . . . This is an election between the social extremists and the radicals against the people who live within the law. What am I talk-

ing about? The Black Panthers . . . the Milton Streets. You could throw in Benjamin Hooks from the NAACP, too. He's black all the time. Vote *black*, vote *black, black, black*—all I hear are black politicians getting up and saying "Vote black, vote black."

Well, I'm gonna tell everybody to *vote white*. And the people who think like me, and there's a lot of them, will help us. Okay, see how easy it is. That's how the lines are being drawn and I welcome it.[83]

Previously Rizzo had capitalized on White fears by suggesting that under a less vigilant mayor the violent crime associated with the Black ghettos could spread to White neighborhoods if low-income public housing projects were built there. But Rizzo's "Vote White" statement marked a new level of rancor. He was no longer talking in code words that would enable him to plausibly deny that he was dividing the city, pitting race against race. Moreover, by focusing on the radical Milton Street, who did not play an important role in the coalition to defend the charter, Rizzo was trying to create a bogeyman against whom he could rally support.[84]

White and Black religious and civic leaders immediately condemned Rizzo for resorting to racial polarization as a campaign tactic.[85] For instance, Rev. William Gray III, a prominent Black minister who had strong ties to White business and civic leaders (and was about to win an election to Congress), said, "It's a blatant attempt to play upon fear and insecurity. But there are too many decent whites in Philadelphia to let him get away with it."[86] The numerous condemnations of Rizzo's attempt to racially polarize the electorate forced a hasty retreat from this strategy.[87]

The many public statements from the business, civic, and religious establishments were evidence of the political bonds that they had developed with the reform segment of the Black leadership. Like Charles Bowser (and Wilson Goode, discussed later), Gray's participation in civic organizations and formal political alliances had enabled him to forge strong ties between the business and civic leadership and a large segment of the Black community.[88] The legitimacy and power of persuasion of groups like the Fellowship Commission and the Greater Philadelphia Partnership was mobilized and amplified by the newspaper coverage such groups commanded to censure those who engaged in such a divisive strategy.[89]

Mayor Rizzo's effort to change the charter was rejected by 67 percent of the voters. The winning coalition comprised Blacks, upper-income WASPs, liberals, and Jewish voters (Jews had previously given Rizzo the bulk of their support).[90] Blacks, displaying unprecedented unanimity, voted 96 percent against changing the charter (in essence, against Rizzo).

As significant as Black unanimity was the degree of mobilization in the Black community. In 1977, 32 percent of Philadelphia's registered voters were Black. The voter registration drives spurred by the charter referendum raised the Black proportion of total registered voters to 38 percent.[91] Moreover, the turnout rate in predominantly Black wards was 63 percent. Only three years earlier, when Charles Bowser had run as an independent mayoral candidate, Blacks had comprised 30 percent of the city's registered voters and Black turnout had been 54 percent. Bowser's mayoral candidacy, which was more of a contest for second place because of Republican Foglietta's presence in the race, had not succeeded in getting unregistered Black voters to register nor in getting registered Black voters to vote in large numbers. However, the challenge of preventing Rizzo from maintaining control of the mayor's office produced massive Black voter registration and turnout. Commenting on the decade-long effort to fight Frank Rizzo through the ballot box, Wilson Goode said, "Biracial coalitions and reformers were dominant forces in city politics. No longer regarded as an anomaly, black and liberal white voters were now taken seriously and had often become pivotal in deciding the outcome of close elections."[92]

Post-Rizzo Politics

With Frank Rizzo out of the running, two serious Democratic mayoral candidates emerged, Congressman Bill Green Jr. and Charles Bowser. Green had run in 1971 and had broad name recognition. While serving in the U.S. Congress, he had built a respected record. He declared his candidacy before the charter referendum and raised about $1 million for the Democratic primary from the city's largest contributors.[93] He won the endorsement of most non-Black organizations in the city, from ADA to the Fraternal Order of Police. The Democratic organization, still dominated by Rizzocrats, also endorsed Green for slating.[94]

Green's headstart forced Bowser to adopt a different strategy than the one he followed in 1975. Although Bowser retained support among White liberals and neighborhood activists, Green had locked up the financial and electoral backing of the White reform-business faction of the Democratic party that Bowser had enjoyed in 1975. Bowser raised less than $250,000. But the increased Black voter registration and turnout levels that the Charter referendum produced suggested that even without a sizable White vote, Bowser could win.[95]

In an attempt to duplicate the Black mobilization produced by the charter referendum, Bowser argued that a Green administration would differ little from the Rizzo years. He claimed that the Democratic organization's endorsement was proof that a vote for Green was a vote for the Rizzo gang.[96] Bowser also claimed to be more sympathetic than Green to those groups struggling to improve the quality of life in the city's neighborhoods.[97] With just a few significant exceptions, the city's Black leadership backed Bowser.[98]

Green captured 53 percent of the vote and defeated Bowser (44 percent) in the Democratic primary. Bowser won every Black ward and two majority White wards. But he did not build the kind of margins in the Black wards that were necessary for victory. Turnout among Black voters was only 46 percent. Although high for a primary election in Philadelphia, this was lower than both the 63 percent in the 1978 charter referendum and the 54 percent in the 1975 mayoral election that Bowser lost to Frank Rizzo.

Green would face former U. S. attorney David Marston, the Republican nominee, in November. Marston's hopes for victory hinged on Black antipathy toward Green. Marston raised the ante for the Black vote by pledging to name a Black as the city's managing director, the second most powerful post in the city government, if he were elected mayor; he also courted Bowser's endorsement.[99]

Meanwhile, many Black leaders continued their efforts to elect the city's first Black mayor. They reasoned that an independent Black candidate would have a better chance in the general election against two White candidates, Marston and Green, than Bowser had had in the head-to-head primary with Green. Councilman Lucien Blackwell soon emerged as an independent Black mayoral candidate.

Green realized that his Black support had been diminished by Bowser's attacks in the primary. Such considerations led Green to strike a deal with Bowser and his ally and strategist Samuel Evans. Bowser and Evans announced their endorsement of Green. In exchange, Green publicly promised (in a written agreement) to appoint a Black managing director, matching Marston's promise.[100] (That managing director would be Wilson Goode.)[101] Once again, in an election that promised to be competitive, the Black vote became pivotal, and Black leaders were able to capture a decisionmaking position that, within the executive branch, was second only to the mayor.

Although Bowser was harshly criticized by Blackwell's supporters, the flood of Black support to Green that followed the Bowser/Evans endorsement insured victory.[102] Green won 53 percent of the vote, Marston received 29 percent, and 17 percent went to Blackwell. Considering Blackwell's presence in the contest, Green did well among Black voters, who turned out at a rate of 55 percent. As table 4–6 indicates, of the 13 wards in which at least 90 percent of the registered voters were Black, Green was able to earn a victory in four, and in three others he lost by less than 55 votes.

In the city council elections, the number of Blacks did not increase from the 5 out of 17 elected in 1975. But two Black reform-oriented Democratic allies of Congressman William Gray—Augusta Clark and John Anderson—replaced GOP councilwoman Dr. Ethel Allen and Democrat Earl Vann. The replacement of Vann, an ally of Rizzo, was an indication that by 1979 Black empowerment had evolved to the point at which the goals and philosophy of Black clientelistic-subordinate leaders had almost no support among the Black electorate.

The Bowser/Evans endorsement of Green rather than Blackwell was a watershed event. Many of the city's Black leaders followed Bowser and endorsed Green, thereby preempting the possibility of a polarizing campaign based on dividing the White vote and mobilizing a Black bloc. Lining up behind Green was not perceived by Blacks to be selling out. Bowser and Evans were not labeled Uncle Toms. This situation presents a contrast to the politics of Chicago, where Blacks who considered supporting White reformers were castigated as Uncle Toms who were selling out to another plantation master.

Why was this not the case in Philadelphia? Why were White reformers seen in a positive light there? This chapter has argued that there was a history of mutually advantageous cooperation and coalition formation between White reformers fighting for good government and Blacks seeking to participate equally, that is, neither as subordinates nor separatists. Biracial reform coalitions yielded an incremental reallocation of power when they were electorally successful. When such coalitions failed to win elections or influence policy, they still served to strengthen the biracial trust that was a byproduct of past alliances. For Blacks, lining up behind Green was not selling out; rather, it meant a major reallocation of power, yielding the prize of a Black managing director and bringing Blacks one step closer to the mayor's office. In Philadelphia, Black voters rejected any conflation of the coalitional-incrementalist leadership with the clientelistic-subordinate leadership.

Table 4–6 1979 Mayoral Vote for Blackwell and Green in
Black Wards

Ward	Candidate	Total vote	Percentage of vote
3	Blackwell	4324	50
	Green	3653	42
4	Blackwell	3401	41
	Green	3975	48
6	Blackwell	2645	50
	Green	2177	41
10	Blackwell	4290	48
	Green	3851	43
11	Blackwell	2432	44
	Green	2428	44
16	Blackwell	2641	47
	Green	2608	46
28	Blackwell	2584	46
	Green	2432	44
29	Blackwell	1959	40
	Green	2575	52
32	Blackwell	4283	50
	Green	3371	40
44	Blackwell	2388	42
	Green	2723	47
47	Blackwell	1252	38
	Green	1822	55
51	Blackwell	4393	55
	Green	2947	37
60	Blackwell	3691	46
	Green	3640	46
Total percentage	Blackwell		46
Black vote	Green		45
	Marston		9

Source: Office of City Commissioners, "Report to the People of Philadelphia, 1979."
All calculations made by me. The Republican mayoral candidate, David Marston, received the remainder of the votes in each of these wards.

Green's Agenda of Procedural Reform

When Green took over the reins of Philadelphia's government, the city was in the
midst of a fiscal disaster, facing a deficit of $167 million and a declining municipal
bond rating. To attack this deficit Green increased taxes, laid off more than 1,200
city employees, including more than seven hundred police officers, and denied city
employees a first-year wage increase. At the end of the first fiscal year of the Green
administration, the city reported a small surplus of $37 million.

Within Green's first two months he delivered on what was undoubtedly the most
pressing issue for the Black citizenry, their fear of harassment and brutality from Frank
Rizzo's police department. A Black aide to Congressman Gray said, "I used to warn
my own son, 'If a cop stops you, smile, do everything he tells you, and pray he doesn't
kill you.' It was very real."[103] The Green administration issued new rules for the use
of firearms by police officers, mandating that use of a gun should come only after all

other methods of suspect apprehension were exhausted. The police rank and file were livid about this new policy that made them subject to a panel of Monday morning quarterbacks. But after only two years of this policy, the incidence of police shooting civilians was halved.[104] This procedural reform produced diffuse support for Green among Black citizens, but the Black political leadership on the city council had a much more ambitious agenda. Green's economic courage and technocratic approach won him the admiration of the fiscally minded members of the community, yet the leaders of the Democratic organization, the unions, and Black leadership were all disappointed he was more committed to the tenets of reform and efficiency than to rewarding his allies. Ultimately, these groups pressed their particularistic agendas without his help. Acting on behalf of the city's unionized workforce, the city council ignored the mayor and city business leaders and enacted the first city-level plant closing legislation in the nation in 1982. The law required firms employing 50 or more to give 60 days of notice prior to closing.[105] Green clashed with Black leaders over an affirmative action hiring program for Black police officers. Although in 1980 only 17 percent of Philadelphia's police force was Black, while 39 percent of the population was Black, Mayor Green opposed legislation to redress this balance because earlier in his administration he had laid off policemen and did not want to now hire new officers. Yet Councilman Blackwell and others argued that Blacks deserved preferential treatment from Green, not only to remedy past discrimination, but also because as crucial members of the mayor's coalition they had earned such rewards. Blacks and White liberals on the city council also clashed with the mayor over set-aside legislation to aid minority-owned firms in winning city contracts on a range of services from construction to consulting. The legislation called for minority-owned businesses to get 15 percent of the city's contracts. Green vetoed this bill, but the city council overrode the veto.[106]

In both these instances, Black elected officials were in a position to advance the progress of Black empowerment through their domination of the city council, a development that came as a result not only of Black electoral mobilization but also of scandals produced by a federal sting operation that forced three conservative Rizzocrats off the city council and gave Blacks and White liberals a dominant coalition in the city council.

Green was also unable to negotiate a compromise with the city council on two other prominent issues, awarding a cable television franchise that would result in the wiring of the city and building a trash incineration plant that would reduce the city's huge landfill costs. Students of political economy should note that the successes on plant closing and set-aside legislation came over the opposition of the city's business community.

The fiscal irresponsibility of the Rizzo administration forced Mayor Green to begin his term with layoffs of city employees. Still, during Green's term the proportion of Blacks holding "Professional"-status jobs (by EEOC standards) increased from 21.7 percent (1978–79) to 25.6 percent (1982–83).[107] In the last year of his administration (1982–83), Blacks represented 28 percent of the overall municipal workforce, Latinos 1 percent, and Whites 70 percent. As of 1980, 39 percent of the city's population were Blacks, making a parity ratio of 66 percent for the well-paying positions of authority in city government and 72 percent for all jobs.

The Green administration also did not enthusiastically attack the problem of racial and gender discrimination in the awarding of contracts with the city. After the city council overrode a mayoral veto of set-aside legislation, the Green administration awarded only a total of $2.4 million to minority- and female-owned firms. Solely because of the appointment of a Black as managing director, the Green administration represented not only an end to the rollback of Black political power under Rizzo but also a leap forward in the empowerment of Blacks. Managing Director Goode was, however, the only Black appointed to Mayor Green's four-man cabinet. Besides the appointment of Goode and the better service delivery that he brought to all neighborhoods, and the decisive actions to reform the police department (in which the office of district attorney Edward Rendell also played an important role), the Green administration marked an improvement over the Rizzo record but still left Black leaders feeling underrewarded.

Black Leadership and Biracial Reform Victory

Before the emerging split between Green and his Black supporters could splinter the biracial coalition, he shocked everyone in Philadelphia by announcing that he would not run for mayor in 1983. Attention immediately focused on two men, Green's predecessor, Frank Rizzo, who sought to regain his former office, and Green's right-hand man and natural successor, Wilson Goode.

Wilson Goode was part of the moderate, reformist Black political leadership network that has long existed in cities like Philadelphia and Atlanta and that distinguishes them from a city like Chicago, which has not fostered a moderate Black political cadre.[108] Like many in this group, Goode had strong ties both to the Black community and to the growth coalition. As a deacon in his church, he was able to develop close ties with many of the city's leading Black clergymen, and his public service was always part of a religious mission. Goode was also an early member of the Black Political Forum, a group of reformers dedicated to Black political empowerment. As president of a nonprofit housing agency from 1967 to 1978, Goode developed a relationship with Black community activists and advocates for the poor. Because this agency was funded by the Ford Foundation, it also put him into contact with many of the city's White reformers and business leaders who were trying to improve innercity conditions without being coopted by Mayor Tate's PAAC. Goode's housing success led to his selection by the GPM in 1967 to participate in their Community Leadership Seminar Program (CLSP), and this enabled him to meet many of the young banking, business, and civic executives who were in line to assume leadership responsibilities in the city over the next 10 years. In 1974 Goode served as chairman of the Program Committee for that year's CLSP.[109] In 1972 the Chamber of Commerce recognized him with its Outstanding Young Leaders Award. As a longtime member of the Philadelphia chapter of ADA and a member of its Committee on Black Political Development, Goode had worked closely with the city's liberals and neighborhood activists. In 1978 Governor Milton Shapp selected him to fill a vacancy on the Public Utilities Commission. There he developed a record as a competent administrator and gained attention for his skillful handling of the Three Mile Island nuclear facility disaster. From there he went to the most powerful post in Philadelphia government aside from the mayor, the office of managing director, where he earned a sterling reputation for effective, nonpolitical service delivery in the Black community and beyond. He won broad respect by meeting with the representatives of more than 30 neighborhood groups to familiarize them with ways that they could influence city hall to improve program and service delivery in their neighborhoods.[110]

Goode's personal contacts with business and civic leaders enabled him to galvanize the business community to make a strong effort on his behalf. The chief executive of one of Philadelphia's largest banks and the president of ARCO Petroleum both said that the support given to Goode by the business community was "the broadest . . . ever seen."[111] Among Goode's backers in the business community, two beliefs were consistently evident: first, that electing him would improve the city's position in the economic competition for new and relocating capital; second, that he would "unify the city" and "balance the legitimate concerns of the neighborhoods with the necessity that the Philadelphia business community thrive."[112] A member of the board of the Greater Philadelphia First Corporation, the present-day incarnation of the GPM, summed up the view of many of his peers when he said, "A Frank Rizzo victory would have given the city such a bad black-eye that it would be impossible to attract new industry."[113]

To the surprise of most observers, the campaign between Rizzo and Goode was free of overt racial divisiveness. When the newspapers did allude to the race factor in the campaign, the discussion was more often about the striking absence of racially divisive rhetoric.[114] What had changed since 1978, when Rizzo had mobilized his base of support with a call for them to "vote White"? Rizzo's campaign had an amicable, nondivisive tenor because that was the most expedient strategy for being elected mayor in the Philadelphia of the 1980s. Given an electorate in which Blacks comprised 39 percent of the registered voters, a Rizzo victory hinged on three factors— a large turnout of White ethnic blue-collar voters; winning some Black votes; and minimizing his losses among White middle- and upper-class reformers. Blacks and White liberals and reformers previously had turned out and voted against Rizzo in heavy numbers because of his racially divisive tactics. Therefore, for the Rizzo campaign, the way to diminish the turnout of Blacks and liberal Whites was to avoid the race issue. In short, although a "vote White" strategy would be successful nationally for George Bush when he used Willie Horton to defeat Michael Dukakis in 1988, it would not work in a city with a 40 percent Black population.

Goode understood the political environment much as Rizzo did. On the one hand, as Hardy Williams's campaign manager in the 1971 Democratic primary, he had seen that the combined votes of White liberals and Blacks would have outpolled Rizzo (and Blacks were only 26 percent of the registered voters then). The cost of that failure to unify was a Rizzo victory that lasted eight years. Conversely, in 1978 Rizzo was stopped by a coalition of registered, mobilized Black voters in alliance with the business community and liberal White voters. Goode reached the same conclusion as Rizzo: the road to victory was not to be found in an overtly racial appeal to Blacks, which might polarize the electorate, but in a more moderate appeal that also attracted White liberals and the business community. Neither the Black vote nor the White ethnic blue-collar vote was big enough to win alone.

Goode's major campaign theme was the imperative of creating and maintaining employment in the city by attracting new firms and preventing present employers from leaving. He also discussed the need to create and refurbish public and private housing and for reform of the criminal justice system, often adding that there was no Black or White way to deliver such city services. He criticized Rizzo's poor administrative record, reminding voters of the corruption that existed in the Rizzo years, the cronyism in City Hall, the huge tax hikes in the second Rizzo term, and the fiscal disaster that the Green administration inherited.[115]

Goode won the primary, capturing 53 percent of the vote, with Rizzo receiving 43 percent. Goode's general election victory over Republican John Egan, a successful businessman, and independent candidate Thomas Leonard, formerly a Democrat and the city's controller, was a virtual replay of the primary vote. In the primary, turnout in predominantly Black wards was 69 percent, while about 70 percent of registered voters in predominantly White wards cast ballots. In the Black wards, Goode won 91 percent of the vote in the primary and 97 percent in the general election; he won about 18 percent of the White vote in the primary and 23 percent in the general election. In the liberal, upper-class areas of Chestnut Hill and Center City (which Bowser had failed to win in the 1979 Democratic primary against Green) Goode captured 70 percent of the vote. In addition, he won 56 percent of the vote in West Philadelphia/Overbrook and in the Logan Circle area, both of which were largely White (65 percent of the registered voters) middle-class areas with growing Black populations. Because of Goode's historic ties to liberal activism and his pervasive presence as a problem-solver while he was managing director, he received substantial support from White liberals.

Who Got What? Evaluating Goode's Record

Evaluating the performance of Goode and his administration is a contentious issue. Goode and his supporters argue that he has compiled a record of accomplishments that, if compared to either his predecessors or mayors in other cities, would inspire praise. Yet what mayor has done anything comparable to the MOVE disaster? MOVE is a radical, back-to-nature group, which has existed in Philadelphia since the 1970s. In Mayor Rizzo's second term, an armed confrontation between the police and MOVE led to the death of an officer. MOVE received virtually no sympathy or support from Philadelphians of any stripe, while in the areas where MOVE settled they quickly alienated their neighbors. In May 1985, after members of the group refused to evacuate a house they were occupying, the mayor approved of a plan in which a Philadelphia police helicopter dropped a bomb on the house. The bomb started a fire that killed 11 MOVE members, including five children, and destroyed 61 homes and two city blocks of the surrounding Black neighborhood.

This outcome shocked and outraged even the most passionate enemies of MOVE. The mayor convened a blue-ribbon commission to investigate the bombing. The commission launched a thorough investigation; it dragged on even after the resignations of the police commissioner and the managing director. Goode was sharply criticized for his lack of involvement and oversight of the police operation. Much ink has been spilled regarding the MOVE disaster, and space limitations preclude an examination of any of the issues. One thing is certain, however: the basis for Goode's political appeal beyond his Black base—his reputation as an effective administrator and manager—was damaged critically in the episode.

Meanwhile, the firms selected to do the reconstruction of the burned-down homes generated cost overruns as well as controversy about the quality of their work. After eight months of such controversy, the construction firms were replaced. A grand jury investigating charges of impropriety against the firms concluded that "[m]uch of the blame for the project's unfortunate waste of resources lies with the mayor and the key people on whom he relied. He often exercised bad judgement and frequently exhibited inflexibility."[116] The reconstruction fiasco hurt the mayor because it further shook the confidence of his former supporters in the White liberal and business communities. It seems that at least one of the contractors involved had a reputation for winning jobs by giving unrealistically low bids and then producing huge cost overruns. Furthermore, though the mayor was apprised of this fact, he insisted on going with minority-owned firms for the reconstruction of this largely Black neighborhood and leaned toward these contractors. Some of his supporters-turned-critics charged that although he had the authority to allow racial considerations to influence the city's contracting process, this did not excuse him from responding to early indications of incompetence that resulted in more than $1 million in overruns.[117]

Aside from the MOVE debacle, the mayor's supporters claim that his performance has been measured, especially by the media, against lofty and, given constraints on mayoral leadership, unrealistic expectations people had of him. One example concerns the quality of city services. The Goode administration argued that it was unfairly blamed for the numerous potholes in the city streets because this condition had existed for at least thirty years and no mayor had been able to address it except in an ad hoc fashion.[118] Moreover, decline in the quality of city services in Philadelphia had more to do with the dramatic cuts in federal funding that the city suffered than with who sits in the mayor's office. During Frank Rizzo's second term, he used CETA (Comprehensive Employment and Training Act) funds to pay the salaries of 4,442 city workers. During Mayor Goode's two terms in office, the Reagan administration's attack on urban America fully eliminated CETA funds. Overall, federal aid to the city fell during the decade Goode was managing director and mayor, from more than $250 million to only $54 million.[119]

A second example of the unfair treatment Mayor Goode received is that he has been blamed for failing to solve problems when the blame should have been shared with the city council. This situation was most notable in the city's inability to solve its expensive garbage disposal crisis. The problem that Goode faced was the same that had stymied the Green administration. The city was paying enormous sums to bury its garbage in landfills outside the city limits. Both mayors and the business community agreed that the best policy was to build a trash incinerator in the city and use the steam produced in the process for energy needs. The city council took a "not in my backyard" approach to the location of an incinerator that some feared was an environmental hazard and potential producer of carcinogens. No location for a trash-to-steam facility could be agreed on by the city council, and the bill for landfill dumping continued to drain the city budget. During the Green years, the city council deservedly received a share of the blame for this stalemate. In the Goode years, the argument was that the mayor lacked the political skills to forge a compromise, which was accurate but constituted only half of the explanation; the city council remained an obstructionist body.

The fiscal crisis that engulfed the city in Goode's second term is a third failure that is unjustly put on his balance sheet. Certainly as chief executive of the city during the crisis, he must share in the responsibility and blame. Yet, as with most fiscal crises, the seeds of the problem were sown long before. One of the most significant aspects of Frank Rizzo's reelection strategy in 1975 was his granting of a 12.5 percent pay increase to municipal unions, a raise that was three times the 4.2 percent increases they had enjoyed in each of the previous two years. Rizzo was running without the party endorsement, and this whopping increase, along with the sweetening of their benefits package, no doubt contributed to his ability to defeat the organization's candidate in a party primary. The fact that Frank Rizzo was President Richard Nixon's favorite mayor ultimately contributed to the city's fiscal crisis as well. Federal revenue-sharing funelled money into Philadelphia at a time when other cities were beginning the belt-tightening process. According to S. A. Paolantonio, "The city got double per capita more than Chicago, reaping $65 million, or about 10 percent of the city's operating budget, in the first 18 months of the program. It enabled the city to balance the budget. In Philadelphia, an inevitable fiscal crisis had been forestalled."[120] During Goode's administration, he was unable to gain the cooperation of Democratic state legislators in his efforts to address the city's mounting debt and its inability to borrow in municipal bond markets because of its junk bond status. To a significant extent, the failure of the Democratically controlled state legislature to rescue the state's largest Democratic stronghold was because the Speaker of the House wanted to be elected governor and recognized that it might be unwise to appear to be the orchestrator of a bailout of the city that many state residents saw as a repository for AIDS victims, welfare recipients, and the homeless. Meanwhile, the two most powerful Black city councilmen, without whom no budget legislation could be passed, refused to offer cooperation or alternative leadership. Lucien Blackwell did not want to support any tax increases because he was planning to run for mayor in 1991 when Goode stepped aside. Appropriations Committee chair John Street wanted to become city council president first (he was the heir apparent but would not be elected until after the 1991 election cycle) and then take as much credit as possible for solving the city's fiscal crisis.

Finally, although Goode took credit for resolving a longstanding impasse that blocked the legislation necessary for establishing cable television franchises in the city, the politics behind the resolution of this issue indicate some of the constraints that a technocratic reformer like Goode faces (and Black mayors increasingly have technocratic backgrounds). Mayor Green believed that the licenses and contracts for cable television service should go to the one company that made the best offers on the basis of cost per customer and extent of service. But enough members of the city council understood that having multiple cable vendors for different parts of the city would enhance the ability of individual council members to forge lucrative relationships with vendors who did not want to risk losing area-wide monopolies. Goode was expected to come in as a strong mayor and force the city council to be a vehicle for "good government." Instead, he balked at confronting the council and chose to cede to it control of the awarding of four separate contracts.

Two other issues that Goode promised to resolve—the future plan for trash disposal in the city and construction of a major convention center—languished in the city council because the mayor, in his own words, refused to "do the kind of political trading that goes with that. . . . We simply can't afford to satisfy the insatiable appetite of members of Council if you're going to base votes on political trading."[121] The mayor offered a number of sound proposals to resolve these issues, yet he could not proceed without the approval of the city council. His administration faltered in much the same way as Green's. Neither mayor was enough of a politician (and Goode was too much the technocrat) to "go along to get along" with the city council's dominant coalition of bipartisan, patronage-minded, neighborhood representatives. The reformist public-regarding faction (mostly Blacks aligned with Congressman William Gray III) were too few to pass legislation in the city council. Both mayors were also good-government advocates who could not bring themselves to threaten to use their power to punish the constituents of their opponents as a tactic for expanding their coalitions. Goode's discussion of this factional split within the Black community is worth quoting at length:

> Over the years black politicians had gained significant power. Bill Gray was now majority whip in Congress. . . . Our reform movement had broken down the racial barriers, but it was threatening to create others as these new "bosses" sought to solidify and hold on to their power, not through merit, but by political control.
>
> Essentially, they were saying they didn't like the way the first wave of reformers had played the political game. It was too altruistic, they didn't like this "community good" stuff—working primarily for the best interests of the community rather than themselves. Basically, they wanted now to play politics the same way the "old boy" establishment had played. Their goal was not to reform politics, but to change the complexion of who was in charge.
>
> Realizing this, I knew the only way I could get some things passed by the council in my final administration would be to work on behalf of their interests. I was out of the equation. So I started strategizing, doing things like getting Blackwell to see that by supporting some of my reforms he wasn't helping me, but painting a favorable portrait of himself as future mayor in the eyes of the people and the business establishment. I made similar suggestions to Street as he pursued his desire to become council president.[122]

When the Philadelphia Eagles professional football team threatened to leave the city for financial reasons, Mayor Goode personally negotiated with the team's ownership and carved out an agreement by which the team, the jobs it generated, and the multiple sources of city revenue connected with it did not leave. Goode received heavy criticism because he agreed to have the city pay the costs—and receive partial rental rights—for deluxe corporate skyboxes to be built atop the stadium. But by September 1987, when the Eagles wanted to buy back the skyboxes because of their popularity, Goode appeared to have scored a coup that promised financial gains for the city. This is but one example of his successes in convincing mobile capital to remain in Philadelphia and in attracting new companies to the city because of his personal involvement. The dramatically changed appearance of center city Philadelphia, with numerous office towers framing the statue of William Penn atop City Hall, is testimony to the service Goode (and the city council) performed on behalf of the growth coalition.[123] Goode deserves credit for facilitating Philadelphia's belated movement into the corporate era. Yet he has been criticized for being too subservient to capital,[124] another criticism his defenders consider unfair. A mayoral aide said, "Scholars are always talking or writing about the tragic consequences of suburban competition with cities. Yet when our mayor takes steps to compete with suburbs and attract good jobs, he is criticized as a lackey for the business elite."[125]

Yet it would be inaccurate to view the Goode administration simply as a corporate-centered regime. Job creation, was, and still is, the number one issue in the Black community. As Goode argued, "Unless I can lay a good, sound economic foundation, no one will benefit from it. If I can build a strong economy here, then the black community benefits most from that, in my view, because they are the most unemployed."[126]

The vast majority of the city's Blacks continued to support Wilson Goode in his successful reelection bid of 1987, not only because he was the city's first Black mayor and not only because he brought Blacks into many positions of real power and responsibility (discussed later), but also because he delivered on his promise by creating 37,000 new jobs.[127]

In Goode's six-person cabinet, there were three Blacks, including one Black female, and three Whites (two female), marking a doubling of the proportion of Blacks in the cabinet. In 1980, 39 percent of the city's population was Black. Goode's appointments went beyond parity for Blacks; 60 percent of the commissioners heading city agencies in the Goode administration were Black. In 1987, after a number of top-level reorganizations, 43 percent of these executive appointments were Black. During Goode's second term in office, he succeeded in removing Police Commissioner Gregore Sambor, whom he blamed for the MOVE disaster.[128] Goode went outside of the department for his next chief, whose tasks included grooming a Black successor. In 1988, Goode appointed the city's first Black police commissioner, Willie Williams, capping a restructuring of the police force that had been begun by Mayor Green and District Attorney Edward Rendell.

In 1985 the Goode administration awarded $63 million worth of contracts to minority-owned firms and $27 million to female-owned firms. Although this was still only 26 percent of the city's aggregate contract expenditures, it represented a dramatic increase from the efforts of the Green administration. When the U.S. Supreme Court struck down set-asides in the Croson case of 1989, Goode refused to modify the city's plan. When a U.S. district judge struck down the city's minority set-aside plan in April 1990, Goode signed an executive order mandating a new set-aside plan.

Critics point to some blemishes in Goode's record regarding Black employment, although defenders would be quick to point out that his actions were designed to protect the tenuous economic position of the city rather than to advance any narrow interests, that is, those of growth barons. For instance, Goode has been criticized for opposing a measure that called for affirmative action hiring preferences for city residents, minorities, and women in construction jobs funded even partially by the city. But Goode was not alone in his opposition to this bill; the city council's two most prominent Black leaders also opposed it. Robert A. Beauregard concluded that

Goode's argument against the legislation—that it would produce similar retaliatory legislation by surrounding suburbs that would hurt Philadelphia construction workers who, in the aggregate, were successful in finding employment outside the city—was sound.[129]

Goode's efforts to restore fiscal discipline to the city led him to refuse the demands of the public employees' union and withstand a 20-day strike by predominantly Black sanitation workers. He eventually endorsed plans for reduction of the size of trash collection crews from three or four to two. This decision seemed reasonable, considering the design of modern trash trucks; nevertheless, it promised to eliminate the jobs of about 1,500 workers.

With respect to affirmative action in the municipal workforce, the record of the Goode administration is also noteworthy. By the end of his second term, Blacks held about 45 percent of the jobs in the city government. The Goode administration was not satisfied with simply raising aggregate numbers of minorities in city jobs. They actively sought to prepare Blacks for the highest-level jobs by implementing the "Upward Mobility Program." This program placed clerical incumbents into special trainee classes and promotional tracks to reduce the degree that White males dominated professional-status, better-paying jobs. The program contributed to an increase in the proportion of Blacks in the top three EEO job classifications from 24 percent under Mayor Green to 31 percent by 1991.

In the neighborhoods, the Goode administration used the meager trickle of federal Urban Development Action Grant dollars to supplement private capital and bring to fruition efforts to revitalize neighborhood shopping areas. This created construction jobs as well as permanent service industry jobs, in addition to upgrading the quality of life in the neighborhoods. Though these projects developed throughout the city, the Goode administration, unlike its predecessors, did not ignore the low-income Black and Latino sections of North Philadelphia, where private capital had been least willing to invest. Goode spent one-half of the city's $60-million block grant on low-income housing rehabilitation in predominantly Black North Philadelphia, yet these efforts were considered disappointing because of the high expectations engendered by his previous involvement with housing issues. This is another example of the positive dialectic of Black leadership; the Goode administration was responding to pressure from an activist neighborhood organization headed by city councilman John Street and his flamboyant brother, Milton. Protest is not enough, but without it, resources probably would have been less forthcoming.

The Goode administration did not ignore the city's poor. The single largest shift in spending in the budget ($2 million in the first year of the program) was toward programs that provided shelter and provisions for the homeless of the city, a program that earned national recognition.[130] Unfortunately, in the midst of the national recession of 1990–92 and impending municipal bankruptcy, spending on the homeless and on AIDS treatment was dramatically cut.[131] With the city's bonds rated at junk bond status and the city council refusing to enact adequate tax increases, services were cut across the board. Wages of municipal employees were also targeted. As one scholar noted, "Mayor W. Wilson Goode, with the support of some very demonstrative advocacy groups, initially attempted to protect [funding to battle homelessness, AIDS, and drug abuse], but the council ultimately prevailed in forcing their reduction. These programs have neither the broad public constituencies of traditional services such as police . . . , nor the federal or state mandates that traditional public welfare services have."[132]

Did Goode fail to deliver to the poorer segment of the black community? Were he and the Black city council members who passed his budget puppets of a growth coalition?[133] Hardly; the Goode administration did not limit political and economic advancement to the middle-class beneficiaries of affirmative action and minority business set-aside programs. Less-educated, less-skilled Blacks also won a greater share of appropriate jobs, the likes of which were disappearing in the private sector. The mayor's efforts improved the employment outlook in the private sector as well. He improved the quality of life in poor neighborhoods that were largely ignored in the past, and his administration temporarily took steps that represented a comprehensive, humanitarian response to the problems of homelessness and AIDS. Although there was certainly much more that needed to be done for the city's disproportionately Black poor, the scope of the problems went far beyond what even a united mayor and city council could do. Federal aid to the cities has declined dramatically, as has been noted. The national epidemic of family breakup that has been correlated with poverty exacerbates the problems of Philadelphia's poor as well; by 1988 "about 45% of the city's black families and 13% of its white families were headed by single women."[134] As the economy of Philadelphia and the greater metropolitan area changes in step with domestic and international rearrangements, demand for a better-educated workforce grows while wages for low-skilled service jobs decline. By the 1980s, according to Carolyn Teich Adams, "three quarters of the black men who had not finished high school were out of the workforce."[135] Educational initiatives should be at the top of the agenda for all big-city mayors, as should strategies for linking employable residents to jobs in the suburbs.

Latinos in Philadelphia

Latinos have until recently played a very minor role in Philadelphia politics. According to Census Bureau data, in 1970 only about 2 percent of the city's population were Latinos; by the 1990 census almost 9 percent were Latino, with nearly three-quarters of these being Puerto Rican. Even with their small numbers, however, the competitiveness of the city's politics has forced politicians seeking citywide offices to give attention to the political demands of Latino voters and elites.

Wilson Goode did so assiduously, and under his administration Black empowerment initiated Latino incorporation. In his initial mayoral campaign, he listed liberal lawyer Angel Ortiz on his sample ballot for an at-large seat on the city council. While Ortiz was not elected, he came very close to winning. As mayor, Goode appointed him to the post of commissioner of records, the first Latino appointment to head of a city department. On the death of a council member, Ortiz ran in a special election and won, with Goode's support, becoming the first Latino to serve on the city council.

Wilson Goode received strong Latino electoral support, garnering approximately 66 percent of the vote in predominantly Latino precincts in the 1983 Democratic primary and 77 percent in the general election. In the 1987 general election, Ortiz, who was again elected to an at-large seat on the city council, campaigned vigorously for Goode against Republican candidate Frank Rizzo, warning that a Rizzo victory would mean a "return to slavery . . . and racism." Goode won about 75 percent of the Latino vote in his narrow victory over Rizzo.

In the final year of the Goode administration, the city's Human Relations Commission held public hearings on discrimination against Latinos in service delivery. The hearings that drew the largest turnout of Latinos were on police abuse, poor relations between the public schools and Latino parents, and the community fire hazard caused by the city's failure to seal vacant buildings in Latino neighborhoods. The low level of Latino employment in the city bureaucracy (2 percent), a product of civil service tests and the absence of political connections (i.e., patronage clout) to circumvent these rules, also received attention.[136]

The most pressing issue for the Latino community seems to be police brutality. Only three percent of the police force are Latino, and in 1994 none held a rank higher than lieutenant. Mayor Edward Rendell's Black police chief has promised to find ways to bring more Latinos (and Asians, who total half the numbers of Latinos) into the department. Latinos have also been vociferous in demanding a strong, independent civilian police review board that would punish and deter brutality. Mayor Rendell (introduced later) originally sought to create a weak advisory police review board, but significant pressure from Black city council members and Latino activists forced him to accede completely to community demands.[137]

The Future of Biracial Politics in Philadelphia

When Frank Rizzo switched to the GOP to challenge Wilson Goode in the 1987 mayoral election, approximately 50,000 ardent supporters gave up their Democratic registration and became Republicans. This increased the Black proportion of registered Democrats, enabling Blacks to outnumber Whites in the Democratic party. Yet Rizzo's move did not divide the city and make the Democrats a "Black" party.

In the Democratic primary, Goode won 57 percent of the vote and defeated Edward Rendell, the very popular former district attorney. Rendell had previously enjoyed the backing of the biracial reform coalition, but in 1987 he was vigorously opposed by the city's Black clergy, who claimed that he had promised not to challenge Goode in exchange for Black support for his unsuccessful 1986 gubernatorial bid. Rendell received the support of many of the White liberals and business executives who had supported Goode in 1983, as well as both of the city's newspapers, which had endorsed Goode in 1983. In personal interviews, these reform-minded former supporters of Mayor Goode indicated that while they were backing away from a mayor whom they perceived to be incompetent, they had not lost faith in the ethos of biracial reform coalitions. Some already were looking toward 1991 and the opportunity to vigorously support another Black reformer for mayor; the names most frequently mentioned included state secretary of welfare John White, schools superintendent Constance Clayton, or Congressman William Gray.

Even Goode's staunchest supporters were not optimistic about the potential for accomplishments by a second Goode administration, largely because they felt that the MOVE disaster had irreparably diminished his political capital. Still, his continued support from both liberal activists and business leaders against Rendell and even more so against Republican mayoral candidate Frank Rizzo—and the stated intent to support Black reformers in future mayoral races—indicated that the incremental empowerment of Blacks and the legitimation of Black leadership through a biracial reform coalition has made and will continue to make a difference in the way political alliances are evaluated in Philadelphia.

The persistence of the biracial reform coalition is not the only reason why party and race do not overlap in Philadelphia. The White ethnic and labor leadership of the Democratic party did not defect from Wilson Goode in 1983 or 1987, even though many of their constituents did. The Democratic party organization, largely because of the unifying leadership of ward leader and former union leader Robert Brady, was able to reach accommodations with Mayor Goode and, even more so, with Black leaders in the city council.[138] Although defections of White Democratic politicians to Rizzo and the Republicans were anticipated, none materialized. Only one of the city's 28-member Democratic delegation to the state house and senate defected to the Rizzo team. Credit for Goode's 1987 mayoral victory goes foremost to Blacks, who turned out at a rate of about 70 percent and gave him 97 percent of their votes. Among Whites, he received 18 percent of the vote. He received diminished but significant support from those living in the city's upper-income reform areas, who gave him 54 percent of their votes. But he could not have eked out his 18,000-vote victory without the support of Democratic party ward leaders who persuaded their friends, families, and city jobholders to vote for him. Even though most of these ward leaders and voters had been lifelong supporters of Rizzo, a significant minority remained loyal to the party's candidate. Party loyalty and precinct-level organization were crucial ingredients in Goode's reelection, suggesting that although his coalition was biracial, it was no longer unequivocally liberal or reformist.

Brady and the Democratic ward leaders, of course, had pragmatic reasons for reelecting Goode. Goode had appointed Brady to head the party in 1986 and knew what he was getting; he gave Brady control over patronage jobs in the court system and Parking Authority.[139] Brady also amassed patronage jobs by becoming a board member of the Pennsylvania Turnpike Authority, the city Redevelopment Authority, and the Delaware River Port Authority. A Republican administration would be a major setback to the resurgent Democratic organization, regardless of the race of the mayor. But more significantly, the White leaders of the Democratic organization believed that in 1991 they might elect a Black Democrat who was not a reformer and was amenable to their machine style of politics, a position Goode was inching toward.

In the post-Rizzo era, the city council has shifted from an arena in which Rizzocrats fought the White reform/Black coalition over the issue of political empowerment to one in which a biracial coalition of politicians who favor a machine style of politics are in conflict with a biracial reform coalition allied with the city's good-government elements. The business community seems comfortable with both coalitions, as long as corruption scandals are avoided by the regular organization and environmentalists and preservationists are not allowed by the reformers to impede development.[140] Black leaders such as former councilman and congressman Lucien Blackwell, state representative Dwight Evans, and city council president John Street have become powerful figures within the Democratic organization that once tried to subordinate them. Street is the early favorite to succeed Rendell. Issues of patronage, the dispensation of city contracts, the selection of candidates for political offices, and spoils for their supporters are all areas in which these Black Democrats can align with conservative White ward politicians and party leaders (including Republicans). But other Black leaders, many of whom are political disciples of former congressman William Gray and former councilman John F. White, remain committed to the good-government tenets they share with the city's White liberal and business communities. In short, two biracial coalitions now exist in Philadelphia. Mayor Goode has walked the line between both groups and, depending on the issue, has been a champion or a disappointment to either group.

Biracial Politics in the Administration of Edward Rendell

Like New York's Rudolph Giuliani and Chicago's Richard M. Daley, Edward Rendell's election in 1991 replaced a Black mayor with a White mayor. Although the three mayors may share certain policy strategies, for instance the privatization of some city services, scholars should not assume that this represents a backlash against Black mayors and reassertion of White political power.[141] That has not been the case in Philadelphia. Councilman Lucien Blackwell was the leading mayoral contender in the Black community, and although he had high negative ratings among White voters, he would have won the Democratic party primary, in which Blacks were a majority of the registered voters, *if he had been the only Black candidate*. He would have received strong support from the Black clergy because his leading opponent was Ed Rendell, who had earned their enmity. He probably would have won the general election because the Democratic party organization would have had little trouble turning out a sizable minority of White voters willing to support this patronage oriented former union leader. The business community would have supported Blackwell because he had engineered the consent of the fractious city council to a number of major development projects, a task for which they could not count on Mayor Goode. Congressman William Gray was, characteristically, two steps ahead of the unfolding events. For personal and ideological reasons, Gray and Blackwell had long been opponents. Even if Blacks would be at the front of the line that included machine-style politicians of both parties, Gray and his biracial reformist allies could not support a candidate who would turn more of the city's coffers into a spoils trough. Moreover, Gray and his Black allies feared that Blackwell's abrasive style and the resentment he shared with his working-class and poor constituents regarding White privilege would foment racial polarization. The efforts that Gray's predecessors and contemporaries had made to demonstrate to Whites that they could work harmoniously with Blacks, particularly middle-class Blacks, for mutual development and advancement would be jeopardized by a Blackwell mayoralty. Gray persuaded one of his city council proteges, Ivy-League-educated George Burrell, to enter the race long before any other Black candidate and to declare that under no circumstances would he withdraw. Gray then twisted the arms of other Black ministers to either support Burrell or refuse to make any endorsements. Either Burrell would be the one Black candidate, in which case he would cruise to victory, or the Black vote would be divided. A term or two with the mayor's office occupied by Ed Rendell or Republican Frank Rizzo (or the other leading GOP candidate) would not do the damage of a Blackwell administration; Rendell would probably hand the mayoral baton to a moderate Black (as Bill Green had done), and Rizzo would unify and rejuvenate the Black-White liberal alliance as he had always done. Even after revelations about Burrell's finances and ethics devastated his candidacy, he refused to withdraw. The Black vote divided, and Rendell easily won the Democratic primary. Rizzo captured the GOP nomination, but he died soon afterward; his replacement was unable to mount a serious campaign.

Rendell has reformer credentials because he broke into politics by defeating an incumbent district attorney who was using the office for personal enrichment. He had the support of ADA, the *Philadelphia Inquirer*, and the Black community. However, he recently said that this image was an accident, that he was only interested in making the district attorney's office work effectively, and "didn't care about making a statement and beating the machine."[142] He earned support in the Black community, in part because of his aggressive actions against police brutality, and this support was not dramatically eroded by his spat with the Black clergy. He became the nation's most esteemed mayor because in his first year he produced a small budgetary surplus in a city that had a junk bond rating and a cumulative deficit of $250 million. Not only is he a friend of President Bill Clinton, he is also a favorite of the *Wall Street Journal*, *The Economist*, and the conservative Manhattan Institute because he rolled back union benefits and froze wages to save $78 million annually. He has also persuaded the state legislature to underwrite some of the city's continuing economic development efforts. The entire budgetary process in his first two years sailed smoothly through the city council because council president John Street received at least half the credit for all of it. Rendell heads a biracial coalition, and Street is his closest advisor aside from the mayor's chief of staff. Rendell has been an exuberant cheerleader for the city and has capitalized on the fiscal crisis environment to divide the city's municipal unions against other unionized workers (whose high taxes pay for the salary and benefit packages that Rendell slashed); he has taken only a few steps toward privatization.[143] He has given no indication that he plans to govern as a reformer and root out patronage, corruption, or abuse of power. He strongly supported a number of changes to the city charter (which failed); they would have increased the power of either the mayor or the president of city council at the expense of independent boards and commissions. When the local Democratic party was implicated in a plot to tamper with and falsify absentee ballots in a crucial state legislative race, the mayor refused to treat the episode as anything deserving of concern, let alone a cause for a thorough housecleaning of the party he now heads. Hence, although he heads a biracial coalition that continues to advance Black empowerment, it is not reformist like its predecessors.

That Rendell is more pragmatist than reformer has significant consequences for the future of Black politics in Philadelphia. His election was not a repudiation of liberal biracial politics, although most Black voters would have preferred either Blackwell or Burrell. Mayor Rendell's first term indicates that his administration does not represent a rollback of Black political empowerment.[144] More data are necessary before one can conclude whether his administration represents a regime change from a liberal, good-government biracial coalition to a biracial form of machine-style politics that unites all those interested in reviving a regular Democratic organization.

But it is clear that these two coalitions, with Blacks in leadership positions of both, are likely to battle for the future control of the city of Philadelphia. If he can complete a second term without a serious scandal, then one of his Black allies, like John Street or Happy Fernandez, could easily follow him and receive the backing of a party that is replenishing its patronage stock and learning to divide the spoils of government equitably between Blacks and Whites.[145] If the Rendell administration is tripped up by a corruption scandal, then the door will reopen for the more liberal reformers in the Black leadership, including councilwoman Marian Tasco, former state official C. Delores Tucker, or two others who may be able to bridge the gap between reformers and organization politicians and garner support among White ward leaders—Congressman Chaka Fattah and the newly elected councilman Michael Nutter. Fattah, who defeated incumbent congressman Lucien Blackwell, stands out as the Black politician with the brightest political future, should he choose to leave the Republican-controlled House of Representatives.

Regardless of who occupies the mayor's office, that person will be operating under some constraints that will circumscribe the economic empowerment of Blacks. With Republican control of Congress, the outlook for cities, particularly eastern and midwestern cities dominated by Democrats, is not good. Federal dollars that in a variety of ways positively impact city residents appear likely to dry up. The ongoing devolution of responsibility for social welfare services from the federal government to states has negative consequences for Philadelphia.[146] This process has gained considerable momentum, unfortunately, from the 1994 GOP congressional sweep. With each census Philadelphia's power in the legislature shrinks. Governors of both parties campaign against the city, casting it as a producer of public assistance recipients, AIDS victims, and prison inmates. The suburban rings that leech off Philadelphia hold a vicious grudge against the city because of the wage tax levied on all workers who hold jobs in the city, including those who reside in suburbs and cannot vote to elect the representatives who set the tax. Moreover, while these suburbs rebounded economically in 1993 and gained 12,000 jobs, employment continued to fall in the city.[147]

The Structure of Political Leadership in Black Philadelphia

Electoral competition in Philadelphia produced all three distinctive groupings of Black leaders—clientelistic-subordinates, separatist-messianics, and coalitional-incrementalists.

Clientelistic-subordinates

One structure of political opportunity for Black leaders has been as a part of the substructure of the Democratic organization. The pattern differed little from the longstanding pattern of Black clientelistic subordination in the Republican party that W. E. B. Du Bois wrote about at the turn of the century.[148] Blacks were anointed as agents of the party, and some were given jobs as city clerks, teachers, or policemen; most merely hoped for these jobs. These were among the best jobs a Black could get; in exchange, these Black party agents had to round up Black voters and find some who were willing to vote repeatedly. If the voters sought anything in return for their votes, the party leadership told them "to go to hell."[149] In the 1930s, when leading Black ministers requested Black representation on the GOP ticket, boss William Vare replied: "Never! Never! The people of Philadelphia would never stand it."[150] Yet Black voters continued to support the local Republican party. When large numbers of Republican ward and precinct workers switched to the Democratic party after scandals toppled the GOP, they brought their *modus operandi* with them.

In the late 1950s and early 1960s, when Democratic party chairman William Green and Mayor James Tate led the regular organization, the Black leaders they relied on were councilmen Thomas McIntosh and Edgar Campbell, councilman and judge Raymond P. Alexander, and Congressman Robert N. C. Nix. Using the state patronage resources of Governor Leader, and turning federal antipoverty programs into patronage sources (all the while benefiting from growing identification among Blacks with the party of FDR), these leaders were able to deliver blocs of Black support to the candidates of the regular Democratic organization. These officeholders were beholden to the organization for their reelection. If subordinates made empowering demands—for instance, when Edgar Campbell sought to become the leader of the Fifty-second Ward, which was 65 percent Black—they were unequivocally rebuffed. Campbell lost the vote for ward leader by a vote of 50–9, even though 41 of the 71 committeemen eligible to vote were Black; Blacks in the party structure were taking orders from the Democratic organization.[151]

Separatist-Messianics

The strength of separatist-messianics in any city is a product of the juxtaposition between the accomplishments of political leaders working through the political system (as subordinates or incrementalists) and the separatist-messianic vision of racial justice and distributive equity. In Philadelphia, when the Tate administration shifted course away from remedying discrimination against Blacks and focused the Democratic party's attention on recapturing White ethnics who were defecting to the GOP (to support candidates like Arlen Specter locally and Richard Nixon at the national level), budding Black political leaders turned toward a more racially separatist vision of political organizing. For instance, Cecil Moore, a cofounder of the Young Independent Political Action Committee, gave up on building electoral alliances with Whites during this period. As president of the Philadelphia NAACP, Moore joined with activists from CORE and followed a separatist strategy in pursuit of a radically redistributive agenda.[152] Because his messianic rhetoric prevented him from making compromises of any sort, Moore was considerably less successful in the use of protest than the group of four hundred Black ministers. Both Moore and the ministers used boycotts and demonstrations to break discriminatory hiring practices in the private sector, but Moore could not jeopardize his reputation by sitting down with White business owners and negotiating "half a loaf" settlements. Lermack commented on the dilemma that negotiating with the Tate administration held for Moore:

> The large campaigns, then, were practical failures but symbolic successes. They were much more important in this regard than anyone will admit. For Moore, riding on the

hatred of the masses, is to a great extent their slave. He can remain the leader of the
lower-class Blacks only so long as he can call forth the hatred of the whites and "Uncle
Toms" that give them unity.[153]

The large numbers of Blacks who were enthused by his rhetoric and marched with
him in protests led Moore, in 1967, to try to duplicate the achievements of Richard
Hatcher and Carl Stokes in Gary and Cleveland by running for the office of mayor.
This race, in which Mayor Tate and district attorney Arlen Specter were sure to divide the White vote, created a unique opportunity for the self-appointed savior of
Philadelphia's Blacks. But as in his two previous congressional races, Moore had no
organization and was soundly defeated; he received less than 1 percent of the mayoral vote. But his forays into electoral politics and his tenure on the city council re-
defined separatist messianism in Philadelphia: participation in the electoral system
was now accepted as long as it did not require forming alliances with Whites.[154]

Coalitional-Incrementalists

Coalitional-incrementalists, the type of Black leadership that distinguishes Philadelphia and Atlanta from Chicago and Gary, are a product of the incentives for biracial
alliance that existed in Philadelphia's competitive political environment. Seeking
support in their struggle against the corrupt Republican party, and later against the
machine-style politics of the resurgent Democratic organization, the liberal-reform
establishment of the GPM, ADA, and the Fellowship Commission helped to develop
and sustain a group of middle-class Black leaders drawn predominantly from the Black
church and the legal profession. These leaders included recorder of deeds and city
councilman Rev. Marshall Shepard, civil service commissioner and fellowship commission vice-president Rev. E. Luther Cunningham, Civilian Police Review Board
member Rev. William Gray (father of the former congressman), OIC chairman Rev.
Leon Sullivan, and Attorney Charles Bowser, who was executive director of the Urban
Coalition.[155] In addition, many middle-class Blacks who obtained civil service jobs
identified with these Black leaders and voted for reform candidates. They delivered
Black electoral support to their senior coalition partners, White good-government
reformers and liberals. In this *functional* way, working through the established electoral channels and institutions of politics and delivering the voting support of sizable groups of Black voters, they acted much like the clientelistic-subordinates. But
in contrast to this group, coalitional-incrementalists did not trade votes solely for
personal advancement; rather, these leaders achieved the removal of discriminatory
barriers to Black advancement and the redistribution of political and economic power
to the Black community. In terms of *goals*, therefore, coalitional-incrementalists
resembled separatist-messianics, except that they accepted the caveat that these goals
would be attained incrementally over decades.

Black Leadership Since 1970

During the Rizzo years, the ranks of the Black subordinates thinned; his pronounce-
ments on public housing and crime made it increasingly difficult for them to maintain credibility while supporting him. The Rizzo team, realistically, invested few

resources to win Black votes. Still, the uneven exchange relationship of electoral support for patronage and other nonempowering preferences (e.g., the filling of potholes) that characterizes subordinate relations did exist between Rizzo and a few Black leaders, such as Campbell, councilman Earl Vann, and state senator Herbert Arlene.[156]

The defeat of Vann in 1979 by a coalitional-incrementalist allied with Congressman William Gray was an indication that Black empowerment had evolved to the point at which the philosophy of clientelistic-subordinate leadership was no longer viable.

By the mid-1970s, state representative Milton Street had emerged as Philadelphia's premier separatist-messianic leader. He become infamous for his harangues in defiance of "the White capitalist establishment."[157] He portrayed himself as a defender of poor, exploited Blacks. He preached that alliances with Whites could produce only cooptation and subordination. Elected to the state legislature, he accomplished little there. More significantly, Councilman Lucien Blackwell and Milton's brother John Street emerged as a team of shrewd politicians who had no inhibitions about publicly voicing their disdain for electoral alliances with Whites.

After the massive Black voter mobilization precipitated by the 1978 charter referendum, a Black mayoral victory without alliance with a White faction seemed possible. Other Black leaders, including some who had formerly frowned on Street's tactics and his separatist agenda, moved closer to him. Among these were state representative David Richardson, Hospital Workers Union president Henry Nichols, and Councilman Blackwell, who was the preferred mayoral candidate of this group in 1979. But Blackwell's candidacy foundered because of the support for reform mayoral candidate Bill Green among coalitional-incrementalists such as Congressman Gray, Councilman Coleman, Wilson Goode, and Charles Bowser.

Although the protest and electoral accomplishments of Moore, Street, and other messianic leaders were limited, as "tree shakers" they played an important role. Often, however, they were not the ones to pick up the fruit that fell from the trees. Rather, the coalitional-incrementalists have had the access to White political and economic leaders that enabled them to negotiate settlements that on occasion were prompted by the militant activities of the messianic leaders. Coalitional-incrementalist leaders and the majority of Black citizens have been beneficiaries of this complementary relationship—the positive dialectic. This success of the Black incrementalist leadership is one of the most important causes of the decline of popular support for the separatist-messianic leaders and their goals.

In the 1970s, leadership of the coalitional-incrementalists passed to Rev. William H. Gray. As the pastor of one of the largest Black churches in the city, Gray had long been active in Black community politics. Additionally, as a member of the Fellowship Commission and a board member of the Greater Philadelphia Partnership, Gray was accustomed to negotiating with representatives of the liberal and business establishment and had gained their confidence.[158] Gray established his preeminence among coalitional-incrementalists by defeating 10-term congressman Robert Nix— the senior member of the subordinate Black leadership group—and winning a seat in the U.S. House of Representatives. Other prominent coalitional-incrementalists were city council members Joseph Coleman, John Anderson, John F. White, George Burrell, and Augusta Clark, NAACP leader Alphonso Deal, attorney Charles Bowser,

Wilson Goode, schools superintendent Constance Clayton, state official C. Delores Tucker, and Congressman Chakah Fattah.[159]

In the 1990s a new leadership group is emerging to compete with and complement the Black coalitional-incrementalists. Leaders like former councilman Blackwell and city council president John Street pursue an agenda of Black empowerment through the Democratic organization and patronage power politics as well as through symbolic attacks on White privilege. Their loyalty is to their Black electoral base, much like the separatist-messianics; they do not work for the benefit of a multiracial community. To some scholars this group will appear to be private-regarding and uninterested in good government, especially in contrast to the coalitional-incrementalists. Their belief that they can work through the party organization and electoral politics in a mutually beneficial relationship with White organization politicians, and their view that those who hold political power have earned the spoils of privileged access and unequal benefits, suggest a lineage to the clientelistic aspect of the subordinates, but they are unwilling to be subordinates to anyone. Whether in practice these Black machine-style politicians will deliver benefits to the Black community with less class skew than the incrementalists—that is, whether they will concentrate more on homelessness, inadequate public housing, and a public school system that delivers its students unready for the workforce—remains unclear.

Now that the coalitional-incrementalists are out from underneath the yoke of Cong. William Gray, who has departed Philadelphia politics, they individually have greater autonomy. They have also been deprived of their source of political guidance and a stellar fundraiser. Some, like Fattah, severed all ties to Gray long ago, but many of the rest are in an unfamiliar situation. This bodes well for John Street and his allies.

Finally, there is the Latino community, which has doubled in size in the last decade and continues to grow, as the Black population is stabilizing and the White population continues to shrink. They represent a wild card, but by the elections of 2003 or 2007 they will be important players in the city's politics.

Five

Political Competition and Black Empowerment in Atlanta, 1946–1992

"The city that was too busy too hate" Mayor William B. Hartsfield once dubbed Atlanta, and this description has stuck. He meant that the city's business and banking leaders refused to allow segregationism and racial polarization to derail their ambition to make it the business hub of the South. Allegedly, that desire led them to build bridges to the Black community and steer a path on the road of race relations that was very different from that of most other cities in Dixie. The conventional wisdom is that Atlanta's business leaders saw green rather than Black versus White; that is, they were pragmatists seeking to insure an environment of racial tranquility where business would thrive and northern businesses would establish southern offices.[1] Atlanta's businessmen feared that if they failed to take a positive leadership role on racial tolerance, the city might evolve as had Birmingham or Little Rock, cities they saw as racially divided and, as a consequence, economically crippled.[2]

This chapter rejects claims that Atlanta's business leaders were innately more ambitious or less racist than elsewhere. I also do not believe that Atlanta's political and economic leaders conceded power when they were not forced to do so. They reflected southern racial attitudes and the typical business desire to advance their financial interests, but their environment created a set of inducements and constraints that forced them to do more than pay lip service to ending segregation and empowering Blacks. Two attributes characterized this environment. First, there were no formal party organizations.[3] Second, two electorally competitive factions defined the city's politics: (a) the aforementioned rapid-growth-oriented big-business, banking, and real estate community, with the backing of the city's newspapers, and White upper-middle- and upper-class voters, constituting almost half the White population; and (b) a segregationist "redneck" faction, with support from small business, lower-middle-class and poor Whites, constituting the other half of the White population, and receiving support from rural Georgia and most of the state's governors. This competition placed a third group, a rapidly growing Black community, into a pivotal electoral position.[4] The growth coalition recognized that capturing the majority of Black votes would facilitate the election of officials who could implement their economic development plans. The segregationist faction feared economic growth because of the concomitant social change that a migration of northerners would bring, most dramatically in race relations. If the segregationist rednecks dominated elections, the progrowth agenda of highway building, airport construction, attraction of new industry, and rabid boosterism was unlikely to receive any encouragement and subsidy from the public sector. This chapter presents data showing that mayoral elections during most of this period were highly competitive. The split of the White vote between the progrowth and segregationist factions enabled Black leaders to deliver decisive blocks of Black voters in exchange for incremental Black empowerment. The Atlanta case, like that of Philadelphia, illustrates Blacks successfully entering the pluralist political arena and gradually claiming a powerful position in political deliberations. In Atlanta Blacks have achieved political power to at least the same extent that the Irish did in cities like Boston in the late nineteenth and early twentieth centuries.[5]

The Origins of the Biracial Coalition

Mobilizing the Black Vote: The Atlanta Negro Voters League

Although the Black population in Atlanta was steadily growing, as table 5–1 indicates, Black voters did not become significant players in Atlanta elections until 1946, when the Supreme Court outlawed the White primary in Georgia (*Chapman v. King*). This court decision profoundly changed the calculus of electoral politics in Atlanta. In March 1946, less than seven thousand Blacks were registered in Atlanta, comprising about 4 percent of the city's electorate. Building on earlier "citizenship school" efforts by the NAACP and Atlanta's Black institutions of higher education, the All-Citizens Registration Committee (ACRC) organized a massive voter registration effort that increased the Black proportion of the electorate to 27 percent by the end of the year.[6]

In 1948, Democrat A. T. Walden, then president of the Atlanta chapter of the NAACP, and Republican J. W. Dobbs founded the nonpartisan Atlanta Negro Voters League (ANVL) to educate and unify the city's novice Black voters. The leaders of the ANVL were primarily preachers with considerable legitimacy among Blacks.[7] The league preserved its nonpartisanship by having two cochairs, one from each party, for each of its eight standing committees. In important respects it was organized and functioned much like a traditional political party organization. It had leaders for every precinct in the city and invited all aldermanic and mayoral candidates to make a presentation before it, answer questions, and solicit its endorsement.[8] It also constructed a street-level network through the Black churches that enabled it to be very success-

Table 5–1 Growth in the Black Proportion of the
Population: Atlanta, 1940–1980

Year	Total city population	Percentage Black
1940	302,288	35
1950	331,314	37
1960	487,455	38
1970	497,024	51
1980	425,022	67

Source: Bureau of the Census, "Negro Population in Selected Places and
Counties" (1940, 1950, 1960, 1970) and "Summary Characteristics of
the Black Population for States and Selected Counties and Places: 1980."

ful in voter registration and mobilization.[9] Because many of its officers were ministers and deacons, the organization could easily arrange for endorsed candidates to speak to voters at the churches. Although it had no patronage incentives to offer, the ANVL captured the loyalty of Black voters because of the moral authority of its leadership and because of the symbolic and substantive benefits that leadership won for Blacks. This unified, well-organized political organization deserves much of the credit for capitalizing on the opportunity for Black political empowerment afforded by Atlanta's competitive politics.

Competitive Politics in Atlanta

In 1949 incumbent mayor William Hartsfield, who had governed with the backing of Coca-Cola owner Robert Woodruff and the rest of the big-business growth coalition, faced Fulton County commissioner Charlie Brown.[10] Both candidates recognized that in the aftermath of *Chapman v. King*, Black voters could make a significant impact on the outcome of the election. Accordingly, both sought the ANVL's endorsement.[11] What the Black leadership sought was a redress of police brutality through the appointment of the city's first Black police officers, a demand that had first been voiced in 1932.[12] Hartsfield struck a deal with one of the ministerial spokesmen that if he was provided with a list of 10,000 newly registered Black voters, after he won reelection he would appoint the city's first eight Black policemen.[13]

In the 1949 mayoral election Hartsfield captured 54 percent of the vote and defeated Brown by 2,825 votes. Column D in table 5–2 shows that in predominantly Black precincts (those in which at least 90 percent of the residents were Black), Hartsfield won about 78 percent of the vote and emerged with a 2,956-vote margin (column E). This "Black margin" represents the difference between the votes that Hartsfield and Brown received in predominantly Black precincts, not among all Black voters. From 1949 through 1961, the period covered in table 5–2, approximately 70 percent of Atlanta's Blacks lived in predominantly Black wards. This estimate of Hartsfield's margin among all Black voters makes two assumptions that are reasonable but nevertheless introduce a possibility of error. First, it assumes that the other 30 percent of the Black population turned out to vote at the same rate as those Blacks living in the most segregated areas. Second, it assumes that this less-segregated 30 percent of the Black population voted with the same preferences (i.e., the percentages of the vote going to each of the candidates) as the voters in predominantly Black wards. Proceeding from these two assumptions, I calculate the "adjusted Black margin" (column F of table 5–2). Because Hartsfield's Black margin was greater than his citywide total margin (column C), it is probable that Hartsfield lost the election among White voters.[14] Column G provides estimates of the White citywide margin, which is the product of the difference between the adjusted Black margin and the total margin. In each election, the mayoral winner lost (quite narrowly) the highly competitive White vote.

In 1953 Hartsfield again faced Brown in the mayoral election. Brown's criticisms of the mayor for his opposition to the unionization of the police force and for his failure to support a streetcar operator's strike were not sufficient to unseat him.[15] In another competitive election, Hartsfield captured 56 percent of the vote. Among White voters only, however, the election was highly competitive; Hartsfield again narrowly lost the election among White voters (see table 5–2), and his victory was again a product of his strong support from Black voters. In predominantly Black precincts he won 78 percent of the votes.

Although race had not been an overt issue in the elections of 1949 and 1953, the rhetoric of the 1957 mayoral election was racially divisive. In part the change was due to the 1954 *Brown v. Board of Education* Supreme Court decision that invigorated Blacks in Atlanta and throughout the country in their fight for school desegregation. But the most important reason for the injection of race into the 1957 election was the candidacy of segregationist Lester Maddox. Maddox claimed that Mayor Hartsfield was controlled by the NAACP and was the "candidate of the colored

Table 5–2 The Decisiveness of the Black Vote in Atlanta, 1949–1961

	A	B	C	D	E	F	G
Year/Election Candidate	Vote	Percentage	Total margin	Percentage Black	Winner's Black margin[a]	Adjusted Black margin[b]	Estimated White margin
1949 Mayoral							
W. Hartsfield	20,080	54	+2,825	78	+2,956	+3,843	
C. Brown	17,255	46		22			+1,018
1953 Mayoral							
W. Hartsfield	32,253	56	+7,139	78	+6,335	+8,235	
C. Brown	25,114	44		22			+916
1957 Mayoral							
W. Hartsfield	41,300	63	+17,313	95	+14,013	+18,217	
L. Maddox	23,987	37		5			+904
1961 Mayoral							
I. Allen	63,670	64	+27,028	99	+21,976	+28,569	
L. Maddox	36,642	36		1			+1541

Source: Tablulations of the complete mayoral vote published in the *Atlanta Constitution*. All calculations made by me.

[a]These figures are based on the vote in predominantly Black precincts only. In 1949 there were 5, in 1953 there were 8, and in 1957 and 1961 there were 13 Black precincts with populations that were 90 percent or more Black.

[b]The adjusted Black margin figure is an estimate of the total margin of victory among Black voters that the winning candidate received city wide, as discussed in the text.

bloc."[16] Hartsfield overwhelmingly defeated Maddox, capturing 63 percent of the vote. His large majority obscures the competitiveness of the 1957 mayoral election among White voters. Among White voters Maddox defeated Hartsfield by an estimated less than a thousand votes. But among Blacks, who constituted about 27 percent of the registered voters, Hartsfield polled 95 percent of the vote and built a lead of more than 18,000 votes. (See table 5–2.) The 80 percent Black turnout rate exceeded the White turnout rate by 12 percent.[17]

The business leaders achieved their goals of electing Hartsfield and turning Atlanta into a southern metropolis in large part because of the votes of Blacks. By the criteria set forth in chapter 1, Hartsfield's 1949 and 1953 elections, won with 54 and 56 percent of the vote, were highly competitive and competitive. However, the narrow margins between the two candidates among White voters makes a compelling case for considering all three elections competitive. The White vote was so closely divided that *Black voters in each instance were placed in the position of providing the decisive votes.* What makes competitive electoral conditions significant is that such circumstances present—to leaders who can mobilize a sizable bloc vote—opportunities to negotiate an exchange of these decisive votes for group empowerment. In each election Hartsfield narrowly lost the White vote, and he and his business-oriented coalition would have lost the election were it not for his overwhelming support among Black voters. Were Black leaders successful in translating this opportunity into Black empowerment?

Incremental Black Empowerment

The mayor earned his considerable Black support in a number of ways. He informally included Blacks in the decisionmaking process on issues such as zoning and municipal employment by consulting with a "kitchen cabinet" of Black leaders.[18] His dismantling of the racial barrier in the police force met stiff resistance in public hearings and in the press and diminished his White support, yet he did not back away from this policy. Conversely, the appointment of Black police officers, which was a prominent item on the Black agenda since the early 1930s, significantly strengthened his Black support.[19] Although Black officers could not arrest Whites until 1959, that fact is somewhat irrelevant because the Black community sought Black police officers primarily as a means to redress police brutality against Black victims. Another accomplishment that seemed quite signficant at the time came in late 1949, when the city installed street lighting along Decatur, Edgewood, and Auburn avenues, an improvement Black leaders had called for to increase public safety in the heart of the Black business district.[20] Hundreds of Blacks turned out to celebrate the lighting of the new lights.[21] The mayor and the business establishment also supported the elevation of a Black to a highly visible post, backing the candidacy of the president of Atlanta University for the Atlanta School Board in 1953.[22] Clarence A. Bacote, an active participant in the politics of the period, listed the following dividends of the relationship between Hartsfield and the Black community:

> Negro policemen have been hired. Police brutality has been reduced to a minimum. Race-baiting groups such as the Klan and the Colombians have been suppressed. City

officials have been more courteous and sensitive to the demands of Negroes. Court-room decorum has improved. In city planning the city fathers began looking at the needs of all citizens regardless of color. Two Negro deputies have been added to the Fulton county Sheriff's office. Better streets, lights, sewers, water, and sidewalks have made Negro neighborhoods attractive. In addition, modern school buildings have been erected to accommodate the growing Negro population.[23]

Plans to expand the number of neighborhoods in which Blacks lived were another significant achievement of the electoral alliance with Hartsfield. The peaceful open-ing up of previously all-White neighborhoods to Blacks in Atlanta is especially no-table. Atlanta's Black and White political leadership recognized that growth in the city's Black population necessitated new areas for Black housing. A Klan-style group known as the Colombians tried to block Black expansion by bombing and burning houses sold to Blacks, as well as through mob action in transitional areas. The White political leadership and the city's two newspapers condemned these actions and helped discredit the Colombians, in salient contrast to the behavior of elites in many cities when faced with White mob violence directed against Blacks. Seeking to maintain law and order, the political leadership worked with the Urban League and organiza-tions of Black real estate brokers to select areas where Black homebuyers could be steered.[24]

Perhaps Blacks' most important achievement during Hartsfield's tenure was also the least tangible—the fostering of what has been labeled an "oasis of racial toler-ance" in the otherwise segregated southern United States of the 1950s and 1960s. M. Kent Jennings and Harmon Zeigler concluded, "If there is anything the coalition fears most, it is seizure of the city government by what are called the 'red neck,' 'wool hat' elements and their urbanized spokesman."[25] One should be careful not to mini-mize the significance of precluding one's enemy from capturing power simply be-cause this achievement is not quantifiable.[26] When arch segregationist Lester Maddox challenged Hartsfield in 1957, Maddox ran a race-baiting campaign. Hartsfield was by no means a liberal.[27] Rather, he was a realist; he recognized that in the competi-tive electoral environment, Black voters, if united, could deliver electoral victory to him and the growth coalition. So he and the city's business leadership did not retreat from their alliance with the Black community but confronted Maddox head-on, ar-guing that only with an amicable racial climate could Atlanta become the financial center of the South.[28] Defeat of the conservative, segregationist position that was shared by the majority of the Whites in the city, state, and region was one of the most important benefits of the biracial alliance for Blacks. For Atlanta's Blacks, the city of Birmingham and the politics and repression of "Bull" Connor presented a picture in living color of the political atmosphere they would face in Atlanta if they refused to join an alliance with the business leadership and the White middle class and en-abled a segregationist victory. As Pat Watters and Reese Cleghorn argued,

[W]ithout Negro votes the moderates most likely would have been overwhelmed by that majority of whites who habitually voted against the city administration. . . .

Perhaps Atlanta would have been spared a Bull Connor anyway, but perhaps it would not have been, for all around it in Georgia in the 1940's and 1950's the racist fires were burning, often higher even than in Alabama, and Atlanta's moderates usually were the objects of the most venal political vituperation in the state.[29]

The fact is that the Colombians were not part of Atlanta's dominant coalition and Blacks were, even though at this point they clearly were not senior partners. Lester Maddox was not mayor in Atlanta, even though he was popular enough to be elected governor of Georgia in 1966. There should be no doubt that Black Atlantans considered this situation an accomplishment that spared many their lives or their property and easily justified their voting for Hartsfield and the other candidates who received the ANVL endorsement. Scholars today should be careful to not dismiss these accomplishments.

The Consolidation of the Biracial Coalition

Protest and Policy Responsiveness in the Allen Era

In early 1961 about 150 students, led by Martin Luther King Jr., initiated demonstrations and sit-ins against segregation in downtown Atlanta restaurants and department stores. At the same time, the efforts of Atlanta's biracial leadership to peacefully desegregate its high schools were culminating. The Atlanta Chamber of Commerce, led by its president, Ivan Allen Jr., had pressured the governor and other state officials to abandon their resistance to school desegregation.[30] Atlanta's business leaders felt that the student-led sit-ins could easily result in violence and jeopardize school desegregation efforts.[31] Both Black and White leaders believed that the eruption of violence would aid the mayoral campaign of Lester Maddox. The protest leaders wanted immediate results, while the business leadership wanted a temporary respite. At this point the protest leaders turned to the older, biracially legitimate Black leadership to open channels of negotiation with the business community, represented by Allen.[32] Allen described the pragmatic approach of local business leaders to the anti-segregation protests:

> The joint opinion of these businessmen was clear: they were in a hell of a pickle. They were being criticized from all directions, and they didn't care to go on much longer like that. *Yes*, they said, *go ahead and work something out. Get us off the hook, even if it means desegregating the stores.* They were more liberal than the balance of the South, but the main thing guiding them was business pragmatism: *what's good for Atlanta is good for us; what's bad for Atlanta is bad for us.*[33]

The business leadership agreed to the desegregation of leading downtown restaurants and department stores, but sought a delay of about six months until the school desegregation battle (and the next mayoral election) had been peacefully settled.[34] This negotiated settlement yielded forward movement to Blacks on problems like the desegregation of schools and public accommodations, while the White business community won the type of positive national publicity that helped attract new business enterprises and investors.[35]

When Hartsfield retired from politics, the business leadership turned to Allen to enter the mayoral race. Allen's main opposition came from insurance executive Milton "Muggsy" Smith and Lester Maddox. Smith won the support of many of the Black student protest leaders who were impatient with incrementalism by advocating a faster pace on school desegregation. The ANVL strongly backed Allen. Black ministers carried to their congregations the message of ANVL leader A. T. Walden that split-ting their vote between Allen and Smith would benefit only Maddox. Walden argued:

> the climate in Atlanta was good and had been good for many years because we have had a strong voting strength and thus we became the balance of power. This balance of power is in danger of being split, which is what happened in city after city in the South. By splitting the Negro strength, one group cancels out the other group and thus the politicians have nothing to fear from Negroes and they can elect whom they wish with the Negro vote having little or no effect.[36]

Allen's campaign strategy was to focus on Maddox as a threat to the city's progress and an enemy against whom Blacks had to unite, behind Allen, to defeat.[37] Allen defeated Smith in the Black precincts by a margin of more than two to one. At the same time, poorer Whites solidly backed Maddox. Because no candidate received a majority of the vote, a runoff between the top two vote-getters, Allen and Maddox, was necessitated. The Black electorate, including the student protesters and their sympathizers, faced again with the threat of an external enemy, arch segregationist Lester Maddox, united behind Allen.

Maddox charged that Allen was controlled by the NAACP, socialists, and com-munists. He condemned Atlanta's school desegregation;[38] he warned that Allen would integrate swimming pools and churches; and he widely disseminated a picture of the Allen primary victory party that showed Whites and Blacks mingling.[39] Allen soundly repudiated Maddox's racially divisive tactics and put together a biracial coalition of the business community, upper-middle-class Whites, and Blacks that delivered 63 percent of the vote.

As table 5–3 indicates, the coalitions that Hartsfield and Allen led against Maddox in 1957 and 1961 were similar; sharp class and racial divisions characterized the city's

Table 5–3 Atlanta Mayoral Voting Percentage by Race and Class, 1957–1961

	Poor White[a]	Middle income white[b]	Affluent White[c]	Black
1957				
Maddox	69	61	29	3
Hartsfield	32	39	71	97
1961 Runoff				
Maddox	69	67	26	1
Allen	32	33	74	99

Source: Norman V. Bartley, *From Thurmond to Wallace: Political Tendencies in Georgia, 1948–1968* (Baltimore: Johns Hopkins University Press, 1970), adapted from table 3–2, p. 47.

[a]Poor Whites earned less than $5,000 (1960 dollars) per year and were not educated beyond the eighth grade.

[b]Middle-income Whites earned $5,000–$10,000 annually and were educated beyond the eighth grade but not beyond high school.

[c]Affluent Whites earned more than $10,000 and had received some education beyond high school.

voting blocs. Allen narrowly lost the White vote; but among affluent Whites, Allen and Hartsfield both captured at least 70 percent of the vote.[40] The divided White vote created competitive electoral conditions that placed the Black vote in a position of crucial importance. Allen won the votes of nearly all of the city's Blacks, which provided him with a deceptively large margin of victory.

From Vetoing Segregation to Black Empowerment

The 1965 Elections

The 1965 elections closed one chapter in Atlanta's political evolution and forced the opening of a new one. Previously, the agenda of the White political and business leaders and their Black coalition partners had been dominated by one concern— defeating the electoral efforts of antigrowth segregationists. But in 1965 no demagogical, segregationist candidate entered the mayoral campaign. Maddox's defeats had proven to other aspiring politicians that in Atlanta a segregationist appeal would provoke a potent countermobilization. Racial segregation and discrimination still typified Georgia and most of the South. This was evident in 1966, when Maddox's segregationist appeal remained powerful enough to elect him governor. But the repeated victories of the biracial coalition in Atlanta denied the utility, and in effect the legitimacy, of an electoral strategy premised on racially polarizing demagoguery.

In the 1965 elections, Allen again faced Milton Smith, whom he easily defeated, capturing 71 percent of the vote. Allen's general popularity was due in part to Atlanta's financial boom and to his promise to bring professional sports to the city.[41] He was popular among Blacks for a number of reasons. In the wake of President Johnson's signing of the historic Civil Rights Act of 1964, Atlanta moved rapidly on the desegregation of hotels, restaurants, and movie theaters. Furthermore, because Allen had been the only southern politician to give testimony before Congress on the need for such federally mandated legislation, he had won considerable respect from Blacks.[42] His administration also was making significant strides in improving the municipal employment opportunities of Blacks in Atlanta. In the first half of 1964, 908 Blacks and 672 Whites were hired by the city; of the jobs filled by Blacks, 188 were in skilled employment categories.[43] All this, it must be remembered, was occuring at the same time that public safety commissioner Eugene "Bull" Connor was unleashing police dogs and water hoses on Black protesters in Birmingham.

After the 1965 elections, the agenda for Blacks shifted from defeating segregationist politicians to electing Blacks to major citywide offices, institutionalizing biracial power-sharing arrangements, and taking other steps that advanced Black empowerment. The first Black alderman was elected to the city council in 1965, and in 1969 another four Blacks were elected. By 1973, 9 of the 18 city council members were African-American, as were 11 of the 14 Atlanta-area state legislators.

Black Atlantans, seeking an increase in their share of power in the biracial coalition, were unwilling to accede to the plans of the White progrowth leadership to construct a rapid transit rail system under the aegis of the Metropolitan Atlanta Rapid Transit Authority (MARTA).[44] Plans had been formulated and transit routes determined without consulting the Black leadership, yet Black leaders were expected to deliver large numbers of favorable votes in a referendum on the issuance of municipal bonds for MARTA. Instead, in a series of moves that caught the White business leadership by surprise, the Atlanta Summit Leadership Conference (the organizational successor to the ANVL), the NAACP, and the Southern Christian Leadership Conference all urged Blacks to defeat the referendum. After its sound defeat in November 1968, Black leaders explained that they had withheld their support because they had not been consulted by MARTA's proponents in the business community. For MARTA's plans to receive Black support, the authority would have to show greater sensitivity to the present and future transportation needs of the Black community, including a commitment to place Blacks in both leadership and staff positions. In this way, Black leaders at this point elevated affirmative action hiring to a priority position on the Black agenda.

The 1969 mayoral elections provided further evidence that Blacks were ready to demand a greater share of power in the biracial coalition. The mayor, his growth coalition colleagues, and the major newspapers committed themselves to Alderman Rodney Cook without consulting the Black leadership.[45] Blacks refused to support Cook, not only because they were not consulted about his selection, but also because he was widely identified with the Republican party.[46]

Three other major candidates entered the race. The most conservative candidate in the race, G. Everett Millican, campaigned for a return to "law and order" in the city and called for a clamping-down on the activities of Atlanta's hippie community.[47] Sam Massell, who had quietly served as Allen's vice mayor (president of the Board of Aldermen) for eight years, was unable to win the support of the growth coalition.[48] He charged that the business leadership snubbed him because he was Jewish; whether true or not, his charges of anti-Semitism further alienated the business community from him but created some empathy among Blacks.[49] He cast himself as a liberal Democrat and promised to increase the number of Blacks in government. He received the endorsements of most of the city's Black political leaders. The other prominent candidate, Dr. Horace Tate, a Black first-term member of the Board of Education, held a Ph.D. in education but had no political experience. The SCLC, led by Rev. Ralph Abernathy, supported Tate. But most Black political and business leaders believed that a Black could not win without significant support from Whites, and they considered Tate and his supporters too militant to do so.[50] These leaders included state senator Leroy Johnson, Rev. Sam Williams, and millionaire insurance executive Jesse Hill.[51] Tate's candidacy was thus doomed because of the absence of Black financial backing, as well as his failure to win the support of any of the city's 15 Black elected officials.[52]

No candidate emerged with a majority, necessitating a runoff election between Massell (31 percent) and Cook (27 percent). Millican and Cook together won about 76 percent of the White vote, while Massell won approximately 22 percent of the White vote and 44 percent of the Black vote (see table 5–4). Tate won nearly 50 percent of the Black vote, but no more than 2 percent of the White vote.

In a race between two White moderates, an antisegregationist appeal could not be used to mobilize Black voters. Recognizing this, Massell successfully pitched the campaign on a more partisan basis as one in which a moderate Republican was pitted against a liberal Democrat.[53] Massell made much of Cook's GOP ties and repeat-

Table 5–4 1969 Atlanta Mayoral Election Voting,
By Race

Candidate	Percentage total vote	Percentage Black vote	Percentage White vote
Massell	31	44	22
Cook	27	6	45
Tate	23	49	2
Millican	19	—	31

Source: Charles Rooks, *The Atlanta Elections of 1969* (Atlanta: Voter Education Project, 1970), chap. 2. Percentages are rounded and do not always total 100 because three other candidates received small proportions of the vote.

edly criticized him for accepting financial support from Republican organizations. Massell called for the same backing from local Democratic organizations and even received the endorsement of Hubert H. Humphrey.

In the runoff election, Cook picked up the votes of Millican's supporters, while Massell added those of Tate's.[54] Massell won by constructing a traditional Democratic coalition of Blacks, White liberals, and organized labor that gave him 55 percent of the votes.[55] He won approximately 27 percent of the White vote (doing better with poorer than more affluent Whites) and about 92 percent of the Black vote.[56]

In the evolution of Black political development in Atlanta, the 1969 elections represented a milestone. Black votes again were decisive in a competitive election, but this time Black leaders engineered this outcome without the support of the White business community. The failure of affluent Whites and Blacks to coalesce behind a single mayoral candidate should not be interpreted as signifying the demise of their long-lived alliance. Although the 1969 mayoral election did disrupt the alliance that elected Hartsfield and Allen, one must be careful not to exaggerate the extent of the fissure.[57] Massell had been Allen's vice-mayor and claimed a share of the credit for his achievements. As Mack Jones said, the contest between Cook and Massell could have been considered "an intrafactional fight among the White business and commercial elite."[58] Massell had not opposed the policies that the business leaders had supported in the Allen administration, and he was unlikely to oppose them on major initiatives.

Moreover, simply looking beyond the mayoral race provides more evidence of the resilience of the business-Black coalition. In the vice-mayoral election, Maynard Jackson faced Alderman Milton Farris, a highly qualified and experienced White candidate.[59] Jackson, the grandson of J. W. Dobbs, cofounder of the ANVL, one year earlier had entered the Democratic primary race for the United States Senate against arch segregationist Eugene Talmadge and achieved a surprise victory within Atlanta while losing heavily statewide. For the vice-mayoral contest, Jackson received the imprimatur of the White business elite in his endorsement by the *Atlanta Constitution*, which stated that he deserved support because he was the kind of Black leader who could help to "bridge the chasm" between races.[60] Jackson captured 58 percent of the vote, winning about 98 percent of the Black and about 28 percent of the White vote. The influence of the business community's support for Jackson was demonstrated by the fact that he won a significantly larger proportion of the most affluent White voters (31 percent) than of poor Whites (17 percent).[61]

In the same election, Black representation on the Board of Aldermen jumped from one to five out of 18 members, or about 28 percent of the aldermanic seats, with Blacks about 50 percent of the city's population. The elections of the five Black aldermen also indicated the support of a biracial coalition, because all aldermen run citywide in Atlanta (although they must reside in the district they represent), so these Black aldermen were not automatically elected because of the existence of aldermanic districts that had majority Black populations. Significantly, three of the five Black winners had defeated White candidates in runoff elections; they won with coalitions similar to Jackson's, receiving a heavy Black vote and significant support (21–32 percent) from Whites, especially from those with higher incomes.[62]

The vigor of the traditional biracial coalition was also exhibited in the Board of Education elections. As with the aldermanic elections, the candidates must reside in the ward they represent, although they are elected at-large. The number of Blacks on the nine-member board rose from two to three. Two of these received more than 80 percent of the Black vote and more than 50 percent of the White vote, while the third won approximately 73 percent of the vote from both Blacks and Whites. All three did significantly better among upper-income Whites than other Whites.[63]

The Attainment of Decisionmaking Power

Mayor Massell augmented the political power of Blacks by his appointment of at least one African-American city councilman to each of the 15 council committees. Because Vice-Mayor Jackson, as president of the city council, was also an ex officio member of all committees, Black representatives had significant power and leverage in the 10 committees that had only three members. Black aldermen began to correct discrimination within the water, police, fire, library, and aviation departments. In only two years, Massell, through the appointment of a Black director of personnel and the creation of an Office of Affirmative Action, was able to raise the proportion of Blacks in the top two municipal job classifications from 11 to 16 percent.[64] Although still far below parity with the Black proportion of the population (51 percent), this fact nonetheless represented positive change.

Massell's record in affairs of concern to the Black community was uneven.[65] But for many in that community, his record was irrelevant; as they had not been in 1969, the majority of the Black political leadership were ready to back a Black mayoral candidate in 1973. Horace Tate had done better than most had expected in the 1969 mayoral election. And Atlanta's Blacks were encouraged by the election of Tom Bradley as the first Black mayor of Los Angeles, where Blacks were less than 20 percent of the population.[66] Both Maynard Jackson and state senator Leroy Johnson gave early indications that they would enter the mayoral race, leaving Massell with little hope for sizable Black support. The largest Black newspaper, the *Atlanta Inquirer*, acknowledged that Massell had been a good mayor and that Black political empowerment had grown with his help. Yet against a Black candidate with the competence of Jackson, the voice of the majority of the Black political leadership could not support Massell.[67]

Midway through his term, Mayor Massell shifted strategy in preparation for a mayoral race against a Black candidate.[68] He curtailed the ability of Vice-Mayor Jackson and the Black aldermen to pursue a legislative agenda by reshuffling committee appointments so that four of the most important committees had no Black membership.[69] In addition, he sponsored legislation in the Georgia assembly to annex to Atlanta new areas that were nearly all White and that included approximately 50,000 new voters who would be eligible to vote in the 1973 elections. Notwithstanding his denials, this legislation was widely viewed as a racially motivated effort to alter the city's electoral demography. The legislation died in the state senate.[70]

Institutionalized Consultation in a Biracial Power Structure

Atlanta was a booming city in a booming region. The Department of Labor found that from 1955 to 1965 Atlanta was among the top four cities in the nation in economic growth. In 1965, department store sales in Atlanta rose faster than in any other city.[71] During the 1960s, only seven cities in the United States had more downtown construction.[72] Rather than risking the demise of the business-Black alliance that had been foreshadowed in both the MARTA referendum and the refusal of Blacks to support Rodney Cook, the business leadership, led by banker Mills Lane, sought new modes of cooperation with Blacks. Lane, real estate agent William Calloway, Jesse Hill, Lonnie King, and a handful of others decided that the time had come to heal the growing rift. This decision led to the creation of the Atlanta Action Forum in 1971.[73]

The creation of the action forum was important because it formalized and institutionalized biracial consultation and power-sharing among the city's economic leadership. Communication between Black and White leaders would no longer be ad hoc. Meeting every month, these leaders became comfortable in discussing strategies for issues of importance to the future of Atlanta. It was at these meetings, according to members of the Action Forum, that Black leaders persuaded their White counterparts that they had nothing to fear from a Black mayor.[74]

One of the first issues the Action Forum grappled with was the formulation of a new MARTA referendum. In November 1971, three years after the first defeat, a new MARTA referendum passed, with strong support from Black economic and political leaders. What had changed? As a result of negotiations conducted by forum members, MARTA had agreed to a number of changes beneficial to the entire Black community, including the expansion of service to poorer, largely Black neighborhoods, a set-aside of 25 percent of project-generated jobs and contracts for minority firms, a restructuring of MARTA to include Blacks in managerial positions, the appointment of a Black member of the Action Forum to the MARTA board of directors, and a reduction of the standard bus fare to 15 cents from 1971 to 1979.[75]

The Action Forum also played a crucial role in resolving the 1973 public school desegregation impasse in Atlanta. The problem was how to desegregate a school system that was already 77 percent Black. Joel L. Fleishman credited the forum with prodding Black and White leaders to take the issue out of the courts and away from national organizations like the NAACP and the ACLU, which favored dividing the few White students evenly across the schools in the system. The Action Forum stimulated negotiations that yielded reduced segregation in the school system while also providing Blacks with the power long sought by community control advocates, that is, substantial executive decisionmaking positions in the public schools bureaucracy, from which they had previously been excluded.[76]

The conflicts surrounding MARTA and the desegregation of the schools were both resolved in a manner that reallocated political power to African-American leaders. Along with the rejection of Rodney Cook and the election of Sam Massell, these events indicated a rearrangement of the relationship between Blacks and the White business leadership within the coalition that governed the city; Blacks were no longer mere junior partners. Even before the election of Maynard Jackson as mayor, the city's African-American leadership cadre had demonstrated that it had the willingness to act unilaterally and the capacity to act forcefully on issues that directly affected Black interests.[77]

Atlanta's First Black Mayor: The Jackson Coalition

In the 1973 election, three major challengers to Mayor Massell emerged: Vice-Mayor Maynard Jackson, state senator Leroy Johnson—both Black—and former congressman Charles Weltner. Johnson received the endorsement of the *Atlanta Constitution*. He was a protege of A. T. Walden with a long history of experience and accomplishments in the state legislature. Many thought he had let his mayoral opportunity slip by when he refused to enter the race in 1969. Weltner, a former member of Congress, was a liberal White with solid credentials among Blacks. In 1966 he had given up the Democratic congressional nomination (from the district that included Atlanta) because he refused to pledge his loyalty to the head of the party ticket, gubernatorial candidate Lester Maddox. Weltner received the endorsement of former mayor Ivan Allen.[78]

As vice-mayor, Maynard Jackson had earned public praise and considerable name recognition. He had been in the forefront of the fight to make the MARTA referendum more beneficial to Blacks. His campaign manager, Atlanta Action Forum leader Jesse Hill, provided Jackson with access and legitimacy in the eyes of the progrowth leadership.[79] Jackson also received support from voters affiliated with the budding neighborhood movements who opposed the construction of freeways that would intersect the city.

No candidate won a majority in the mayoral election, resulting in a runoff between Jackson, who had garnered 47 percent of the vote, and Massell, who had won only 20 percent, just slightly ahead of Weltner. Turnout was about 47 percent among registered Whites and about 53 percent among Blacks.[80] During the runoff, Mayor Massell pitched a racially divisive campaign at Atlantans. He tried to equate Maynard Jackson's candidacy with that of Hosea Williams, a candidate for the city council presidency who was a fiery civil rights activist and the director of the Atlanta branch of the SCLC. Massell's new campaign literature, and his slogan, "Atlanta's Too Young to Die," bluntly suggested that a Jackson-Williams administration would result in "an end to progress, an end to opportunity, an end to faith."[81]

No evidence of any relationship between Maynard Jackson and Hosea Williams—other than the color of their skin—existed. Nor was any such coordination of the two candidacies likely, considering that Williams had not entered the race until very late.

Williams was seeking to ruin an alleged deal between Jackson and the business community, in which Jackson had promised his support in the race for the city council presidency (formerly the office of vice-mayor) to Wade Mitchell, the candidate most closely allied to the business community.[82] In exchange, that community, it was claimed, would support Jackson's mayoral campaign.[83] In fact, when Mitchell lost, and Wyche Fowler and Williams emerged as the two runoff candidates, Jackson made no moves to support Williams.

Massell's strategy of trying to smear Maynard Jackson by linking him to Hosea Williams, whose messianic rhetoric seemed radical to both Blacks and Whites, was widely repudiated, and his tactics helped convince both major newspapers to endorse Jackson in the runoff. The *Atlanta Constitution* voiced the growth coalition's sentiment when it editorialized, "Mayor Sam Massell acts as if he were running for mayor of a South African city which practices apartheid rather than mayor of a fully integrated city."[84]

Jackson won 63 percent of the vote. At the same time, Fowler won about 64 percent of the vote and defeated Williams. Nine Blacks and an equal number of Whites were elected to the city council. While Jackson won more than 90 percent of the Black vote, he also won nearly 25 percent of the White vote. Similarly, Fowler won approximately 40 percent of the Black vote and 82 percent of the White vote.[85] These data suggest that even when a credible politician like Mayor Massell attempted to polarize the electorate racially, a significant number of Atlantans refused to be swayed.[86]

How was Maynard Jackson's election read by the power structure? What did his victory mean for the special relationship between the White progrowth coalition and the growing group of Black politicians and politically active civic leaders? The power structure was divided in its support in the 1973 mayoral election. Former mayor Allen supported Weltner, the *Constitution* supported Johnson, and, as the incumbent, Massell surely received business support. But Maynard Jackson received considerable support from the power structure.[87] He had the support of the two Black business leaders who had made the furthest penetration into the power structure, Atlanta Life Insurance CEO Jesse Hill and contractor Herman Russell. Hill had been the first Black to become president of the Chamber of Commerce in 1968, and Russell had followed him in this position in 1971. Both were also members of Atlanta Action Forum. Support among the White business leadership came from J. Paul Austin (chairman of the board of Coca-Cola, and the successor to Robert Woodruff), Richard Kattel (chairman of the board of Citizens and Southern National Bank and the successor to Mills Lane), and architect-developer John Portman, the kingpin of Atlanta's growth coalition since the 1960s. In the Hartsfield and Allen years, the two business leaders who had stood head-and-shoulders above their peers were Woodruff and Lane. Certainly from a reputational perspective, support from this triumvirate would be the equivalent of an endorsement of Jackson by the power structure.

Jackson's first two years in office were characterized by strained relations with the White business leadership; both programatically and personally they clashed. The reallocation of political and economic power that he sought through affirmative action in the bureaucracy and the setting aside of 25 percent of the city's contracts for minority-owned firms was resisted by the White business leadership; they tried to turn the Black leadership against him. His demands were in fact an extension, albeit a hefty one, of the earlier programs of power-sharing developed by the Action Forum, Leadership Atlanta, and other organizations that had institutionalized biracial consultation in the resolution of the MARTA crisis and the school desegregation impasse. To argue, as Clarence N. Stone does, that Jackson's election "had shaken profoundly the past foundations of biracial cooperation in Atlanta" is correct only with respect to his support for neighborhood interests (discussed later).[88] But with respect to the agenda that was most important to Jackson, Black empowerment, Stone's view diminishes the significance of the fact that both the MARTA referendum crisis and the school desegregation impasse were resolved only after the growth elite capitulated to the Black leadership's demands for reallocation of political and economic power. The policies of the Jackson administration continued down a trail blazed by the institutionalized power sharing arrangements and the fact that the resolution of these two crises produced Black empowerment. This is why Atlanta's growth elite failed in resisting a redistributive challenge whereas Cleveland's succeeded. In Cleveland, the growth coalition's claims that Mayor Dennis Kucinich's policies were poisoning the business climate were accepted by his supporters and precipitated defection from his coalition.[89] In Atlanta the White growth elite was unable to drive a wedge between Jackson and the Black coalitionist leadership by claiming that the mayor's policies were bad for Atlanta's business climate, because the affirmative action and minority business set-aside policies that Jackson advocated had historic support from the majority of Black leaders and voters. Because neither Black leaders nor Black voters urged Jackson to back down on his demands for African-American empowerment, these policies did not cripple his administration.

The larger stumbling block in the relations between Jackson and the White business elite was the personal and procedural problem of access. The White business elite had long been accustomed to informal access to the city's mayors. In a letter addressed to him that marked the low point in his relationship with the growth coalition, many of the city's business leaders expressed the concern that their lack of easy access to him would lead to the the the breakdown of Atlanta's public-private partnership.[90]

When Mayor Allen described his relationship with Atlanta's business community, he said, "[W]hen I looked around to see who was with me in this new group of leaders, I found my lifelong friends. Almost all of us had been born and raised within a mile or two of each other in Atlanta. We had gone to the same churches, to the same golf courses, to the same summer camps. We had played within our group, married within our group, partied within our group, and worked within our group."[91] Maynard Jackson could not possibly duplicate the relationship that business leaders had enjoyed with Allen and Hartsfield because he was not one of them. As an African-American, he had not belonged to this club, and he had never been invited to their houses. Social gatherings like golf games and debutante balls would no longer serve as opportunities to discuss the business of the city, because the mayor would not be present. Mayor Sam Massell had had a similarly rocky relationship with the business community because he too did not fit in socially.[92]

Issues of access were eventually resolved and the mayor agreed to offer the growth elite formalized access. He inaugurated Pound Cake Summits, meetings with leading executives at early morning breakfasts at city hall. Reflecting back on this period, Jackson said:

> The difficult relations that I had with them [business leaders] received more attention and focus than they deserved. But the power structure, and the newspaper, did not know what to do with the first black mayor and I must tell you that I had no background in what to do with the power structure. The main thing, I believe now, is that I lost the eye-to-eye contact with the power structure, the personal relationship and assurance. This may sound naive, but I thought these people would do what was good for Atlanta with or without a personal relationship.[93]

Jackson came into office not only with the support of the business community and overwhelming support from Black voters but also with the backing of a budding neighborhood movement that challenged unfettered growth and the destruction of neighborhoods. Neighborhood activists were not as successful in achieving a reallocation of power vis-à-vis the growth coalition as was the Black leadership. A brief examination of this differential success reveals why Blacks were successful in winning political empowerment in Atlanta. In part, neighborhood groups were not successful simply because they often took a noncompromise stance in their dealings with the business and growth advocates.[94] Furthermore, Mayor Jackson expended more political capital on behalf of the empowerment agenda of Blacks. He threatened the city's bankers that if they did not name women and minorities to their boards and improve their opportunities for executive-level positions, he would deposit the city's money in Birmingham banks. He also threatened to "let grass grow on the runways" if minority firms were not brought into the construction process of the new sections of the airport.[95] He refused to issue highly visible ultimatums on behalf of his allies in the neighborhood movement, however, because to do so would have placed him alone, out on a limb. He would have been alone because other Black coalitional-incrementalist leaders did not see neighborhood activists as important allies. That is, the neighborhood movement's opposition to the externalities of a growth strategy was not an issue on which either the Black leadership or the Black electorate could easily be mobilized. Floyd Hunter's important insight into the approach the Black leadership took toward White liberals probably applies equally well to their approach to the neighborhood activists:

> The relative powerlessness of white liberals, except as a small voting bloc, was never lost on black politicians. Astutely, as only black men could, blacks saw their white helpers as hired hands in the white community, hired for their brains and talents but generally denied positions of great power. Black politicians, public or private, have left the liberals to fend for themselves as they have moved toward the greater prizes of the system. They not only reached for the prizes of power, they demonstrated how well they had learned the more basic strategies of personal and group survival. With the exception of perhaps one or two, one finds few, but very few, liberal thinkers in the board rooms of power; indeed, continued associations with such liberals could be a distinct liability.[96]

To the extent that Mayor Jackson did advocate the slow-growth neighborhood agenda, this advocacy placed him out of step with the coalitional-incrementalist Black leadership cadre. This dissonance was in sharp contrast to the united front that the Black leadership and Black voters presented on the extension of rapid transit to Black neighborhoods, affirmative action hiring, and minority business set-aside programs. Jackson did not win these battles alone, nor could he have done so. Blacks on the city council, in the Action Forum and Leadership Atlanta, in the Chamber of Commerce and in the voting booths stood with Jackson when he issued ultimatums. Few if any of these allies saw the neighborhood agenda as a priority.

To understand the tenure of Mayor Jackson, it is crucial to maintain a distinction between Jackson and the Black coalitional-incrementalist leadership cadre. He was their representative and their leader by virtue of his office. But what distinguishes Atlanta (and Philadelphia) is that the fate of the Black agenda and Black representation has not been tied to one person. Atlanta's Black coalitionist leadership had a history, a momentum, and a network of biracial institutionalized relationships that existed independent of Maynard Jackson. Probably every Black leader in Atlanta wanted Jackson to be a successful mayor, but if he failed, his failure would not void the consensual relationship that had long been evolving and had been cemented by recent episodes such as the resolution of the differences over MARTA and the decision by the business leadership to back Jackson's candidacy. Thus, whether or not Jackson's style or personality clashed with the growth coalition, the Black leadership cadre, which had equal claim to representing the Black electorate, would continue to pursue quite successfully an agenda of political and economic empowerment.

Black Empowerment Through Mayoral Power

Mayor Jackson accelerated the political empowerment of Blacks. During his mayoral campaign he had repeatedly raised the issues of police brutality and the underrepresentation of Blacks on the police force. In 1973 Atlanta's population was 52 percent Black, but only 21 percent of the police force was Black. This problem had been exacerbated by the refusal of Massell's police chief, John Inman, to obey the city personnel board's recommendation that two-thirds of all newly hired police officers be Black until the racial imbalance was eliminated. Chief Inman became identified with a policy of racial insensitivity and tolerance of police brutality. After considerable struggle in the courts, Jackson scored a victory for his Black constituents by replacing Inman with a Black chief of public safety, Reginald Eaves. Eaves curbed police brutality and pursued affirmative action; within two years the proportion of Blacks on the police force rose to 35 percent.[97] Similarly, while the total municipal workforce was slashed by 18 percent in Jackson's first term, the proportion of Blacks holding city jobs rose from 42 percent in 1973 to 51 percent in 1977 (when Blacks were about 61 percent of Atlanta's population). More significantly, the proportion of Blacks in the top two municipal employment categories rose from 16 percent under Massell (when Blacks were 52 percent of the population, for a parity score of 31 percent) to 33 percent in the final year of Mayor Jackson's first term (when Blacks were 61 percent of the population, for a parity score of 54 percent).[98]

Aggregate data such as these obscure the effort Mayor Jackson's administration was making to empower Blacks, because those who are newly hired are mixed into a much larger pool of employees. Data that isolate new hires by the administration show that in the final year of Jackson's first term, 80 percent of all newly hired, permanent, full-time employees were African-American. Within the top two job classifications, 59 percent of the permanent, full-time new hires were African-Americans.[99] Jackson also appointed 12 Whites and 15 Blacks to head the city's departments and agencies, and 252 Whites and 237 Blacks were appointed to the various boards and commissions that helped run the city.[100]

One of Jackson's most significant accomplishments was to institutionalize the practice of apportioning significant shares of city construction and service contracts to minority firms, begun during the MARTA project. He threatened to hold up the construction of both the Atlanta OMNI convention and sports arena and Hartsfield International Airport until proportional targets for contracts to minority firms were met. In 1973 when he took office, approximately 1 percent of the city's contracts went to minority firms. By 1977, when his first term ended, 19 percent of all city contracts went to minority business enterprises (MBEs); by 1981, when he finished his second term, that figure was 34 percent.[101] He frequently said that from the airport construction alone, 21 Black millionaires were created.[102] Many in the business community, the fulcrum of the so-called power structure, resisted minority business set-asides and refused to become involved in projects that targeted proportional goals of participation by minority-owned businesses. They felt that the mayor's policies did not "reflect the needs and objectives of the entire community and virtually ignored the interests of the business sector," and that his administration was creating a climate that was perceived as bad for business.[103] Yet the Black leadership prevailed.

The minority business set-aside programs created by Mayor Jackson (and imitated in many U.S. cities) indicate Black empowerment not merely because they were legislated over the resistance of powerful White economic and political elites but, more important, because they delivered political and economic benefits to the Black community. Opportunities that had been closed to Black-owned businesses were opened; small-scale Black-owned businesses that faced high hurdles due to their inability to take advantage of economies of scale and their lack of experience with the competitive bidding process were boosted over these hurdles. Moreover, MBE policies did not just expand the Black business class; they also expanded employment opportunities for Blacks who were not business owners. For example, an analysis of payroll data for runway construction at Hartsfield Airport found that 95 percent of those employed by MBEs on the project were minority workers. Furthermore, a broad survey of Atlanta MBEs found that 71 percent of their employees were minority workers.[104]

Mayoral Succession and the Legitimation of Black Leadership

From Maynard Jackson's breakthrough election to the present, Blacks have held the mayor's office in Atlanta. Blacks have held the city council presidency since Wyche Fowler resigned in 1977, and they have won the majority of both district and at-large seats on the city council since 1978. Have Black elected officials merely offered trickle-down policies to the majority of Black voters and delivered selective benefits to the narrow Black upper class? If Black voters were offered a more redistributive alternative to the Black coalitional-incrementalist leadership, would they flock to this choice? The empirical evidence forces a negative answer for both of these questions.

Maynard Jackson was reelected in 1977, defeating Emma Darnell and five other candidates. Darnell was one of the African-Americans Jackson had appointed to head a city department. She ran from Jackson's left, as a critic who believed that the mayor was not doing enough to advance the interests of both the Black middle class and his working-class Black constituency, yet she was soundly beaten.

Jackson was forced to step aside after his second consecutive term by city law. The 1981 mayoral election was won by Andrew Young, the former associate of Martin Luther King Jr., who had also served in Congress and as President Carter's ambassador to the United Nations. He defeated Sidney Marcus, a White state legislator with business community backing, and Reginald Eaves, the former public safety commissioner (superchief of police) in Jackson's administration. Eaves had been dismissed after police department scandals; however, he remained popular among Blacks and was elected to the Fulton County Commission. Even though Young ran a campaign that often seemed targeted at the business community—he promised to make Atlanta the headquarters for business with nonwestern nations—he received about three times the support that Eaves did among Black voters.[105] During Young's two terms he continued to advance the political and economic empowerment of African-Americans. By the close of his first term, Blacks held about 59 percent of the decisionmaking positions in the bureaucracy.[106] The city's nine executive departments were headed by five Blacks and four Whites. In 1982 he expanded affirmative action in the city. Previously, 25 percent of all workers on city-funded projects had to be from minorities. The first Young administration added rules that required that 25 percent of the total money spent on each city-funded project had to go to minority-owned firms. In Young's second term, that share was increased to 35 percent.[107] Increased Black employment, the growth of Black businesses, and capital formation in the Black community were all consequences of these policies. In some instances the Young administration was able to force businesses to agree to even greater commitments than these rules required. For instance, when a major railroad company sought to build a piggyback facility in a racially mixed, working-class neighborhood, Young blocked this proposal in response to neighborhood concerns about truck traffic. His veto came even though the company had agreed to a joint-venture arrangement with minority-owned firms. The company ultimately won the acquiescence of some neighborhood opponents and the approval of Mayor Young after it agreed to create a fund for neighborhood improvement and to construct a community center.[108]

In 1989, after Young was forced to step aside by the two consecutive term limit, Maynard Jackson was reelected. He faced competition from two well-known Black candidates, Fulton County Commission chairman Michael Lomax, and former city council member and civil rights activist Hosea Williams. Lomax withdrew two months before the election when his polling indicated that he could not beat Jackson. Into this void stepped Williams, who believed that Maynard Jackson was not an adequate voice for the interests of lower-class African-Americans. A poll conducted by Georgia State University indicated that Jackson, Lomax, and Williams each received about 30 percent of the support of those who identified themselves as "poor." This finding contradicted Williams's assertion that Jackson (and Lomax) would only advance the interests of middle- and upper-income Blacks, unless one makes the troublesome assumption that Black voters were unable to discern which of the three well-known candidates could best represent their interests. Ultimately Williams won about 17 percent of the citywide vote, with Jackson gathering about 80 percent.[109] The support Jackson and Young received from the Black community against more progressive, redistributionist Black challengers like Darnell, Eaves, and Williams belies the prediction of "revolt against the city's Black political leadership" by lower-class Blacks that some scholars have articulated.[110] Given well-known candidates who advocated redistributionist policies that were even more dramatic than those articulated by the coalitional-incrementalist leaders, Black voters overwhelmingly voted for the less radical but by no means subordinate leadership.

The argument that the policies of Black leadership are identical to those of pro-growth White elites, that the policy preference of Black administrations "denies redistribution as a policy option," that the upshot of Black empowerment "for most of its constituents could only be symbolic," and that "the black community did not figure into the list of real beneficiaries" of the policies of either Maynard Jackson or Andrew Young is an empirically incorrect distortion of reality.[111] I do not debate the contention that the Black middle class has benefited *more* from the gains of Black political empowerment than lower-status Blacks. This pattern has obtained for every ethnic group that has struggled for power and wealth in capitalist America. Yet, as I have repeatedly demonstrated, lower-status Blacks have gained much from the biracial coalition that began back in the Hartsfield era. One of the most crucial benefits has been the incremental reduction in police brutality in Atlanta.[112] Moreover, many Blacks in Atlanta have gained from the affirmative action hiring policies that have been implemented informally in the Allen and Massell years and formally in the Jackson and Young administrations. Opportunities that did not exist before were opened specifically for African-Americans at all levels of the urban bureaucracy, much as the capture of office enabled the Irish and Italians to influence the distribution of patronage jobs in the nineteenth and early twentieth centuries. In *Subordination or Empowerment?* I have stressed the penetration of the upper levels of the urban bureaucracy by Blacks, because these are where the decisionmaking that is crucial for the reallocation of power that defines Black empowerment takes place. But many more African-Americans benefit from these policies at the middle and lower levels of the bureaucracy. These successful affirmative action strategies must be distinguished from the strategy of economic expansion, trickle-down benefits, and the alleged "lifting of all boats by a rising tide," a scenario that does not disrupt the distributional queue. Affirmative action mandates the disruption of previous, often deeply entrenched allocational patterns, and it substitutes a redistributive policy that could not happen without a political struggle being fought and won by and for Blacks and other subordinated groups.

Minority business programs that mandate joint ventures or the inclusion of minority-owned firms and require a certain proportion of total employment to go to minority workers are also redistributive policies. The rhetoric that only a handful of businesses benefit from such programs is false. During Andrew Young's administration more than five hundred minority-owned businesses received over $180 million in contracts from the city. Of the $308,432,644 expended for the 10 largest contracts, $94,088,028 went to MBEs. Only 16 percent of that went to the city's four very large Black firms.[113] The benefits of these contracts go beyond the hundreds of business owners, because Black-owned firms employ Black workers at a much higher rate than White firms.[114] These policies were resisted vigorously by White business leaders, who viewed them as "social experiments" and "reverse racism." Resistance to policies that give preference to Blacks in hiring, promotion, and the allocation of contracts continues in Atlanta and throughout the nation. Yet African-American politicians like Jackson, Young, and numerous other leaders in Atlanta were able to force other powerful interests to accept these policies and their consequent reallocation of power.

The Structure of Black Political Leadership in Atlanta

In Atlanta the lines of demarcation between clientelistic-subordinates, coalitional-incrementalists, and separatist-messianics are less stark than in the other cities in this study. The explanation rests with the success that the ministers, educators, business leaders, and politicians who constitute the coalitional-incrementalist leadership cadre have had in the dual legitimizing tasks of incrementally achieving the goals of the Black community and delivering solid blocs of Black votes that have meant the difference between victory and defeat.

Coalitional-Incrementalist Leadership

In the late 1930s and throughout the 1940s, the efforts of A. T. Walden, John Wesley Dobbs, Martin Luther King Sr., and others to organize the Black community did not meet with the unanimous support of Blacks. Daddy King, in his autobiography, discussed many Blacks in leadership roles who fit the clientelistic-subordinates leadership type. They did not want to jeopardize their privileges within the southern system of segregation in a fight for the rights of all Blacks. He wrote:

> My vote alone would mean nothing until social and political change could be more than a vision of a distant future. I organized a few meetings and sounded out a few close friends, among them several other Atlanta churchmen. There were arguments, healthy kinds of disagreement in the beginning. Eventually, though, I began to sense the formation of a strong opinion based, for the most part, on the theory that the comfortable passenger is the last one who should think about rocking the boat. . . .
>
> At one of these meetings I proposed that black churches become central headquarters for a voter drive. . . .
>
> The idea fell on deaf ears. When any of my fellow clergy spoke, it was to suggest that I keep such notions to myself, there was far too much at stake for Negroes in Atlanta to risk anything over some actions that could only bring trouble. Some others made the point that there was no need for everybody in the black community to vote as long as those who knew what government was really all about exercised that right wisely for themselves and for those folks who attended church.[115]

Coalitional-incrementalist leaders, including organizers of the ACRC and the ANVL, differed significantly from the subordinates King described. Their goal was to register as many Black voters as possible and then to unify in support of the candidate who promised Blacks the most benefits.[116]

The goals of the coalitional-incrementalist leadership and the differences between them and the clientelistic-subordinates went beyond voter registration. There was also the question of who gets what, that is, who was to benefit from the political influence of the Black vote. Although Walden, Dobbs, and King all enjoyed heightened status in the Black community and the ability to intercede personally with Mayor Hartsfield, as leaders they were not satisfied with such particularistic benefits. They were critical of those who, because they owned cars, took no interest in the desegregation of public transportation, or because they could afford private education, showed no concern for upgrading the low quality of public education available in segregated schools.[117] Their desire to win benefits for all Black citizens rather than just a select few can be seen in the goals they pursued. For instance, persuading Mayor Hartsfield to hire Black policemen to patrol Black neighborhoods resulted in reducing police brutality that affected all Blacks. Convincing the mayor to seek improvements in living conditions in Black Atlanta—streets, lights, sewers, sidewalks—and the expansion of housing opportunities benefited all Blacks. The Black leadership and Mayor Hartsfield also jointly planned the arrest of a Black minister for refusal to sit in the area designated for Blacks on city buses to force the state court system to rule that segregation on public transportation was unconstitutional.[118]

The competitive electoral environment created the potential for Black political leverage; because the Black vote was unified by leaders who recognized their opportunity, it could play a decisive electoral role. The ANVL was formed in order to preempt partisan divisions among Blacks, deliver a bloc vote, and capitalize on the opportunity presented by competitive elections. Leaders of the progrowth coalition developed respect for their coalitional partners' ability to deliver votes, came to trust their integrity, and in exchange worked to satisfy many of their demands. Black voters in turn accorded the coalitional-incrementalist leadership increasing legitimacy because of their achievement of aspects of the Black agenda: desegregation (of water fountains, lunch counters, schools, and transportation) and the reduction of police brutality. Additionally, by repeatedly defeating Lester Maddox, the coalitional-incrementalists forced Atlanta's White voters to accept that segregationism was not a viable part of the political discourse in Atlanta, even while it remained triumphant in the rest of Georgia and much of the South. Maddox's defeats also signalled the resolution of one of the major crises of development for Blacks in any polity, the delegitimization of racially divisive and polarizing tactics.

Coalitional-incrementalist Black leaders were considered legitimate by the White electorate as well. The public's response to Sam Massell's attempt to racially polarize the electorate in 1973 was testimony to this fact. Furthermore, the absence of public panic during the turmoil between the business community and Maynard Jackson contrasts with the success that growth coalitions have had in other cities in sowing anxiety about the consequences of redistribution by other Black mayoral candidates and White populist mayors.

Because of the successes of Black coalitional-incrementalist leaders, the numbers of potential leaders who believed that biracial elite bargaining was the most effective means of conflict resolution and demand satisfaction grew. The successors to the ANVL defined two additional goals: Black penetration of public and private decisionmaking posts, and the reallocation of economic power to African-Americans. Blacks steadily increased their numbers on the city council, then captured the office of vice-mayor, and have held the mayor's office since 1973. Genuine biracial consultation on issues that affect the future of the metropolitan area has been institutionalized in the Atlanta Action Forum, the Chamber of Commerce, and other organizations. This biracial consultation appears likely to continue long after the city council becomes almost all Black. Progress has been made on African-American economic empowerment through affirmative action hiring practices, as well as an ambitious minority business enterprise program. Both these programs functionally mimic the patronage policies that historically have enabled White ethnic groups to translate group political power into group economic advancement.

Finally, the successes of the coalitional-incrementalists have had an inverse affect on the legitimacy and appeal of the two other segments of Black political leadership. The leverage that Black voters had in electoral politics in Atlanta made the subordinates' anxiety that any demands made of the White business leadership might jeopardize the relationship seem unnecessarily accommodationist. More interesting and more complex is the relationship between the coalitional-incrementalists and the separatist-messianics.

Clientelistic-Subordinate Leadership

The subordinate Black leaders already mentioned, who opposed the ANVL's efforts to register Black voters during the 1930s and 1940s, feared that if Walden and King Sr. rocked the boat, White leaders might rescind the few privileges that they as Black leaders enjoyed. This anxiety characterized Atlanta's subordinate Black leadership of the 1960s and 1970s as well.

During and after the lunch-counter desegregation efforts led by Atlanta University students, some Black leaders feared a backlash by previously sympathetic White leaders. C. A. Scott and the *Atlanta Daily World*, which he published, advocated the acceptance of Black subordination throughout the 1950s and 1960s while the coalitionist leadership was expanding to include many of the protest leaders. The *Daily World* was a constant critic of the activities of the Southern Christian Leadership Conference during the 1950s and early 1960s. Scott editorially warned Black voters to show restraint in the aftermath of the 1965 Voting Rights Act, not to try to exercise too much political power at the ballot box too soon, and to divide their votes between parties and factions rather than voting as a bloc.[119] In the 1969 mayoral election, the *Daily World* feared disruption of the business-Black alliance and endorsed Rodney Cook for mayor. In 1973 the paper endorsed Sam Massell over Maynard Jackson and refused to withdraw its endorsement even after Massell injected racial demagoguery into the campaign. The paper claimed that Jackson was too radical, warning that his election would "accelerate white flight to the suburbs," and admonished Blacks to "show appreciation where it is due."[120]

The very small numbers of Blacks who supported mayoral candidates Rodney Cook in 1969 or Sam Massell in 1973 is one indication of the clientelistic-subordinates' lack of followers. Their acceptance of White political domination was discredited by the coalitional-incrementalists' ability to win Black political empowerment without provoking a White backlash.

Separatist-Messianic Leadership

As president of Morehouse College and a venerated Black leader, Dr. Benjamin Mays was able to bridge the gap between the more youthful protest leaders and the coalitional-incrementalists. He pointed out that after the admixture of protest and negotiation leaders and the formation of such new organizations as the Atlanta Summit Leadership Conference, those protest leaders who refused to recognize the benefits of biracial negotiation became increasingly isolated and militant. The character of the Student Nonviolent Coordinating Committee (SNCC) changed—in Atlanta and throughout the country—in the latter part of the 1960s, becoming both more separatist and more conflict-oriented.

The SNCC leadership was responsible for the only disturbances in Atlanta that approached being riots. In 1966 and 1967, mobs caused much destruction of property in the impoverished Black neighborhoods of Summerhill, Vine City, and Dixie Hills. While SNCC drew greater attention to neighborhood inequity through these efforts, the community's demands for street repairs and additional parks were not calls for Black separatism, nor were these issues that necessarily pitted White against Black. Rather, the problems of poor quality service delivery resulted from inadequate representation of the interests of Black neighborhoods at city hall.[121] A petition signed by more than a thousand residents after the Dixie Hills disturbance demanded that SNCC and Stokely Carmichael "get out of the community and allow the people to handle their own affairs."[122] Instead of yielding neighborhood leadership, Black politicians and ministers worked together with residents to help restore order and prevent additional violence. Not only was an ombudsman organization created for Atlanta's neighborhoods, but another consequence of this mobilization was the election of four more Black members of the city council in 1969 (up from one in 1965).[123]

Even Atlanta's most renowned protest leader, Hosea Williams, mixed the tactics of biracial elite bargaining with protest. Williams, Ralph Abernathy, and Andrew Young were Martin Luther King Jr.'s closest advisors in the SCLC. Young was known as the moderate who had the negotiating skills and demeanor to win concessions from Whites over a bargaining table, while Williams believed in mobilizing Black citizenry for marches, boycotts, and any other activities that brought opposing parties to the brink of confrontation. He said:

> Yes, I never believed that any progress can be made other than through confrontation. Andy [Young] believed that a lot of things could be accomplished around a table, and I just didn't believe it 'cause I think a mental thing had to take place first in white people's mind. . . . I thought you really had to take him to some type of physical confrontation and hurt his pocketbook was the main way—boycotts and things of that sort—to bring him around, to really convince him.[124]

Because of Blacks' history of success in incrementally gaining greater political empowerment in Atlanta, Williams's militancy never had a separatist, reject-the-system accent to it. He organized and led boycotts against such major Atlanta employers as Sears, Coca-Cola, and Rich's Department Store, with the goals of increasing the numbers of Blacks hired by these firms and speeding the pace of promotions for Blacks. He used these tactics to bring the chief executives of these companies to the bargaining table to negotiate settlements.[125] His goals, and even the companies he targeted for economic boycotts in Atlanta, were often the same as those of leaders like Jesse Hill who preferred more quiet negotiations.[126]

Two *Atlanta Constitution* reporters recognized the function of the positive dialectic of Black leadership when they explained that Hosea Williams and other separatist-messianics in Atlanta "serve a very useful function in the Black community. They go on and on, calling for this and that, getting everything stirred up. Then some other Black can come in and whatever he says short of their position looks like the greatest kind of moderation."[127] Because of the responsiveness of White political and business leaders to the demands of coalitional-incrementalist Black leaders—whom they could not afford to alienate because of the electoral calculus of the city's politics—Atlanta was not a fertile area for the cultivation of separatist-messianic sentiments. Severing interdependence with White political leaders, as Black separatist and Black nationalist leaders advocated, was an unpopular strategy in a city where Blacks had gained considerable benefits as a result of just such biracial alliances.[128]

The Positive Dialectic

The differences that emerged in the early 1960s between the coalitionist leadership and student groups were not over goals but tactics. Both groups were fighting to end racial discrimination and the denial of civil rights to Blacks. Direct action protests and boycotts were the only tactics available to the Atlanta University students who refused to leave segregated lunch counters or to patronize segregated businesses. In contrast, the tactics that brought the ANVL its victories were negotiation with White political and business leaders, the exchange of electoral support for the satisfaction of salient Black demands, and reliance on the federal court system.

The different tactics of older coalitionist leaders and students were *complementary* because the two groups were pursuing the same goals. The protest leaders could attract attention and create an atmosphere of urgency much more quickly than the ANVL leadership. But the protest leaders had no contacts with the White political leadership and no experience in negotiating solutions to political problems that amounted to significant redistributions of political power. Ultimately, the successful desegregation of lunch counters in downtown Atlanta stores was negotiated by the established Black leadership, led by Benjamin Mays. Jack L. Walker interviewed a member of the coalitional-incrementalist leadership, who "acknowledged the importance of the student protests in bringing 'more integration in less than two years than we gained in ten,' but he argued that 'they will never get anything done on their own because they are cut off; they work in a righteous vacuum over there.'"[129]

Another example of the complementarity of the separatist-messianic and the coalitional-incrementalist leaderships involved the previously mentioned problem of inequitable distribution of city services that typified poor Black neighborhoods in Atlanta and across the nation. Beginning in 1963 the SNCC organized protests, rent strikes, and sit-ins to call attention to problems such as irregular garbage pickup, poor libraries, inadequate recreational facilities, unpaved streets, and substandard housing. The SNCC presented a grievance statement that demanded "that *all* the grievances of our communities be met—and met at once."[130] At about the same time, the Atlanta Summit Leadership Conference was forming with a similar agenda that included school desegregation, equality in housing, equal access to all public facilities, and the improvement of neighborhood services. Mayor Allen appointed a committee to work with the Summit group, but most of their attention was given to school issues rather than neighborhood problems. After the Watts riot in 1965, and a visit to Atlanta by Martin Luther King Jr., the mayor briefly gave his attention to the problems of Atlanta's poor neighborhoods.[131] When rioting erupted in 1966–67, the mayor blamed and marginalized the SNCC and Stokely Carmichael as "outside agitators" interested in violence; he also took comfort from the fact that Black political and civic leaders came to his side and helped resolve the disturbances. But when the NAACP, the Anti-Defamation League, the Southern Regional Council, the Council of Human Relations of Greater Atlanta, and even the city's newspapers pleaded with the mayor to take quicker, more forceful action on behalf of the neighborhoods, he stepped up the city's plodding efforts. The 10 worst slums of the city were identified, and service delivery as well as housing code enforcement were improved dramatically in an ad hoc manner. The biracial Community Relations Commission was also created as an ombudsman organization to institutionalize the city's ability to respond to neighborhood grievances. Finally, in response to the perception that inadequate housing was the biggest problem of the lot, the mayor appointed the Housing Resources Committee, which set a five-year goal of 17,000 new units of low- and moderate-income housing, with more than half to be completed in the first two years.[132] Ronald Bayor is correct in concluding that the "riot clearly speeded up the process of change already begun."[133] Yet it is important to recognize that change was possible because the mayor had an alternative to the SNCC—he could turn to a set of Black leaders whom he considered legitimate and who would not issue ultimatums—and the neighborhood activists had an alternative to protest, violence, and police reprisals—they could trust that the same Black leaders would wrest significant concessions from the city administration and guarantee that their battle was not in vain.

The protest leadership initially considered Walden and the ANVL leadership Uncle Toms who had "done little but feather their own nests."[134] But such charges did not jeopardize the legitimacy of the coalitionist leadership, because these leaders had a record of incremental accomplishments and diffuse legitimacy. Ultimately, the protest leaders recognized that the hard bargaining of the coalitionist leadership was, if not sufficient, certainly necessary for the advancement of Black empowerment. This resulted in an expansion of the ranks of the coalitionist leadership, as "some of the younger Black professional people who had sided with the students in their earlier confrontations with the older leadership groups joined with the remnants of the Walden cadre to form a new leadership class."[135] This next generation of coalitional-incrementalist leadership included the owner of the newly established *Atlanta Inquirer* and confidant of the protest leadership, Jesse Hill, Walden's protege state Senator Leroy Johnson (elected in 1963), and the first Black alderman, Q. V. Williamson (elected in 1965). Together they helped to establish the Atlanta Summit Leadership Conference, which superseded the ANVL as the organizational vehicle of Atlanta's Black coalitional-incrementalist leadership. By 1969 student protest leader Lonnie King was president of the Atlanta branch of the NAACP. He headed the efforts to resolve the school desegregation impasse, in which the Atlanta Action Forum, another organizational vehicle for coalitionist leadership, played a crucial role.[136]

The fruits of the relationship with the growth coalition, directly under Hartsfield and Allen, and through such organizations as the Action Forum in the Massell and Jackson tenures, resulted in the growth of the legitimacy of the coalitional-incrementalist leadership as well as an expansion of their ranks.[137] These leaders supported the candidacies of Maynard Jackson and Andrew Young, who emerged from their ranks with biracial support, and joined these mayors in governing the city of Atlanta.

Six

Subordination or Empowerment?

This book has posited answers to two broad questions. First, it has sought to explain why some cities with sizable Black populations that remain a minority of the electorate have been the sites of incremental Black empowerment—as measured by participation in a dominant coalition, Black office-holding, and achievement of political agenda items—when other similar cities have long remained sites of Black political subordination. Second, as is captured in its subtitle, which emphasizes the development of Black leadership, this book proffers both a dynamic theory to explain the emergence and evolution of Black political leaders and a typology of Black leadership. To the layperson, the uneven distribution of talented Black leaders who are perceived as legitimate by Black and White voters is enough to explain cities' differing levels of success in Black political empowerment. Some cities seem blessed with Black leaders who can forge biracial coalitions, and other cities have no such luck, according to this perspective. The structural theory of leadership formation I have posited shows that the distribution of biracially legitimate leaders is nonrandom.

Electoral Competition

My studies of Philadelphia and Atlanta, as well as early-twentieth-century Chicago, confirmed the hypothesis that electoral competitiveness creates opportunities for leaders in the Black community to mobilize a united Black vote to play a decisive role in electoral outcomes. Under such conditions, Black leaders had the negotiating leverage to win incrementally a genuine reallocation of political power. Conversely, the examination of Chicago and Gary showed that when elections were noncompetitive, Black leaders had almost no leverage with which they could bargain for group empowerment; the dominant party coalition did not need Black votes, and the opposition coalition was too small to win elections and facilitate the reallocation of political power.

In Philadelphia, a long-lived Republican machine that blocked the political advancement of Blacks was defeated in 1951 after a series of political scandals depleted confidence in the Republican administration. Intraparty electoral competition between a liberal-reform faction and a rejuvenated Democratic organization soon emerged. Black votes became a pivotal battlefield in this competition, and Black voters won numerous benefits that were empowering or potentially empowering, including civil service reforms that brought numerous well-educated Blacks into the city workforce, the election or appointment of Blacks to citywide offices, the nation's first civilian police review board, and Philadelphia's first Black Democratic member of the House of Representatives. The Democratic organization got the upper hand in this struggle during the mid-1960s and the 1970s and elected the city's first Irish and Italian mayors, James Tate and Frank Rizzo. Yet throughout this period intraparty factional competition and interparty competition continued unabated and contributed to the resilience of the biracial liberal-reform alliance. The highlight of this coalition's efforts during the 1970s was the defeat of Frank Rizzo's effort to change the city charter's prohibition of more than two consecutive mayoral terms. When Rizzo stepped aside, the biracial liberal-reform alliance elected Bill Green in 1979. The 1979 elections again demonstrated the bargaining and empowerment leverage that Black voters possessed when their votes could have a decisive impact on electoral outcomes. After Green defeated the city's top Black candidate in the Democratic primary, the Republican mayoral candidate actively wooed the Black vote. This action raised the ante for the endorsements of Black leaders and forced Green to promise to appoint a Black to the city's number-two post. The appointment went to Wilson Goode, who became the city's first Black mayor four years later.

Atlanta represents a second demonstration that electoral competition creates the conditions for minority empowerment. In Atlanta's nonpartisan political system, political competition between a progrowth faction of the White community that sought to make Atlanta the economic capital of the South and an insular, traditionalist faction that sought to maintain racial segregation and feared interaction with northern economic elites emerged in the 1940s. Initially Black voters aligned with the progrowth faction of the White community, because the traditionalist or "wool hat" faction advocated strict segregationism. By electing progrowth mayors, Blacks accomplished the first priority on their political agenda, the preclusion of segregationists like Lester Maddox from local office and the exclusion of race-baiting groups like the Colombians from even junior membership status in the city's governing coalition. Aside from fostering this "oasis of racial tolerance," other achievements included a redress of police brutality through the appointment of the city's first Black police officers; the reduction in the inequity of the distribution of certain city services, such as street lighting, that helped reduce crime and improve the climate along the main streets of the Black community, the election of a Black to the Atlanta School Board, and the peaceful desegregation of public accommodations and schools in Atlanta. By the late 1960s this biracial coalition had matured significantly. Blacks, no longer junior partners, bolted from the progrowth candidate and elected a liberal Democrat in 1969. Black voters also successfully scuttled the growth elite's plans for a rapid transit system. By 1973 the coalition between the Black community and White growth elites was reconstructed, but leading the coalition was the city's first Black mayor, Maynard Jackson. The rapid transit system was approved but only after the city's new allocation of political power was recognized through significant concessions in administrative hiring and transit routes that benefited Blacks.

Politics in the early part of the century in Chicago are a third demonstration that conditions of electoral competition create opportunities for Black leaders to play a decisive role in electoral outcomes and create leverage for incremental Black political empowerment. In Chicago, Republican mayor William "Big Bill" Thompson won the mayoralty in 1915, 1919, and 1927 in highly competitive elections that could not have been won without a Black bloc vote. With the mayor's support, Blacks won positions as alderman, committeeman, and member of the House of Representatives and enough jobs in the city bureaucracy to be just shy of parity with their proportion of the city's population. In the era of Democratic mayor Edward Kelly (1933–47), mayoral politics remained competitive. Black voters slowly withdrew their loyalty to the GOP as Kelly assiduously wooed their votes. Indicative of incremental Black empowerment was the election of a Black Democrat to Congress, the appointment of another Black as chairman of the Chicago Housing Authority, and the initiation by Mayor Kelly of desegregation policies in schools and housing that produced vigorous White protests. When Mayor Kelly left office in 1947, competition for the Black vote in Chicago ended, and during subsequent decades Black power was rolled back.

The studies of Chicago and Gary also verify the relationship between electoral competition and Black empowerment by demonstrating that under noncompetitive conditions in which Black votes were superfluous to the electoral coalition, no advances were made in Black political empowerment. Black leaders who sought to reallocate political power had few tools and little leverage with which to do so. The Democratic party organizations in both cities constructed their political monopolies by combining White ethnic, ward-based electoral support with support or at least acquiescence from a business community that refrained from bankrolling either Republican or reformist opponents. Black votes came cheaply to these organizations because of Democratic party identification and a plethora of low-level patronage jobs that members of White ethnic groups no longer coveted. But Black votes were in any case superfluous to the victories of the Daley and Chacharis organizations in most municipal elections, and Black defections to whatever opposition existed did not threaten the Democratic organizations' political domination. Because Black political leaders had no electoral leverage with which to demand political empowerment, they either capitulated and cooperated with the organization to maintain Black subordination (as illustrated by the behavior of so many Black politicians and ministers described in chapters 2 and 3) or they challenged their domination, albeit ineffectively, by preaching separatism, advocating protests, and offering a messianic vision.

Finally, *Subordination or Empowerment?* has demonstrated that even with the constraints that local elected officials faced, Black mayors and city councils that were led by biracial reformers did much to advance minority empowerment. Even though they came to power at a time when the cities are losing ground in a battle with the suburbs for economic dynamism and statewide political clout, Black leaders and Black constituents captured a much greater share of the still quite sizable benefits that are the upshot of political control in these cities. Even though they were working within a capitalist framework that typically delivers greater rewards to those minority group members with more resources than less, coalitional-incrementalist Black leaders still delivered political and economic empowerment to all group members. Moreover, the disproportionate benefits that middle-class Blacks receive in the process of Black empowerment moves Blacks forward in the pluralist distributional queue in the same way that White ethnic immigrants gained political and economic power. The Black underclass of today faces more severe conditions than the comparable poorest of each White immigrant group, but this has more to do with changes in the international and domestic political economies and the job structure in American cities than with the shortcomings of Black mayors. My conclusions regarding the empowering accomplishments of Black elected and appointed officials and biracial reform coalitions represent an empirical counterpoint to the largely theoretical work of Adolph Reed Jr., Robert C. Smith, and James Jennings.[1]

Even though coalitional-incrementalists often climb to power as junior partners in urban growth coalitions, there is no imperative that they remain junior partners. In Philadelphia and Atlanta, Black-led dominant coalitions were neither puppets nor the executive committee of some ruling group of influentials. On this matter of the power that Black representatives have within the biracial coalition I differ significantly with Clarence N. Stone's interpretation of Atlanta politics. To equate the record of Atlanta's biracial leadership with the Chicago of Richard J. Daley, as Stone does, is not only wrong but is a dangerous dismissal of the efforts and accomplishments of coalitional-incrementalists in Atlanta.[2] Both cities do face "major unaddressed social problems"; all large cities in the United States share these unfortunate circumstances. But Atlanta has struggled to achieve much more than the "occasional hint" of Black empowerment with which Stone credits the city. Even though this achievement has not cured the problems of poverty, poor schools, crime, or inadequate housing, the extent of Atlanta's successes is most obvious when it is compared to Chicago. In Atlanta, African-Americans are senior partners in the governing coalition. They have used politics to achieve some of the agenda of the Black community and deliver benefits, albeit unevenly, to Black constituents. In Atlanta, Black leadership is considered legitimate by White political, economic, and civic leaders. In Chicago, Black leaders have been unable to achieve these accomplishments.

Of Strong Machines, Liberal Coalitions, and Great Leaders

The argument about the independent explanatory value of electoral competition presented in this book complements three other important arguments in the literature that purported to explain the process of minority empowerment. The first argument, focusing on urban political party machines, claims that where such organizations exist, they play a crucial role as the ladder for the political advancement of subordinated minorities. Ample evidence for this hypothesis comes from the historical record; the

Irish and Italians did indeed penetrate party organizations in numerous cities and gradually captured party and municipal offices and political power. The sensibility of this argument led both analysts and politicians, from James Q. Wilson in *Negro Politics* to the Kerner Commission, to lament publicly the weakening of urban political machines because of the presumed detrimental effect it would have on the empowerment of Blacks and Latinos.[3] Yet there are also numerous instances of party machines serving not as ladders but as lids on minority empowerment, blocking the ascendance and maintaining the subordination of members of White ethnic groups and African-Americans.[4] The shortcoming of this perspective is its failure to specify under what conditions political parties serve either as ladders for group empowerment or as lids on it. *Subordination or Empowerment?* shows that when party organizations competed with each other, or when factions within a dominant party produced intraparty electoral competition, the party served as a channel for the upward mobility of the subordinated Black population that found itself in a decisive position with respect to electoral outcomes. Philadelphia and early-twentieth-century Chicago offer, as discussed, numerous examples of the pressures of electoral competition and the potential decisiveness of Black votes forcing the party organization to cede political power to Blacks. Conversely, I have demonstrated that in the absence of electoral competition, that is, when a party organization attained the stature of a monopolistic machine—as was the case in both Chicago and Gary—the party represented a major impediment to the empowerment of Blacks. Political party organizations can be ladders for the empowerment of subordinated minority groups when these organizations are forced by electoral competition to reach out to new constituencies and further democratize the polity. Political party organizations function as lids that block minority empowerment when noncompetitive polities enable these organizations to become monopolistic parties that can afford to view subordinated minority group voters as superfluous.

A second argument in the literature that attempts to explain minority empowerment is derived from the pathbreaking work of Rufus Browning, Dale Rogers Marshall, and David Tabb. In *Protest Is Not Enough* and *Racial Politics in American Cities*, they argued that when the growing populations of Blacks and Latinos joined with White liberals in an electoral coalition that accounted for nearly half (or more) of the electorate, they could form a "liberal coalition" that could win citywide elections. This coalition could defeat formerly dominant antiempowerment "conservative coalition" candidates, elect sympathetic officials, and influence policy so that minority empowerment would be expanded.[5] Browning, Marshall, and Tabb have pushed the field forward dramatically, and their work deserves the lavish praise it has received. But at least one crucial step in their argument remains unexplored. Given the presence of the ingredients necessary for minority empowerment—a minority population and a White liberal segment that together approach half of the electorate—how can one explain why only some of the time such biracial reform coalitions are formed and minority empowerment is pursued? Do such liberal coalitions emerge to challenge and defeat conservative coalitions only under certain conditions, and, if so, what are these conditions? To be fair, Browning, Marshall, and Tabb recognize this problem; they note that in a number of their cases, "some of the fundamental resources for a minority-oriented coalition were present—in particular, sufficient numbers of minority population and liberal supporters—but coalitions did not form or could not be sustained because of conflict among potential partners or lack of unifying leadership."[6] The question remains: Can we say something systematic about the conditions that mitigate conflict among potential partners or otherwise lead the potential members of liberal coalitions to join together and seize their opportunity to defeat the conservative coalition that is blocking minority empowerment and urban democratization?

The case studies demonstrated that, when the dominant conservative polity appeared invincible—as it did in Chicago after the election of Richard J. Daley and in Chacharis's Gary—sizable segments of the Black electorate and White liberals as well either allowed themselves to be coopted or withdrew from the electorate (in local as opposed to state and national elections). That is, even though a coalition of White liberals, Blacks, and other disaffected groups could have totaled almost half of the electorate, such a coalition did not emerge because the requirements for victory seemed too daunting and the penalties for failure against a coalition that dominated most aspects of city politics were perceived to be too steep. However, the pattern that Browning, Marshall, and Tabb describe did occur in the cases I describe when electoral politics was competitive. White liberals and Blacks (and other subordinated groups) recognized that if they joined forces they might be able to defeat the dominant conservative coalition. A track record of victories or near victories (i.e., competitive elections) against the dominant conservative coalition existed and helped to form trust, a crucial ingredient in any coalition. The plausibility of electoral victory that is synonymous with competitive elections is a key ingredient in minimizing defection and mobilizing the kind of turnout that is usually necessary for victory.

A third argument in the literature on minority empowerment focuses on the variability of leadership talent. This argument suggests that where great leaders emerge, the political empowerment of formerly subordinated groups will follow. Where political subordination is maintained, the explanation is found in the absence of leadership in the subordinated group.[7] When looking at individual cases, this "great man" approach to history has appeal. But from a comparative perspective, its unsatisfactory nature becomes apparent: the question of why great leaders emerge in certain places and at certain times, in other words, the search for structural factors that create the conditions for great leadership, demands attention. Particularly when we recognize that certain cities (like Philadelphia and Atlanta) have had an abundance of White and Black leaders who were able to claim biracial legitimacy and advance Black empowerment, while other cities (like Chicago), have gone for long periods without such leadership, such nonrandom distribution of leadership talent further warrants attention to structural factors.

Yet leadership is a crucial, albeit dependent, variable, and the preceding two arguments about minority empowerment also emphasize the role and functions of leaders in producing successful minority empowerment. In cities where political party organizations served as ladders for minority empowerment, it is clear that a special type of minority leadership has emerged that can exist within the organization without being compromised and delegitimized by it. The converse is equally clear; in cities where party organizations function more like lids, the Black regular organization leadership appears coopted and is seen as illegitimate in many quarters. From the Browning, Marshall, and Tabb perspective, leadership is also crucial. The statement from their work cited earlier suggests that the absence of certain kinds of leaders is one of the reasons why liberal, empowering polities fail to form even when the other ingredients for such coalitions seem to exist. Only a certain type of leadership can at once mobilize large numbers of Blacks and Latinos and win the confidence of White liberals. Both these important strands of scholarship on minority empowerment point to the importance of a certain kind of leader who can command broad, biracial legitimacy. For this reason I undertook in this book to analyze a second puzzle about the emergence and evolution of Black political leadership.

A Typology of Black Leadership

A number of useful typologies of Black leadership can be found in the literature, as was noted in chapter 1. My goal was to construct a typology that elucidated the different leadership roles that contributed to the struggle for political empowerment. I presented a detailed elaboration of my typology of leadership in chapter 1, and in each case study I applied that typology to the Black political leadership structure. Here I summarize the findings.

In the two cases of noncompetitive polities that illustrated the pattern of the maintenance of political subordination, only two types of the tripartite leadership typology were in evidence. Clientelistic-subordinates who organized Black support for, and compliance with, the dominant organization that subordinated Blacks politically were present, particularly among Black elected officials and clergy. In contrast, fledgling Black leaders, like Lu Palmer in Chicago, refused to condone Black subordination and harangued against the situation of White political and economic domination. Sometimes they formed ad hoc organizations, such as the Fair Share Organization in Gary, to protest their political impotence and economic exploitation; they also supported the idea of independent Black candidacies. They dogmatically maintained their separatism by shunning any consideration of coalition formation with White groups who were also opposed to the dominant regime. All those who advocated biracial coalitions were vilified as Uncle Toms who would merely maintain Black subordination to Whites. This dynamic created what I have labeled the negative dialectic of Black leadership, in which separatist-messianics condemn and delegitimate fledgling coalitional-incrementalists, while clientelistic-subordinates criticize the same group for being dangerous radicals. In the absence of electoral success and the incremental reallocation of power to Blacks, coalitional-incrementalists are vulnerable to such charges.

In contrast, in the cases of competitive polities, not only these two types of Black leaders but also an ultimately crucial third type of leader, coalitional-incrementalists, were in evidence. Black coalitional-incrementalist leaders sought to end the political subordination of their constituents, and they chose to do this through participation in the electoral arena. Coalitional-incrementalists typically formed biracial coalitions with groups amenable to a reallocation of political power to Blacks. When Black support appeared decisive for electoral outcomes, coalitional-incrementalists and their constituents were in a position in which their votes could not be taken for granted and they had leverage that enabled them to make claims for incremental political empowerment. Electoral competition gave coalitional-incrementalists in Philadelphia and Atlanta what their fledgling counterparts in Chicago and Gary did not have: the opportunity to demonstrate that electoral mobilization could deliver group empowerment. Initially, the ability to deliver good jobs in the city bureaucracy to educated Blacks who faced private-sector discrimination and the ability to take credit for the nation's first civilian police review board won broad legitimacy for coalitional-incrementalist Black politicians and clergy in Philadelphia, such as Marshall Shepard and Raymond Pace Alexander. Separatist-messianics like Cecil Moore who scorned coalitions with Whites could not persuade voters that the coalitional-incrementalists were Uncle Toms who were no different than the Black clientelistic-subordinates. A decade later, leaders like William Gray, Charles Bowser, Samuel Evans, and Joseph Coleman played a key role in organizing a coalition and delivering Black votes that prevented Mayor Frank Rizzo from running for a third consecutive term. Although these leaders wanted a Black to head the biracial coalition, when Bill Green, a White reformer, won the Democratic party primary, the coalitional-incrementalists did not abrogate their coalition to support an independent, separatist-oriented candidacy. Instead they persuaded half of the Black voters in the city to support Green's mayoral bid. Among the steps taken by Mayor Green to advance Black empowerment, none was more significant than the appointment of Wilson Goode to the city's second highest post, managing director. Opposition to Goode's candidacy and to his administration was never cast in a polarized Black-versus-White manner, because Whites had grown accustomed to and comfortable with Blacks in decisionmaking positions.

Similarly, in Atlanta, separatist-messianics were unable to delegitimize the leadership of A. T. Walden or Martin Luther King Sr. after they (and their White business community allies) were able to claim credit for the hiring of the city's first Black police officers and the electoral repudiation of arch segregationist Lester Maddox. The success of Black leaders like Jesse Hill and Leroy Johnson in negotiating a reallocation of power during the 1960s led some separatist-messianics like Lonnie King to renounce their dogmatic disdain for biracial coalitions and to become prominent leaders of the coalitional-incrementalist type. In the late 1960s, separatist-messianics like Hosea Williams proffered charges that Black leaders like Maynard Jackson were participants in unholy alliances with Whites that would result in the advancement of a few Black politicians but no reallocation of power. But Black voters knew that biracial coalitions had delivered genuine political and economic empowerment that benefited middle- and working-class Blacks. These coalitions continued to deliver empowerment in the Massell administration, in Jackson's first two terms as mayor, and in subsequent administrations.

In both Philadelphia and Atlanta I observed the positive dialectic of Black leadership between the coalitional-incrementalists and the separatist-messianics. The separatist-messianics had to combat significant empirical evidence that demonstrated the utility of biracial coalitions for the advancement of Black empowerment. Their claims that progress could be made more rapidly and the benefits of empowerment distributed more equitably still resonated with many Black voters, including most of the coalitional-incrementalist leaders. Such charges prodded the coalitional-incrementalists to increase their efforts and set bolder terms for the allocation of power over public policy issues. But when given the opportunity to choose between coalitional-incrementalists and separatist-messianic leaders who charged that their opponents were not delivering genuine empowerment, voters overwhelmingly sided with the coalitional-incrementalists, who had a record of accomplishments.

As the coalitional-incrementalists grew stronger, the clientelistic-subordinates lost almost all of the support they had among Black voters. Their counsel to make more modest demands from White allies was based on a fear of backlash and disruption of the biracial coalition. Yet this fear was repeatedly proven to be unfounded as the competitive electoral environment forced White factions to accede to Black political leaders' demands.

Transformations from Monopolistic to Competitive Polities

Like so many endeavors that investigate large questions, this work has raised and addressed an additional question. I have argued that competitive electoral politics is the condition that creates opportunities for Black leaders to engineer incremental political empowerment. I have also argued that when minorities struggle for political power in a noncompetitive polity, the result will be the maintenance of political subordination. But the question remains: why and how do polities transform from noncompetitive to competitive electoral conditions? In other words, why do subordinated Blacks and other power-seeking groups who were previously fragmented, easily coopted, or demobilized, suddenly develop intragroup unity and intergroup coalitions that are necessary conditions for the empowerment of subordinated minorities? And why do power-holding groups that were part of the conservative monopolistic coalition abandon that coalition and help to make polities more competitive? The answers to these questions that I tentatively proffer here are significant for scholars interested in regime change, the dynamics of coalition formation, the engendering of ethnic or racial consciousness, and the creation of community.

One can hypothesize a few answers based on historically informed intuition. For instance, just as national governments that have long been stable often encounter turbulence or disruption when a long-lived leader dies, one would hypothesize that when a longstanding mayor or city boss who has presided over a noncompetitive polity dies, that polity is prone to instability and transformation. Critical elections theory also shows that dramatic events like the Great Depression transformed the national political alignment and destabilized longstanding Republican regimes in many big cities. One would hypothesize that rare events that reverberate throughout a region or a nation, like the depression, may account for a transformation from noncompetitive to competitive politics (and vice versa). Unfortunately, my case studies do not shed light on these two hypotheses, but they do illustrate two other explanations for such transformations: (1) an external enemy and (2) political scandals.

An External Enemy: Source of Coalitional Unity

The problematic tasks for coalitional-incrementalist leadership are the creation of unity among Black voters and the mobilization of a quiescent electorate in support of a coalition that challenges an anti-Black organization. As has been shown, a significant share of the Black population is often willing to support the subordinating coalition at the polls, and there are numerous leaders in politics and the clergy who follow a clientelistic-subordinate path. How, then, is Black anti–status quo unity forged in the face of the multiple incentives (e.g., patronage benefits, party identification and loyalty, inertia, fear of retribution) for supporting the dominant cooptative coalition? How are subordinated nonvoters mobilized? Of course, the fact that competition among White factions creates the opportunities for coalitional-incrementalist leaders is understood by some Black citizens, who recognize the leverage a united and mobilized Black electorate might have in a competitive polity. However, as the case studies demonstrate, it was primarily the emergence of highly visible and powerful political leaders who were zealously dedicated to maintaining or exacerbating the conditions of Black political subordination, functioning as a rallying point for Blacks, that led them to mobilize and unify. Much as Bull Connor's brutality functioned as a symbol against which Blacks and northern liberals rallied, leaders like Frank Rizzo, Jane Byrne, and Lester Maddox actually helped Black leaders both to discredit the clientelistic-subordinate leadership alternative and to mobilize former nonvoters. These external enemies did not maintain the status quo; rather, they increased Black subordination. The Black mobilizations to defeat Maddox's mayoral bids, Rizzo's attempts to change the city charter and later to win reelection, and Byrne's reelection bid were each turning points in their respective cities. Black voters' enmity for these individuals overcame lack of unity and acquiescence to subordination. Successful mobilization against these external enemies then provided Black voters with powerful examples of the successes that could be gained through participation in electoral politics in a competitive opposition coalition. Defeating these external enemies provided crucial legitimacy for coalitional-incrementalists. As has been shown, defeating enemies who seek to roll back even meager Black political power is not the same as winning Black empowerment; yet empirically these external enemies were steppingstones to minority empowerment. The importance of an external enemy against which a fledgling coalition can rally, a coalition that may not yet share programmatic common ground but does share diffuse antiregime sentiment, has been neglected in the theoretical literature on minority empowerment.

Chapter 4 showed that the Black vote in Philadelphia was divided along socioeconomic status lines. Blacks living in middle-class, better-educated wards gave the majority of their support to the liberal-reform faction (ADA and the GPM) led by Joseph Clark and Richardson Dilworth, which instituted civil service testing for public-sector jobs. Conversely, Black voters living in predominantly lower-status wards gave the majority of their support to the reborn Democratic organization, which doled out patronage. But Frank Rizzo's candidacy united Black voters and mobilized nonvoters to the point where 77 percent of them crossed party lines to vote for Republican Thacher Longstreth, and Black turnout reached 64 percent. This level of mobilization could not be reached in the 1975 election in which two opponents split the anti-Rizzo vote. But in the 1978 charter change referendum, the opportunity to vote up or down on Mayor Rizzo again united and mobilized Blacks in impressive numbers. Black voter registration efforts raised the Black proportion of the electorate from 32 to 38 percent, and Black turnout was 63 percent, nine points higher than in Rizzo's three-way race in 1975. Black unity in this mobilization was unprecedented;

96 percent of the Black vote opposed allowing Rizzo to run for a third consecutive term. Black candidates Hardy Williams and Charles Bowser could not mobilize and unify Black voters in multiple candidate races. But in a head-to-head race with a White Republican and a yes/no referendum vote on Rizzo's future, the virulent animosity that Black Philadelphians had for this external enemy produced quite historical unity and mobilization. These levels would be surpassed only in the mayoral election of Wilson Goode.

Mayor Jane Byrne exemplifies the same phenomenon. Many observers of Chicago politics give Byrne a major share of the credit for bringing to fruition the efforts of organizers in the Black community. Paul Kleppner wrote, "Byrne's actions and patronizing insults to the black community sowed the seeds of the political revolution that came to fruition in 1983."[8] What did Jane Byrne do? Her desire was two-fold: She did not want to cede the White ethnic vote to her likely opponent, Richard M. Daley, eldest son of the former mayor, and her strategy in this battle was to appear to be the staunchest defender of the color line. She also wanted to provoke a Black candidate to enter the mayoral race against her, so that she would face another opponent in the 1983 Democratic mayoral primary aside from Daley. She had captured the anti–status quo vote of Blacks simply because she was the only alternative to Bilandic, and she sought to insure that Daley would not reap a similar harvest. She had no fear of inciting the Black community, and she did not consider a Black candidate as a threat to her election; she was well aware of how poorly both Richard Newhouse and Harold Washington had done, even among Black voters, in their earlier bids. Her tactics for simultaneously accomplishing both these goals included the following: She angered Black Chicagoans and appealed to many Whites by refusing to promote the acting superintendent of police, who was Black, to the top public safety position and instead appointing a White candidate; by replacing two Black members of the school board with two White women who had gained notoriety as leaders of the antibusing movement; by choosing a White woman to be superintendent of schools rather than the sitting deputy superintendent, who was Black; and by replacing two Black Chicago Housing Authority board members with two Whites.

Byrne's outrageous behavior led separatist-messianic Lu Palmer to create the organization Chicago Black United Communities (CBUC) and to make his first foray into voter registration and mobilization. Palmer and CBUC made contributions to Washington's mayoral efforts without which he would not have won.

In Atlanta, Black unity was organized by the ANVL so that Black votes could be used as a weapon against segregationism. Following the quid pro quo offered by William Hartsfield, the appointment of Black police officers, the ANVL registered Black voters and organized them to turn out and vote for him. Blacks were also included in his "kitchen cabinet," and they won an expansion of Black residential areas and housing opportunities for the growing Black population. These Black achievements provoked a general hostile reaction from segregationist elements, including the Colombians, who tried to burn houses sold to Blacks, and a political neophyte named Lester Maddox. Maddox galvanized the considerable resentment toward Blacks and combined it with the latent racism of many Atlanta residents to produce a powerful political movement. He ran for the office of mayor in 1957 against Hartsfield, and he opposed Ivan Allen in 1961. Maddox won the White vote in both contests, but he lost the elections because he also galvanized Black voters to oppose him. Black unity was phenomenal, as more than 97 percent of Black voters voted for his opponents. This was far more unity than affluent Whites had offered the progrowth mayors (as table 5–3 showed).

Neglect of the theoretical and empirical significance of rallying subordinated forces against an external enemy results, I believe, from an underemphasis on conflict as a motivating factor in urban politics. In the initial phase of *coalition formation*, I see conflict against common opponents as a more likely basis for coalition than ideological affinity, trust among elites, or selective incentives. It is hard to dispute that these other factors played some minor role in coalition formation, and they are often the most important factors in explaining *coalition maintenance*.[9] But the coordination of opposition to a common enemy, be it an individual or an interest, is the major factor that explains coalition formation and, for our purposes, the development of Black unity and mobilization.

Clarence N. Stone's recent analysis of Black politics in Atlanta is a good example of how an exclusive theoretical emphasis on cooperation can obscure the empirical relevance of conflict. For example, his analysis of Atlanta's biracial coalition emphasizes two factors: that Atlanta's White business leadership and Black leaders cooperated to pursue a common interest in economic prosperity and that they subsequently developed a reservoir of skill in biracial negotiation over many years. But he gives little theoretical significance to the fact that the electoral alliance was imperative for both groups if their common enemy was to be defeated. This is an important distinction that is not subsumed by recognizing that the common enemy—the redneck, wool hat segregationists—were neither part of the business community nor progrowth boosters. I contend that, for Blacks, delegitimizing segregationism and ending the politics of exclusion was a more pressing issue in the early decades of the coalition, when the reservoir of biracial trust was still dry, than was economic growth.[10]

My analysis of Atlanta's biracial coalition also differs from Stone's in a more fundamental way. His argument focuses on informal arrangements to coordinate efforts between groups and promote *cooperation*; he states, "[M]y line of argument here points to another way of viewing urban communities; it points to the need to think about cooperation, its possibilities and limitations—not just any cooperation, but cooperation of the kind that can bring together people based in different sectors of a community's institutional life and that enables a coalition of actors to make and support a set of governing decisions.[11] Certainly, the selective incentives the business community could offer Black leadership became increasingly important; and the trust that was built through iterations of biracial bargaining was also a salient factor in the continuity and maintenance of Atlanta's biracial coalition. But these two variables do not address the more important question of the origins of this coalition. Why did Atlanta's business elite seek to form an electoral alliance with Blacks in the first place? Why didn't they try to entice working-class Whites with the lure of progrowth prosperity and jobs, for instance? What factor precluded a coalition of cooperation for financial gain by the have-nots, poor Whites and Blacks? A theory of urban politics that has cooperation as its point of departure, as Stone's regime theory does, is not adept at answering these questions because politics in the urban trenches quite often is a blood sport. *Conflict*, as well as cooperation, is central to urban politics, and one cannot understand the formation of Atlanta's biracial coalition (or many of the other important coalitions discussed in this book) without recognizing the importance of conflict and the political competition that is a surrogate for conflict. Both the business community and the Black community perceived the working-class "redneck" faction as their enemy, but for different reasons. The rednecks opposed rapid economic expansion and feared the social and cultural changes that would result from the relocation of northern business executives to what the local growth elites envisioned as the New York City of the South. The Black community naturally viewed the segregationist rednecks as their bitter enemies, and not because of redneck antipathy to economic restructuring; Black animosity toward Lester Maddox had nothing to do with his opposition to turning Atlanta into a national business headquarters. The basis for the biracial coalition that began in 1946 and yielded the history of trust and cooperation that Stone emphasizes was, therefore, a common external enemy that both the progrowth business faction and the Black community wanted to preclude from gaining mayoral power. The mutuality of interests in the benefits of economic growth did not become the raison d'être of the biracial coalition until the late 1960s—after segregationist candidates no longer appeared on Atlanta's ballots—when Blacks made their first demands about affirmative action hiring and minority business set-asides in the construction of MARTA. Although the segregationist conflict with Blacks is region- and time-specific, the forming of an alliance against a common enemy surely is not. The examples of Maddox, Rizzo, and Byrne demonstrate the role that conflict with a common external enemy plays in creating empowering coalitions; the concept of the external enemy as a source of unity, mobilization, and polity transformation is a fertile area for future scholarship.

Political Scandals and Polity Change

As the case studies reveal, a second factor, political scandals, created opportunities for coalitional-incrementalist Black leadership to emerge and work toward coalitional realignment that transformed polities from noncompetitive to competitive conditions. Political scandals discredited longstanding coalitions that appeared electorally invincible and that had subordinated Blacks in both Philadelphia and Gary. In Philadelphia, the Republican party organization dominated politics for the first half of the twentieth century. Even the depression and the popularity of FDR's New Deal policies could not interrupt the GOP's domination of the city. But a series of scandals that shocked the city toppled the corrupt Republican machine. Patricians and business leaders who had been important supporters of the GOP, as well as White ethnics and Black supporters, defected and joined the reform elements who had futilely battled the GOP for years. As shown in chapter 4, all Blacks, but especially the better-educated, benefited from the policies of the administrations of Joseph Clark and Richardson Dilworth. The competition between these reformers and an invigorated Democratic party continued to yield Black political empowerment.

In Gary, as shown in chapter 3, political scandals also played a crucial role in the transformation from Black political subordination to empowerment. The *New York Times* reported that the scandals uncovered "a maze of undercover manipulations that the Government charged were designed to disguise construction company kick-backs paid to the Gary Mayor" to win preferential economic treatment in the award-ing of city contracts.[12] Mayor Chacharis and more than 10 other high-ranking asso-ciates pled not guilty to a variety of charges that included money laundering and tax evasion. After federal prosecutors presented 75 witnesses and more than four hun-dred pieces of evidence, Chacharis pled guilty, and the charges against all others were dropped.[13] He resigned in January 1963, was convicted on all counts, and was sen-tenced to three years in federal prison. Only two months into his interim term, the scandals then brought down Mayor John Visclosky.[14] Because the scandals were in-vestigated by the Justice Department, Gary drew the attention of the nation's major newspapers and weekly journals. William E. Nelson and Philip Meranto wrote, "Dur-ing the long and controversial trial that ensued, Gary gained a national reputation as a city whose governance lay in the hands of an administration that was corrupt from top to bottom."[15] The crumbling Democratic organization turned to Black voters in an attempt to rebuild support against a growing reform movement. The organization picked Richard Hatcher to run for city council as part of its attempt to coopt Black support. But the Democratic machine had not stabilized, and Gary was transformed from a noncompetitive polity to a competitive polity. Four years later, the voters of Gary made history when Richard Hatcher became one of the first Black mayors of a major city of the United States.

Undoubtedly, other factors contributed to these polity transformations. The be-havior of external enemy Jane Byrne is not the only explanatory variable of the break-through election of Harold Washington; nor are the Chacharis scandals the complete explanation for the displacement of that regime by the Hatcher coalition. My goal is more modest than to find single, overarching explanatory variables. I do believe, however, that the evidence presented in the cases shows that both external enemies and political scandals are factors that contribute very significantly to the creation of opportunities for Black leaders and their allies to forge unity where it was absent, to mobilize formerly acquiescent electorates, and most critically to transform polities' electoral conditions from noncompetitive to competitive.

Notes

Chapter 1. Electoral Competition and the Emergence
of Political Leadership

1. Although economic inequality is typically exacerbated by political inequality, and the reduction of the latter often brings amelioration of the former, they are not the same, and democratization should not be evaluated by measures of economic inequality. Economic inequality is a product of market capitalism, and politics can affect this inequality only through regulatory and redistributive policies.

2. Nathan Glazer, "Blacks and Ethnic Groups: The Difference, and the Political Difference It Makes," *Social Problems* 18 (1971), pp. 444–461.

3. Martin Kilson, "Political Change in the Negro Ghetto, 1900–1940s," in *Key Issues in the Afro-American Experience*, ed. Nathan J. Huggins, Martin Kilson, and Daniel M. Fox (New York: Harcourt Brace Jovanovich, 1971), 2:182.

4. See Richard A. Keiser, "Explaining African-American Political Empowerment: 'Windy City' Politics from 1900 to 1983," *Urban Affairs Quarterly* 29:1 (September 1993), pp. 84–116.

5. See Ralph Bunche, "The Thompson-Negro Alliance," *Opportunity* 7 (1929), p. 78. For a flawed yet provocative discussion of the contemporary decline of urban Black political power, see Jim Sleeper, "The End of the Rainbow," *New Republic* (November 1, 1993), pp. 20–25.

6. The intellectual antecedents of these definitions can be found in the distinction between formal and informal cooptation in the work of Philip Selznick. See Selznick, *TVA and the Grass Roots* (Berkeley: University of California Press, 1949), pp. 14–15, 261.

7. The following discussion of the indicators of growing minority political power builds on much earlier work by political scientists, including Elmer E. Cornwell Jr., "Party Absorp-

tion of Ethnic Groups: The Case of Providence, Rhode Island," *Social Forces* 38 (March 1960), pp. 205–210; Theodore J. Lowi, *At the Pleasure of the Mayor* (New York: Free Press, 1964); and particularly Rufus P. Browning, Dale Rogers Marshall, and David H. Tabb, *Protest Is Not Enough: The Struggle of Blacks and Hispanics for Equality in Urban Politics* (Berkeley: University of California Press, 1984).

8. A third type of influence over public policy that might indicate group empowerment is the distribution of city services, such as garbage pickup, street repairs, police protection, or recreational facilities. If a group that was previously discriminated against subsequently receives a favorable distribution of such services, this might be evidence of the incremental political empowerment of that group. Yet there is some evidence that neutral bureaucratic rules govern the distribution of city services. If this were the case, then a shift from discrimination to equal treatment of the group in the provision of city services might merely indicate a better enforcement of neutral rules, rather than incremental empowerment. Because of this ambiguity, this measure is not used in this study. For a sampling of the debate, see Kenneth Mladenka, "Rules, Service Equity and Distributional Decisions," *Social Science Quarterly* 59 (1978), pp. 192–202, and Bryan D. Jones, "Party and Bureaucracy: The Influence of Intermediary Groups on Urban Public Service Delivery," *American Political Science Review* 75:3 (September 1981), pp. 688–700.

9. See the discussion of the significance of middle-class leadership for ethnic politics in Raymond E. Wolfinger, *The Politics of Progress* (Englewood Cliffs, N.J.: Prentice Hall, 1974), pp. 57–73.

10. A number of democratic theorists have argued that political competition is a crucial explanatory variable for the emergence of democracy and participatory rights. Participation is clearly far from empowerment, but participatory rights are a necessary condition for political empowerment. For Joseph A. Schumpeter, democracy was simply "a competitive struggle for the people's vote." Robert A. Dahl posited two variables, political competitiveness and the diffusion of participatory rights, in his explanation of the transformation from political hegemonies to polyarchies. E. E. Schattschneider argued that the losers in the competitive political struggle were responsible for expansion of the scope of conflict. Myron Weiner and Harry Eckstein, in discussions of the achievement of participatory rights in the postcolonial world, each argued that competition between governing elites and their opponents triggered mass political participation. See Schumpeter, *Capitalism, Socialism, and Democracy* (New York: Harper and Row, 1942), p. 269; Dahl, *Polyarchy: Participation and Opposition* (New Haven: Yale University Press, 1971), chap. 1; Schattschneider, *The Semisovereign People* (Hinsdale, Ill.: Dryden Press, 1960), p. 16; Weiner, "Political Participation: Crisis of the Political Process," in *Crises and Sequences in Political Development*, ed. Leonard Binder (Princeton: Princeton University Press, 1971), p. 172; and Eckstein, "The Idea of Political Development: From Dignity to Efficiency," *World Politics* 34:4 (July 1982).

11. William H. Standing and James A. Robinson, "Inter-Party Competition and Primary Contesting: The Case of Indiana," *American Political Science Review* 52:4 (December 1958), pp. 1066–1077.

12. Many similar measures of electoral competition exist. See, for example, Julius Turner, "Primary Elections as the Alternative to Party Competition in 'Safe' Districts," *Journal of Politics* 15:2 (May 1953); Austin Ranney and Wilmoore Kendall, "The American Party Systems," *American Political Science Review* 48 (June 1954), pp. 477–485; Austin Ranney, "Parties in State Politics," chap. 3, in *Politics in the American States*, ed. Herbert Jacob and Kenneth Vines (Boston: Little Brown, 1971), pp. 84–89; Joseph A. Schlesinger, "A Two-Dimensional Scheme for Classifying the States According to Degree of Inter-Party Competition," *American Political Science Review* 49 (1955), pp. 1120–1128; Robert T. Golembiewski, "A Taxonomic Approach to State Political Party Strength," *Western Political Quarterly*

11:3 (September 1958), pp. 494–513; Charles E. Gilbert and Christopher Clague, "Electoral Competition and Electoral Systems in Large Cities," *Journal of Politics* 24 (1962), pp. 323–349; Richard Dawson and James Robinson, "Inter-Party Competition, Economic Variables, and Welfare Policies in the American States," *Journal of Politics* 25 (1963), pp. 265–289; David G. Pfeiffer, "The Measurement of Inter-Party Competition and Systemic Stability," *American Political Science Review* 61 (1967), pp. 457–467; Richard E. Zody and Norman R. Luttbeg, "An Evaluation of Various Measures of State Party Competition," *Western Political Quarterly* 21 (1968), pp. 723–724; and William H. Flanigan and Nancy H. Zingale, "Measures of Electoral Competition," *Political Methodology* 1:4 (Fall 1974), pp. 31–60.

13. Golembiewski, "Taxonomic Approach to Political Party Strength," p. 498.

14. Martin Shefter, "Political Incorporation and the Extrusion of the Left: Party Politics and Social Forces in New York City," in *Studies in American Political Development*, vol. 1, ed. Karen Orren and Stephen Skowronek (New Haven: Yale University Press, 1986).

15. Cities in which African-Americans are a majority of the electorate prior to the election of the first Black mayor are not the subject of this book because, in my opinion, they do not represent cases that illuminate the problems and prospects that African-Americans and other subordinated minorities face in trying to win political empowerment. The leader of a numerical majority can afford to approach dealings with other power contenders and the formulation of a policy agenda differently from the way the leader of a numerical minority would, subordinated or not. Therefore, the experience of the struggle for empowerment in cities in which African-Americans were not a numerical minority should not be used to test the validity of the arguments presented.

16. These labels are respectively used in Gunnar Myrdal, *An American Dilemma* (New York: Harper, 1944), pp. 18–23; Oliver C. Cox, "Leadership among Negroes in the United States," in *Studies in Leadership*, ed. Alvin W. Gouldner (New York: Harper, 1950), pp. 228–271; James Q. Wilson, *Negro Politics: The Search for Leadership* (Glencoe, Ill.: Free Press, 1960), especially pp. 214–254; Daniel C. Thompson, *The Negro Leadership Class* (Englewood Cliffs, N.J.: Prentice Hall, 1963); Hanes Walton Jr. and Leslie Burl McLemore, "Portrait of Black Political Styles," *Black Politician* 2:2 (October 1970), pp. 9–13; and Donald L. Tryman, "A Typology of Black Leadership," *Western Journal of Black Studies* 1:1 (March 1977), pp. 18–22.

17. Kilson, "Political Change in the Negro Ghetto," pp. 167–192, quotation on p. 183.

18. Carter G. Woodson, *The Mis-Education of the Negro* (Washington, D.C.: Associated Publishers, 1933), pp. 115–116.

19. Cox, "Leadership among Negroes in the United States," p. 245.

20. Adolph Reed Jr., "The Black Urban Regime: Structural Origins and Constraints," *Comparative Urban and Community Research* 1 (1988), pp. 138–189; Robert C. Smith, "Recent Elections and Black Politics: The Maturation or Death of Black Politics?" *PS* 23:2 (June 1990), pp. 160–162; Tryman, "A Typology of Black Leadership"; Manning Marable, *The Crisis of Color and Democracy* (Monroe, Me.: Common Courage Press, 1992); and James Jennings, *The Politics of Black Empowerment: The Transformation of Black Activism in Urban America* (Detroit: Wayne State University Press, 1992). Even Cornel West in *Race Matters* makes the unfortunate mistake of issuing a blanket dismissal of the accomplishments of Black mayors.

21. See Cox, "Leadership among Negroes in the United States," pp. 228–271; Wilson, *Negro Politics*, especially pp. 214–254; Alphonso Pinkney, *Red, Black and Green: Black Nationalism in the United States* (New York: Cambridge University Press, 1976); Walton and McLemore, "Portrait of Black Political Styles"; Tryman, "A Typology of Black Leadership"; and Adolph Reed, "Pan-Africanism: Ideology for Liberation?" in *Pan-Africanism*, ed. Robert Chrisman and Nathan Hare (Indianapolis and New York: Bobbs Merrill, 1974).

22. A good discussion of the minutiae that constitute differences among these subtypes can be found in Manning Marable, "Black Nationalism in the 1970s: Through the Prism of Race and Class," *Socialist Review* 10:2–3 (March–June 1980), pp. 57–108.

23. Pinkney, *Red, Black and Green*, p. 4.

24. On Carmichael's less well-known odyssey across the spectrum of Black nationalism, see Robert L. Allen, *Black Awakening in Capitalist America* (New York: Doubleday, 1969), pp. 247–253.

25. Wilson discusses the "militant's" attitude toward the White power structure. See Wilson, *Negro Politics*, pp. 226–227.

26. Jennings, *Politics of Black Empowerment*.

27. Francis Fox Piven and Richard Cloward, *Poor Peoples Movements* (New York: Pantheon Books, 1977), p. 36.

28. Marable, "Black Nationalism in the 1970s," p. 94.

29. Manning Marable, "Black Politics and the Challenges for the Left," *Monthly Review* 41:11 (April 1990), pp. 22–31.

30. On the growth, size, and significance of the Black middle class, compare Bart Landry, *The New Black Middle Class* (Berkeley: University of California Press, 1987) and Thomas Boston, *Race, Class and Conservatism* (Boston: Unwin Hyman, 1988).

31. For example, Marxist-Leninist–inclined African-American leaders and followers believe that the Black working class and poor are the vanguard of the proletariat and that the forces of history dictate their eventual triumph. Similarly, the Nation of Islam preaches that Blacks are the world's "original" race, that Elijah Muhammad was divinely inspired, and that in the imminent providential ascendance of a moral order, Louis Farrakhan will be the redeemer. On the similarity between the eschatology of Marxism and Catholicism, which both prophesy a millennium in which the select, true believers triumph over the hedonistic, immoral oppressors, see Bertrand Russell, *A History of Western Philosophy* (New York: Simon and Schuster, 1945), pp. 363–364.

32. Wilson Jeremiah Moses, *Black Messiahs and Uncle Toms: Social and Literary Manipulations of a Religious Myth*, (1982), rev. ed. (University Park: Pennsylvania State University Press, 1993), pp. 7–8.

33. See Ronald Radosh, "From Protest to Black Power: The Failure of Coalition Politics," in *The Great Society Reader*, ed. Marvin E. Gettleman and David Mermelstein (New York: Random House, 1967), and Raymond Hall, *Black Separatism in the United States* (Hanover, N.H.: University Press of New England, 1978).

34. Lewis M. Killian, "The Significance of Extremism in the Black Revolution," *Social Problems* 20 (1972), pp. 41–48.

35. In his discussion of Black leadership, Daniel C. Thompson wrote, "As a rule the Uncle Tom type of leader employs one basic strategy—protest." Yet many would intuitively associate protest tactics with messianic leadership. See Thompson, *The Negro Leadership Class*, p. 166.

36. The Kerner Commission explained:

> Black Power rhetoric and ideology actually express a lack of power. . . . Powerless to make any fundamental changes in the life of the masses—powerless, that is, to compel white America to make those changes—many advocates of Black Power have retreated into an unreal world, where they see an outnumbered and poverty-stricken minority organizing itself independently of whites and creating sufficient power to force white America to grant its demands.

National Advisory Commission on Civil Disorders (Kerner Commission), *Report* (New York: Bantam Books, 1968), pp. 234–235.

37. Ann Ruth Wilner, *The Spellbinders: Charismatic Political Leadership* (New Haven: Yale University Press, 1984), p. 93. Also see H. H. Gerth and C. Wright Mills, *From Max Weber: Essays in Sociology* (New York: Oxford University Press, 1946), p. 249.

38. See James C. Scott, *Domination and the Arts of Resistance* (New Haven: Yale University Press, 1990).

39. Adolph Reed Jr. has argued, "Farrakhan has been successful in filling auditoriums and titillating rallies, but he has neither won mass adherence to the Nation of Islam nor ever demonstrated a capacity to galvanize popular action toward any end. . . . [The] characteristic Nation of Islam stance . . . [is] a militant rhetorical posture that preserves an aversion to real political mobilization." Reed, "The Rise of Louis Farrakhan," *Nation*, January 21, 1991, pp. 1, 51–56 (quotation on p. 54).

40. The unusual combination of "cathartic, feel-good militancy" and conservative bootstrap capitalism is what explains the appeal of Louis Farrakhan to normally moderate middle-class and older Blacks, according to Reed. See Adolph Reed Jr., "All for One and None for All," *Nation*, January 28, 1991, pp. 86–92.

41. In a critique of Black nationalism, Robert L. Allen wrote, "Black culture has become a badge to be worn rather than an experience to be shared. African robes, dashikis, dresses, and sandals have become standard equipment not only for the well-dressed black militant, but even for middle-class hipsters who have gone Afro. . . . How this activity relates to black liberation is difficult to understand." Allen, *Black Awakening in Capitalist America*, p. 168.

42. Cox writes, "The ruling class, possessing the power, is able to endow the conservative leader with sufficient vicarious authority and control of material things to make it obvious to the people that his way is the correct one and that those who oppose him, because of the material emptiness of their leadership, are utopian dreamers." Cox, "Leadership among Negroes in the United States," pp. 245–246. Also see Kilson, "Political Change in the Negro Ghetto," p. 172.

43. Moses, *Black Messiahs and Uncle Toms*, pp. 226–227.

44. See James Q. Wilson, "Two Negro Politicians: An Interpretation," *Midwest Journal of Political Science* 4:4 (November 1960), pp. 352–353. Also see the discussion of the "racial style" of Black politics in Thomas Dye, *The Politics of Equality* (New York: Bobbs Merrill, 1971), p. 164.

45. Reed, "Rise of Louis Farrakhan," p. 56; Cornel West, *Race Matters* (Boston: Beacon Press, 1993).

46. Thompson, *The Negro Leadership Class*, p. 63.

47. Ronald Walters, "Imperatives of Black Leadership: Policy Mobilization and Community Development," *Urban League Review* 9:1 (Summer 1985), pp. 20–41.

48. This discussion assumes political power is zero sum. If new sources of power are added to the political system, such as new bureaucratic agencies or programs funded by new monies (e.g., the federal antipoverty programs of the 1960s), one group can win control of such sources of political power without the diminution or reallocation of power from other groups.

49. At the same time, each instance in which the Black coalitional-incrementalist leadership delivers a solid Black bloc vote that provides a decisive electoral margin, their credibility and legitimacy increases in the eyes of the leadership of the other power-contending groups as well.

50. The 1964 presidential election between Democrat Lyndon Johnson, who had come into his own as an advocate of civil rights for Blacks, and Republican Barry Goldwater, who pioneered the so-called Southern strategy for presidential elections, signaled the end of competition for the Black vote at the presidential level. See Thomas Byrne Edsall and Mary Edsall, *Chain Reaction: The Impact of Race, Rights, and Taxes on American Politics* (New York: W. W. Norton, 1991).

51. Another strategy has been pursued by organizations like the National Association for the Advancement of Colored People (NAACP) and the Legal Defense and Education Fund (LDEF). The leadership of such organizations established political institutions to advance the empowerment of African-Americans incrementally, in the manner of coalitional-incrementalists. Although operating through the judicial process is extra-electoral, struggling for Black empowerment through legal channels is clearly not the same as separatism, which rejects the strategy of working through the established political system, defining it as institutionally racist. Moreover, those who have pursued Black empowerment through the courts have never proceeded in an invidious manner that excluded working together with non-Blacks to advance this goal.

52. See Henry Lee Moon, *Balance of Power: The Negro Vote* (Garden City, N.Y.: Doubleday, 1948), pp. 35–36, and Robert P. Turner, *Up to the Front of the Line: Blacks in the American Political System* (Port Washington, N.Y.: Kennikat Press, 1975), p. 143.

53. Moon, *Balance of Power*, pp. 205–206.

54. Turner, *Up to the Front of the Line*, p. 145. Also see Oscar Glantz, "The Negro Voter in Northern Industrial Cities," *Western Political Quarterly* 13:4 (December 1960), pp. 999–1010.

55. Henry Lee Moon, "The Negro Vote in the Presidential Election of 1956," *Journal of Negro Education* 26:3 (Summer 1957), pp. 219–230; Samuel Lubell, "The Future of the Negro Voter in the United States," *Journal of Negro Education* 26:3 (Summer 1957), pp. 408–417; Turner, *Up to the Front of the Line*, pp. 125–126, 167; and Lawrence J. Hanks, *Black Political Empowerment in Three Georgia Counties* (Knoxville: University of Tennessee Press, 1978), p. 26.

56. Nancy J. Weiss, *Farewell to the Party of Lincoln: Black Politics in the Age of FDR* (Princeton: Princeton University Press, 1983), p. 93.

57. Hanes Walton Jr., *Invisible Politics: Black Political Behavior* (Albany: State University of New York Press, 1985), p. 29.

58. On the complementarity between these two leadership types, also see John E. Jacob, "Black Leadership in a Reactionary Era," *Urban League Review* 9:1 (Summer 1985), pp. 20–41, and Herbert Haines Jr., *Black Radicals and the Civil Rights Mainstream, 1954–1970* (Knoxville: University of Tennessee Press, 1988).

59. Lewis M. Killian, "Significance of Extremism in the Black Revolution," p. 44.

60. Much of the literature is discussed in Charles Henry, *Jesse Jackson: The Search for Common Ground* (Oakland, Calif.: Black Scholar Press, 1991).

61. Adolph L. Reed Jr., *The Jesse Jackson Phenomenon* (New Haven: Yale University Press, 1986), p. 37.

62. Henry, *Jesse Jackson*, p. 102.

63. Thomas H. Landess and Richard M. Quinn, *Jesse Jackson and the Politics of Race* (Ottawa, Ill.: Jameson, 1985), pp. 57–61.

Chapter 2. Black Political Subordination in Chicago

1. Ralph Bunche, "The Thompson-Negro Alliance," *Opportunity* 7 (March 1929), p. 78.

2. Harold Gosnell, *Negro Politicians* (Chicago: University of Chicago Press, 1935), p. 11; also see Martin Kilson, "Adam Clayton Powell, Jr.: The Militant As Politician," in *Black Leaders of the Twentieth Century*, ed. John Hope Franklin and August Meier (Chicago: University of Illinois Press, 1982), p. 260.

3. Allan H. Spear, *Black Chicago: The Making of a Negro Ghetto, 1890–1920* (Chicago: University of Chicago Press, 1967), p. 191.

4. See Michael Preston, "Black Politics in the Post-Daley Era," in *After Daley: Chicago Politics in Transition*, ed. Samuel Gove and Louis Masotti (Urbana: University of Illinois Press, 1982), pp. 88–117, and Diane Pinderhughes, *Race and Ethnicity in Chicago Politics* (Urbana: University of Illinois Press, 1987).

5. Aside from providing evidence in support of the hypothesized relationship between political competition and opportunities for the empowerment of Blacks, the first part of this chapter has an additional purpose. Showing that Blacks won significant political power should disabuse readers of the view that Whites in Chicago are uniquely racist and that this explains the extreme degree of Black political subordination since the late 1950s. This view was expressed to me many times in casual conversations in Chicago. Many with whom I spoke in Philadelphia and in Gary felt the same way about their own city.

6. Joseph A. Logsdon, "The Rev. Archibald J. Carey and the Negro in Chicago Politics" (master's thesis, University of Chicago, 1961), p. 36. Also see John Allswang, *Bosses, Machines, and Urban Voters* (Baltimore: Johns Hopkins University Press, 1986), pp. 96–98.

7. Gosnell, *Negro Politicians*, pp. 49–50; Logsdon, "Rev. Archibald J. Carey and the Negro," pp. 36–38.

8. For a discussion of factional politics in this period, see Charles Merriam, *Chicago: A More Intimate View of Urban Politics* (New York: Macmillan, 1929), chap. 6. Also see Carter H. Harrison, *Stormy Years* (New York: Bobbs Merrill, 1935).

9. Logsdon, "Rev. Archibald J. Carey and the Negro," p. 43.

10. For the interesting story of DePriest's introduction to ward politics, see St. Clair Drake and Horace Cayton, *Black Metropolis* (New York: Harcourt, Brace, 1945), pp. 361–362.

11. Gosnell, *Negro Politicians*, pp. 40–41; Logsdon, "Rev. Archibald J. Carey and the Negro," pp. 48–49. Also see Lloyd Wendt and Herman Kogan, *Big Bill of Chicago* (New York: Bobbs Merrill, 1953), pp. 114–115.

12. Gosnell, *Negro Politicians*, pp. 36–62; quotations from pp. 40–41, 43.

13. Ibid., p. 181; also see Elmer William Henderson, "A Study of the Basic Factors Involved in the Change in the Party Alignment of Negroes in Chicago, 1932–1938" (master's thesis, University of Chicago, 1939), pp. 10–11.

14. Gosnell, *Negro Politicians*, p. 201.

15. Henderson, "A Study of the Basic Factors," pp. 10–11.

16. Pinderhughes, *Race and Ethnicity in Chicago Politics*, p. 200.

17. Logsdon, "Rev. Archibald J. Carey and the Negro," pp. 50–56; Gosnell, *Negro Politicians*, pp. 86–87.

18. Drake and Cayton, *Black Metropolis*, p. 358.

19. Gosnell, *Negro Politicians*, p. 200.

20. Spear, *Black Chicago*, pp. 124, 188; Logsdon, "Rev. Archibald J. Carey and the Negro," pp. 50–51; Drake and Cayton, *Black Metropolis*, p. 348; Gosnell, *Negro Politicians*, p. 199.

21. Gosnell, *Negro Politicians*, p. 239.

22. Gosnell commented that DePriest "did not regard himself as bound by party loyalty, by personal loyalty to any white man, or by loyalty to any abstract cause. In local politics he shifted from Republican to Democratic candidates when he thought that such a move would serve his purposes best. In national politics he advised Negroes to vote Democratic in sections where the Democrats had the most to offer them." Gosnell, *Negro Politicians*, pp. 193–194. Also see John Allswang, *A House for All Peoples: Ethnic Politics in Chicago, 1890–1936* (Lexington: University Press of Kentucky, 1971), pp. 148–149.

23. Logsdon, "Rev. Archibald J. Carey and the Negro," pp. 24–25; Spear, *Black Chicago*, p. 64; and Drake and Cayton, *Black Metropolis*, p. 345.

24. Logsdon, "Rev. Archibald J. Carey and the Negro," p. 25. Also see Charles Branham, "Black Chicago: Accommodationist Politics before the Great Migration," in *The Ethnic Frontier: Essays in the History of Group Survival in Chicago and the Midwest*, ed. Melvin Holli and Peter d'A. Jones (Grand Rapids, Mich.: William Eerdmans, 1977).

25. The Second and Third wards were more than 80 percent and 70 percent Black, respectively. Unless otherwise noted, all wards termed predominantly Black are at least 90 percent Black.

26. Gosnell, *Negro Politicians*, pp. 44, 177.

27. Ben Joravsky and Eduardo Camacho, *Race and Politics in Chicago* (Chicago: Community Renewal Society, 1987), p. 13.

28. Logsdon commented that "the respect and reputation [Carey] retained among white politicians only increased his prestige among the members of his own race." "Rev. Archibald J. Carey and the Negro," p. 39.

29. See Alex Gottfried, *Boss Cermak of Chicago: A Study of Political Leadership* (Seattle: University of Washington Press, 1962), and Paul M. Green, "Irish Chicago: The Multiethnic Road to Machine Success," in *Ethnic Chicago*, ed. Peter d'A. Jones and Melvin G. Holli (Grand Rapids, Mich.: William Eerdmans, 1981).

30. Wendt and Kogan, *Big Bill of Chicago*, pp. 329–31.

31. Dempsey J. Travis, *An Autobiography of Black Politics* (Chicago: Urban Research Press, 1987), pp. 94–96.

32. Pinderhughes argued that the Kelly era marked the end of electoral competition between the two parties. See Pinderhughes, *Race and Ethnicity in Chicago Politics*, p. 39.

33. Christopher Robert Reed, "Black Chicago Political Realignment during the Great Depression and New Deal," *Illinois Historical Journal* 78:4 (Winter 1985), pp. 242–256.

34. Harold Gosnell discounts the importance of the 1935 election, and argues that Kelly's Republican opponent "was actually chosen by the Democrats on the basis of a bipartisan deal" and waged a "powder-puff campaign." See Gosnell, *Machine Politics Chicago Model* (Chicago: University of Chicago Press, 1937), p. 19.

35. Further evidence of continued strength of the GOP among Blacks in Chicago is provided by Nancy J. Weiss. In Chicago, of the seven major U.S. cities with sizable Black populations, President Franklin D. Roosevelt received the smallest proportion of the Black vote in the 1940 election—52.2 percent. Next on the list was Cleveland, at 64.7 percent. The largest proportion was in Pittsburgh—82 percent. See the excellent study, Nancy J. Weiss, *Farewell to the Party of Lincoln: Black Politics in the Age of FDR* (Princeton: Princeton University Press, 1983), p. 287.

36. Gosnell, *Negro Politicians*, p. 201; Travis, *Autobiography of Black Politics*, pp. 120–126.

37. The civil service commissioner and the judge were the same person. See Roger Biles, *Big City Boss in Depression and War: Mayor Edward J. Kelly of Chicago* (Dekalb: Northern Illinois University Press, 1984), p. 91; Drake and Cayton, *Black Metropolis*, p. 353.

38. John M. Allswang, "The Chicago Negro Voter and the Democratic Consensus," *Journal of the Illinois State Historical Society* 60:2 (Summer 1967), p. 173.

39. Michael W. Homel, "The Politics of Public Education in Black Chicago, 1910–1941," *Journal of Negro Education* 45 (1976), pp. 185–186; Travis, *Autobiography of Black Politics*, pp. 120–125.

40. Homel, "Politics of Public Education in Black Chicago," p. 182.

41. Martin Meyerson and Edward Banfield, *Politics, Planning, and the Public Interest* (Glencoe, Ill.: Free Press, 1955), pp. 83–86; Arnold Hirsch, *Making the Second Ghetto: Race and Housing in Chicago, 1940–1960* (Cambridge: Cambridge University Press, 1983), pp. 219–220; and Manning Marable, *Black American Politics* (London: Verso, 1985), p. 203.

42. Meyerson and Banfield, *Politics, Planning, and the Public Interest*, p. 128.

43. See Arvarh Strickland, *History of the Chicago Urban League* (Urbana: University of Illinois Press, 1966), pp. 141–142. Also see Hirsch, *Making the Second Ghetto*, p. 177.

44. Biles, *Big City Boss in Depression and War*, pp. 97–98.

45. See Weiss, *Farewell to the Party of Lincoln*. Also see Drake and Cayton, *Black Metropolis*, pp. 353–355, and Rita Werner Gordon, "The Change in the Political Alignment of Chicago's Negroes during the New Deal," *Journal of American History* 56 (December 1969).

46, Reed, "Black Chicago Political Realignment," p. 244. Also see Michael F. Funchion, "The Political and Nationalist Dimensions," in *The Irish in Chicago*, ed. Laurence J. McCaffrey et al. (Urbana: University of Illinois Press, 1987), pp. 85–86.

47. Rakove, *We Don't Want Nobody Nobody Sent: An Oral History of the Daley Years*, (Bloomington: Indiana University Press, 1979), p. 12. On Kelly's school scandals, see Paul Peterson, *School Politics Chicago Style* (Chicago: University of Chicago Press, 1976), pp. 82–87.

48. See Hirsch, *Making the Second Ghetto*, ch. 6.

49. Biles, *Big City Boss in Depression and War*, p. 146.

50. Kennelly had developed a reputation for fighting corruption as the director of the Chicago Crime Commission. As mayor, he also established an independent school board, and he inaugurated a centralized purchasing system for the city government that reduced the potential for graft by each department head. See James Q. Wilson, *Negro Politics* (New York: Free Press, 1960), pp. 81–82; Meyerson and Banfield, *Politics, Planning, and the Public Interest*; and Eugene Kennedy, *Himself: The Life and Times of Mayor Richard J. Daley* (New York: Viking Press, 1978), p. 97.

51. According to Meyerson and Banfield, "Dawson's organization was built in part on patronage and in part on financial contributions from 'policy kings' and, perhaps, from other illegitimate enterprises as well." See Meyerson and Banfield, *Politics, Planning, and the Public Interest*, pp. 77–78.

52. For accounts of Daley's early life, his rise in the ranks of the Democratic party organization, and his emergence as the choice of the ward leaders to replace Mayor Kennelly, see Len O'Connor, *Clout: Mayor Daley and His City* (New York: Avon, 1975); Mike Royko, *Boss: Richard J. Daley of Chicago* (New York: E.P. Dutton, 1971); and Kennedy, *Himself*.

53. The characterization is from the *Chicago Tribune*, quoted in James Winters, "Democracy in Chicago," *Notre Dame Magazine* (January 1984), p. 17. The following excerpt from a *Chicago Sun Times* editorial is exemplary:

> While Dawson did not singlehandedly execute the coup, there is no doubt that he wielded more influence than any other one man in the organization's decision to deny Kennelly the Democratic machine's support in the February 22 mayoral primary. Dawson has long been a force for evil within the local Democratic organization. He is a political overlord of a district where policy rackets and narcotics peddling flourish as they do nowhere in the city.

"Policy, Narcotics, and Mayoral Politics," *Chicago Sun Times*, February 1, 1955.

54. See "Dawson Not a Candidate, but Key Man in Election," *Chicago Defender*, February 12, 1955. In fact, getting Mayor Kennelly to halt police raids on policy wheels in Dawson's congressional district was one of Dawson's top priorities. See the illuminating anecdote told by Ira Bach in Hirsch, *Making the Second Ghetto*, p. 130. Also see Joel Weisman and Ralph Whitehead, "Untangling Black Politics," *Chicagoan* (July 1974), p. 44.

55. See *Chicago Defender*, February 5, 1955.

56. Polish-Americans are the largest White ethnic group in the city. Although the Census Bureau found 258,657 people who labeled themselves as Polish in 1960, Rakove stated that

the number for all people of Polish origin may be as high as six hundred thousand. Milton Rakove, *Don't Make No Waves, Don't Back No Losers* (Bloomington: Indiana University Press, 1975), p. 151. For a discussion of the respective sources of support of each candidate, see Joseph Zikmund, "Mayoral Voting and Ethnic Politics in the Daley-Bilandic-Byrne Era," in Gove and Masotti *After Daley*.

57. Merriam had fought for an ordinance to outlaw segregation in publicly financed housing, as well as other legislation in the areas of housing, police, sanitation, and education that would benefit the Black community. See Alfred de Grazia, "The Limits of External Leadership over a Minority Electorate," *Public Opinion Quarterly* 20:1 (Spring 1956), p. 116.

58. Rakove, *We Don't Want Nobody Nobody Sent*, p. 42.

59. William Grimshaw, *Black Politics in Chicago* (Chicago: Loyola University Center for Urban Policy, 1980), pp. 11–12, 22.

60. These three aldermen, plus three other Daley-anointed Black aldermen, came to be known as the Silent Six. They earned this epithet by never speaking up when the interests of the Black community clashed with the interests of the Daley machine.

61. Edward Banfield, *Political Influence* (New York: Free Press, 1961), p. 251.

62. See Royko, *Boss*, pp. 100–101. Also see John Allswang, *Bosses, Machines, and Urban Voters* (Port Washington, N.Y.: Kennikat Press, 1977), pp. 128, 146.

63. Rakove has also noted this basic rule of Daley's corporatist approach to governance.

> In accordance with his concept of the proper functioning of government, Daley's strategy as mayor is to deal with the business leaders of the city on matters of interest to the business community; with labor leaders on labor problems; with religious leaders of the various denominations in the city on matters which concern their flocks; with ethnic spokesmen on ethnic interests; with sympathetic black spokesmen on racial matters; and with representatives of all interest groups who can demonstrate power, responsibility, and support from their constituents.

Rakove, *Don't Make No Waves, Don't Back No Losers*, pp. 83–84. Rakove's view is corroborated by a story told by Father George Clements, who was part of a group of priests who were called to Daley's office after they voiced support for issues raised by the Afro-American Patrolman's League against the Police Department. Daley turned to one of the priests, who was holding a prayer book, and said, "If you read that book more, you wouldn't have time to be getting into my book. You see, the city of Chicago is my book. Therefore, I'm suggesting that you stay out of my book and stay in your book." Travis, *Autobiography of Black Politics*, pp. 291–292.

64. For example, a two-year effort by the Chicago Urban League to persuade the business community of the need for special funding for Black education and job training programs in order to enhance the future manpower potential of the city produced programs for cab drivers, gas station attendants, and typists with an annual funding of only $17,500. See Strickland, *History of the Chicago Urban League*, pp. 213–214, 225–227.

65. Ralph Whitehead Jr. and Joel Weisman, "Is LaSalle Street Grooming the Black Mayor?" *Chicagoan* (August 1974), p. 48.

66. Interview by author, October 22, 1987.

67. Malcolm Wise, "Civic Leaders Rally behind Daley for Re-election," *Chicago Sun Times*, February 13, 1959, p. 24. Also see Rakove, *We Don't Want Nobody Nobody Sent*, pp. 259–306.

68. Rakove, *Don't Make No Waves, Don't Back No Losers*, p. 160.

69. James Q. Wilson discusses the internal divisions and political ineffectiveness of the IVI in *The Amateur Democrat* (Chicago: University of Chicago Press, 1962), chap. 3. The

IPO was a north Lakefront organization created in 1968, while the IVI was primarily located in the Hyde Park area, near the University of Chicago.

70. Rakove, *Don't Make No Waves, Don't Back No Losers*, pp. 212–13.

71. On the origins of the tax revolt, see Royko, *Boss*, pp. 129–132. On its significance, see the excellent analysis of the relationship between the Irish and Democratic machines in Steven Erie, *Rainbow's End: Irish-Americans and the Dilemmas of Urban Machine Politics, 1840–1985* (Berkeley: University of California Press, 1988), pp. 157, 161, 245–46.

72. See "Daley Predicts Victory," *Chicago Tribune*, April 2, 1963, in which Daley repeatedly refused to answer a reporter's questions about his stance on open occupancy housing. Also see Allswang, *Bosses, Machines, and Voters*, p. 130, and Winters, "Democracy in Chicago," p. 20.

73. Grimshaw, *Black Politics in Chicago*, pp. 23–24.

74. See Hirsch, *Making the Second Ghetto*, pp. 242–243.

75. Some months after President Johnson overruled the Office of Education, Francis Keppell, the commissioner of education, left his office under a cloud formed during his clash with Daley. See Gary Orfield, *The Reconstruction of Southern Education* (New York: Wiley, 1969), chap. 4. Similar pressure from Daley led the Johnson administration to remove the midwest regional director of the Office of Equal Opportunity after he denied Chicago additional funding until the city increased the "participation of the poor" in the city's antipoverty program. See J. David Greenstone and Paul E. Peterson, *Race and Authority in Urban Politics* (Chicago: University of Chicago Press, 1973), p. 22.

76. Greenstone and Peterson, *Race and Authority in Urban Politics*, pp. 125–162.

77. One should not forget that Daley's first elected office was president of the Hamburg Social and Athletic Club in 1924. In 1919 the Hamburgers were reputed to have been leaders of the four-day race riot that ensued after a Black tried to use a beach that was all-White. No evidence linked Daley to participation in the brutal beatings of Blacks; nor does any evidence suggest that the nature of the club had changed at all in the interim. See O'Connor, *Clout: Mayor Daley and His City*, pp. 18–20.

78. Adding Hanrahan's votes to those of Singer and Newhouse would not change the view expressed here that Daley still dominated the city's electoral politics in 1975. But to include Hanrahan in an anti-Daley coalition would be misleading. Hanrahan's votes were antiliberal, anti-Black, White ethnic solidarity votes. Hanrahan did best in the same wards where Daley did best (e.g., Wards 12, 13, 23, 36, and 41). Hanrahan's supporters were Daley supporters as well, and probably would not have voted for Singer or Newhouse.

79. Interview with Timothy Sheehan (pp. 270–71), and interview with John Waner in Rakove, *We Don't Want Nobody Nobody Sent*, pp. 282–83. Also see Rakove, *Don't Make No Waves, Don't Back No Losers*, ch. 6.

80. Predominantly Black wards are representative of the Black population in terms of education and income. Because of racial steering by real-estate brokers and mortgage lenders, Blacks rarely lived for long in areas where they were a small proportion of the population; so whatever effects isolation may have on the voting of a minority population probably had little impact on Blacks in Chicago. Moreover, I am not trying to arrive at the precise number of Black votes received by Daley; rather, I wish to illustrate the magnitude of his margins of electoral victory and the superfluousness of Black votes. Inexact but quite reasonable and logical estimates seem appropriate for this endeavor.

81. Bilandic came from Daley's Eleventh Ward in Bridgeport, was the chairman of the Finance Committee of the city council, and was Daley's floor leader in the city council.

82. Leader of the Hyde Park–Kenwood IVI, Interview by author, October 14, 1986.

83. For a description of the long personal relationship between Metcalfe and Washington

and an explanation of Metcalfe's failure to back Washington based on personal feuding, see Florence Hamlish Levinsohn, *Harold Washington: A Political Biography* (Chicago: Chicago Review Press, 1983), pp. 123–124. A different interpretation suggesting that Metcalfe was seeking to reingratiate himself with the machine is offered in Vernon Jarrett, "Ralph Metcalfe Takes His Stand," *Chicago Tribune*, January 23, 1977.

84. Washington did win five Black South Side wards with pluralities of about 43 percent.

85. Basil Talbott Jr. wrote: "When the Democratic Party bosses picked [Stewart], they showed they had no respect for their black members or the voters. The party leaders demonstrated they take the black vote, light as it is, for granted." "Getting the City Hall Shaft," *Chicago Sun Times*, October 19, 1978, p. 69.

86. Basil Talbott Jr., "Pick Stewart in Secret to Replace Metcalfe," *Chicago Sun Times*, October 13, 1978, p. 7. Unlike many in the IVI, Ackerman was not merely a "procedural" liberal interested in popular elections rather than smoke-filled-room appointments. He knew that defeating the machine in an election to replace Congressman Metcalfe could be an important step in Black political empowerment.

87. Joravsky and Camacho, *Race and Politics in Chicago*, pp. 52–53.

88. On Byrne's nontraditional rise to political power in Chicago, which circumvented precinct and ward organization service, see Bill Granger and Lori Granger, *Fighting Jane: Mayor Jane Byrne and the Chicago Machine* (New York: Dial Press, 1980), chaps. 13–14.

89. Milton Rakove, "Jane Byrne and the New Chicago Politics," in Gove and Masotti, *After Daley*, p. 229.

90. Paul Kleppner, *Chicago Divided: The Making of A Black Mayor* (Dekalb: Northern Illinois University Press, 1985), p. 117.

91. See Meyerson and Banfield, *Politics, Planning, and the Public Interest*; Hirsch, *Making the Second Ghetto*; and Devereux Bowly Jr., *The Poorhouse: Subsidized Housing in Chicago, 1895–1976* (Carbondale: Southern Illinois University Press, 1978).

92. Meyerson and Banfield, *Politics, Planning, and the Public Interest*, pp. 29–30.

93. Arnold R. Hirsch, "Martin H. Kennelly: The Mugwump and the Machine," in *The Mayors*, ed. Melvin G. Holli and Paul M. Green (Carbondale: Southern Illinois University Press, 1987), pp. 126–143.

94. Under Daley's CHA director, Alvin Rose, White aldermen were given virtual veto power over the siting of public housing in their wards. See Hirsch, *Making the Second Ghetto*, p. 241.

95. See *Gautreaux v. Chicago Housing Authority*, 296 F. Supp. 907 (1969), and 304 F. Supp. 736 (1969).

96. Hirsch, *Making the Second Ghetto*, pp. 265–268.

97. Michael Wallace Homel, "Negroes in the Chicago Public Schools, 1910–1941" (Ph.D. diss., University of Chicago, 1972), p. 79.

98. Biles, *Big City Mayor in Depression and War*, pp. 92–94, and Orfield, *Reconstruction of Southern Education*, pp. 154–155.

99. Orfield, *Reconstruction of Southern Education*, p. 162.

100. Ibid., p. 189.

101. Gosnell, *Negro Politicians*, table 8, p. 239.

102. Jesse E. Hoskins, Commissioner of Personnel, "Official Report of the Task Force on Affirmative Action, City of Chicago," (Chicago: City Hall, December 1985). Data are for "All categories/Full time" positions.

103. Gosnell, *Negro Politicians*; Pinderhughes, *Race and Ethnicity in Chicago Politics*.

104. Harold Baron et al., "Black Powerlessness in Chicago," *TRANS-action* 6:1 (November 1968), pp. 27–33.

105. See Vernon Jarrett, "City Hall Displays More Than Racism," *Chicago Tribune*, October 20, 1978.

106. "Black Political Power Grows in Wake of Protest Victories," *Chicago Reporter* 8:12 (December 1979), pp. 5, 8.

107. Weisman and Whitehead, "Untangling Black Politics," p. 75.

108. Travis, *Autobiography of Black Politics*, pp. 234–235. When Daley took office he vowed that he would never permit a Black to have the power that William Dawson had when he led the party organization to dump Kennelly. See Levinsohn, *Harold Washington*, p. 143. Grimshaw has argued that even before Daley was elected mayor he had begun efforts to weaken Dawson. See Grimshaw, *Black Politics in Chicago*, pp. 5–14. As mayor he tried to rid himself of the threat Dawson represented by persuading President John F. Kennedy to make Dawson the first Black cabinet member by appointing him postmaster general, but Dawson refused the appointment. See Travis, *Autobiography of Black Politics*, p. 301.

109. On the rivalry between Dawson and Metcalfe, see Grimshaw, *Black Politics in Chicago*, pp. 11–12.

110. Travis, *Autobiography of Black Politics*, pp. 234–235.

111. Wilson, *Negro Politics*, p. 80.

112. For studies of voting behavior on the Chicago city council, see Dick Simpson, "Chicago Government," in *Chicago: An Agenda for Change*, ed. Dick Simpson and Pierre de Vise (Chicago: University of Illinois at Chicago Circle, 1975); and Ross Lathrop, "Improving the City Council," in *Chicago's Future: In a Time for Change*, ed. Dick Simpson (Champaign, Ill.: Stipes, 1988).

113. Most of the White city council members also voted as instructed by Daley and did not criticize the mayor. But the White council members and their constituents (except White liberals) were almost unanimously in favor of segregated schools and the construction of high-rise ghettos in already overcrowded Black neighborhoods rather than scattered-site public housing. Blacks sought desegregated schools and scattered-site public housing, as numerous protest demonstrations in the 1960s indicated, but Black city council members did not reflect these views. Former officer of the Coordinating Committee of Community Organizations, interview by author, October 17, 1986.

114. Wife of the pastor of major Black church, interview by author, October 16, 1986; civil rights activist and producer of a gospel music radio program, interview by author, October 23, 1986.

115. Travis recounts how Daley stalled the construction of a Black church by deterring a local bank from making a loan to the minister. The minister was being punished for his support of the Martin Luther King Jr.'s political activities in Chicago. See Travis, *Autobiography of Black Politics*, p. 355.

116. Quoted in Travis, *Autobiography of Black Politics*, p. 244.

117. Quoted in Travis, *Autobiography of Black Politics*, pp. 346–347. Further confirmation of Daley's capture of the Black clergy and their opposition to King can be found in Eddie Stone, *Jesse Jackson: Biography of an Ambitious Man* (Los Angeles: Holloway House, 1979), pp. 57–58.

118. David Lewis, *King: A Critical Biography* (New York: Praeger, 1970), pp. 336–337. Also see Charles Hamilton, *The Black Preacher in America* (New York: William Morrow, 1972), pp. 26–27.

119. For a more detailed look at declining turnout in mayoral elections among Blacks, see Michael Preston, "The Resurgence of Black Voting in Chicago: 1955–1983," in *The Making of the Mayor*, ed. Marvin G. Holli and Paul M. Green (Grand Rapids, Mich.: William Eerdmans, 1984).

120. See Alan B. Anderson and George W. Pickering, *Confronting the Color Line: The Broken Promise of the Civil Rights Movement in Chicago* (Athens: University of Georgia Press, 1986).

121. The Kerner Commission offered the following incisive explanation:

> Black Power rhetoric and ideology actually express a lack of power. The slogan emerged when the Negro protest movement was slowing down, when it was finding increasing resistance to its changing goals, when it discovered that nonviolent direct action was no more a panacea than legal action. . . . This combination of circumstances provoked anger deepened by impotence. Powerless to make any fundamental changes in the life of the masses—powerless, that is, to compel white America to make those changes— many advocates of Black Power have retreated into an unreal world, where they see an outnumbered and poverty-stricken minority organizing itself independently of whites and creating sufficient power to force white America to grant its demands.

National Advisory Commission on Civil Disorders (Kerner Commission), *Report* (New York: Bantam Books, 1968), pp. 234–235.

122. Gregory, a famous comedian and political activist, entered the 1967 mayoral election and won less than 2 percent of the vote. Landry was cochairman of the Chicago Area Friends of the Student Nonviolent Coordinating Committee and the chairman of the Coordinating Council of Community Organizations (CCCO). Lucas was chairman of the Chicago branch of the Congress Of Racial Equality. Lu Palmer was a militant Black journalist and community leader who founded the Chicago Black United Communities, a Black nationalist, working-class organization that shunned alliances with Whites. See Marable, *Black American Politics*, p. 222.

123. The one exception deserving mention is The Woodlawn Organization (TWO), a Saul Alinsky–inspired neighborhood organization, which forced Daley to allow it to represent the Woodlawn neighborhood in its struggle against the University of Chicago. But TWO differed from extraelectoral groups in a number of ways. It did not shun electoral participation but won the respect of Daley by registering huge numbers of voters. TWO also set short-range goals that were easily accomplishable and could therefore build its credibility. Finally, TWO, through Alinsky, had the support of the Chicago archdiocese. See John Hall Fish, *Black Power, White Control* (Princeton: Princeton University Press, 1973), especially chaps. 3–5. Also see Sanford Horwitt, *Let Them Call Me Rebel* (New York: Alfred A. Knopf, 1989).

124. Ralph Metcalfe, quoted in Barbara Reynolds, *Jesse Jackson: the Man, the Movement, the Myth* (Chicago: Nelson-Hall, 1975), pp. 220–221. Sammy Rayner also complained that he had expected much more from Jackson than he and his supporters were able to deliver. See Reynolds, *Jesse Jackson*, p. 219.

125. The story of the CCCO struggle for school desegregation can be found in Anderson and Pickering, *Confronting the Color Line.*

126. Preston has shown that turnout in primary and general mayoral elections during the 1970s fell more sharply in middle-class than non-middle-class Black wards. At the same time, Black middle-class turnout in presidential elections remained high. See Preston, "Black Politics in the Post-Daley Era," in Gove and Massatti, *After Daley.*

127. Anderson and Pickering, *Confronting the Color Line*, pp. 121, 284–285.

128. Wards 6, 8, and 17, discussed hereafter, were inhabited by middle-class Blacks in the early 1960s.

129. Richard J. Daley had persuaded committeeman Ralph Metcalfe to rejuvenate the Young Democrats in order to attract young Blacks into the party organization. Metcalfe gave this recruitment task to his chief lieutenant, Harold Washington. But when the Young Democrats' meetings shifted from training in constituency servicing and get-out-the-vote techniques

to how Blacks could capture greater political power and how the themes of the civil rights movement could be pursued in Chicago, Daley disbanded the organization. See Levinsohn, *Harold Washington*, pp. 80–95; and John Camper, Cheryl Devall, and John Kass, "The Road to City Hall," *Chicago Tribune Magazine*, November 16, 1986, p. 35.

130. Rakove wrote that independent Black politicians "are clearly little more that a nuisance to the machine at large, and to the black machine politicians in particular. And, while it may be possible for other black political independents to make it to the city council in the future, it is also unlikely that their numbers will increase significantly or their power radically." See Rakove, *Don't Make No Waves, Don't Back No Losers*, p. 263.

131. Chew was replaced as alderman by committeeman William Shannon, who held both posts until 1979. Shannon dutifully followed the orders of Daley.

132. Travis, *Autobiography of Black Politics*, p. 245.

133. See Travis, *Autobiography of Black Politics*, pp. 245–247, and Rakove, *Don't Make No Waves, Don't Back No Losers*, p. 264.

134. Member of the IVI State Board of Directors and chairman of the IVI Political Action Committee, interview by author, October 24, 1986.

135. In 1975 he stepped down to run successfully for a judgeship. It was widely rumored that the Democratic party organization gave Cousins behind-the-scenes aid in that campaign in order to be rid of him.

136. See "IVI Backing Hubbard, Stevens, Singer in March 11 Elections," *Chicago Defender*, January 2, 1969, and "'Liberal Bloc' Indorses Two for Aldermanic Elections," *Chicago Tribune*, January 31, 1969.

137. Former cochairman of the Committee for an Effective City Council, interview by author, July 1986.

138. Quoted in Vernon Jarrett, "Fred Hubbard's Actual Crime," *Chicago Tribune*, January 10, 1973.

139. Many believe that the Daley organization crafted a deal with Hubbard early on and clandestinely supported Hubbard in the race against Woods because Woods had been tainted by corruption charges. See Robert Davis, "Former Alderman Hubbard Gets 2-Year Prison Sentence," *Chicago Tribune*, January 6, 1973, and Rakove, *Don't Make No Waves, Don't Back No Losers*, pp. 103–104.

140. For examples from the state House of Representatives, see David Halberstam, "Daley of Chicago," in *The City Boss in America*, ed. Alexander B. Callow (New York: Oxford University Press, 1976), p. 302.

141. Singer's major claim to fame came in 1972 when he and Jesse Jackson led a successful challenge of Daley's slate of delegates to the presidential nominating convention. Daley had refused to abide by the new rules, which required a quota of Blacks, Hispanics, women, and people under 30, as well as guidelines for the "open" election of the delegates.

142. Frank Zahour, "Singer Hits Black Hopefuls Chances," *Chicago Tribune*, September 19, 1974.

143. Columnist, *Chicago Sun Times*, interview by author, July 14, 1986.

144. Some Blacks saw Newhouse as an opportunist trying to stake a claim to be the front-running Black in future mayoral races. Another reason for Newhouse's unpopularity among some Blacks was the fact that he had a White wife. See Clarence Page, "The Real Goal, Some Indicate, Is To Build for a '79 Victory," *Chicago Tribune*, September 22, 1974, pp. 49–50, and Ted Seals, "Black Candidates Lay Their Mayoral Cards on the Table," *Chicago Sun Times*, December 1, 1974.

145. Basil Talbott, Jr., "Black Group Drops Newhouse, Eyes Singer," *Chicago Sun Times*, January 11, 1975.

146. Black political activist who worked for the Singer campaign, interview by author,

October 21, 1986. Also see Jerry DeMuth, "Three Black Hopefuls Slow Singer's Mayoral Wagon," *Chicago Sun Times*, September 26, 1974; Eleanor Randolph, "Jesse Hints PUSH May O.K. Singer," *Chicago Tribune*, January 12, 1975; Roger Flaherty, "Newhouse Asked To Back Singer," *Chicago Sun Times*, January 20, 1975; and Eleanor Randolph, "Metcalfe Severs Daley Ties, Backs Singer for Mayor," *Chicago Tribune*, January 26, 1975.

147. Talbott, "Black Group Drops Newhouse, Eyes Singer," and Michael Hirsley, "Daley Unqualified, Black Group Says," *Chicago Tribune*, February 13, 1975, p. 2:10.

148. "The Hot Skillet," *Chicago Metro News*, February 1, 1975. Also see "Newhouse Endorsed for Mayor by Six Black Publishers Here," *Chicago Daily News*, January 21, 1975.

149. "'Mayor' Group Called 'toms'" *Chicago Defender*, November 12, 1974.

150. Jerry DeMuth, "Three Black Hopefuls Slow Singer's Mayoral Wagon."

151. Barbara Reynolds, "Blacks Blast Jesse on Newhouse Snub," *Chicago Tribune*, January 13, 1975, p. 2:1.

152. A fourth candidate who challenged Daley from the law-and-order right wing, Edward Hanrahan, won 5 percent.

153. Singer won Wards 5 (Hyde Park), 43, and 44 (Lakefront liberal). Together with Newhouse, they would have won Wards 2, 6, 7, 8, 17, 21, 28, 34, and 49 (all predominantly Black except Ward 49, which was Lakefront liberal).

154. See *Chicago Tribune*, February 11, 1975, p. 2:1.

155. Byrne's goals, beliefs, and stratagems were discussed by an alderman who was one of her closest allies and most ardent supporters, interview by author, October 16, 1986.

156. For additional examples, see Abdul Alkalimat and Doug Gills, "Chicago," in *The New Black Vote*, ed. Rod Bush (San Francisco: Synthesis Publications, 1984), pp. 68–83, and Travis, *Autobiography of Black Politics*, pp. 529–554.

157. Paul M. Green, "The Primary: Some New Players—Same Old Rules," in Holli and Green, *Making of the Mayor*, p. 23.

158. Travis, *Autobiography of Black Politics*, p. 537.

159. Sickening examples of the depths to which Washington's enemies stooped are provided in Levinsohn, *Harold Washington*.

160. See Stephen C. Baker and Paul Kleppner, "Race War Chicago Style: The Election of a Black Mayor, 1983," *Research in Urban Policy* 2 (Los Angeles: JAI Press, 1986), p. 222.

161. This theme is discussed in *Harold Washington and the Neighborhoods*, ed. Pierre Clavel and Wim Wiewel (New Brunswick, N.J.: Rutgers University Press, 1991). Also see Gary Rivlin, *Fire on the Prairie: Chicago's Harold Washington and the Politics of Race*, (New York: Henry Holt, 1992), p. 309.

162. Ann Marie Lipinski and James Strong, "Ethics Code Takes Aim at Aldermen, Lobbyists," *Chicago Tribune*, February 15, 1987, p. 1; Lynn Sweet and Don Terry, "Mayor Signs Ethics Bill; Byrne Hits Fund-Raising," *Chicago Sun-Times*, February 19, 1987, p. 1.

163. Clavel and Wiewel, *Harold Washington and the Neighborhoods*.

164. Thomas Hardy, "Could the Game Be Complete without Our Local Stassen?" *Chicago Tribune*, December 18, 1988.

165. John Camper and Jerry Thornton, "Without Washington, Black Support Splinters," *Chicago Tribune*, December 15, 1988.

166. David Moberg, "How's He Doing? A Daley Report Card," *Chicago Reader* 20:20 (February 22, 1991), p. 25. Also see David Jackson, "Double Vision," *Chicago Magazine*, (October 1989), p. 159.

167. Greg Hinz, "The Pothole Mayor," *Chicago Magazine* (February 1995), p. 123.

168. James Strong, "Whites Have Most Top-Level City Jobs," *Chicago Tribune*, November 1, 1989, p. 1; Robert Davis, "Daley Hiring More Minorities," *Chicago Tribune*, February

1, 1991, p. 1. On the impact of layoffs on Black personnel, see David Jackson, "City Layoffs Affect Minorities Mostly," *Chicago Tribune*, February 11, 1992, pp. 1, 8.

169. Dirk Johnson, "Blacks Plan Rights March in Chicago," *New York Times*, October 20, 1989, p. 7; David Jackson, "Legal Frights," *Chicago Magazine* (November 1990), pp. 15–17.

170. Green, quoted in Dirk Johnson, "Chicago's Mayor Pursuing Quiet Quest To Win Trust of Blacks," *New York Times*, November 12, 1989, p. 28.

171. Professor Robert Starks, interview by author, July 1986.

172. Rivlin, *Fire on the Prairie*, p. 133.

173. Palmer asked, "Why do black people have to be fairer than fair? My principle is problack. I don't believe in coalitions." Quoted in David Moberg, "One Year without Washington, What Did He Accomplish?" *Chicago Reader* 18:10 (November 25, 1988), p. 20.

174. Rivlin, *Fire on the Prairie*, pp. 290–292.

175. Ibid., p. 249.

176. Evans *could* work with Whites, but only progressive Whites, not liberals or ethnics. The difference was that progressive Whites favored large-scale redistribution of political and economic power to Blacks (and Latinos), an equality-of-outcomes policy. Separatist-messianics could abide by this policy because it delivered the spoils of politics to the victors. Ethnic voters as nonvictors and as the displaced group opposed such a policy, of course. Lakefront liberals, when they differed with bungalow-belt ethnic voters (and many on the Lakefront were recent upwardly mobile émigrés from that belt, which had regularly elected Richard J. Daley), preferred a policy of procedural equality that called for a strict merit-based personnel policy and a policy of best-bid disbursement of city contracting. To progressives, merit was a euphemism for the enshrinement of the results of longstanding inequities.

177. James Strong and Jacqueline Heard, "Council Meeting Fails as Evans Rally," *Chicago Tribune*, December 2, 1988, p. 1; Mike Royko, "Daley and Evans: A Perfect Shootout," *Chicago Tribune*, December 6, 1988.

Chapter 3. Political Monopoly and the Maintenance of Black Subordination in Gary

1. Powell A. Moore, *The Calumet Region: Indiana's Last Frontier* (East Chicago: Indiana Historical Bureau, 1959), pp. 331–333; Raymond A. Mohl and Neil Betten, *Steel City: Urban and Ethnic Patterns in Gary, Indiana, 1906–1950* (New York: Holmes and Meir, 1986), p. 4. Good discussions of the early history of Gary can also be found in Roger K. Oden, "Black Political Power in Gary, Indiana: A Theoretical and Structural Analysis" (Ph.D. diss., University of Chicago, 1977), chaps. 2, 4; Edward Greer, *Big Steel* (New York: Monthly Review Press, 1979); James B. Lane, *City of the Century: A History of Gary, Indiana* (Bloomington: Indiana University Press, 1978); and William E. Nelson, Jr., "Black Political Mobilization: The 1967 Mayoral Election in Gary" (Ph.D. diss., University of Illinois, 1971).

2. Mohl and Betten, *Steel City*, p. 5.

3. Bureau of the Census, *Fifteenth Census of the U.S., 1930, Population: Composition and Characteristics* (Washington, D.C., 1932), pp. 37–39; Mohl and Betten, *Steel City*, p. 51; Lane, *City of the Century*, p. 7.

4. Dolly Millender, *Yesterday in Gary: History of the Negro in Gary* (Gary: Dolly Millender, 1967), pp. 23–27.

5. Mohl and Betten, *Steel City*, pp. 84–85.

6. Gregory received a judicial appointment in 1920, Hueston was named assistant solicitor general in the Post Office Department, and in 1921 Whitlock became the first Black to be slated and elected to the city council.

7. Mohl and Betten, *Steel City*, p. 63.

8. Millender, *Yesterday in Gary*, pp. 57–60; Mohl and Betten, *Steel City*, pp. 55–63, 86; Lane, *City of the Century*, p. 69.

9. Lane, *City of the Century*, pp. 145–146.

10. Johnson's involvement, indictment, and imprisonment for violation of Prohibition is discussed in Moore, *Calumet Region*, pp. 548–49.

11. Lane, *City of the Century*, pp. 127–129.

12. Millender, *Yesterday in Gary*, pp. 64–65.

13. Richard J. Meister, "A History of Gary, Indiana: 1930–1940" (Ph.D. diss., University of Notre Dame, 1966), pp. 257–258.

14. Ibid.," p. 260.

15. Smith lost in Gary by about seven thousand votes. But the approximately 12,000 votes he received was almost four times the total cast for the Democratic presidential candidate in 1924 in Gary.

16. Meister, "History of Gary, Indiana: 1930–1940," p. 265.

17. Ibid., pp. 272–273.

18. A. Brown, "To Protest Redistricting of Precincts," *Gary American*, March 19, 1932, p. 1.

19. "Democratic County Ticket Wins by Wide Majorities," *Gary Post-Tribune*, November 8, 1934, pp. 1, 8.

20. The operation of the numbers game and the links between Kelly and Clayton are discussed in Meister, "History of Gary, Indiana: 1930–1940," pp. 264–265.

21. Ibid., pp. 289–290.

22. Democratic mayor Barney Clayton was endorsed by the editor of the *Gary American* in "A Mayor Who Has Not Failed Us," *Gary American*, October 28, 1938, p. 8. Meister claims that the *Gary American* was controlled by the Gary Democratic organization, which held the mortgage for the paper, and by numbers boss Walter Kelly, a close ally of Mayor Clayton. See Meister, "A History of Gary, Indiana: 1930–1940," pp. 297, 306.

23. Editorial, *Gary Post-Tribune*, November 17, 1938, p. 1.

24. Seven precincts (Precincts 40–44 and 54–55) were more than 80 percent Black. Predominantly Black precincts are identified in the *Gary American* and the WPA Housing Survey of 1936. All calculations made by me.

25. Meister, "History of Gary, Indiana: 1930–1940," p. 34.

26. Lane, *City of the Century*, p. 192.

27. The involvement of politicians and organized crime was extreme in Gary, as evidenced by the murder of a bootlegger in Mayor Clayton's home and the gangland killing of Mayor Finerty's brother. See Lane, *City of the Century*.

28. Finerty's ascendance was evident in the 1940 elections when his candidates, Eugene Swartz (who served as mayor after Finerty) and Frank Martin, defeated Ray Madden and Matt Vlasic of the Clayton faction for the county offices of auditor and treasurer. See Meister, pp. 312–313. For a profile of Finerty's long political career, see "Finerty Asks Support from Every Citizen," *Gary Post-Tribune*, November 4, 1942, p. 21.

29. "Finerty Piles Up 5,277 Vote Lead to Win," *Gary Post-Tribune*, November 4, 1942, pp. 1, 18.

30. The Urban League director was not sure whether this program had any impact. "Interview with Joseph C. Chapman," in *Steel Shavings: The Postwar Period in the Calumet Region 1945–1950*, ed. James B. Lane and Stephen G. McShane, vol. 14 (Gary: Indiana University Northwest, 1988), pp. 10–13.

31. See "Froebel Strike," in Lane and McShane, *Steel Shavings*, p. 9.

32. White parents were able to force the School Board to rescind the integration of the

pool and instead allow Blacks to use it only on the day before it was cleaned. See Lane, *City of the Century*, pp. 232–239.

33. Ibid., p. 238.

34. Ibid., pp. 238–239.

35. Ibid., p. 239.

36. Finerty's brother Lawrence was murdered in what appeared to be a gangland killing. He had allegedly been involved in gambling and prostitution, and it was rumored that former associates of Al Capone had killed him. When Mayor Finerty retired from his $8,000-a-year job, he had a personal estate worth more than three million dollars, including yachts, mansions, an airplane, and Florida real estate. See James B. Lane, "Anxious Years," Chris Yugo, "Trends," Alfred L. Gordon, "Gary Scene," and Lynette Jones, "Bottom of the Tea Cup," in Lane and McShane, *Steel Shavings*, pp. 1–17.

37. In the 1942 elections the GOP scored one sensational upset, when Charles W. Gannon won the office of Lake County prosecutor. The ticket-splitting that produced Gannon's election amid staggering Democratic victories indicated that many Democratic voters were fed up with Gary's wide-open attitude toward vice. See "Gannon Wins as Demos Take Major Offices," *Gary Post-Tribune*, November 4, 1942, p. 1 and "Gannon Ready for Whoopee Cleanup," *Gary Post-Tribune*, November 4, 1942, p. 20.

38. "Davis Lone GOP Council Choice," *Gary Post-Tribune*, November 3, 1947, p. 1.

39. See "Complete Vote Totals," *Gary Post-Tribune*, November 5, 1947, p. 1.

40. See "Reminiscences of Lydia Grady," in Lane and McShane, *Steel Shavings*, pp. 40–42.

41. See "Interview with Joseph C. Chapman," in Lane and McShane, *Steel Shavings*, pp. 10–13; L. K. Jackson, "An Open Letter to the Citizens of Gary!" Rev. L. K. Jackson Collection, Booklets, Calumet Regional Archives (n.d.).

42. John Stanley, "Mayor Chacharis at Apex of Long Political Career," *Gary Post-Tribune*, November 8, 1959, p. 6.

43. Matthew A. Crenson, *The Un-Politics of Air Pollution* (Baltimore: Johns Hopkins University Press, 1971), p. 56. For details on Club SAR, see George Chacharis, "Tales of Steel," *Gary Post-Tribune*, June 17, 1956, p. 12. Also see Albert Renslow, "The Immigrants' Climb to Legitimacy: The Rise of George Chacharis, Gary's Immigrant Mayor," 1976, paper, Calumet Regional Archives.

44. Kelley Bauldridge, "Young Democrats," in Lane and McShane, *Steel Shavings*, p. 55. Renslow claimed that Swartz secretly supported Mandich and that Bauldridge was Finerty's choice. See Renslow, "Immigrants' Climb to Legitimacy," pp. 25–26.

45. For details of the political upheaval caused by Cheever's murder see Lane, *City of the Century*, pp. 247–251; Louisa A. Medina, "Not Soon Forgotten," in Lane and McShane, *Steel Shavings*.

46. "Dobis, Burton Trail in Gary Demo Ballot," *Gary Post-Tribune*, May 9, 1951, p. 5.

47. See the story of Black attorney Hilbert Bradley's decision to quit the GOP after learning that they were not serious in their efforts to bring Black voters into their coalition in "Negro Vote To Be Deciding Factor in Election Tuesday," *Gary American*, November 2, 1951, p. 3. Bradley would become a prominent Democratic politician in the Hatcher era.

48. "Smith Uses Race Insult To Answer Beach Question," *Gary American*, November 2, 1951, p. 3.

49. "Heavy District Demo Vote Sweeps in Mandich, Elich, 3 Councilmen," *Gary American*, November 9, 1951, p. 1.

50. "Gary Names Demo Mayor, GOP Judge," *Gary Post-Tribune*, November 7, 1951, pp. 1, 26 and "Gary Results," *Gary Post-Tribune*, November 7, 1951, pp. 24–25. All calculations made by me.

51. Quotation from "Negro Voters Prove Again that They Refuse To Be Intimidated,"

Gary American, November 9, 1951, p. 3. Also see "We Cannot Lose Sight of the Negro Demo's Support nor Rats in the Party," *Gary American*, November 16, 1951, p. 3.

52. Thomas F. Thompson, "Public Administration in the Civil City of Gary, Indiana" (Ph.D. diss., Indiana University, 1960), pp. 31–32.

53. See "Negro Voters Prove Again that They Refuse To Be Intimidated," and "We Cannot Lose Sight of the Negro Demo's Support nor Rats in the Party."

54. Thompson, "Public Administration in the Civil City of Gary," pp. 57, 73.

55. Lane, *City of the Century*, p. 263.

56. Ibid., p. 261.

57. Millender, *Yesterday in Gary*, p. 70.

58. All across the country President Roosevelt's rhetoric and the passage of the 1935 Labor Relations Act, which legalized the formation of industry-wide unions, galvanized the relationship between organized labor and the Democratic party. In Gary, Democratic party leaders integrated the leaders of the union into the party structure in exchange for financial support and manpower that supplemented the machine's electoral organization. At least 25 unions were active in Gary politics, including the United Steelworkers of America, the American Federation of Teachers, the United Auto Workers, and the American Federation of Labor building trades. See Lane, *City of the Century*, pp. 231, 257–59.

59. See Charles H. Levine, *Racial Conflict and the American Mayor* (Lexington, Mass.: Lexington Books, 1974), p. 69; Nelson, "Black Political Mobilization," pp. 146–154, 170; and Peter H. Rossi and Phillips Cutright, "The Impact of Party Organization in an Industrial Setting," in *Community Political Systems*, ed. Morris Janowitz, International Yearbook of Political Behavior Research, vol. 1 (Glencoe, Ill.: Free Press, 1961), p. 90.

60. Warner Bloomberg Jr., "The Power Structure of an Industrial Community" (Ph.D. diss., University of Chicago, 1961), p. 208, and Rossi and Cutright, "Impact of Party Organization in an Industrial Setting," pp. 81–116, especially p. 106.

61. Lane, *City of the Century*, p. 263. On Mayor Chacharis's orchestration of all city council activities, see Thompson, "Public Administration in the Civil City of Gary," pp. 133–34.

62. See Lane, *City of the Century*, p. 264; also see "Dowling Beats G.O.P. Mayor in Hammond Race," *Chicago Daily Tribune*, November 9, 1955, p. 3; and "Lake County, Indiana, Won by Democrats," *Chicago Daily Tribune*, November 4, 1959, p. 3.

63. Lane, *City of the Century*, pp. 263–268; Levine, *Racial Conflict and the American Mayor*, pp. 69–70.

64. Nelson, "Black Political Mobilization," p. 184; Oden, "Black Political Power in Gary, Indiana," p. 141. Also see Bloomberg, "Power Structure of an Industrial Community," p. 208.

65. Thompson, "Public Administration in the Civil City of Gary," pp. 30, 72–73.

66. "Means Quits Group; Pastor Charges FEPC Head with Misrepresenting Facts," *Gary American*, January 13, 1956, p. 1.

67. Jackson, "Open Letter to the Citizens of Gary!"

68. Lane, *City of the Century*, p. 275.

69. Ibid., p. 276.

70. Ibid., pp. 271–277.

71. Edward Banfield and James Q. Wilson, *City Politics* (New York: Vintage, 1963), p. 116. Also see Levine, *Racial Conflict and the American Mayor*, p. 70.

72. William E. Nelson and Philip J. Meranto, *Electing Black Mayors: Political Action in the Black Community* (Columbus: Ohio State University Press, 1977), p. 174.

73. Thompson, "Public Administration in the Civil City of Gary," pp. 31–32.

74. Nelson, "Black Political Mobilization," pp. 364–365. This fact is, of course, in keeping with the findings of J. David Greenstone and Paul Peterson regarding the intolerance of

political machines for other organizations that jeopardize their monopoly of the functions of interest articulation and political mobilization. See Greenstone and Peterson, *Race and Authority in Urban Politics* (Chicago: University of Chicago Press, 1973).

75. Dave Samuels, "Prison Term Starts Next Wednesday," *Gary Post-Tribune*, January 18, 1962, p. 1.

76. Running on the Democratic slate, Katz had been elected city judge in 1955 with about 66 percent of the vote and was reelected in 1959 with 75 percent of the vote.

77. Nelson, "Black Political Mobilization," p. 183.

78. Ibid., p. 268.

79. Ibid., p. 269.

80. Ibid., p. 269, and Levine, *Racial Conflict and the American Mayor*, p. 71.

81. Alex Poinsett, *Black Power: Gary Style* (Chicago: Johnson Publishing, 1970), pp. 64–70; Nelson, "Black Political Mobilization," pp. 254–262; and Hal Higdon, "Richard G. Hatcher: Soul Mayor," in *The Politics of the Powerless*, ed. Robert Binstock and Katherine Ely (Cambridge, Mass.: Winthrop, 1971), p. 148.

82. Nelson, "Black Political Mobilization," pp. 186–196.

83. According to Levine, Katz did not carry a single White precinct in either the primary or general elections of 1963. *Racial Conflict and the American Mayor*, p. 71.

84. Oden, "Black Political Power in Gary, Indiana," p. 148; also see Nelson, "Black Political Mobilization," p. 184.

85. See "Tell It Like It Is—Hatcher Can Win," Chacharis Collection, Pamphlets, Political Campaigns (18:1:38), Calumet Regional Archives, and Poinsett, *Black Power*, p. 107.

86. Nelson, "Black Political Mobilization," pp. 201–202; also see Oden, "Black Political Power in Gary, Indiana," pp. 155–156.

87. See Nelson, "Black Political Mobilization," pp. 249–254, 271–280. After a resignation from the city council enabled Mayor Katz to appoint a new council member, an open occupancy ordinance was passed.

88. Oden, "Black Political Power in Gary, Indiana," pp. 153–154.

89. Ibid., pp. 153–154.

90. Nelson, "Black Political Mobilization," pp. 323–365.

91. Ibid., pp. 382–384.

92. Lane, *City of the Century*, p. 287, emphasis added.

93. The Justice Department ruled in favor of charges brought by the Hatcher organization that the election board had illegally stricken the names of five thousand Black voters from the rolls and substituted the names of fictitious Whites. See Jeffrey K. Hadden, Louis Masotti, and Victor Thiessen, "The Making of the Negro Mayors, 1967," *TRANS-action* 5:1 (January–February 1968), p. 28, and Lane, *City of the Century*, pp. 289–290.

94. Nelson and Meranto, *Electing Black Mayors*, p. 273; Also see Poinsett, *Black Power*, p. 81, and Lane, *City of the Century*, p. 288.

95. Krupa also said that he had supported Blacks for public office in the past, and the 'only color I am against is red'; Nelson, "Black Political Mobilization," p. 418. Krupa also said, "I feel I'm standing shoulder to shoulder with the boys in Vietnam. They're fighting Communism and I'm fighting it here." Lane, *City of the Century*, p. 288.

96. Nelson, "Black Political Mobilization," pp. 402–409; Poinsett, *Black Power*, p. 81; Levine, *Racial Conflict and the American Mayor*, pp. 72–74; and Lane, *City of the Century*, p. 288.

97. Nelson, "Black Political Mobilization," pp. 403–405; Nelson and Meranto, *Electing Black Mayors*, p. 275; Levine, *Racial Conflict and the American Mayor*, p. 74; and Oden, "Black Political Power in Gary, Indiana," p. 159.

98. Levine, *Racial Conflict and the American Mayor*, p. 75.

99. Ibid., p. 79.

100. Ibid., pp. 79–80.

101. The candidate was Dr. Alexander Williams, who had been Lake County coroner and a loyal machine subordinate. Hatcher won with 60 percent of the vote, comprising 92 percent of the Black vote and about 9 percent of the White vote.

102. See Greer, *Big Steel*.

103. Robert A. Catlin, *Racial Politics and Urban Planning* (Lexington: University Press of Kentucky, 1993), pp. 2, 114.

104. See Robert A. Catlin, "The Decline and Fall of Gary, Indiana," *Planning* 54:6 (June 1988), pp. 10–15.

105. Nelson, "Black Political Mobilization," p. 177.

106. Millender, *Yesterday in Gary*, p. 69.

107. Nelson, "Black Political Mobilization," p. 178. Also see Lane, *City of the Century*, p. 287.

108. Nelson, "Black Political Mobilization," p. 177.

109. Levine, *Racial Conflict and the American Mayor*, pp. 70–71. Also see Rossi and Cutright, " Impact of Party Organization in an Industrial Setting," p. 106.

110. Oden, "Black Political Power in Gary, Indiana," p. 151.

111. Thompson, "Public Administration in the Civil City of Gary," p. 33. Also see Bloomberg, "Power Structure of an Industrial Community," p. 208.

112. Nelson, "Black Political Mobilization," p. 179.

113. Millender, *Yesterday in Gary*, p. 41.

114. Thompson, "Public Administration in the Civil City of Gary," pp. 28–29, and Nelson, "Black Political Mobilization," pp. 178–179.

115. Nelson, "Black Political Mobilization," pp. 297, 312.

116. Ibid., p. 181.

117. Ibid., pp. 172, 182.

118. According to Nelson, "[B]lacks became less interested in finding ways of making the machine responsive to their needs than in developing strategies for overthrowing the machine and instituting black control as a necessary step toward eventual black social, economic, and political liberation." Nelson, "Black Political Mobilization," p. 254.

119. The activities of the direct action leadership brought White anxieties about Black mobilization to the surface and produced such reactions as the formation of the National Association for the Advancement of White People. See Nelson, "Black Political Mobilization," pp. 229–230.

120. The NAACP's response to the formation of FSO was a front-page condemnation of its tactics in the *Gary Post-Tribune*. See Nelson, "Black Political Mobilization," pp. 213–215.

121. Nelson, "Black Political Mobilization," p. 228.

122. Ibid., pp. 229–243.

123. William E. Nelson Jr., *Black Politics in Gary: Problems and Prospects* (Washington, D.C.: Joint Center for Political Studies, 1972), pp. 15–16. Also see Nelson, "Black Political Mobilization," pp. 529–539.

124. Levine, *Racial Conflict and the American Mayor*, p. 74. Also see Oden, "Black Political Power in Gary, Indiana," p. 166.

125. Nelson, "Black Political Mobilization," pp. 174–175, emphasis added.

126. Gary's worsening economic conditions were caused by the decline of the domestic steel industry as a result of foreign competition and the cost of the technology needed to reduce air pollution, as well as by cuts made by the Nixon administration in federal aid to cities. See Seth S. King, "Steel Slowdown Brings Clear Skies to Gary, Ind., but City's Workers

Are Gloomy," *New York Times*, December 14, 1971, p. 35; Godfrey Hodgson and George Crile, "Gary: Epitaph for a Model City," *Washington Post*, March 4, 1973; Joel D. Weisman, "Every Major City Problem Seems More Acute in Gary," *Washington Post*, December 2, 1974; and Lane, *City of the Century*, pp. 302–303.

127. Levine, *Racial Conflict and the American Mayor*, p. 78, and Lane, *City of the Century*, p. 304.

128. Oden, "Black Political Power in Gary, Indiana," p. 181.

Chapter 4. Not Quite Brotherly Love

1. See The Committee of Seventy, *The Charter: A History* (Philadelphia: Committee of Seventy, 1980), pp. 7–8.

2. The New Deal markedly improved the electoral performance of the Philadelphia Democratic party in the 1935 and 1939 mayoral elections. But, as the table indicates, by 1943 and 1947 the GOP seemed to have successfully beaten back the Democratic party's challenge.

Republican Domination of Mayoral Politics, 1919–1947

Year	Percentage of vote Republican	Percentage of vote Democrat	Percentage of vote Other
1919	83	11	6
1923	88	12	—
1927	67	30	3
1931	92	8	—
1935	53	47	—
1939	52	48	—
1943	59	41	—
1947	56	44	—

Source: Office of City Commissioners, Voter Registration Division, "Annual Report of the City Commissioners to the People of Philadelphia" (1919, 1923, 1927, 1931, 1935, 1939, 1943, 1947).

3. Kirk Petshek, *The Challenge of Urban Reform: Policies and Programs in Philadelphia* (Philadelphia: Temple University Press, 1973), p. 65. Petshek, who was an official in the Clark administration, offers a thorough chronicle of the reform movement. On the Republican machine and Philadelphia politics since the 1920s, see Alan Frazier, "City of Brotherly Loot," *American Mercury* 47:187 (July 1939); John T. Salter, *Boss Rule: Portraits in City Politics* (York, Pa.: McGraw-Hill, 1935); James A. Reichley, *The Art of Government: Reform and Organization Politics in Philadelphia* (New York: Fund for the Republic, 1959); and Jeanne Lowe, *Cities in a Race with Time: Progress and Poverty in America's Renewing Cities* (New York: Random House, 1967), p. 319.

4. About 1,300 Republican committeemen, out of approximately 3,000, switched to the Democratic party. See Robert Freedman, *A Report on the Politics of Philadelphia* (Cambridge: Joint Center for Urban Studies of the Massachusetts Institute of Technology and Harvard University, 1963), 2:49.

5. There is wide agreement that the GPM was the most powerful civic group in the city. See Freedman, *Report on the Politics of Philadelphia*, 5:3; John G. McCullough, "Philadelphia's Movers and Shakers: Potent Core of Civic Giants Molds City's Destiny," *Philadelphia Bulletin*, June 6, 1965, and McCullough, "Philadelphia's Movers and Shakers: No. 2," *Philadelphia Bulletin*, June 7, 1965; and David Rogers, *The Management of Big Cities* (Beverly Hills: Sage, 1971), p. 76.

6. Among other things, the charter stripped the city council of much power and vested that power in the mayor, including the power to appoint a four-person cabinet of managing director, director of finance, city representative/director of commerce, and city solicitor. It also encouraged civil service, stipulated that applicants for important municipal positions be selected by nonpolitical panels, and combined Philadelphia County with the city. See Committee of Seventy, *The Charter.*

7. Petshek, *Challenge of Urban Reform*, pp. 16–30.

8. See John Guinther, "Light a Candle for the City Charter," *Philadelphia Magazine* (April 1976). The Committee of Seventy and the Fellowship Commission were also prominent organizations in the reform movement.

9. Petshek, *Challenge of Urban Reform*, pp. 63–64.

10. See Oscar Glantz, "Recent Negro Ballots in Philadelphia," p. 67, and Charles A. Ekstrom, "The Electoral Politics of Reform and Machine: The Political Behavior of Philadelphia's 'Black' Wards, 1943–1969," p. 92, table 6–3, both in *Black Politics in Philadelphia*, ed. Miriam Ershkowitz and Joseph Zikmund II (New York: Basic Books, 1973).

11. Ekstrom, "Electoral Politics of Reform and Machine," especially table 6–4, p. 94.

12. See Robert Bendiner, "The Negro Vote and the Democrats," *Reporter* 14:8, May 31, 1956, quoted in Glantz, "Recent Negro Ballots in Philadelphia," p. 69.

13. See William J. McKenna, "The Changing Pattern of Philadelphia Politics, 1914–1955," *Economics and Business Bulletin of the School of Business and Public Administration, Temple University* 8:3 (March 1956), especially table 13.

14. Joseph R. Daughen, "Parties Court Negroes, Who Hold Key to Power," *Philadelphia Bulletin*, January 24, 1965, p. A–3.

15. Blacks attained the positions of staff inspector, sergeant, lieutenant, and captain on the police force. See Lowe, *Cities in a Race with Time*, p. 353.

16. Conrad Weiler concluded that "reform has provided, in Philadelphia at least, much more of an avenue of political mobility for blacks than the party organizations that normally make ethnicity their business." See Weiler, *Philadelphia: Neighborhood, Authority, and the Urban Crisis* (New York: Praeger, 1974), p. 164. Also see "Struggle of Negro in Philadelphia from Slave to Citizen," *Philadelphia Bulletin*, January 24, 1965, p. 2.

17. Lowe, *Cities in a Race with Time*, p. 353.

18. Ibid., p. 353.

19. Lowe, *Cities in a Race with Time*, pp. 334–335, 354–356. Also see John F. Bauman, *Public Housing, Race, and Renewal: Urban Planning in Philadelphia, 1920–1974* (Philadelphia: Temple University Press, 1988), chaps. 5–6.

20. Reichley, *Art of Government.*

21. For instance, the composition of the city council shifted. Five of the six votes that Clark had marshalled to defeat charter amendments, sponsored by party chairman Green to weaken its antipatronage statutes, were no longer available on the city council. One reform-oriented Republican was not reslated, one Democratic independent city council member was defeated, and two others who had supported Clark's defense of the charter were won over by the organization. Soon after the election another independent Democrat died.

22. Reichley suggests that Leader's decision came after Green pledged that the organization would back Leader in his planned bid for the U.S. Senate. Reichley, *Art of Government*, p. 14. On the importance of gubernatorial patronage for machine-building, see Steven Erie, *Rainbow's End: Irish Americans and the Dilemmas of Urban Machine Politics, 1840–1985* (Berkeley: University of California Press, 1988).

23. John Strange, "The Negro in Philadelphia Politics: 1963–1965" (Ph.D. diss., Princeton University, 1966), p. 57.

24. Just how many patronage jobs are available to Philadelphia through the governor's office is a subject of some debate. See Reichley, *Art of Government*, p. 9, especially n. 5.

25. See Petshek, *Challenge of Urban Reform*, p. 293

26. As a city councilman, Tate had proposed amendments to weaken the charter that were sponsored by Green and defeated by Mayor Clark.

27. See Edward Banfield, *Big City Politics* (New York: Random House, 1965), p. 107; also see Edward Banfield and James Q. Wilson, *City Politics* (New York: Vintage Books, 1963), pp. 116, 125.

28. James H. J. Tate, "In Praise of Politicians," *Philadelphia Bulletin*, January 20, 1974, p. 27. Prior to the 1963 election, unions were very weak politically in the city. See Reichley, *Art of Government*, pp. 19–20. The major unions in Philadelphia are the Building and Construction Trades Council, the United Steel Workers, the ILGWU, the Transport Workers, the Retail Clerks, and the Teamsters.

29. Daughen, "Parties Court Negroes, Who Hold Key to Power."

30. Jewish liberals supported 'Darlin' Arlen Specter, who promised to fight corruption in city hall, whereas Italians and members of other White ethnic groups were drawn to his tough "law and order" declarations. The movement of White ethnic voters away from the party was evident in Richard Nixon's 1968 presidential victory and was already noticeable in 1965 with Specter, and in Chicago in 1963 when Benjamin Adamowski gave Richard J. Daley a serious challenge.

31. William J. McKenna, "The Negro Vote in Philadelphia Elections," in Ershkowitz and Zikmund, *Black Politics in Philadelphia*.

32. Ekstrom, "Electoral Politics of Reform and Machine."

33. This, of course, is the infamous and usually accurate characterization of antimachine political reformers by Tammany Hall ward leader George Washington Plunkitt. See William Riordon, *Plunkitt of Tammany Hall* (New York: E. P. Dutton, 1963), p. 17.

34. Another vehicle—mentioned repeatedly in interviews I conducted—through which the White business and liberal communities developed organizational ties with moderate Black leaders and institutionalized a reform orientation in the city's government was the Philadelphia Fellowship Commission. The Fellowship Commission is an interracial organization comprised of religious, business, and labor groups dedicated to combating racial bias in opportunities for employment, housing, and education. The city charter designated the Fellowship Commission one of five organizations represented on the panel that nominates officers for the Civil Service Commission. The Fellowship Commission's role has historically been to seek out talented minority individuals as members, and a number of the city's most prominent Black leaders have become known to the White reform leadership through their membership in the commission. See Strange, "The Negro in Philadelphia Politics: 1963–1965," pp. 58–59.

35. In 1967 controller Alexander Hemphill, an anticorruption watchdog, ran against Mayor Tate and won about 35 percent of the primary vote, including 38 percent of the vote in predominantly Black middle-class wards.

36. See Banfield, *Big City Politics*, p. 107; Alex Gottfried, "Political Machines," *The International Encyclopedia of the Social Sciences*, vol. 12 (New York: Crowell, Collier and Macmillan, 1968), p. 249; also see David Mayhew, *Placing Parties in American Politics* (Princeton: Princeton University Press, 1986), pp. 55–64.

37. Melvin G. Holli and Peter A. Jones, *Biographical Dictionary of American Mayors, 1820–1980* (Westport, Conn.: Greenwood Press, 1981), p. 356.

38. See Ershkowitz and Zikmund, *Black Politics in Philadelphia*, p. 58.

39. On the funneling of PCCA money to Sullivan's OIC and other efforts to create em-

ployment in the Black community, see minutes of meeting of the Community Relations Committee (February 15, 1966), GPM Records, Urban Archives Center, Temple University Libraries. Wilson Goode got his political start as a housing activist in the PCCA. See W. Wilson Goode with Joann Stevens, *In Goode Faith* (Valley Forge, Pa.: Judson Press, 1992), chap. 6.

40. See Peter Marris and Martin Rein, *Dilemmas of Social Reform* (New York: Atherton Press, 1969), chaps. 4.

41. PAAC election rules "eliminated politicians, clergymen, and middle class leaders," insuring that there would be no infiltration by Blacks sympathetic to the reformers and no allegiances other than to Bowser, Evans, and Tate. See Paul Peterson, "City Politics and Community Action: The Implementation of the Community Action Program in Three American Cities" (Ph.D. diss., University of Chicago, 1967), p. 111. Also see Elliot White, "Articulateness, Political Mobility, and Conservatism: An Analysis of the Philadelphia Antipoverty Election," in Ershkowitz and Zikmund, *Black Politics in Philadelphia*, pp. 188–205.

42. Workers were pressured to help pass a city bond issue in 1966 and do campaign work in the 1967 mayoral race. See Harry A. Bailey Jr., "Poverty, Politics, and Administration," in Ershkowitz and Zikmund, *Black Politics in Philadelphia*, p. 179.

43. Strange argues that the vast majority of the positions in city government that Blacks obtained during the Tate years were low-paying manual jobs exempted from civil service. Blacks held less than 1 percent of the municipal jobs that paid over $7,000 a year. In the Philadelphia public schools almost all the Black teachers were paid at the lowest tenure scale. See Strange, "The Negro in Philadelphia Politics: 1963–1965," pp. 133–137.

44. John H. Strange, "Black Politics in Philadelphia," in Ershkowitz and Zikmund, *Black Politics in Philadelphia*, p. 110.

45. A second Black was elected in 1967 to one of the six at-large seats on the city council, but he was nominated by the Republican party.

46. See John H. Strange, "The Negro and Philadelphia Politics," in *Urban Government*, ed. Edward Banfield (New York: Free Press, 1969), pp. 409–410.

47. See "Police Board Ruled Illegal," *New York Times*, November 15, 1968, p. 33, and "Police Advisory Board Abolished in Philadelphia," *New York Times*, December 28, 1969, p. 33.

48. James H. J. Tate, "Tate Felt a Rizzo Win Would Save Democratic Control," *Philadelphia Bulletin*, January 23, 1974.

49. See Ekstrom, "Electoral Politics of Reform and Machine," and Thomas Byrne Edsall and Mary Edsall, *Chain Reaction: The Impact of Race, Rights, and Taxes on American Politics* (New York: Norton, 1991).

50. Gaeton Fonzi, "Cecil Storms In," *Greater Philadelphia Magazine* (July 1963), pp. 21–23, 45–57.

51. Moore advised Crippens to decline the post of PAAC legal counsel; after he accepted it, Moore severed their relationship. See Bailey, "Poverty, Politics, and Administration," and White, "Articulateness, Political Mobility, and Conservatism."

52. See Strange, "The Negro and Philadelphia Politics," p. 413, and Paul Lermack, "Cecil Moore and the Philadelphia Branch of the National Association for the Advancement of Colored People: The Politics of Negro Pressure Group Organization," in Ershkowitz and Zikmund, *Black Politics in Philadelphia*, pp. 145–160.

53. Lermack, "Cecil Moore and the Philadelphia Branch of the National Association for the Advancement of Colored People," pp. 155–158.

54. See Minutes, Board of Directors Meeting (October 26, 1966), GPM Records.

55. See Claude Sitton, "An Uneasy Racial Truce Prevails in Philadelphia," *New York Times*, August 3, 1963, p. 14; and Barbara Reynolds, *Jesse Jackson: The Man, The Movement, The Myth* (Chicago: Nelson-Hall, 1975). Also see the discussion of the strategy and

success of the four hundred ministers by one of their spokesmen, Leon Sullivan, in *Build Brother Build* (Philadelphia: Macrae Smith, 1969), pp. 70–77.

56. For another example of a successful employment training program sponsored by the private sector in the Black community, see Chamber of Commerce, Urban Action Clearinghouse, "Philadelphia Utility Offers Jobs and Advancement to Minorities," Case Study Number 7 (Washington, D.C., 1968).

57. See "Philadelphia Poor Pledged $1 Million by Business Group," *New York Times*, May 12, 1968, p. 34, and "Negro Help Is Planned in Pa. City," *New York Times*, November 24, 1968, p. 17.

58. See Orrin Evans, "Black Coalition Disbands; Leaders Ask New Program," *Philadelphia Bulletin*, April 9, 1969, and "Directors OK Plan To Merge 2 Coalitions," *Philadelphia Bulletin*, April 29, 1969.

59. Kos Semonski, "Bowser Ready to Quit Tate, Lead Civic Unit," *Philadelphia Bulletin*, April 27, 1969. Wilson Goode later rose to a position of leadership in this organization, which institutionalized business-Black consultation.

60. See Sullivan, *Build Brother Build*, pp. 86–92.

61. See Joint Economic Committee, U.S. Congress, *Employment and Manpower Problems in the Cities: Implications of the Report of the National Advisory Commission on Civil Disorders*, Hearings of the Joint Economic Committee, 90th Congress, Second Session, May 28, 29, June 4, 5, 6, 1968. Also see Bernard E. Anderson, *The Opportunities Industrialization Centers: A Decade of Community-Based Manpower Services*, University of Pennsylvania, Wharton School, Industrial Research Unit, Manpower and Human Resources Studies, no. 6 (Philadelphia, 1976).

62. Tate's memoirs appeared as a series of articles entitled "In Praise of Politicians," *Philadelphia Bulletin*, January 13–24, 1974. He admits that he never imagined Rizzo would turn out to be the kind of mayor he became. See "In Praise of Politicians," *Philadelphia Bulletin*, January 23, 1974, pp. 16–17.

63. Peter C. Buffum and Rita Sagi, "Philadelphia: Politics of Reform and Retreat," in *Crime in City Politics*, ed. Anne Heinz, Herbert Jacob, and Robert L. Lineberry (New York: Longman, 1983), p. 141; Jonathan Newman and William K. Marimow, "The Homicide Files," *Philadelphia Inquirer*, April 24–27, 1977; "Cops on Trial," *Time*, August 27, 1979.

64. Green was sent to Congress in a special election necessitated by the death of his father. See "Democrats Choose Rep. Green to Head Philadelphia Party," *New York Times*, December 29, 1967, p. 11. Five other unknowns filed for the Democratic primary and together received less than eight thousand votes.

65. The NDC, Central City Reform Democrats, the Black Political Forum, and the Women's Political Caucus were all formed to articulate the liberal-reform viewpoint once direct access to the mayor's office was closed after Dilworth's departure. Some of these groups worked to perpetuate the cooperation between White reformers and Blacks that began in the Clark period. For instance, the NDC built an alliance with progressive Blacks in the Black Political Forum, and they agreed to run joint slates in some wards. The existence and success of these organizations provides further evidence that reform did not die in Philadelphia during the Tate period. See Peter A. McGrath, "Bicentennial Philadelphia: A Quaking City," in *Philadelphia: 1776–2076*, ed. Dennis Clark (Port Washington, N.Y.: Kennikat Press, 1975), p. 10.

66. There were 268,707 registered Black voters in 1971, comprising 30 percent of the total registered voter population, according to the Philadelphia Board of Election Commissioners.

67. Joseph Daughen and Peter Binzen, *The Cop Who Would Be King: Mayor Frank Rizzo* (Boston: Little, Brown, 1977), p. 175.

68. Gene Harris, "Sullivan Plays 'Dirty Pool,' Rizzo Says," *Philadelphia Bulletin*, October 21, 1971.

69. All calculations made by me. For the data, see Richard A. Keiser, "Black Political Incorporation or Subordination? Political Competitiveness and Leadership Formation Prior to the Election of Black Mayors," (Ph.D. diss., University of California, Berkeley, 1989), p. 201A.

70. See William K. Mandel, "Citizens Group Boosts Hardy Williams for Mayor," *Philadelphia Bulletin*, November 22, 1970; Acel Moore and Gerald McKelvey, "Hardy Williams: Underdog Insists 'My Time Is Now,'" *Philadelphia Inquirer*, April 30, 1971; and Henry R. Darling, "Hardy Williams: Soft Spoken, Tough on Shoes," *Philadelphia Bulletin*, March 26, 1971.

71. Almost 80 percent of the voters in these Black wards were registered as Democrats. Citywide, 62 percent of the voters were registered Democrats, and 35 percent were Republican.

72. See the perceptive article by John Guinther, "Party Pooper," *Philadelphia Magazine* 63:9 (September 1972), pp. 44–54. Rizzo's independence of organizational intermediation was evident in his ability to mobilize registered Republicans to switch parties and become registered Democrats in order to vote for him in the Democratic primary. Comparison of the voter registration figures for 1970 and 1971 indicates that almost 20,000 Republicans, largely in Italian-American areas of the city, had switched their registration to Democrat.

73. Camiel's success in pyramiding resources resulted in his control of all the city's patronage from Governor Shapp. See John Guinther, "Up the Organization," *Philadelphia Magazine* 63: 5 (May 1972).

74. Daughen and Binzen recount numerous stories of firing and hiring by Rizzo and his aides in the final month before the 1975 mayoral election for what seem to be purely political reasons. They enumerate 5,500 jobs paying salaries that totalled at least $65,000,000, and they suggest other possible sources of jobs. See Daughen and Binzen, *Cop Who Would Be King*, pp. 254–264.

75. See Daughen and Binzen, *Cop Who Would Be King*, p. 208 and Gerard McCullough, "Rizzo's Strategy: Meet the Voters," *Philadelphia Bulletin*, September 14, 1975, p. 25. Managing Director Hillel Levinson was indicted on 35 criminal counts of extortion, illegally demanding political contributions and perjury. See "Philadelphia Aide Cited in Extortion," *New York Times*, April 17, 1975, p. 42.

76. On Black dissatisfaction with Hill, see Joseph R. Daughen, "Hill Must Gain Support of Blacks To Win Primary," *Philadelphia Bulletin*, March 16, 1975, and Jerome Mondesire, "Black Voters Stayed at Home Tuesday," *Philadelphia Inquirer*, May 22, 1975.

77. Wayne King, "Rizzo Is Strong Victor in Philadelphia," *New York Times*, May 21, 1975, p. 14; Wayne King, "Rizzo Aides Planning To Unseat Party Regulars in Philadelphia," *New York Times*, May 22, 1975, p. 22; and "Rizzo Solidifies Power in Philadelphia," *New York Times*, May 26, 1976, p. 11.

78. The total number of registered voters declined from 1971 to 1975 among both Whites and Blacks. For Whites, the decline was proportionately larger, with the result that in 1975 Whites comprised 69 percent of the electorate and Blacks totalled 31 percent.

79. Charles Bowser and former Mayor Clark were among the leaders of the movement. See "Rizzo Recall Drive," *New York Times*, April 1, 1976, p. 34, and "A Petition Drive to Remove Rizzo Begins at Philadelphia Ceremony," *New York Times*, April 18, 1976, p. 32.

80. "Court Explains Its Ruling Opposing Recall of Rizzo," *New York Times*, November 20, 1976, p. 10.

81. In the 1978 charter referendum, however, Rizzo received the tacit support of Republican party chairman William Meehan, who recognized that under a reform Democrat mayor

the GOP would not receive even the patronage crumbs they obtained from Rizzo. See Mike Mallowe, "Should the City Charter Be Changed So That Frank Rizzo Can Be Mayor for Life?" *Philadelphia Magazine* 69:10 (October 1978), pp. 195–196, 250–263.

82. See Acel Moore, "The Rev. Gray is suddenly a political force," *Philadelphia Inquirer*, November 11, 1978; Paul Taylor, "Third Term Opponents Form Alliance," *Philadelphia Inquirer*, September 6, 1978; Paul Taylor, "Meet the Men Fighting the Charter Change," *Philadelphia Inquirer*, September 24, 1978; and Mallowe, "Should the City Charter Be Changed So That Frank Rizzo Can Be Mayor for Life?"

83. See Bob Frump, "Rizzo Warns of Radicals," *Philadelphia Inquirer*, September 22, 1978, and Bob Frump, "Rizzo's Message As Clear As Black and White," *Philadelphia Inquirer*, September 24, 1978.

84. Street was a confrontational political leader who was notorious for leading disruptive demonstrations in center city. Few Black leaders would have defined themselves as his allies.

85. A representative of the Fellowship Commission said: "[S]uch rhetoric poisons the atmosphere, setting group against group, and threatens to divide future generations along racial lines long after the question of the Charter change is resolved." Editorial, *Philadelphia Inquirer*, October 5, 1978.

86. Quoted in Mike Mallowe, "The White Hope," *Philadelphia Magazine* 69:11 (November 1978), p. 269.

87. Paul Taylor, "Rizzo To Downplay Racially Based Issues," *Philadelphia Inquirer*, September 26, 1978, and Bob Frump, Ray Holton, and Paul Taylor, "A Black Defends Rizzo As 'Vote White' Debate Intensifies," *Philadelphia Inquirer*, September 28, 1978.

88. Hiley Ward, "The Gray Tradition May End at Bright Hope Church," *Philadelphia Inquirer*, September 16, 1978, p. 4–A, and Moore, "Rev. Gray Is Suddenly a Political Force," *Philadelphia Inquirer*, November 11, 1978.

89. See Bob Frump and Acel Moore, "City's Religious Leaders Censure Racial Rhetoric," *Philadelphia Inquirer*, September 30, 1978, and Bob Frump, "Rizzo on the Clergy," *Philadelphia Inquirer*, October 1, 1978.

90. Featherman and Rosenberg have calculated the percentage of support for the charter change vote by racial/ethnic group. They found that Blacks gave the charter change 4 percent of their support, Poles 62 percent, Italians 85 percent, Irish 61 percent, Jews 31 percent, Puerto Ricans 23 percent, and WASP 15 percent. Their figures should be treated with some caution because they are based on calculations from voting divisions (precincts) in which registered voters comprised only 50 percent or more of the respective ethnic group. See Sandra Featherman and William L. Rosenberg, *Jews, Blacks, and Ethnics: The 1978 "Vote White" Charter Campaign in Philadelphia* (Philadelphia: American Jewish Committee, 1979).

91. According to the Voter Registration Division of the Office of City Commissioners, from November 1977 to November 1978 the number of registered Black voters rose by approximately 90,000, while the number of registered Whites increased by about 18,000.

92. Goode, *In Goode Faith*, p. 148.

93. See Paul Green, "Green Started the Race Early—Perhaps Too Early," *Philadelphia Inquirer*, May 16, 1979.

94. See Gregory Jaynes, "Green and Marston Win Philadelphia Races," *New York Times*, May 16, 1979, p. 12.

95. See Paul Taylor, "Now Everyone Is Chasing Green," *Philadelphia Inquirer*, March 18, 1979; Green, "Green Started the Race Early—Perhaps Too Early"; and Mike Mallowe, "The Pretenders," *Philadelphia Magazine* 70:5 (May 1979), p. 125.

96. Green's disdain for the feeble organization was demonstrated when he abandoned his neutral stance on candidates for city council and endorsed a slate of five Blacks and liberals who were running in opposition to the Rizzocrat Democratic City Committee slate. Three of

the five insurgents were victorious. See Ronald Goldwyn, "Rizzo Names His 6 Candidates," *Philadelphia Bulletin*, July 24, 1979, and Paul Taylor, "Two Reply to Rizzo Criticism," *Philadelphia Inquirer*, July 20, 1979.

97. Mallowe, "Pretenders," p. 234.

98. One prominent Black leader who refused to support Bowser was councilman Joseph Coleman, who, like Gray, had built strong ties to the White business and civic establishments. Gray hesitated for a long time before actually endorsing Bowser. See Ronald Goldwyn, "Voters Will Have To Come Out As They Did in Charter Fight," *Philadelphia Bulletin*, April 29, 1979. Animosity existed between Gray and Bowser because Bowser, a member of Gray's Bright Hope Baptist Church, endorsed Congressman Nix in his 1976 race against Gray. Gray lost this first challenge by only a few hundred votes, and Bowser's support might well have made the difference.

99. See Ronald Goldwyn, "Bowser Endorses Green in Mayor's Race," *Philadelphia Bulletin*, July 12, 1979.

100. Ibid.

101. The managing director, whose position is similar to that of city manager, manages service delivery in the areas of police, fire, health, streets, recreation, welfare, water, public property, licenses and inspections, and records. The 10 commissioners of these service areas report directly to the managing director. The businessmen who wrote the city charter liked the idea of a city manager and were in favor of that form of government. However, Cincinnati's city manager, Charles Taft, advised the charter writers that Philadelphia was too large for this form of government. So the office of managing director was created. See Freedman, *Report on the Politics of Philadelphia*, 2:4.

102. See Ronald Goldwyn, "Bowser Leaves Green Standing at the Altar," *Philadelphia Bulletin*, July 13, 1979, and Joe Davidson, "Bowser Accused of Stealing Show," *Philadelphia Bulletin*, July 15, 1979.

103. S. A. Paolantonio, *Frank Rizzo: The Last Big Man in Big City America* (Philadelphia: Camino Books, 1993), p. 247; also see Goode, *In Goode Faith*, p. 104.

104. Paolantonio, *Frank Rizzo*, p. 254, and Goode, *In Goode Faith*, p. 149.

105. John Portz, *The Politics of Plant Closings* (Lawrence: University Press of Kansas, 1990), p. 165.

106. Green and the Black community leaders also clashed over his refusal to divest the city's pension fund from its investments in companies doing business in South Africa. See "Philadelphia Mayor in Trouble over Minority Aid," *New York Times*, May 17, 1982.

107. Personal correspondence with office of Orville W. Jones, director, Personnel Department, City of Philadelphia, September 23, 1987.

108. Richard A. Keiser, "Explaining African-American Political Empowerment: 'Windy City' Politics from 1900 to 1983," *Urban Affairs Quarterly* 29:1 (September 1993), pp. 84–116.

109. Community Leadership Seminar Program, GPM Records. "Community Leadership Seminar Program, 1974."

110. In meetings throughout the city, Goode explained how the budget was formulated, where the money went, the effects of federal government funding cutbacks, and how citizens would make the city government more accountable to their demands. An agenda that included the issues most commonly raised throughout the city was presented to Mayor Green and the city council. Prominent neighborhood organizer, interview by author, April 1987. Also see Carolyn Acker, "Wilson Goode: He Transformed the Job," *Philadelphia Daily News*, November 30, 1982, p. 6.

111. See Peter Binzen, "Business Leaders Give Less to Goode for This Campaign," *Philadelphia Inquirer*, October 31, 1983.

112. See Edwin Guthman, "Philadelphia Was Also a Winner in the Primary," *Philadelphia Inquirer*, May 22, 1983; Binzen, "Business Leaders Give Less to Goode for this Campaign."

113. Officer of the Greater Philadelphia First Corporation, interview by author, July 1984.

114. "Race Is a Muted Issue in Philadelphia," *New York Times*, April 12, 1983.

115. Goode had impressive credentials to discuss government administration; he had earned a master's degree in government administration from the University of Pennsylvania's Wharton School in 1968.

116. "For Goode, Year of Recovery," *Philadelphia Inquirer*, January 24, 1987.

117. Goode's choice of incompetent and/or corrupt administrators and his failure to quickly remove them again became evident in the scandals surrounding the Inner City Organizing Network (ICON), the recipient of a major share of the city's federal housing funds. Its director, Charles L. "Boo" Burrus, an associate of the mayor, was charged with theft and misuse of housing money.

118. "Goode's Bright Promise Beset by MOVE, Strike,"*Christian Science Monitor*, July 22, 1986; "Goode Pulled Black Vote for a Range of Reasons," *Philadelphia Inquirer*, May 24, 1987.

119. Carolyn Teich Adams, "Philadelphia: The Slide toward Municipal Bankruptcy," in *Big City Politics in Transition*, ed. H. V. Savitch and John Clayton Thomas, Sage Urban Affairs Annual Reviews, vol. 38 (Newbury Park, Calif., 1991).

120. Paolantonio, *Frank Rizzo*, p. 154.

121. "For Goode, a Year of Recovery," *Philadelphia Inquirer*, April 12, 1987.

122. Goode, *In Goode Faith*, pp. 279–280.

123. Anita Summers and Thomas Luce, *Economic Development within the Philadelphia Metropolitan Area* (Philadelphia: University of Pennsylvania Press, 1987).

124. James Jennings, *The Politics of Black Empowerment: The Transformation of Black Activism in Urban America* (Detroit: Wayne State University Press, 1992), p. 138.

125. Supervisory member of Mayor Goode's office staff, interview by author, July 1986.

126. Mike Mallowe, "The No-Frills Mayor," *Philadelphia Magazine*, 74:12 (December 1984), pp. 169–172, 226–289.

127. "Goode Pulled Black Vote for a Range of Reasons."

128. Goode, *In Goode Faith*, pp. 245–247.

129. Robert A. Beauregard, "Local Politics and the Employment Relation: Construction Jobs in Philadelphia," in *Economic Restructuring and Political Response*, ed. Robert A. Beauregard, Sage Urban Affairs Annual Reviews, vol. 34 (Newbury Park, Calif., 1989), p. 168.

130. U.S. Conference of Mayors, *A Status Report on Homeless Families in America's Cities* (Washington, D.C., 1987).

131. Michael deCourcy Hinds, "50% Cutback in Funds for Homeless Is Fiercely Protested," *New York Times*, September 15, 1989.

132. Bruce E. Caswell, "Machine, Reform, Interest, and Race: The Politics of the Philadelphia Fiscal Crisis," (paper presented at the annual meeting of the American Political Science Association, Chicago, Ill., August 1992).

133. Jennings, *Politics of Black Empowerment*, p. 168.

134. Adams, "Philadelphia: The Slide toward Municipal Bankruptcy," p. 31.

135. Ibid., p. 31.

136. Murray Dubin, "The City Gets a Rude Awakening on Latinos' Plight," *Philadelphia Inquirer*, June 17, 1990, p. 5.

137. Doreen Carvajal, "Marching Side by Side along a Divide," *Philadelphia Inquirer*, September 27, 1993, pp. B1–2; Sergio R. Bustos, "Police Accused of Beating up Latinos," *Philadelphia Inquirer*, January 15, 1994, p. B1, B5; and Jeff Gammage, "Response Time," *Philadelphia Inquirer Magazine*, February 6, 1994, p. 24.

138. Vernon Loeb, "The Soul of an Old Machine," *Philadelphia Inquirer Magazine*, April 17, 1994, pp. 20–28.

139. Mary Ellen Balchunis, "A Study of the Old and New Campaign Politics Models: A Comparative Analysis of Wilson Goode's 1983 and 1987 Philadelphia Mayoral Campaigns" (Ph.D. diss., Temple University, 1992), p. 77.

140. Ginny Weigand, "Rendell's Panel Fails To Mollify Preservationists," *Philadelphia Inquirer*, March 27, 1994, p. B1.

141. See Jim Sleeper, "The End of the Rainbow," *New Republic*, November 1, 1993, pp. 20–25.

142. Dan Rottenberg, "Ed Rendell: The Eternal Sophomore as America's Mayor," *Pennsylvania Gazette* (May 1994), p. 24.

143. Amy S. Rosenberg, "Layoff Notices Sent to 350 City Workers," *Philadelphia Inquirer*, January 7, 1994, p. B1.

144. In a battle for the presidency of the Board of Education, Rendell insured that a Black candidate would win. The leading opponent, an Italian, would have been the first Italian to hold this office and was backed by the most powerful White ethnic politician in Philadelphia. See Dale Mezzacappa, "A Controversial Year Later, Lee Looks Like a Shoo-in," *Philadelphia Inquirer*, November 20, 1993, p. B2. In the awarding of contracts for work with the Philadelphia Housing Authority, Rendell and Street have refused to consider contractors who do not agree to make a good faith effort to hire from a list of qualified, trained tenants. See Amy S. Rosenberg, "PHA Imposes Tenant-Hiring Policy on Bids," *Philadelphia Inquirer*, March 1, 1994, p. B1.

145. Neither Lucien Blackwell nor William Gray III are any longer active players in Philadelphia politics.

146. The state of Pennsylvania has failed to fully reimburse its counties for court costs and child welfare expenditures. As a result, Philadelphia (which is both a city and a county) has been dramatically affected by increases in homelessness and drug abuse, which directly affect these costs.

147. Jerry W. Byrd, "After Years of Losses, Area Jobs Up," *Philadelphia Inquirer*, April 17, 1994, p. A1, A8.

148. W. E. B. Du Bois, *The Philadelphia Negro* (Philadelphia: University of Pennsylvania Press, 1899), and "The Black Vote in Philadelphia," *Charities* 15 (1905), pp. 31–35.

149. W.E.B. Du Bois, "The Black Vote of Philadelphia," in Ershkowitz and Zikmund, *Black Politics in Philadelphia*, p. 36.

150. Reichley, *Art of Government*, p. 69.

151. Strange, "Blacks and Philadelphia Politics," p. 111.

152. On Moore, see Lermack, "Cecil Moore and the Philadelphia Branch of the National Association for the Advancement of Colored People," and Fonzi, "Cecil Storms In." Other Black separatist-messianic leaders active in the 1960s were Stanley Branche, "Freedom George" Brower, Jeremiah X, and Malik Yulmid.

153. Lermack, "Cecil Moore and the Philadelphia Branch of the National Association for the Advancement of Colored People," p. 151.

154. See Carl Gilbert, "From 'Integration' to 'Black Power': The Civil Rights Movement in the City of Philadelphia, 1960–67" (master's thesis, Temple University, n.d.), especially pp. 57–87.

155. Others who would be included among the coalitional-incrementalists were Rev. Henry Nichols (president of the Philadelphia Council of Churches), attorney Harvey Schmidt, and GPM executive director James Lineberger.

156. See Frump, Holton, and Taylor, "A Black Defends Rizzo As 'Vote White' Debate Intensifies," *Philadelphia Inquirer*, September 28, 1978.

157. Street's first major publicity came when he handcuffed himself to the lectern in city council chambers to protest a proposed ordinance that placed restrictions on street vendors, jobs that were increasingly held by Blacks. He protested against the spending of community development funds on downtown redevelopment by organizing mass marches on the new Gallery, a downtown shopping mall. See Mallowe, "White Hope."

158. At the Philadelphia Partnership, Gray, together with James Bodine, president of First Pennsylvania Bank, and M. Todd Cooke, president of the Philadelphia Savings Fund Society—two of the city's largest banks—created the Philadelphia Mortgage Plan. This plan represented a commitment by these and other major banks to erase the de facto redlining (the denial of mortgages to Blacks seeking to move into White neighborhoods) that characterized the city's housing and real estate markets.

159. Goode also served as William Gray's campaign manager in 1978 and was part of the network of people over which Gray exerted considerable influence. Coleman had strong credentials in the White liberal community because of his longstanding membership in the Philadelphia ADA, where he served as the chairman of the Anti-Poverty Committee in the mid-1960s and was an outspoken critic of Mayor Tate's PAAC. See Nicholas Stroh, "ADA Proposes Changes in Staff Policies of PAAC," *Bulletin of the Americans for Democratic Action*, December 13, 1966, ADA Records, Urban Archives Center, Temple University Libraries.

Chapter 5. Political Competition and Black Empowerment in Atlanta, 1946–1992

1. Alton Hornsby Jr., "A City That Was Too Busy To Hate," in *Southern Businessmen and Desegregation*, ed. Elizabeth Jacoway and David R. Colburn (Baton Rouge: Louisiana State University Press, 1982), pp. 120–136. See Ivan Allen Jr., with Paul Hemphill, *Mayor: Notes on the Sixties* (New York: Simon and Schuster, 1971), p. 93, and Fred Powledge, "A New Politics in Atlanta," *New Yorker*, December 31, 1973, p. 31.

2. Little Rock's image, in the eyes of Northern capital seeking to relocate to the nonunion South, was severely damaged by Arkansas Governor Orval Faubus's 1957 decision to use national guardsmen to block the integration of Little Rock's Central High School. According to Cobb, Little Rock had attracted eight new industrial plants in 1957, but during the next four years the city was unable to attract a single new industry. Leaders from the Little Rock Chamber of Commerce visited Atlanta with letters from companies that had stopped considering relocating to Arkansas because of the school desegregation publicity. See James S. Cobb, *The Selling of the South: The Southern Crusade for Industrial Development, 1936–1940* (Baton Rouge: Louisiana State University Press, 1982), pp. 124–126.

3. In Atlanta, local elections are nonpartisan, although elections to state offices are partisan.

4. On this tripartite description of political groups, see Jack Walker, "Negro Voting in Atlanta: 1954–1961," *Phylon* 24 (Winter 1963B), p. 381. The split between large- and small-scale business was reflected in the formation of the Central Atlanta Improvement Association in 1941. This organization was a vehicle for the interests of major downtown property holders, whereas the Chamber of Commerce continued to reflect the diversity of interests among big and small businesses.

5. On Boston and the Irish, see Peter K. Eisinger, "Ethnic Political Transition in Boston, 1884–1933: Some Lessons for Contemporary Cities," *Political Science Quarterly* 91:2 (Summer 1978), pp. 217–239.

6. See Clarence A. Bacote, "The Negro in Atlanta Politics," *Phylon* 16:4 (1955), pp. 348–349.

7. Atlanta's White politicians viewed the Black ministers "as perhaps the most power-ful of all influences on the Negro voter." See Mary Louise Frick, "Influences on Negro Political Participation in Atlanta, Georgia" (master's thesis, Georgia State College, 1967), pp. 47–55, with quotation p. 63. Also see Francena Edwina Culmer, "Changing Patterns of Leadership in the Black Community of Atlanta, Georgia: 1960–1969" (master's thesis, Georgia State College, 1967), pp. 47–55.

8. Under the city charter of 1874 (replaced in 1973) aldermanic candidates were quali-fied from each ward but were elected citywide. Records of the ANVL precinct and ward leaders, together with letters to and from aldermanic candidates regarding the group's endorsement, can be found in the Atlanta Negro Voters League Series, Austin T. Walden Papers, Atlanta History Center, Atlanta.

9. According to Pat Watters and Reese Cleghorn, in politics the Black community of Atlanta was "better organized, more interested, and more likely to produce a better election-day turnout" than the White community. See Watters and Cleghorn, *Climbing Jacob's Lad-der: The Arrival of Negroes in Southern Politics* (New York: Harcourt, Brace, and World, 1967), p. 85.

10. Harold H. Martin, *William Berry Hartsfield* (Athens: University of Georgia Press, 1978), pp. 23–24.

11. See "Mayor Candidate Refuses To Attend Dodd Meeting," *Atlanta Constitution*, September 4, 1949, p. 10–A.

12. Three prominent Black leaders approached Mayor James L. Key about the appoint-ment of the first police officer of their race in 1932. See Herbert Jenkins, *Keeping the Peace: A Police Chief Looks at His Job* (New York: Harper and Row, 1970), p. 10.

13. See James W. English, *Handyman of the Lord: The Life and Ministry of the Rev. William Holmes Borders* (New York: Meredith Press, 1967), p. 15.; Herbert T. Jenkins, *Forty Years on the Force, 1932–1972* (Atlanta: Center for Research in Social Change, Emory Uni-versity, 1973), p. 45.

14. Herbert T. Jenkins, police chief under Mayor Hartsfield (and the next mayor, Ivan Allen Jr.), also claimed that Brown won the majority of White votes. See Jenkins, *Forty Years on the Force*, p. 48.

15. Martin, *William Berry Hartsfield*, p. 72.

16. Maddox's staunch prosegregation stance is documented in Bradley R. Rice, "Lester Maddox and the 'Liberal' Mayors," *Proceedings and Papers of the Georgia Association of Historians* (Marietta, Ga.: Kennesaw College, 1981), pp. 80–81.

17. Walker, "Negro Voting in Atlanta: 1954–1961," p. 384.

18. For evidence of consultation between Hartsfield and the ANVL on the commercial rezoning of Auburn Avenue, the main artery of Black Atlanta, as well as the discussion of the municipal hiring of Blacks, see Atlanta Negro Voters League Series, Austin T. Walden Papers. Also see Bradley R. Rice, "If Dixie Were Atlanta," in *Sunbelt Cities*, ed. Richard M. Bernard and Bradley Rice (Austin: University of Texas Press, 1983), p. 46.

19. Jenkins, *Keeping the Peace*, p. 26.

20. Atlanta Negro Voters League Series, and Atlanta City Executive Commission, Aus-tin T. Walden Papers, Atlanta History Center, Atlanta.

21. "Whiteway Add Hailed by Negroes," *Atlanta Constitution*, December 9, 1949.

22. Georgia Ann Persons asserts that business community support for this candidacy was not important because most White voters did not know that the candidate was Black. But the important point is that the White leadership was willing to back a Black candidate for a vis-ible public office in which people soon enough would learn that he was Black. By supporting a Black candidate for the School Board, the White business leaders were affirming their will-ingness to take such a bold step, even though it would make them vulnerable to the attacks of

segregationists. See Persons, "Atlanta: Black Mayoral Leadership and the Dynamics of Political Change" (Ph.D. diss., Massachusetts Institute of Technology, 1978), p. 93.

23. Bacote, "The Negro in Atlanta Politics," pp. 349–350. In this book I strive not to be present-minded and not to minimize the importance of past events by looking at them through the lens of the present. If participants in the events saw them as decisive, I hesitate to challenge this interpretation without evidence from that era. Scholars such as Banfield and Eisinger have minimized the significance of Hartsfield's actions. But Bacote, a scholar and Black political leader who negotiated with Hartsfield, thought the mayor was following "progressive lines." Discussing the decision to appoint Black police officers, Police Chief Jenkins said, "It was perhaps the most emotional meeting ever held in police headquarters. As we look back on it today, it is hard to understand, but at this time it was an issue that created a great deal of controversy and hard feelings." Jenkins, *Forty Years on the Force*, p. 46; Edward Banfield, *Big City Politics* (New York: Random House, 1965), p. 30; and Peter Eisinger, *The Politics of Displacement* (New York: Academic Press, 1980), p. 65.

24. See Robert A. Thompson, Hylan Lewis, and Davis McEntire, "Atlanta and Birmingham: A Comparative Study in Negro Housing," in *Studies in Housing and Minority Groups*, ed. Nathan Glazer and Davis McEntire (Berkeley: University of California Press, 1960), p. 30.

25. M. Kent Jennings and Harmon Zeigler, "Class, Party, and Race in Four Types of Elections: The Case of Atlanta," *Journal of Politics* 28 (1966), p. 406.

26. See Clarence Stone, *Regime Politics: Governing Atlanta 1946–1988* (Lawrence: University Press of Kansas, 1989), chap. 3.

27. In advocating the eligibility of Blacks for jobs in a WPA-sponsored sewerage construction project, Hartsfield had said, "surely if there is any place for the negro on our city payroll it would be at the place where sewerage is treated." Douglas L. Smith, *The New Deal in the Urban South* (Baton Rouge: Louisiana State University Press, 1988), p. 222.

28. Bradley R. Rice, "The Battle of Buckhead: The Plan of Improvement and Atlanta's Last Big Annexation," *Atlanta Historical Journal* 25 (1981), pp. 80–81.

29. Watters and Cleghorn, *Climbing Jacob's Ladder*, p. 86.

30. The influential banker Mills B. Lane disagreed with the Supreme Court's decision, which he characterized as "an invasion of state's rights." Yet he realized that school desegregation was a necessary price to pay to maintain the electoral coalition with Blacks that perpetuated the progrowth regime. See Cobb, *Selling of the South*, p. 128.

31. Hornsby interviewed business leaders who recalled thinking that all Atlanta's advances in commerce and industry "could be set back by prolonged turmoil over desegregation" of the schools. Instead, Atlanta won national recognition, and the personal congratulations of President John F. Kennedy, for its success in peacefully integrating previously all-White high schools. See Hornsby, "City That Was Too Busy To Hate."

32. See Jack L. Walker, "Protest and Negotiation: A Case Study of Negro Leadership in Atlanta, Georgia," *Midwest Journal of Political Science* 7:2 (May 1963), p. 103.

33. Allen, *Mayor*, p. 38. Additional evidence of racial pragmatism by business leaders who were personally opposed to desegregation can be found in Cobb, *Selling of the South*, p. 128.

34. Two of the young sit-in organizers, Julian Bond and Lonnie King, present their accounts of this episode in Howell Raines, *My Soul Is Rested* (New York: G. P. Putnam's Sons, 1977), pp. 83–93. Also see Benjamin Mays, *Born to Rebel* (New York: Scribners, 1971), pp. 287–299.

35. For example, see "The Second Battle of Atlanta," *Look*, April 25, 1961, p. 34; "Glad to See You," *Newsweek*, September 11, 1961, p. 93; "Atlanta's Peaceful Blow for Justice," *Life*, September 15, 1961, pp. 35–36.

36. Atlanta Negro Voters League Series, Austin T. Walden Papers.

37. Banfield, *Big City Politics*, p. 26.

38. Commenting on the issue of school desegregation, Maddox scored Allen for "planning to invade every white high school in Atlanta, with negro students, in September this year. . . . After a few years of this, stories about young white girls being found in negro hotels will not even make the newspapers." See Hornsby, "City That Was Too Busy To Hate," p. 135.

39. Rice, "Battle of Buckhead," p. 83.

40. Walker, "Negro Voting in Atlanta," pp. 381–385. Also see Numan V. Bartley, *From Thurmond to Wallace: Political Tendencies in Georgia, 1948–1968* (Baltimore: Johns Hopkins University Press, 1970A), p. 47.

41. Allen, *Mayor*, pp. 131–134, and Rice, "If Dixie Were Atlanta," p. 38.

42. Allen carried a transcript of his testimony with him whenever he campaigned among Blacks. See Eisinger, *Politics of Displacement*, p. 66.

43. Alton Hornsby Jr., "The Negro in Atlanta Politics, 1961–1973," *Atlanta Historical Bulletin* 21 (Spring 1977), pp. 17–18.

44. Information about MARTA is drawn from the following: Timothy Almy, William B. Hildreth, and Robert Golembiewski, "Case Study I—Assessing Electoral Defeat: New Directions and Values for MARTA," in *Mass Transit Management: Case Studies of the Metropolitan Atlanta Rapid Transit Authority*, report, Department of Transportation, Urban Mass Transportation Administration (Washington, D.C.: 1981); Mack Jones, "Black Political Empowerment in Atlanta," *Annals of the American Academy of Political and Social Science* 439 (September 1978), p. 103; Alex Coffin, "Blacks Basic Transit Plan," *Atlanta Constitution*, September 24, 1971, p. 12; and Bill Seddon, "Blacks Claim Credit for MARTA Win," *Atlanta Constitution*, November 11, 1971, p. 13.

45. Hornsby, "The Negro in Atlanta Politics," p. 22.

46. See Raleigh Bryans, "Race Called Key to City's Future," *Atlanta Constitution*, September 7, 1969, pp. 1, 19–A.

47. See Alex Coffin, "Cook, Millican Swap Attacks," *Atlanta Constitution*, September 3, 1969, p. 8–A.

48. Eisinger, *Politics of Displacement*, p. 67.

49. See Bartley, *From Thurmond to Wallace*, p. 53.

50. See Alex Coffin, "Candidates' Support Picture Is Blurred," *Atlanta Constitution*, October 6, 1969, p. 18–A, in which Tate's supporters are described as the "newer, more militant leadership" in the Black community.

51. Before Maynard Jackson's mayoral election, Hill probably was the most influential Black in Atlanta. He was the first Black named to the board of MARTA and the first Black president of the Atlanta Chamber of Commerce. His credentials in the African-American community went back to the lunch-counter protests of the 1960s, when he was an adviser to Lonnie King and other leaders of the student movement. He played a leadership role in the ACRC's voter registration efforts and in bargaining over school desegregation. He was also one of the founding members of both the Atlanta Summit Leadership Conference and the Atlanta Action Forum. He served as campaign manager for Jackson in his successful mayoral bid in 1973. On Hill, see Raleigh Bryans, "Jesse Hill Gets Leery of 'Token Black' Role," *Atlanta Journal and Constitution*, May 13, 1973, p. 14–A.

52. For details on the strategy of the Black political leadership, see Alex Coffin, "Negro Leaders Endorse Massell; Cook Questions Experience Claim," *Atlanta Constitution*, October 3, 1969, p. 1–A. Both Maynard Jackson and state senator Leroy Johnson considered entering the mayoral race of 1969, and both concluded that a Black could not yet win. On Jackson, see Bruce Galphin, "They Laughed When He Ran—Now Jackson's a Winner," *Atlanta*

Constitution, October 12, 1969, p. 19–B. On Johnson's decision to pass up the 1969 mayoral race, see Hornsby, "The Negro in Atlanta Politics," pp. 23–25.

53. Alex Coffin, "Massell and Cook Vow Strong Races for Oct. 21 Runoff," *Atlanta Constitution*, October 9, 1969, p. 1–A; "Massell Climbed to Power, Fell As the Guard Changed," *Atlanta Constitution*, March 27, 1973, p. 19–A.

54. This was the case even though Tate endorsed Cook. Alex Coffin, "Tate's Nod Goes to Cook," *Atlanta Constitution*, October 18, 1969, p. 1. Also see "Cook Is Backed By Millican," *Atlanta Constitution*, October 16, 1969, p. 6–A.

55. Raleigh Bryans, "Politics Getting Heated Up, So Are Atlanta's Voters," *Atlanta Journal and Constitution*, October 19, 1969, p. 1, 6–A. Also see Numan Bartley, "Atlanta Elections and Georgia Political Trends," *New South* (Winter 1970), p. 23.

56. Charles Rooks, *The Atlanta Elections of 1969* (Atlanta: Voter Education Project, 1970), pp. 19–21.

57. Clarence Stone offers the contrary view that the 1969 elections signified the dissolution of the traditional Black-White coalition. See Stone, *Regime Politics*, p. 79.

58. Jones, "Black Political Empowerment in Atlanta," p. 99.

59. On Farris, see Alex Coffin, "Farris, Jackson Equated," *Atlanta Journal and Constitution*, September 1, 1969, p. 14–A.

60. See Editorial, *Atlanta Constitution*, October 2, 1969.

61. Rooks, *Atlanta Elections of 1969*, pp. 34–38. Also see Bartley, *From Thurmond to Wallace*, p. 101, especially table 6–12.

62. Rooks, *Atlanta Elections of 1969*, pp. 41–51.

63. Ibid., p. 54.

64. Jones, "Black Electoral Empowerment in Atlanta," p. 101, table 6; also see Alex Coffin, "City Hiring of Blacks Boosted by 20 Percent," *Atlanta Constitution*, August 17, 1972, p. 9–A.

65. Massell disappointed Black supporters in 1970 by refusing to negotiate with striking sanitation workers, most of whom were Black. He offered a pay increase that was considerably less than the union had originally demanded, and the union capitulated. Numerous articles on the strike and the mayor's stiff resistance can be found in the *Atlanta Constitution*, March 2–14, 1970.

66. See Sam Hopkins, "L.A. Vote Omen for Atlanta?" *Atlanta Constitution*, May 31, 1973, p. 12–A.

67. Duncan R. Jamieson, "Maynard Jackson's 1973 Election as Mayor of Atlanta," *Midwest Quarterly* 18 (1976), pp. 7–26.

68. See Hornsby, "The Negro in Atlanta Politics," pp. 28–30.

69. Jones, "Black Electoral Empowerment in Atlanta," p. 102.

70. For students enamored of the metropolitanization panacea offered by David Rusk in *Cities without Suburbs* (Baltimore: Johns Hopkins University Press, 1993), this rejection of annexation proposals offers a healthy reality check.

71. Department of Labor, Bureau of Labor Statistics, Special Regional Report, *Atlanta: Ten Years of Growth, 1955–1965* (Washington, D.C.: 1966), p. 1.

72. Rice, "If Dixie Were Atlanta," pp. 38–39.

73. At its founding, there were twelve White and twelve Black members of the Action Forum. The majority were CEOs who had the ability to make decisions for their companies without consultation. See Powledge, "New Politics in Atlanta," pp. 35–39.

74. See Bryans, "Jesse Hill Gets Leery of 'Token Black' Role"; Hopkins, "L.A. Vote Omen for Atlanta?"; and Hank Ezell, "Power Structure Hunting Candidates?" *Atlanta Journal and Constitution*, June 3, 1973, p. 7–A.

75. Jonathan Kaufman, "Atlanta: Open Doors Abounding," *Boston Globe*, December 21,

1983; Alex Coffin, "Blacks Back Transit Plan," *Atlanta Constitution*, September 24, 1971, p. 12–A; Bill Seddon, "Blacks Claim Credit for MARTA Win," *Atlanta Constitution*, November 11, 1971, p. 13–A.

76. See Joel L. Fleishman, "The Real Against the Ideal—Making the Solution Fit the Problem: The Atlanta Public School Agreement of 1973," in *Roundtable Justice: Case Studies in Conflict Resolution*, ed. Robert B. Goldmann (Boulder, Colo.: Westview Press, 1980), pp. 129–180.

77. Clarence Stone argues that Maynard Jackson, because he was an outsider and not part of the Black leadership cadre that had traditionally been junior partners with the White power structure, was responsible for changing the relationship. "Jackson's independent stance altered the understandings about power relationships that had long been in place. The black community traditionally had beseeched favors or concessions from the community's "top" leaders. For Jackson to inform the business elite what their obligations were—whether about bank hiring or city contracts—upset that understanding." (Stone, *Regime Politics*, p. 94.) I argue that it was the Black coalitionist leadership that altered the relationship (i.e., the allocation of power) between Blacks and the growth coalition, and that Black leaders in organizations like Action Forum paved the way for Jackson's election by demonstrating that, as full partners, they could work effectively with Whites for the good of the city at the same time that they negotiated reallocations of political and economic power that benefited the Black community.

78. Tom Linthicum and Chuck Bell, "Allen Backs Weltner for Mayor," *Atlanta Constitution*, September 21, 1973, p. 1–C.

79. Among the White executives who supported Jackson were the chairmen of the boards of Coca-Cola, Citizens and Southern National Bank, and the Trust Company of Georgia. Together with the most visible Black leaders, many of whom had formed good working relations with the White leaders through the Atlanta Action Forum, they comprised Jackson's kitchen cabinet during the campaign. See M. Dale Henson and James King, "The Atlanta Public-Private Romance: An Abrupt Transformation," in *Public-Private Partnership in American Cities*, ed. R. Scott Fosler and Renee A. Berger (Lexington, Mass.: D.C. Heath, 1982), p. 306. Also see Ezell, "Power Structure Hunting Candidates?"

80. Stan Alexander, Sharon Broussard, and Barnetta Jackson, *The 1973 Atlanta Elections* (Atlanta: Voters Education Project, 1973), pp. 9–14.

81. See Jim Gray, "Jackson, Williams Are 'Racists,' Says Massell," *Atlanta Constitution*, October 8, 1973; Tom Linthicum, "Massell's Strategy—Play on White Fears," *Atlanta Constitution*, October 8, 1973; and Tom Linthicum, "Jackson Calls for Rejection of 'Fear Mongers,'" *Atlanta Constitution*, October 9, 1973, p. 11–A.

82. In the new city charter enacted in 1973, the name of the city's governing body was changed from Board of Aldermen to City Council and that of the city's second highest elective office from Vice-Mayor to City Council President. Just as was the case with the vice-mayor, the city council president is elected at large. The president appoints all members and chairpersons of the legislative committees; the mayor had this power in the past.

83. See Sam Hopkins, "'Deal' by Jackson charged by Massell," *Atlanta Constitution*, July 10, 1973, p. 11–A; Tom Linthicum, "Mitchell Warns of Last Minute Stories That Charge a 'Deal,'" *Atlanta Constitution*, September 15, 1973; Jim Merriner, "Runoff Likely with Hosea; Mitchell Third," *Atlanta Constitution*, October 3, 1973; and Editorial, *Atlanta Constitution*, October 8, 1973.

84. Editorial, *Atlanta Constitution*, October 12, 1973. Also see "Atlanta Elects a Black Mayor, but Hosea Williams Is Defeated," *New York Times*, October 17, 1973, pp. 1, 9.

85. Alexander, Broussard, and Jackson, *The 1973 Atlanta Elections*, pp. 22–30.

86. See Editorial, *Atlanta Constitution*, October 18, 1973; also see Powledge, "New Politics in Atlanta," p. 30.

87. According to Jackson's campaign treasurer, the White business leadership gave large sums of money to the campaign. See Colleen Teasley, "Mayor Execs Put on Show of Unity," *Atlanta Journal and Constitution*, November 24, 1974, p. 20–D.

88. Stone, *Regime Politics*, p. 81.

89. On Cleveland, see Todd Swanstrom, *The Crisis of Growth Politics* (Philadelphia: Temple University Press, 1985).

90. See Henson and King, "Atlanta Public-Private Romance," pp. 331–333.

91. Allen, *Mayor*, p. 50.

92. Henson and King, "Atlanta Public-Private Romance," p. 305.

93. Mayor Maynard Jackson, interview with author, July 1993.

94. Stone, *Regime Politics*, p. 93.

95. Ibid., pp. 87–88.

96. Floyd Hunter, *Community Power Succession* (Chapel Hill: University of North Carolina Press, 1980), p. 74.

97. Jones considered Inman and police brutality to be a "major concern to the black electorate." See Jones, "Black Political Empowerment in Atlanta," pp. 108–09, 116, with quotation p. 109.

98. Ibid., p. 116.

99. Atlanta Bureau of Personnel and Human Resources, Affirmative Action Division, "Survey of Current Employment, November 30, 1977" (Atlanta: Department of Administrative Services, 1977). All computations and calculations made by me.

100. Eisinger, *Politics of Displacement*, table 7.1, p. 160.

101. See Research Atlanta, *The Impact of Local Government Programs to Encourage Minority Business Development* (Atlanta: Research Atlanta, 1986), table 3–1, p. 41.

102. Marshall Ingwereson, "Atlanta Business Mecca for Black Middle Class in America," *Christian Science Monitor*, May 29, 1987, p. 1.

103. Henson and King, "Atlanta Public-Private Romance," pp. 331–333.

104. See Research Atlanta, *Impact of Local Government Programs*, p. 54.

105. See Wendell Rawls Jr., "Atlanta Sees Role As Global Trader," *New York Times*, December 12, 1982, p. 31. On Young and Eaves, see Charles S. Bullock III and Bruce A. Campbell, "Racist or Racial Voting in the 1981 Municipal Elections," *Urban Affairs Quarterly* 20:2 (December 1984), pp. 149–164.

106. Atlanta Bureau of Personnel and Human Resources, Affirmative Action Division, "1985 City Work Force Profile" (Atlanta: Department of Administrative Services, 1985).

107. Ronald Smothers, "Affirmative Action Booms in Atlanta," *New York Times*, January 27, 1989, p. 17.

108. See Stone, *Regime Politics*, p. 118.

109. See Carol Pierannunzi and John D. Hutcheson Jr., "Electoral Change and Regime Maintenance: Maynard Jackson's Second Time Around," *PS* 23:2 (June 1990), pp. 151–153.

110. See, for instance, Stone, *Regime Politics*, p. 167, and the works of Adolph Reed Jr. cited hereafter.

111. See Adolph Reed Jr., "Black Urban Administrations," *Telos* 65 (Fall 1985), pp. 51–54, and "A Critique of Neo-Progressivisim in Theorizing about Local Development Policy: A Case from Atlanta," in *The Politics of Urban Development*, ed. Clarence N. Stone and Heywood T. Sanders (Lawrence: University Press of Kansas, 1987), p. 203. Also see Stephen Burman, "The Illusion of Progress: Race and Politics in Atlanta, Georgia," *Ethnic and Racial Studies* 2:4 (October 1979), pp. 441–454.

112. Both Jones and Eisinger cite changes in police behavior toward Blacks and reductions in police brutality as major accomplishments. See Jones, "Black Political Empowerment in Atlanta," p. 115, and Eisinger, *Politics of Displacement*, pp. 154–55.

113. Rodney Strong, director, Office of Contract Compliance, City of Atlanta, letter to Anita Sharp, Editor, *Atlanta Business Chronicle*, February 28, 1989.

114. Timothy Bates, *Banking on Black Enterprise* (Washington, D.C.: Joint Center for Political and Economic Studies, 1993).

115. Martin Luther King Sr., with Clayton Riley, *Daddy King: An Autobiography* (New York: William Morrow, 1980), pp. 98–99. Mays also notes the resistance that A. T. Walden faced in the Black community when, in the 1950s, he led the struggle for equal pay for Black and White teachers in Atlanta. See *Born to Rebel*, p. 205.

116. An ANVL meeting was described as a forum at which candidates "out-promise each other" to secure endorsement. "Mayor Candidate Refuses To Attend Dodd Meeting."

117. King, *Daddy King*, pp. 138–139.

118. Martin, *William Berry Hartsfield*, pp. 118–119.

119. Jamieson, "Maynard Jackson's 1973 Election As Mayor of Atlanta," pp. 20–22; also see Frick, "Influences on Negro Political Participation in Atlanta, Georgia."

120. Jamieson, "Maynard Jackson's 1973 Election as Mayor of Atlanta," pp. 20–22. In contrast, the *Atlanta Inquirer*, which was owned by Jesse Hill, endorsed Massell in 1969 and Jackson in 1973. See Virginia H. Hein, "The Image of 'A City Too Busy to Hate': Atlanta in the 1960s," *Phylon* 33:3 (Fall 1972), p. 212.

121. Anne Rivers Siddons, "The Seeds of Sanity," *Atlanta Magazine*, (July 1967).

122. Hein, "Image of 'A City Too Busy to Hate,'" pp. 215–216.

123. Siddons, "Seeds of Sanity," and Bill Schemmel, "Atlanta's 'Power Structure' Faces Life," *New South* 27:2 (Spring 1972).

124. *My Soul Is Rested*, pp. 435–436.

125. Williams discusses this process and the settlement he personally negotiated with a Sears executive in "Hosea Taught Business Leaders a New Lesson in Uses of Power," *Atlanta Constitution*, March 26, 1975, pp. 1–A, 15–A. In his earliest civil rights experiences in Savannah, Williams had learned that when threatened with the disruption of business activity, a community's business leaders would come forward and could effectively pressure even the most hardheaded segregationist politicians into acceding to desegregation plans. See Raines, *My Soul Is Rested*, pp. 438–445.

126. Bryans, "Jesse Hill Gets Leery of 'Token Black' Role."

127. Jim Merriner and Rex Granum, "Atlanta's Black Power Structure," *Atlanta Constitution*, September 22, 1975, pp. 1, 12.

128. The separatist-messianic leadership group also includes housing tenant advocate Louise Watley and Rev. Ted Clark, an antigrowth zealot.

129. Walker, "Protest and Negotiation: A Case Study of Negro Leadership in Atlanta, Georgia," p. 117.

130. Ronald Bayor, "The Civil Rights Movement as Urban Reform: Atlanta's Black Neighborhoods and a New 'Progressivism,'" *Georgia Historical Quarterly* 77:2 (Summer 1993), p. 295.

131. Clarence Stone, *Economic Growth and Neighborhood Discontent* (Chapel Hill: University of North Carolina Press, 1976), pp. 107–124.

132. Ibid., pp. 127–128; also see Stone, *Regime Politics*, pp. 72–73.

133. Bayor, "Civil Rights Movement as Urban Reform," p. 303.

134. See Banfield, *Big City Politics*, pp. 34–35.

135. Hornsby, "The Negro in Atlanta Politics," p. 19; Culmer, "Changing Patterns of Leadership in the Black Community of Atlanta, Georgia: 1960–1969," p. 40.

136. Fleishman, "The Real against the Ideal—Making the Solution Fit the Problem: The Atlanta Public School Agreement of 1973."

137. Aside from the coalitional-incrementalists mentioned in the text, the high-profile ranks of this group would include Mrs. Grace Hamilton, a state legislator and matriarch of the Atlanta civil rights movement; state representative Ben Brown; W. C. "Bill" Calloway, a wealthy real estate broker; attorney David Franklin, once considered to be Maynard Jackson's closest adviser; Bill Campbell, who served for 12 years on the city council and was elected mayor in 1993; city council president Marvin Arrington; city council member Myrtle Davis; Fulton County commissioner Martin Luther King III; and one-time city council Finance Committee chairman Ira Jackson.

Chapter 6. Subordination or Empowerment?

1. This hypothesis was stimulated by four sources to which I owe intellectual debts: Robert Dahl, *Polyarchy: Participation and Oppostion* (New Haven: Yale University Press, 1971); J. David Greenstone and Paul E. Peterson, *Race and Authority in Urban Politics: Community Participation and the War on Poverty* (New York: Sage, 1973); Charles E. Gilbert and Christopher Clague, "Electoral Competition and Electoral Systems in Large Cities," *Journal of Politics* 24 (1962), pp. 323–349; and Henry Lee Moon, *Balance of Power: The Negro Vote* (Garden City, N.Y.: Doubleday, 1948). See Adolph Reed Jr., "The Black Urban Regime: Structural Origins and Constraints," *Comparative Urban and Community Research* 1 (1988), pp. 138–189; Robert C. Smith, "Recent Elections and Black Politics: The Maturation or Death of Black Politics?" *PS* 23 (1990), pp. 160–162; and James Jennings, *The Politics of Black Empowerment: The Transformation of Black Activism in Urban America* (Detroit: Wayne State University, 1992).

2. Clarence N. Stone, *Regime Politics: Governing Atlanta, 1946–1988* (Lawrence: University Press of Kansas, 1989), p. 213.

3. Robert K. Merton first argued that one of the latent functions of the political machine was the provision for subgroups otherwise disadvantaged in society. James Q. Wilson developed this thesis with specific reference to Blacks, and he argued that the absence of "machine control" placed Blacks in weak machine, nonmachine, and nonpartisan cities at a "profound disadvantage" in the construction of Black organizations, the promotion of Black interests, and the capturing of "important political roles." He contended that "the structure and style of Negro politics reflect the politics of the city as a whole." The existence of a unified Black political machine in Chicago was dependent on the existence of White machine. In cities where White political groups were factionalized and competitive, Wilson argued, Blacks would also be factionalized and would engage in debilitating competition rather than presenting a united front to negotiate benefits. Furthermore, he argued that "[i]n non-machine and weak-machine cities, the active intervention of another strong force which has a vested interest in mobilizing Negroes seems to be necessary to bring them into important political roles."

Wilson erred in two ways. First, he did not recognize that the most significant examples of Black empowerment from 1919 to 1955 were the result of competition between Republican and Democratic organizations for blocs of Black votes (as I argue in detail in chapter 2) rather than of the existence of either a Democratic or Republican machine. Second, he presumed that Blacks in Chicago would be successful in obtaining "important political roles" from the Daley machine because they had been successful in capturing low-level offices. But these entry-level offices did not lead any further than comfortable cooptation for Blacks in noncompetitive Chicago. See Merton, *Social Theory and Social Structure* (1949; reprint, New York: Free Press, 1968), p. 132, and James Q. Wilson, *Negro Politics: The Search for Leadership* (Glencoe, Ill.: Free Press, 1960), pp. 23–26. For an important caveat on the success of the Irish through machine politics, see Steven Erie, *Rainbow's End: Irish-Americans and the Dilemmas of Urban Machine Politics, 1840–1985* (Berkeley: University of California Press, 1988). The Kerner Report concluded that one of the reasons the political system "has not worked for the Negro as it has for other groups" was because of "the demise of the historic urban political machines." See National Advisory Commission on Civil Disorders (Kerner Commission), *Report* (New York: Bantam Books, 1968), p. 287. This view is endorsed in Nathan Glazer, "Blacks and Ethnic Groups: The Difference, and the Political Difference It Makes," *Social Problems* 18:4 (Spring 1971), p. 457.

4. For examples of this argument see William E. Nelson and Philip Meranto, *Electing Black Mayors* (Columbus: Ohio State University Press, 1977); Erie, *Rainbow's End*; and Richard A. Keiser, "Explaining African-American Political Empowerment: 'Windy City' Politics from 1900 to 1983," *Urban Affairs Quarterly* 29:1 (September 1993), pp. 84–116.

5. Rufus P. Browning, Dale Rogers Marshall, and David H. Tabb, *Protest Is Not Enough: The Struggle of Blacks and Hispanics for Equality in Urban Politics* (Berkeley: University of California Press, 1984), pp. 18–19.

6. Rufus P. Browning, Dale Rogers Marshall, and David H. Tabb, eds., *Racial Politics in American Cities* (New York: Longman, 1990), pp. 19–20.

7. One of the most sophisticated versions of this argument was offered by Michael Preston in his analysis of Chicago politics. He argued that the subordination of Blacks by the Daley organization should have catalyzed an independent Black movement or a biracial reform movement, but failed to do so because of the absence of Black leadership. In fact, however, independent Black leaders did emerge in Chicago, but they were either coopted and subordinated by the Daley organization or chose to withdraw from participation in local politics. Preston's argument begs the question of why they chose these two paths, neither of which leads to Black empowerment, in Chicago. This question demands attention to the structural factors that create opportunities and shape the cost-benefit calculations of Black leaders. See Preston, "Black Politics in the Post-Daley Era," in *After Daley*, ed. Samuel K. Gove and Louis H. Masotti (Urbana: University of Illinois Press, 1982), pp. 104–105.

8. Paul Kleppner, *Chicago Divided: The Making of a Black Mayor* (Dekalb, Ill.: Northern Illinois University Press, 1985), p. 144. Alkalimat and Gills argue that Mayor Byrne "gave virtually every aspect of the movement fuel for building a protest against the machine." See Abdul Alkalimat and Doug Gills, "Black Power vs. Racism: Harold Washington Becomes Mayor," in *The New Black Vote*, ed. Rod Bush (San Francisco: Synthesis Publications, 1984), pp. 53–179, with quotations p. 68; also see William J. Grimshaw, *Bitter Fruit: Black Politics and the Chicago Machine 1931–1991* (Chicago: University of Chicago Press, 1992), pp. 159–166.

9. In addition to Clarence Stone's work, discussed hereafter, see Raphael J. Sonenshein, *Politics in Black and White: Race and Power in Los Angeles* (Princeton: Princeton University Press, 1993).

10. See Stone, *Regime Politics*, pp. 161–163.

11. Stone, *Regime Politics*, pp. 8–9; also see p. 5.

12. Donald Janson, "Tax Fraud Denied by Mayor of Gary," *New York Times*, February 25, 1962, p. 74.

13. Victor S. Navasky, *Kennedy Justice* (Kingsport, Tenn.: Kingsport Press, 1970), p. 375.

14. "Gary Mayor and 2 Indicted in City Buying without Bids," *New York Times*, March 9, 1963, p. 4.

15. Nelson and Meranto, *Electing Black Mayors*, p. 180.

Bibliography

Acker, Carolyn. "Wilson Goode: He Transformed the Job." *Philadelphia Daily News*, November 30, 1982.

Adams, Carolyn Teich. "Philadelphia: The Slide toward Municipal Bankruptcy." In *Big City Politics in Transition*, edited by H. V. Savitch and John Clayton Thomas, Sage Urban Affairs Annual Reviews, vol. 38. Newbury Park, Calif.: 1991.

Alexander, Stan, Sharon Broussard, and Barnetta Jackson. *The 1973 Atlanta Elections* (Atlanta: Voters Education Project, 1973).

Alkalimat, Abdul, and Gills, Doug. "Black Power vs. Racism: Harold Washington Becomes Mayor." In *The New Black Vote*, edited by Rod Bush. San Francisco: Synthesis Publications, 1984.

———. "Chicago." In *The New Black Vote*, edited by Rod Bush. San Francisco: Synthesis Publications, 1984.

Allen, Ivan, Jr., with Paul Hemphill. *Mayor: Notes on the Sixties*. New York: Simon and Schuster, 1971.

Allen, Robert L. *Black Awakening in Capitalist America*. New York: Doubleday, 1969.

Allswang, John. *Bosses, Machines, and Urban Voters*. Baltimore: Johns Hopkins University Press, 1986.

———. *Bosses, Machines, and Urban Voters.* Port Washington, N.Y.: Kennikat Press, 1977.

———. *A House for all Peoples: Ethnic Politics in Chicago, 1890–1936.* Lexington: University Press of Kentucky, 1971.

Allswang, John M. "The Chicago Negro Voter and the Democratic Consensus." *Journal of the Illinois State Historical Society* 60:2 (Summer 1967).

Almy, Timothy, William B. Hildreth, and Robert Golembiewski. "Case Study I—Assessing

Electoral Defeat: New Directions and Values for MARTA." In *Mass Transit Management: Case Studies of the Metropolitan Atlanta Rapid Transit Authority* report, U.S. Department of Transportation: Urban Mass Transportation Administration, Washington, D.C.: 1981.

Anderson, Alan B., and George W. Pickering. *Confronting the Color Line: The Broken Promise of the Civil Rights Movement in Chicago.* Athens: University of Georgia Press, 1986.

Anderson, Bernard E. *The Opportunities Industrialization Centers: A Decade of Community-Based Manpower Services.* University of Pennsylvania, Wharton School, Industrial Research Unit, Manpower and Human Resources Studies, no. 6. Philadelphia: 1976.

Atlanta Bureau of Personnel and Human Resources, Affirmative Action Division. "1985 City Work Force Profile."

———. "Survey of Current Employment, November 30, 1977." (Atlanta: Department of Administrative Services, 1977).

"Atlanta Elects a Black Mayor, but Hosea Williams is Defeated." *New York Times*, October 17, 1973.

"Atlanta's Peaceful Blow for Justice." *Life*, September 15, 1961.

Bacote, Clarence A. "The Negro in Atlanta Politics." *Phylon* 16:4 (1955).

Bailey, Harry A., Jr. "Poverty, Politics, and Administration." In *Black Politics in Philadelphia*, edited by Miriam Ershkowitz and Joseph Zikmund II (New York: Basic Books, 1973).

Baker, Stephen C., and Paul Kleppner. "Race War Chicago Style: The Election of a Black Mayor, 1983." *Research in Urban Policy* 2 (Los Angeles: JAI Press, 1986).

Balchunis, Mary Ellen. "A Study of the Old and New Campaign Politics Models: A Comparative Analysis of Wilson Goode's 1983 and 1987 Philadelphia Mayoral Campaigns." Ph.D. diss., Temple University, 1992.

Banfield, Edward. *Big City Politics.* New York: Random House, 1965.

———. *Political Influence.* New York: Free Press, 1961.

Banfield, Edward, and James Q. Wilson. *City Politics.* New York: Vintage Books, 1963.

Baron, Harold, et al. "Black Powerlessness in Chicago." *TRANS-action* 6:1 (November 1968).

Bartley, Numan V. "Atlanta Elections and Georgia Political Trends." *New South* (Winter 1970).

———. *From Thurmond to Wallace: Political Tendencies in Georgia, 1948–1968.* Baltimore: Johns Hopkins University Press, 1970.

Bates, Timothy. *Banking on Black Enterprise.* Washington, D.C.: Joint Center for Political and Economic Studies, 1993.

Bauman, John F. *Public Housing, Race, and Renewal: Urban Planning in Philadelphia, 1920–1974.* Philadelphia: Temple University Press, 1988.

Bayor, Ronald. "The Civil Rights Movement as Urban Reform: Atlanta's Black Neighborhoods and a New 'Progressivism.'" *Georgia Historical Quarterly* 77:2 (Summer 1993).

Beauregard, Robert A. "Local Politics and the Employment Relation: Construction Jobs in Philadelphia." In *Economic Restructuring and Political Response*, edited by Robert A. Beauregard. Sage Urban Affairs Annual Reviews, vol. 34. Newbury Park, Calif.: 1989.

Biles, Roger. *Big City Boss in Depression and War: Mayor Edward J. Kelly of Chicago.* Dekalb: Northern Illinois University Press, 1984.

Binzen, Peter. "Business Leaders Give Less to Goode for This Campaign." *Philadelphia Inquirer*, October 31, 1983.

"Black Political Power Grows in Wake of Protest Victories." *Chicago Reporter* 8:12 (December 1979).

"Black Vote in Philadelphia, The." *Charities* 15 (1905).

Bloomberg, Warner, Jr. "The Power Structure of an Industrial Community." Ph.D. diss., University of Chicago, 1961.

Boston, Thomas. *Race, Class and Conservatism*. Boston: Unwin Hyman, 1988.

Bowly, Devereux, Jr. *The Poorhouse: Subsidized Housing in Chicago, 1895–1976*. Carbondale: Southern Illinois University Press, 1978.

Branham, Charles. "Black Chicago: Accommodationist Politics before the Great Migration." In *The Ethnic Frontier: Essays in the History of Group Survival in Chicago*, edited by Melvin Holli and Peter d'A. Jones. Grand Rapids, Mich.: William Eerdmans, 1977.

Brisbane, Robert H. *Black Activism: Racial Revolution in the United States, 1954–1970*. Valley Forge, Pa.: Judson Press, 1974.

Brown, A. "To Protest Redistricting of Precincts." *Gary American*, March 19, 1932.

Browning, Rufus P., Dale Rogers Marshall, and David H. Tabb. *Protest Is Not Enough: The Struggle of Blacks and Hispanics for Equality in Urban Politics*. Berkeley: University of California Press, 1984.

Browning, Rufus P., Dale Rogers Marshall, and David H. Tabb, eds. *Racial Politics in American Cities*. New York: Longman, 1990.

Bryans, Raleigh. "Jesse Hill Gets Leery of 'Token Black' Role." *Atlanta Journal and Constitution*, May 13, 1973.

———. "Politics Getting Heated up, So Are Atlanta's Voters." *Atlanta Journal and Constitution*, October 19, 1969.

———. "Race Called Key to City's Future." *Atlanta Constitution*, September 7, 1969.

Buffum, Peter C., and Rita Sagi. "Philadelphia: Politics of Reform and Retreat." In *Crime in City Politics*, edited by Anne Heinz, Herbert Jacob, and Robert L. Lineberry. New York: Longman, 1983.

Bullock, Charles S., III, and Bruce A. Campbell. "Racist or Racial Voting in the 1981 Municipal Elections." *Urban Affairs Quarterly* 20:2 (December 1984).

Bunche, Ralph. "The Thompson-Negro Alliance." *Opportunity* 7 (1929).

Burman, Stephen. "The Illusion of Progress: Race and Politics in Atlanta, Georgia." *Ethnic and Racial Studies* 2:4 (October 1979).

Bustos, Sergio R. "Police Accused of Beating up Latinos." *Philadelphia Inquirer*, January 15, 1994.

Byrd, Jerry W. "After Years of Losses, Area Jobs Up." *Philadelphia Inquirer*, April 17, 1994.

Camper, John, Cheryl Devall, and John Kass. "The Road to City Hall." *Chicago Tribune Magazine*, November 16, 1986.

Camper, John, and Jerry Thornton. "Without Washington, Black Support Splinters." *Chicago Tribune*, December 15, 1988.

Carvajal, Doreen. "Marching Side by Side Along a Divide." *Philadelphia Inquirer*, September 27, 1993.

Caswell, Bruce E. "Machine, Reform, Interest, and Race: The Politics of the Philadelphia Fiscal Crisis." Paper presented at the annual meeting of the American Political Science Association, Chicago, Illinois, August 1992.

Catlin, Robert A. "The Decline and Fall of Gary, Indiana." *Planning* 54:6 (June 1988).

———. *Racial Politics and Urban Planning*. Lexington: University Press of Kentucky, 1993.

Chacharis, George. "Tales of Steel." *Gary Post-Tribune*, June 17, 1956.

Clavel, Pierre, and Wim Wiewel, eds. *Harold Washington and the Neighborhoods*. New Brunswick, N.J.: Rutgers University Press, 1991.

Clay, Nate. "Hot Skillet, The." Chicago Metro News, February 1, 1975.

Cobb, James S. *The Selling of the South: The Southern Crusade for Industrial Development, 1936–1940*. Baton Rouge: Louisiana State University Press, 1982.

Coffin, Alex. "Blacks Back Transit Plan." *Atlanta Constitution*, September 24, 1971.

———. "Candidates' Support Picture Is Blurred." *Atlanta Constitution*, October 6, 1969.

———. "City Hiring of Blacks Boosted by 20 Pct." *Atlanta Constitution*, August 17, 1972.

———. "Cook, Millican Swap Attacks." *Atlanta Constitution*, September 3, 1969.

———. "Farris, Jackson Equated." *Atlanta Journal and Constitution*, September 1, 1969.

———. "Massell and Cook Vow Strong Races for Oct. 21 Runoff." *Atlanta Constitution*, October 9, 1969.

———. "Negro Leaders Endorse Massell; Cook Questions Experience Claim." *Atlanta Constitution*, October 3, 1969.

———. "Tate's Nod Goes To Cook." *Atlanta Constitution*, October 18, 1969.

Committee of Seventy, The. *The Charter: A History*. Philadelphia: Committee of Seventy, 1980.

"Complete Vote Totals." *Gary Post-Tribune*, November 5, 1947.

"Cook Is Backed by Millican." *Atlanta Constitution*, October 16, 1969.

"Cops on Trial." *Time*, August 27, 1979.

Cornwell, Elmer E., Jr., "Party Absorption of Ethnic Groups: The Case of Providence, Rhode Island." *Social Forces* 38 (March 1960).

Cox, Oliver C. "Leadership among Negroes in the United States." In *Studies in Leadership*, edited by Alvin W. Gouldner. New York: Harper, 1950.

Crenson, Matthew A. *The Un-Politics of Air Pollution*. Baltimore: Johns Hopkins University Press, 1971.

Culmer, Francena Edwina. "Changing Patterns of Leadership in the Black Community of Atlanta, Georgia: 1960–1969." Master's thesis, Georgia State College, 1967.

Dahl, Robert A. *Polyarchy: Participation and Opposition*. New Haven: Yale University Press, 1971.

"Daley Predicts Victory." *Chicago Tribune*, April 2, 1963.

Darling, Henry R. "Hardy Williams: Soft Spoken, Tough on Shoes." *Philadelphia Bulletin*, March 26, 1971.

Daughen, Joseph, and Peter Binzen. *The Cop Who Would Be King: Mayor Frank Rizzo*. Boston: Little, Brown, 1977.

Daughen, Joseph R. "Hill Must Gain Support of Blacks to Win Primary." *Philadelphia Bulletin*, March 16, 1975.

———. "Parties Court Negroes, Who Hold Key to Power." *Philadelphia Bulletin*, January 24, 1965.

Davidson, Joe. "Bowser Accused of Stealing Show." *Philadelphia Bulletin*, July 15, 1979.

"Davis Lone GOP Council Choice." *Gary Post-Tribune*, November 3, 1947.

Davis, Robert. "Daley Hiring More Minorities." *Chicago Tribune*, February 1, 1991.

———. "Former Alderman Hubbard Gets 2-Year Prison Sentence." *Chicago Tribune*, January 6, 1973.

Dawson, Richard, and James Robinson. "Inter-Party Competition, Economic Variables, and Welfare Policies in the United States." *Journal of Politics* 25 (1963).

"Dawson Not a Candidate, but Key Man in Election." *Chicago Defender*, February 12, 1955.

de Grazia, Alfred. "The Limits of External Leadership over a Minority Electorate." *Public Opinion Quarterly* 20:1 (Spring 1956).

DeMuth, Jerry. "Three Black Hopefuls Slow Singer's Mayoral Wagon." *Chicago Sun Times*, September 26, 1974.

"Democratic County Ticket Wins by Wide Majorities." *Gary Post-Tribune*, November 8, 1934.

"Directors OK Plan To Merge 2 Coalitions." *Philadelphia Bulletin*, April 29, 1969.

"Dobis, Burton Trail in Gary Demo Ballot." *Gary Post-Tribune*, May 9, 1951.

"Dowling Beats G.O.P. Mayor in Hammond Race." *Chicago Daily Tribune*, November 9, 1955.

Drake, St. Clair, and Horace Cayton. *Black Metropolis*. New York: Harcourt, Brace, 1945.

Du Bois, W. E. B. *The Philadelphia Negro*. Philadelphia: University of Pennsylvania Press, 1899.

————. "The Black Vote of Philadelphia." In *Black Politics in Philadelphia*, edited by Miriam Ershkowitz and Joseph Zikmund II. New York: Basic Books, 1973.

Dubin, Murray. "The City Gets a Rude Awakening on Latinos' Plight." *Philadelphia Inquirer*, June 17, 1990.

Dye, Thomas. *The Politics of Equality*. New York: Bobbs Merrill, 1971.

Eckstein, Harry. "The Idea of Political Development: From Dignity to Efficiency." *World Politics* 34:4 (July 1982).

Edsall, Thomas Byrne, and Mary Edsall. *Chain Reaction: The Impact of Race, Rights, and Taxes on American Politics*. New York: W. W. Norton, 1991.

Eisinger, Peter. *The Politics of Displacement*. New York: Academic Press, 1980.

Eisinger, Peter K. "Ethnic Political Transition in Boston, 1884–1933: Some Lessons for Contemporary Cities." *Political Science Quarterly* 91:2 (Summer 1978).

Ekstrom, Charles A. "The Electoral Politics of Reform and Machine: The Political Behavior of Philadelphia's 'Black' Wards, 1943–1969." *Black Politics in Philadelphia*, edited by Miriam Ershkowitz and Joseph Zikmund II. New York: Basic Books, 1973.

English, James W. *Handyman of the Lord: The Life and Ministry of the Rev. William Holmes Borders*. New York: Meredith Press, 1967.

Erie, Steven. *Rainbow's End: Irish-Americans and the Dilemmas of Urban Machine Politics, 1840–1985*. Berkeley: University of California Press, 1988.

Evans, Orrin. "Black Coalition Disbands; Leaders Ask New Program." *Philadelphia Bulletin*, April 9, 1969.

Ezell, Hank. "Power Structure Hunting Candidates?" *Atlanta Journal and Constitution*, June 3, 1973.

Featherman, Sandra and, William L. Rosenberg. *Jews, Blacks, and Ethnics: The 1978 "Vote White" Charter Campaign in Philadelphia*. Philadelphia: American Jewish Committee, 1979.

"Finerty Asks Support from Every Citizen." *Gary Post-Tribune*, November 4, 1942.

"Finerty Piles Up 5,277 Vote Lead To Win." *Gary Post-Tribune*, November 4, 1942.

Fish, John Hall. *Black Power, White Control*. Princeton: Princeton University Press, 1973.

Flaherty, Roger. "Newhouse Asked To Back Singer." *Chicago Sun Times*, January 20, 1975.

Flanigan, William H., and Nancy H. Zingale. "Measures of Electoral Competition." *Political Methodology* 1:4 (Fall 1974).

Fleishman, Joel L. "The Real Against the Ideal—Making the Solution Fit the Problem: The Atlanta Public School Agreement of 1973." In *Roundtable Justice: Case Studies in Conflict Resolution*, edited by Robert B. Goldmann. Boulder, Colo.: Westview Press, 1980.

Fonzi, Gaeton. "Cecil Storms In." *Greater Philadelphia Magazine* (July 1963).

"For Goode, a Year of Recovery." *Philadelphia Inquirer*, January 24, 1987.

Frazier, Alan. "City of Brotherly Loot." *American Mercury* 47:187 (July 1939).

Freedman, Robert. *A Report on the Politics of Philadelphia*. Cambridge, Mass.: Joint Center for Urban Studies of the Massachusetts Institute of Technology and Harvard University, 1963.

Frick, Mary Louise. "Influences on Negro Political Participation in Atlanta, Georgia." Master's thesis, Georgia State College, 1967.

Frump, Bob, and Acel Moore. "City's Religious Leaders Censure Racial Rhetoric." *Philadelphia Inquirer*, September 30, 1978.

Frump, Bob, Bob Holton, and Paul Taylor. "A Black Defends Rizzo as 'Vote White' Debate Intensifies." *Philadelphia Inquirer*, September 28, 1978.

Frump, Bob. "Rizzo on the Clergy." *Philadelphia Inquirer*, October 1, 1978.

———. "Rizzo's Message as Clear as Black and White." *Philadelphia Inquirer*, September 24, 1978.

———. "Rizzo Warns of Radicals." *Philadelphia Inquirer*, September 22, 1978.

Funchion, Michael. "The Political and Nationalist Dimensions." In *The Irish in Chicago*, edited by Laurence J. McCaffrey et al. Urbana: University of Illinois Press, 1987.

Galphin, Bruce. "They Laughed When He Ran—Now Jackson's a Winner." *Atlanta Constitution*, October 12, 1969.

Gammage, Jeff. "Response Time." *Philadelphia Inquirer Magazine*, February 6, 1994.

"Gannon Ready for Whoopee Cleanup." *Gary Post-Tribune*, November 14, 1942.

"Gannon Wins As Demos Take Major Offices." *Gary Post-Tribune*, November 4, 1942.

"Gary Mayor and 2 Indicted in City Buying without Bids." *New York Times*, March 9, 1963.

"Gary Names Demo Mayor, GOP Judge." *Gary Post-Tribune*, November 7, 1951.

"Gary Results." *Gary Post-Tribune*, November 7, 1951.

Gerth, H. H., and C. Wright Mills. *From Max Weber: Essays in Sociology*. New York: Oxford University Press, 1946.

Gilbert, Carl. "From 'Integration' to 'Black Power': The Civil Rights Movement in the City of Philadelphia, 1960–67." Master's thesis, Temple University, n.d.

Gilbert, Charles E., and Christopher Clague. "Electoral Competition and Electoral Systems in Large Cities." *Journal of Politics* 24 (1962).

"Glad to See You." *Newsweek*, September 11, 1961.

Glantz, Oscar. "Recent Negro Ballots in Philadelphia." In *Black Politics in Philadelphia*, edited by Miriam Ershkowitz and Joseph Zikmund II. New York: Basic Books, 1973.

Glantz, Oscar. "The Negro Voter in Northern Industrial Cities." *Western Political Quarterly* 13:4 (December 1960).

Glazer, Nathan. "Blacks and Ethnic Groups: The Difference, and the Political Difference It Makes." *Social Problems* 18 (1971).

Goldwyn, Ronald. "Bowser Endorses Green in Mayor's Race." *Philadelphia Bulletin*, July 12, 1979.

———. "Bowser Leaves Green Standing at the Altar." *Philadelphia Bulletin*, July 13, 1979.

———. "Rizzo Names His 6 Candidates." *Philadelphia Bulletin*, July 24, 1979.

———. "Voters Will Have To Come out as They Did in Charter Fight." *Philadelphia Bulletin*, April 29, 1979.

Golembiewski, Robert T. "A Taxonomic Approach to State Political Party Strength." *Western Political Quarterly* 11:3 (September 1958).

"Goode's Bright Promise Beset by MOVE, Strike."*Christian Science Monitor*, July 22, 1986.

"Goode Pulled Black Vote for a Range of Reasons." *Philadelphia Inquirer*, May 24, 1987.

Goode, W. Wilson, with Joann Stevens. *In Goode Faith*. Valley Forge, Pa: Judson Press, 1992.

Gordon, Rita Werner. "The Change in the Political Alignment of Chicago's Negroes During the New Deal." *Journal of American History* 56 (December 1969).

Gosnell, Harold. *Machine Politics Chicago Model*. Chicago: University of Chicago Press, 1937.

———. *Negro Politicians*. Chicago: University of Chicago Press, 1935.

Gottfried, Alex. *Boss Cermak of Chicago: A Study of Political Leadership*. Seattle: University of Washington Press, 1962.

————. "Political Machines." In *International Encyclopedia of the Social Sciences*, vol. 12. New York: Crowell, Collier and Macmillan, 1968.

Granger, Bill, and Lori Granger. *Fighting Jane: Mayor Jane Byrne and the Chicago Machine.* New York: Dial Press, 1980.

Gray, Jim. "Jackson, Williams Are 'Racists,' Says Massell." *Atlanta Constitution*, October 8, 1973.

Green, Paul. "Green Started the Race Early—Perhaps Too Early." *Philadelphia Inquirer*, May 16, 1979.

Green, Paul M. "Irish Chicago: The Multiethnic Road to Machine Success." In *Ethnic Chicago*, edited by Peter d'A. Jones and Melvin G. Holli. Grand Rapids, Mich.: William Eerdmans, 1981.

————. "The Primary: Some New Players—Same Old Rules." In *The Making of the Mayor*, edited by Melvin G. Holli and Paul M. Green. Grand Rapids, Mich.: William Eerdmans, 1984.

Greenstone, J. David, and Paul E. Peterson. *Race and Authority in Urban Politics: Community Participation and the War on Poverty.* Chicago: University of Chicago Press, 1973.

Greer, Edward. *Big Steel.* New York: Monthly Review Press, 1979.

Grimshaw, William. *Bitter Fruit? Black Politics and the Chicago Machine 1931–1991.* Chicago: University of Chicago Press, 1992.

————. *Black Politics in Chicago.* Chicago: Loyola University Center for Urban Policy, 1980.

Guinther, John. "Light a Candle for the City Charter." *Philadelphia Magazine* (April 1976).

————. "Party Pooper." *Philadelphia Magazine* 63:9 (September 1972).

————. "Up the Organization." *Philadelphia Magazine* 63: 5 (May 1972).

Guthman, Edwin. "Philadelphia Was Also a Winner in the Primary." *Philadelphia Inquirer*, May 22, 1983.

Hadden, Jeffrey K., Louis Masotti, and Victor Thiessen. "The Making of the Negro Mayors, 1967." *TRANS-action* 5 (January–February 1968).

Haines, Herbert, Jr. *Black Radicals and the Civil Rights Mainstream, 1954–1970.* Knoxville: University of Tennessee Press, 1988.

Halberstam, David. "Daley of Chicago." In *The City Boss in America*, edited by Alexander B. Callow. New York: Oxford University Press, 1976.

Hall, Raymond. *Black Separatism in the United States.* Hanover, N.H.: University Press of New England, 1978.

Hamilton, Charles. *The Black Preacher in America.* New York: William Morrow, 1972.

Hanks, Lawrence J. *Black Political Empowerment in Three Georgia Counties.* Knoxville: University of Tennessee Press, 1978.

Hardy, Thomas. "Could the Game Be Complete without Our Local Stassen?" *Chicago Tribune*, December 18, 1988.

Harris, Gene. "Sullivan Plays 'Dirty Pool,' Rizzo Says." *Philadelphia Bulletin*, October 21, 1971.

Harrison, Carter H. *Stormy Years.* New York: Bobbs Merrill, 1935.

"Heavy District Demo Vote Sweeps in Mandich, Elich, 3 Councilmen." *Gary American*, November 9, 1951.

Hein, Virginia H. "The Image of 'A City Too Busy to Hate': Atlanta in the 1960's." *Phylon* 33:3 (Fall 1972).

Henderson, Elmer William. "A Study of the Basic Factors Involved in the Change in the Party Alignment of Negroes in Chicago, 1932–1938." Master's thesis, University of Chicago, 1939.

Henry, Charles. *Jesse Jackson: The Search for Common Ground.* Oakland, Calif.: Black Scholar Press, 1991.

Henson, Dale, and James King. "The Atlanta Public-Private Romance: An Abrupt Transformation." In *Public-Private Partnership in American Cities*, edited by R. Scott Fosler and Renee A. Berger. Lexington, Mass.: D.C. Heath, 1982.

Higdon, Hal. "Richard G. Hatcher: Soul Mayor." In *The Politics of the Powerless*, edited by Robert Binstock and Katherine Ely. Cambridge, Mass: Winthrop, 1971.

Hinds, Michael deCourcy. "50% Cutback in Funds for Homeless is Fiercely Protested." *New York Times*, September 15, 1989.

Hinz, Greg. "The Pothole Mayor." *Chicago Magazine* (February 1995).

Hirsch, Arnold R. "Martin H. Kennelly: The Mugwump and the Machine." In *The Mayors*, edited by Melvin G. Holli and Paul M. Green. Carbondale: Southern Illinois University Press, 1987.

Hirsch, Arnold. *Making the Second Ghetto: Race and Housing in Chicago, 1940–1960*. Cambridge: Cambridge University Press, 1983.

Hirsley, Michael. "Daley Unqualified, Black Group Says." *Chicago Tribune*, February 13, 1975.

Hodgson, Godfrey, and Godfrey Crile. "Gary: Epitaph for a Model City." *Washington Post*, March 4, 1973.

Holli, Melvin G., and Peter d'A Jones. *Biographical Dictionary of American Mayors, 1820–1980*. Westport, Conn.: Greenwood Press, 1981.

Homel, Michael W. "The Politics of Public Education in Black Chicago, 1910–1941." *Journal of Negro Education* 45 (1976).

Homel, Michael Wallace. "Negroes in the Chicago Public Schools, 1910–1941." Ph.D. diss., University of Chicago, 1972.

Hopkins, Sam. "'Deal' by Jackson charged by Massell." *Atlanta Constitution*, July 10, 1973.

———. "L.A. Vote Omen for Atlanta?" *Atlanta Constitution*, May 31, 1973.

Hornsby, Alton Jr. "A City That Was Too Busy To Hate." In *Southern Businessmen and Desegregation*, edited by Elizabeth Jacoway and David R. Colburn. Baton Rouge: Louisiana State University Press, 1982.

———. "The Negro in Atlanta Politics, 1961–1973." *Atlanta Historical Bulletin* 21 (Spring 1977).

Horwitt, Sanford. *Let Them Call Me Rebel*. New York: Alfred A. Knopf, 1989.

"Hosea Taught Business Leaders a New Lesson in Uses of Power." *Atlanta Constitution*, March 26, 1975.

Hoskins, Jesse E. Commissioner of Personnel, "Official Report of the Task Force on Affirmative Action, City of Chicago." Chicago: City Hall, December, 1985.

Hunter, Floyd. *Community Power Succession*. Chapel Hill: University of North Carolina Press, 1980.

Ingwereson, Marshall. "Atlanta Business Mecca for Black Middle Class in America." *Christian Science Monitor*, May 29, 1987.

"IVI Backing Hubbard, Stevens, Singer in March 11 Elections." *Chicago Defender*, January 2, 1969.

Jackson, David. "City Layoffs Affect Minorities Mostly." *Chicago Tribune*, February 11, 1992.

———. "Double Vision." *Chicago Magazine* (Oct. 1989).

———. "Legal Frights." *Chicago Magazine* (Nov. 1990).

Jackson, Dr. L. K. "An Open Letter to the Citizens of Gary!" Rev. L. K. Jackson Collection, Booklets, Calumet Regional Archives (n.d.).

Jacob, John E. "Black Leadership in a Reactionary Era." *Urban League Review* 9:1 (Summer 1985).

Jamieson, Duncan R. "Maynard Jackson's 1973 Election as Mayor of Atlanta." *Midwest Quarterly* 18 (1976).

Janson, Donald. "Tax Fraud Denied by Mayor of Gary." *New York Times*, February 25, 1962.

Jarrett, Vernon. "City Hall Displays More Than Racism." *Chicago Tribune*, October 20, 1978.

———. "Fred Hubbard's Actual Crime." *Chicago Tribune*, January 10, 1973.

———. "Ralph Metcalfe Takes His Stand." *Chicago Tribune*, January 23, 1977.

Jaynes, Gregory. "Green and Marston Win Philadelphia Races." *New York Times*, May 16, 1979.

Jenkins, Herbert T. *Forty Years on the Force, 1932–1972*. Atlanta: Center for Research in Social Change, Emory University, 1973.

———. *Keeping the Peace: A Police Chief Looks at His Job*. New York: Harper and Row, 1970.

Jennings, James. *The Politics of Black Empowerment: The Transformation of Black Activism in Urban America*. Detroit: Wayne State University, 1992.

Jennings, M. Kent, and Harmon Zeigler. "Class, Party, and Race in Four Types of Elections: The Case of Atlanta." *Journal of Politics* 28 (1966).

Johnson, Dirk. "Blacks Plan Rights March in Chicago." *New York Times*, October 20, 1989.

———. "Chicago's Mayor Pursuing Quiet Quest to Win Trust of Blacks." *New York Times*, November 12, 1989.

Jones, Bryan D. "Party and Bureaucracy: The Influence of Intermediary Groups on Urban Public Service Delivery." *American Political Science Review* 75:3 (September 1981).

Jones, Mack. "Black Political Empowerment in Atlanta." *Annals of the American Academy of Political and Social Science* 439 (September 1978).

Joravsky, Ben, and Eduardo Camacho. *Race and Politics in Chicago*. Chicago: Community Renewal Society, 1987.

Kaufman, Jonathan. "Atlanta: Open Doors Abounding." *Boston Globe*, December 21, 1983.

Keiser, Richard A. "Black Political Incorporation or Subordination? Political Competitiveness and Leadership Formation Prior to the Election of Black Mayors." Ph.D. diss., University of California, Berkeley, 1989.

———. "Explaining African-American Political Empowerment: 'Windy City' Politics from 1900 to 1983." *Urban Affairs Quarterly* 29:1 (September 1993).

Kennedy, Eugene. *Himself: The Life and Times of Mayor Richard J. Daley*. New York: Viking Press, 1978.

Killian, Lewis M. "The Significance of Extremism in the Black Revolution." *Social Problems* 20 (1972).

Kilson, Martin. "Adam Clayton Powell, Jr.: The Militant as Politician." In *Black Leaders of the Twentieth Century*, edited by John Hope Franklin and August Meier. Chicago: University of Illinois Press, 1982.

———. "Political Change in the Negro Ghetto, 1900–1940's." In *Key Issues in the Afro-American Experience*, edited by Nathan J. Huggins, Martin Kilson, and Daniel M. Fox. Vol. 2. New York: Harcourt Brace Jovanovich, 1971.

King, Martin Luther, Sr. with Clayton Riley. *Daddy King: An Autobiography*. New York: William Morrow and Company, 1980.

King, Seth S. "Steel Slowdown Brings Clear Skies to Gary, Ind. but City's Workers Are Gloomy." *New York Times*, December 14, 1971.

King, Wayne. "Rizzo Aides Planning to Unseat Party Regulars in Philadelphia." *New York Times*, May 22, 1975.

———. "Rizzo is Strong Victor in Philadelphia." *New York Times*, May 21, 1975.

Kleppner, Paul. *Chicago Divided: The Making of a Black Mayor*. Dekalb: Northern Illinois University Press, 1985.

"Lake County, Indiana, Won by Democrats." *Chicago Daily Tribune*, November 4, 1959.

Landess, Thomas H., and Richard M. Quinn. *Jesse Jackson and the Politics of Race*. Ottawa, Ill.: Jameson, 1985.

Landry, Bart. *The New Black Middle Class*. Berkeley: University of California Press, 1987.

Lane, James B. *City of the Century: A History of Gary, Indiana*. Bloomington: Indiana University Press, 1978.

Lane, James B., and Stephen G. McShane, eds. *Steel Shavings: The Postwar Period in the Calumet Region 1945–1950*. Vol. 14. (Gary: Indiana University, Northwest, 1988).

Lathrop, Ross. "Improving the City Council." In *Chicago's Future: In a Time for Change*, edited by Dick Simpson. Champaign, Ill.: Stipes, 1988.

Lermack, Paul. "Cecil Moore and the Philadelphia Branch of the National Association for the Advancement of Colored People: The Politics of Negro Pressure Group Organization." In *Black Politics in Philadelphia*, edited by Miriam Ershkowitz and Joseph Zikmund II. New York: Basic Books, 1973.

Levine, Charles H. *Racial Conflict and the American Mayor*. Lexington, Mass.: Lexington Books, 1974.

Levinsohn, Florence Hamlish. *Harold Washington: A Political Biography*. Chicago: Chicago Review Press, 1983.

Lewis, David. *King: A Critical Biography*. New York: Praeger Publishers, 1970.

"'Liberal Bloc' Indorses Two for Aldermanic Elections." *Chicago Tribune*, January 31, 1969.

Linthicum, Tom. "Jackson Calls for Rejection of 'Fear Mongers.'" *Atlanta Constitution*, October 9, 1973.

———. "Massell's Strategy—Play on White Fears." *Atlanta Constitution*, October 8, 1973.

———. "Mitchell Warns of Last Minute Stories That Charge a 'Deal.'" *Atlanta Constitution*, September 15, 1973.

Linthicum, Tom, and Chuck Bell. "Allen Backs Weltner for Mayor." *Atlanta Constitution*, September 21, 1973.

Lipinski, Ann Marie, and James Strong. "Ethics Code Takes Aim at Aldermen, Lobbyists." *Chicago Tribune*, February 15, 1987.

Loeb, Vernon. "The Soul of an Old Machine." *Philadelphia Inquirer Magazine*, April 17, 1994.

Logsdon, Joseph A. "The Rev. Archibald J. Carey and the Negro in Chicago Politics." Master's thesis, University of Chicago, 1961.

Lowe, Jeanne. *Cities in a Race with Time: Progress and Poverty in America's Renewing Cities*. New York: Random House, 1967.

Lowi, Theodore J. *At the Pleasure of the Mayor*. New York: Free Press, 1964.

Lubell, Samuel. "The Future of the Negro Voter in the United States." *Journal of Negro Education* 26:3 (Summer 1957).

Mallowe, Mike. "Should the City Charter Be Changed So That Frank Rizzo Can Be Mayor for Life?" *Philadelphia Magazine* 69:10 (October 1978).

———. "The No-Frills Mayor." *Philadelphia Magazine* 76:12 (December 1984).

———. "The Pretenders." *Philadelphia Magazine* 70:5 (May 1979).

———. "The White Hope." *Philadelphia Magazine* 69:11 (November 1978).

Mandel, William K. "Citizens Group Boosts Hardy Williams for Mayor." *Philadelphia Bulletin*, November 22, 1970.

Marable, Manning. *Black American Politics*. London: Verso, 1985.

———. "Black Nationalism in the 1970s: Through the Prism of Race and Class." *Socialist Review* 10:2–3 (March–June 1980).

———. "Black Politics and the Challenges for the Left." *Monthly Review* 41:11 (April 1990).

———. *The Crisis of Color and Democracy*. Monroe, Me.: Common Courage Press, 1992.

Marris, Peter, and Martin Rein. *Dilemmas of Social Reform*. New York: Atherton Press, 1969.

Martin, Harold H. *William Berrry Hartsfield*. Athens: University of Georgia Press, 1978.

"Massell Climbed to Power, Fell as the Guard Changed." *Atlanta Constitution*, March 27, 1973.

Mayhew, David. *Placing Parties in American Politics*. Princeton: Princeton University Press, 1986.

"Mayor Candidate Refuses To Attend Dodd Meeting." *Atlanta Constitution*, September 4, 1949.

"Mayor Chacharis at Apex of Long Political Career." *Gary Post-Tribune*, November 8, 1959.

"'Mayor' Group Called 'Toms.'" *Chicago Defender*, November 12, 1974.

"Mayor Who Has Not Failed Us, A." *Gary American*, October 28, 1938.

Mays, Benjamin. *Born to Rebel*. New York: Scribners, 1971.

McCullough, Gerard. "Rizzo's Strategy: Meet the Voters." *Philadelphia Bulletin*, September 14, 1975.

McCullough, John G. "Philadelphia's Movers and Shakers: Potent Core of Civic Giants Molds City's Destiny." *Philadelphia Bulletin*, June 6, 1965.

———. "Philadelphia's Movers and Shakers: No. 2." *Philadelphia Bulletin*, June 7, 1965.

McGrath, Peter A. "Bicentennial Philadelphia: A Quaking City." In *Philadelphia: 1776–2076*, edited by Dennis Clark. Port Washington, N.Y.: Kennikat Press, 1975.

McKenna, William J. "The Changing Pattern of Philadelphia Politics, 1914–1955." *Economics and Business Bulletin of the School of Business and Public Administration, Temple University* 8:3 (March 1956).

———. "The Negro Vote in Philadelphia Elections." In *Black Politics in Philadelphia*, edited by Miriam Ershkowitz and Joseph Zikmund II. New York: Basic Books, 1973.

"Means Quits Group; Pastor Charges FEPC Head with Misrepresenting Facts." *Gary American*, January 13, 1956.

Meister, Richard J. "A History of Gary, Indiana: 1930–1940." Ph.D. diss., University of Notre Dame, 1966.

Merriam, Charles. *Chicago: A More Intimate View of Urban Politics*. New York: Macmillan Co., 1929.

Merriner, Jim. "Runoff Likely with Hosea; Mitchell Third." *Atlanta Constitution*, October 3, 1973.

Merriner, Jim, and Rex Granum. "Atlanta's Black Power Structure." *Atlanta Constitution*, September 22, 1975.

Merton, Robert K. *Social Theory and Social Structure*. 1949. Reprint, New York: Free Press, 1968.

Meyerson, Martin, and Edward Banfield. *Politics, Planning, and the Public Interest*. Glencoe: Free Press, 1955.

Mezzacappa, Dale. "A Controversial Year Later, Lee Looks Like a Shoo-in." *Philadelphia Inquirer*, November 20, 1993.

Millender, Dolly. *Yesterday in Gary: History of the Negro in Gary*. Gary: Dolly Millender, 1967.

Mladenka, Kenneth. "Rules, Service Equity, and Distributed Decisions." *Social Science Quarterly* 59 (1978).

Moberg, David. "How's He Doing? A Daley Report Card." *Chicago Reader* 20:20 (February 22, 1991).

———. "One Year Without Washington, What Did He Accomplish?" *Chicago Reader* 18:10 (November 25, 1988).

Mohl, Raymond A., and Neil Betten. *Steel City: Urban and Ethnic Patterns in Gary, Indiana, 1906–1950*. New York: Holmes and Meir, 1986.

Mondesire, Jerome. "Black Voters Stayed at Home Tuesday." *Philadelphia Inquirer*, May 22, 1975.

Moon, Henry Lee. *Balance of Power: The Negro Vote*. Garden City, N.Y.: Doubleday, 1948.

———. "The Negro Vote in the Presidential Election of 1956." *Journal of Negro Education* 26:3 (Summer 1957).

Moore, Acel. "The Rev. Gray Is Suddenly a Political Force." *Philadelphia Inquirer*, November 11, 1978.

Moore, Acel, and Gerald McKelvey. "Hardy Williams: Underdog Insists 'My Time Is Now.'" *Philadelphia Inquirer*, April 30, 1971.

Moore, Powell A. *The Calumet Region: Indiana's Last Frontier*. East Chicago: Indiana Historical Bureau, 1959.

Moses, Wilson Jeremiah. *Black Messiahs and Uncle Toms: Social and Literary Manipulations of a Religious Myth*. Rev. ed. University Park: Pennsylvania State University Press, 1982, 1993.

Myrdal, Gunnar. *An American Dilemma*. New York: Harper and Bros., 1944.

National Advisory Commission on Civil Disorders (Kerner Commission). *Report*. New York: Bantam Books, 1968.

Navasky, Victor S. *Kennedy Justice*. Kingsport, Tenn: Kingsport Press, 1970.

"Negro Help Is Planned in Pa. City." *New York Times*, November 24, 1968.

"Negro Vote To Be Deciding Factor in Election Tuesday." *Gary American*, November 25, 1951.

"Negro Voters Prove Again That They Refuse To Be Intimidated." *Gary American*, November 9, 1951.

Nelson, William E., and Philip J. Meranto. *Electing Black Mayors: Political Action in the Black Community*. Columbus: Ohio State University Press, 1977.

Nelson, William E., Jr. "Black Political Mobilization: The 1967 Mayoral Election in Gary." Ph.D. diss., University of Illinois, 1971.

———. *Black Politics in Gary: Problems and Prospects*. Washington, D.C.: Joint Center for Political Studies, 1972.

"Newhouse Endorsed for Mayor by Six Black Publishers Here." *Chicago Daily News*, January 21, 1975.

Newman, Jonathan, and William K. Marimow. "The Homicide Files." *Philadelphia Inquirer*, April 24–27, 1977.

O'Connor, Len. *Clout: Mayor Daley and His City*. New York: Avon, 1975.

Oden, Roger K. "Black Political Power in Gary, Indiana: A Theoretical and Structural Analysis." Ph.D. diss., University of Chicago, 1977.

Orfield, Gary. *The Reconstruction of Southern Education*. New York: Wiley, 1969.

Page, Clarence. "The Real Goal, Some Indicate, Is To Build for a '79 Victory." *Chicago Tribune*, September 22, 1974.

Paolantonio, S. A. *Frank Rizzo: The Last Big Man in Big City America*. Philadelphia: Camino Books, 1993.

Persons, Georgia Ann. "Atlanta: Black Mayoral Leadership and the Dynamics of Political Change." Ph.D. diss., Massachusetts Institute of Technology, 1978.

Peterson, Paul. "City Politics and Community Action: The Implementation of the Community Action Program in Three American Cities." Ph.D. diss., University of Chicago, 1967.

———. *School Politics Chicago Style*. Chicago: University of Chicago Press, 1976.

"Petition Drive to Remove Rizzo Begins at Philadelphia Ceremony, A" *New York Times*, April 18, 1976.

Petshek, Kirk. *The Challenge of Urban Reform: Policies and Programs in Philadelphia*. Philadelphia: Temple University Press, 1973.

Pfeiffer, David G. "The Measurement of Inter-Party Competition and Systemic Stability." *American Political Science Review* 61 (1967).

"Philadelphia Aide Cited in Extortion." *New York Times*, April 17, 1975.

"Philadelphia Mayor in Trouble over Minority Aid." *New York Times*, May 17, 1982.

"Philadelphia Poor Pledged $1 Million by Business Group." *New York Times*, May 12, 1968.

Pierannunzi, Carol, and John D. Hutcheson, Jr. "Electoral Change and Regime Maintenance: Maynard Jackson's Second Time Around." *PS* 23:2 (June 1990).

Pinderhughes, Diane. *Race and Ethnicity in Chicago Politics*. Urbana: University of Illinois Press, 1987.

Pinkney, Alphonso. *Red, Black and Green: Black Nationalism in the United States*. New York: Cambridge University Press, 1976.

Piven, Francis Fox, and Richard Cloward. *Poor Peoples Movements*. New York: Pantheon Books, 1977.

Poinsett, Alex. *Black Power: Gary Style*. Chicago: Johnson Publishing, 1970.

"Police Advisory Board Abolished in Philadelphia." *New York Times*, December 28, 1969.

"Police Board Ruled Illegal." *New York Times*, November 15, 1968.

"Policy, Narcotics, and Mayoral Politics." *Chicago Sun Times*, February 1, 1955.

Portz, John. *The Politics of Plant Closings*. Lawrence: University Press of Kansas, 1990.

Powledge, Fred. "A New Politics in Atlanta." *New Yorker*, December 31, 1973.

Preston, Michael. "Black Politics in the Post-Daley Era." In *After Daley: Chicago Politics in Transition*, edited by Samuel Gove and Louis Masotti. Urbana: University of Illinois Press, 1982.

———. "The Resurgence of Black Voting in Chicago: 1955–1983." In *The Making of the Mayor*, edited by Melvin G. Holli and Paul M. Green. Grand Rapids, Mich.: William Eerdmans, 1984.

"Race Is a Muted Issue in Philadelphia." *New York Times*, April 12, 1983.

Radosh, Ronald. "From Protest to Black Power: The Failure of Coalition Politics." In *The Great Society Reader*, edited by Marvin E. Gettleman and David Mermelstein. New York: Random House, 1967.

Raines, Howell. *My Soul Is Rested*. New York: G. P. Putnam's Sons, 1977.

Rakove, Milton. *Don't Make No Waves, Don't Back No Losers*. Bloomington: Indiana University Press, 1975.

———. "Jane Byrne and the New Chicago Politics." In *After Daley: Chicago Politics in Transition*, edited by Samuel Gove and Louis Masotti, Urbana: University of Illinois Press, 1982.

———. *We Don't Want Nobody Nobody Sent*. Bloomington: Indiana University Press, 1979.

Randolph, Eleanor. "Jesse Hints PUSH May O.K. Singer." *Chicago Tribune*, January 12, 1975.

———. "Metcalfe Severs Daley Ties, Backs Singer for Mayor." *Chicago Tribune*, January 26, 1975.

Ranney, Austin, and Wilmoore Kendall. "The American Party Systems." *American Political Science Review* 48 (June 1954).

———. "Parties in State Politics." In *Politics in the American States*, edited by Herbert Jacob and Kenneth Vines. Boston: Little, Brown, 1971.

Rawls, Wendell, Jr., "Atlanta Sees Role as Global Trader." *New York Times*, December 12, 1982.

Reed, Adolph, Jr. "A Critique of Neo-Progressivisim in Theorizing about Local Development Policy: A Case from Atlanta." In *The Politics of Urban Development*, edited by Clarence N. Stone and Heywood T. Sanders. Lawrence: University Press of Kansas, 1987.

———. "Black Urban Administrations." *Telos* 65 (Fall 1985).

———. "The Black Urban Regime: Structural Origins and Constraints." *Comparative Urban and Community Research* 1 (1988).

———. "The Rise of Louis Farrakhan." *Nation*, January 21, 1991.

———. *The Jesse Jackson Phenomenon*. New Haven: Yale University Press, 1986.

———. "Pan-Africanism: Ideology for Liberation?" In *Pan-Africanism*, edited by Robert Chrisman and Nathan Hare. Indianapolis and New York: Bobbs Merrill, 1974.

Reed, Christopher Robert. "Black Chicago Political Realignment during the Great Depression and New Deal." *Illinois Historical Journal* 78:4 (Winter 1985).

Reichley, James A. *The Art of Government: Reform and Organization Politics in Philadelphia*. New York: Fund for the Republic, 1959.

Renslow, Albert. "The Immigrants' Climb to Legitimacy: The Rise of George Chacharis, Gary's Immigrant Mayor." Paper, 1976. Calumet Regional Archives.

Research Atlanta. *The Impact of Local Government Programs to Encourage Minority Business Development*. Atlanta: Research Atlanta, 1986.

Reynolds, Barbara. "Blacks Blast Jesse on Newhouse Snub." *Chicago Tribune*, January 13, 1975.

————. *Jesse Jackson: The Man, The Movement, The Myth*. Chicago: Nelson-Hall, 1975.

Rice, Bradley R. "The Battle of Buckhead: The Plan of Improvement and Atlanta's Last Big Annexation." *Atlanta Historical Journal* 25 (1981).

————. "If Dixie Were Atlanta." In *Sunbelt Cities*, edited by Richard M. Bernard and Bradley Rice. Austin: University of Texas Press, 1983.

————. "Lester Maddox and the 'Liberal' Mayors." *Proceedings and Papers of the Georgia Association of Historians*. Marietta, Ga: Kennesaw College, 1981.

Riordon, William. *Plunkitt of Tammany Hall*. New York: E. P. Dutton, 1963.

Rivlin, Gary. *Fire on the Prairie: Chicago's Harold Washington and the Politics of Race*. New York: Henry Holt, 1992.

"Rizzo Recall Drive." *New York Times*, April 1, 1976.

"Rizzo Solidifies Power in Philadelphia." *New York Times*, May 26, 1976.

Rogers, David. *The Management of Big Cities*. Beverly Hills: Sage, 1971.

Rooks, Charles. *The Atlanta Elections of 1969*. Atlanta: Voter Education Project, 1970.

Rosenberg, Amy S. "Layoff Notices Sent to 350 City Workers." *Philadelphia Inquirer*, January 7, 1994.

————. "PHA Imposes Tenant-hiring Policy on Bids." *Philadelphia Inquirer*, March 1, 1994.

Rossi, Peter H., and Phillips Cutright. "The Impact of Party Organization in an Industrial Setting." In *Community Political Systems*, edited by Morris Janowitz. International Yearbook of Political Behavior Research, vol. 1. Glencoe, Ill.: Free Press, 1961.

Rottenberg, Dan. "Ed Rendell: The Eternal Sophomore as America's Mayor." *Pennsylvania Gazette* (May 1994).

Royko, Mike. *Boss: Richard J. Daley of Chicago*. New York: E.P. Dutton, 1971.

————. "Daley and Evans: A Perfect Shootout." *Chicago Tribune*, December 6, 1988.

Rusk, David. *Cities without Suburbs*. Baltimore: Johns Hopkins University Press, 1993.

Russell, Bertrand. *A History of Western Philosophy*. New York: Simon and Schuster, 1945.

Salter, John T. *Boss Rule: Portraits in City Politics*. York, Pa.: McGraw-Hill, 1935.

Samuels, Dave. "Prison Term Starts Next Wednesday." *Gary Post-Tribune*, January 18, 1962.

Schattschneider, E. E. *The Semisovereign People*. Hinsdale, Ill.: Dryden Press, 1960.

Schemmel, Bill. "Atlanta's 'Power Structure' Faces Life." *New South* 27:2 (Spring 1972).

Schlesinger, Joseph A. "A Two-Dimensional Scheme for Classifying the States according to Degree of Inter-Party Competition." *American Political Science Review* 49 (1955).

Schumpeter, Joseph A. *Capitalism, Socialism, and Democracy*. New York: Harper and Row, 1942.

Scott, James C. *Domination and the Arts of Resistance*. New Haven: Yale University Press, 1990.

Seals, Ted. "Black Candidates Lay Their Mayoral Cards on the Table." *Chicago Sun Times*, December 1, 1974.

"Second Battle of Atlanta, The." *Look*, April 25, 1961.

Seddon, Bill. "Blacks Claim Credit for MARTA Win." *Atlanta Constitution*, November 11, 1971.

Selznick, Philip. *TVA and the Grass Roots*. Berkeley: University of California Press, 1949.

Semonski, Kos. "Bowser Ready To Quit Tate, Lead Civic Unit." *Philadelphia Bulletin*, April 27, 1969.

Shefter, Martin. "Political Incorporation and the Extrusion of the Left: Party Politics and Social Forces in New York City." In *Studies in American Political Development*, edited by Karen Orren and Stephen Skowronek. Vol. 1. New Haven: Yale University Press, 1986.

Siddons, Anne Rivers. "The Seeds of Sanity." *Atlanta Magazine* (July 1967).

Simpson, Dick. "Chicago Government." In *Chicago: An Agenda For Change*, edited by Dick Simpson and Pierre de Vise. Chicago: University of Illinois at Chicago Circle, 1975.

Sitton, Claude. "An Uneasy Racial Truce Prevails in Philadelphia." *New York Times*, August 3, 1963.

Sleeper, Jim. "The End of the Rainbow." *New Republic* (November 1, 1993).

"Smith Uses Race Insult to Answer Beach Question." *Gary American*, November 2, 1951.

Smith, Douglas L. *The New Deal in the Urban South*. Baton Rouge: Louisiana State University Press, 1988.

Smith, Robert C. "Recent Elections and Black Politics: The Maturation or Death of Black Politics?" *PS* 23:2 (June 1990).

Smothers, Ronald. "Affirmative Action Booms in Atlanta." *New York Times*, January 27, 1989.

Sonenshein, Raphael J. *Politics in Black and White: Race and Power in Los Angeles*. Princeton: Princeton University Press, 1993.

Spear, Allan H. *Black Chicago: The Making of a Negro Ghetto, 1890–1920*. Chicago: University of Chicago Press, 1967.

Standing, William H., and James A. Robinson. "Inter-Party Competition and Primary Contesting: The Case of Indiana." *American Political Science Review* 52:4 (December 1958).

Stanley, John. "Mayor Chacharis at Apex of Long Political Career." *Gary Post-Tribune*, November 8, 1959.

Stone, Clarence. *Economic Growth and Neighborhood Discontent*. Chapel Hill: University of North Carolina Press, 1976.

Stone, Clarence N. *Regime Politics: Governing Atlanta, 1946–1988*. Lawrence: University Press of Kansas, 1989.

Stone, Eddie. *Jesse Jackson: Biography of an Ambitious Man*. Los Angeles: Holloway House, 1979.

Strange, John H. "Black Politics in Philadelphia." In *Black Politics in Philadelphia*, edited by Miriam Ershkowitz and Joseph Zikmund II. New York: Basic Books, 1973.

———. "The Negro and Philadelphia Politics." In *Urban Government*, edited by Edward Banfield. New York: Free Press, 1969.

———. "The Negro in Philadelphia Politics: 1963–1965." Ph.D.diss., Princeton University, 1966.

Strickland, Arvarh. *History of the Chicago Urban League*. Urbana: University of Illinois Press, 1966.

Stroh, Nicholas. "ADA Proposes Changes in Staff Policies of PAAC." *Bulletin of the Americans for Democratic Action*, December 13, 1966, ADA Records, Urban Archives Center, Temple University Libraries.

Strong, James. "Whites Have Most Top-level City Jobs." *Chicago Tribune*, November 1, 1989.

Strong, James, and Jacqueline Heard. "Council Meeting Fails as Evans Rally." *Chicago Tribune*, December 2, 1988.

Strong, Rodney, Director, Office of Contract Compliance, City of Atlanta, to Anita Sharp, Editor, Atlanta Business Chronicle, February 28, 1989.

"Struggle of Negro in Philadelphia from Slave to Citizen." *Philadelphia Bulletin*, January 24, 1965.

Sullivan, Leon. *Build Brother Build*. Philadelphia: Macrae Smith, 1969.

Summers, Anita, and Thomas Luce. *Economic Development within the Philadelphia Metropolitan Area*. Philadelphia: University of Pennsylvania Press, 1987.

Swanstrom, Todd. *The Crisis of Growth Politics*. Philadelphia: Temple University Press, 1985.

Sweet, Lynn, and Don Terry. "Mayor Signs Ethics Bill; Byrne Hits Fund-raising." *Chicago Sun-Times*, February 19, 1987.

Talbott, Basil, Jr. "Black Group Drops Newhouse, Eyes Singer." *Chicago Sun Times*, January 11, 1975.

————. "Getting the City Hall Shaft." *Chicago Sun Times*, October 19, 1978.

————. "Pick Stewart in Secret to Replace Metcalfe." *Chicago Sun Times*, October 13, 1978.

Tate, James H. J. "In Praise of Politicians." *Philadelphia Bulletin*, January 13–24, 1974.

————. "Tate Felt a Rizzo Win Would Save Democratic Control." *Philadelphia Bulletin*, January 23, 1974.

Taylor, Paul. "Meet the Men Fighting the Charter Change." *Philadelphia Inquirer*, September 24, 1978.

————. "Now Everyone Is Chasing Green." *Philadelphia Inquirer*, March 18, 1979.

————. "Rizzo to Downplay Racially Based Issues." *Philadelphia Inquirer*, September 26, 1978.

————. "Two Reply to Rizzo Criticism." *Philadelphia Inquirer*, July 20, 1979.

————. "Third Term Opponents Form Alliance." *Philadelphia Inquirer*, September 6, 1978.

Teasley, Colleen. "Mayor Execs Put on Show of Unity." *Atlanta Journal and Constitution*, November 24, 1974.

"Tell It Like It Is—Hatcher Can Win." Chacharis Collection, Pamphlets, Political Campaigns (18:1:38), Calumet Regional Archives.

Thompson, Daniel C. *The Negro Leadership Class*. Englewood Cliffs, N.J.: Prentice Hall, 1963.

Thompson, Robert A., Hylan Lewis, and Davis McEntire. "Atlanta and Birmingham: A Comparative Study in Negro Housing." In *Studies in Housing and Minority Groups*, edited by Nathan Glazer and Davis McEntire. Berkeley: University of California Press, 1960.

Thompson, Thomas F. "Public Administration in the Civil City of Gary, Indiana." Ph.D. diss., Indiana University, 1960.

Travis, Dempsey J. *An Autobiography of Black Politics*. Chicago: Urban Research Press, 1987.

Tryman, Donald L. "A Typology of Black Leadership." *Western Journal of Black Studies* 1:1 (March 1977).

Turner, Julius. "Primary Elections as the Alternative to Party Competition in 'Safe' Districts." *Journal of Politics* 15:2 (May 1953).

Turner, Robert P. *Up to the Front of the Line: Blacks in the American Political System*. Port Washington, N.Y.: Kennikat Press, 1975.

U. S. Chamber of Commerce. Urban Action Clearinghouse. "Philadelphia Utility Offers Jobs and Advancement to Minorities." Case Study Number 7. Washington, D.C.: 1968.

U.S. Bureau of the Census. *Fifteenth Census of the U.S., 1930, Population: Composition and Characteristics*. Washington, D.C.: 1932.

U.S. Conference of Mayors, *A Status Report on Homeless Families in America's Cities*. Washington, D.C.: 1987).

U.S. Congress. Joint Economic Committee. *Employment and Manpower Problems in the Cities: Implications of the Report of the National Advisory Commission on Civil Disorders*. Hearings of the Joint Economic Committee, May 28, 29, June 4, 5, 6, 1968.

U.S. Department of Labor, Bureau of Labor Statistics. *Atlanta: Ten Years of Growth, 1955–1965*. Special Regional Report. Washington, D.C.: 1966.

Walker, Jack L. "Protest and Negotiation: A Case Study of Negro Leadership in Atlanta, Georgia." *Midwest Journal of Political Science* 7:2 (May 1963).

Walker, Jack. "Negro Voting in Atlanta: 1954–1961." *Phylon* 24 (Winter 1963).

Walters, Ronald. "Imperatives of Black Leadership: Policy Mobilization and Community Development." *Urban League Review* 9:1 (Summer 1985).

Walton, Hanes, Jr. *Invisible Politics: Black Political Behavior*. Albany: State University of New York Press, 1985.

Walton, Hanes, Jr., and Leslie Burl McLemore. "Portrait of Black Political Styles." *Black Politician* 2:2 (October 1970).

Ward, Hiley. "The Gray Tradition May End at Bright Hope Church." *Philadelphia Inquirer*, September 16, 1978.

Watters, Pat, and Reese Cleghorn. *Climbing Jacob's Ladder: The Arrival of Negroes in Southern Politics*. New York: Harcourt, Brace, and World, 1967.

"We Cannot Lose Sight of the Negro Demo's Support nor Rats in the Party." *Gary American*, November 16, 1951.

Weigand, Ginny. "Rendell's Panel Fails To Mollify Preservationists." *Philadelphia Inquirer*, March 27, 1994.

Weiler, Conrad. *Philadelphia: Neighborhood, Authority, and the Urban Crisis*. New York: Praeger, 1974.

Weiner, Myron. "Political Participation: Crisis of the Political Process." In *Crises and Sequences in Political Development*, edited by Leonard Binder. Princeton: Princeton University Press, 1971.

Weisman, Joel, and Ralph Whitehead. "Untangling Black Politics." *Chicagoan* (July 1974).

Weisman, Joel D. "Every Major City Problem Seems More Acute in Gary." *Washington Post*, December 2, 1974.

Weiss, Nancy J. *Farewell to the Party of Lincoln: Black Politics in the Age of FDR*. Princeton: Princeton University Press, 1983.

Wendt, Lloyd, and Herman Kogan. *Big Bill of Chicago*. New York: Bobbs-Merrill, 1953.

West, Cornel. *Race Matters*. Boston: Beacon Press, 1993.

White, Elliot. "Articulateness, Political Mobility, and Conservatism: An Analysis of the Philadelphia Antipoverty Election." In *Black Politics in Philadelphia*, edited by Miriam Ershkowitz and Joseph Zikmund II. New York: Basic Books, 1973.

Whitehead, Ralph, Jr., and Joel Weisman. "Is LaSalle Street Grooming the Black Mayor?" *Chicagoan* (August 1974).

"Whiteway Add Hailed by Negroes." *Atlanta Constitution*, December 9, 1949.

Wilner, Ann Ruth. *The Spellbinders: Charismatic Political Leadership*. New Haven: Yale University Press, 1984.

Wilson, James Q. *The Amateur Democrat*. Chicago: University of Chicago Press, 1962.

———. *Negro Politics: The Search for Leadership*. Glencoe, Ill.: Free Press, 1960.

———. "Two Negro Politicians: An Interpretation." *Midwest Journal of Political Science* 4:4 (November 1960).

Winters, James. "Democracy in Chicago." *Notre Dame Magazine* (January 1984).

Wise, Malcolm. "Civic Leaders Rally behind Daley for Re-election." *Chicago Sun Times*, February 13, 1959.

Wolfinger, Raymond E. *The Politics of Progress*. Englewood Cliffs, NJ: Prentice Hall, 1974.

Woodson, Carter G. *The Mis-Education of the Negro*. Washington, D.C.: Associated Publishers, 1933.

Zahour, Frank. "Singer Hits Black Hopefuls Chances." *Chicago Tribune*, September 19, 1974.

Zikmund, Joseph. "Mayoral Voting and Ethnic Politics in the Daley-Bilandic-Byrne Era." In *After Daley: Chicago Politics in Transition*, edited by Samuel Gove and Louis Masotti. Urbana: University of Illinois Press, 1982.

Zody, Richard E., and Norman R. Luttbeg. "An Evaluation of Various Measures of State Party Competition." *Western Political Quarterly* 21 (1968).

Index